D1087315

Character and Culture

Studies in Social, Political, and Legal Philosophy

General Editor: James P. Sterba, University of Notre Dame

This series analyzes and evaluates critically the major political, social, and legal ideals, institutions, and practices of our time. The analysis may be historical or problem-centered; the evaluation may focus on theoretical underpinnings or practical implications. Among the recent titles in the series are:

Character and Culture

LESTER H. HUNT

ROWMAN & LITTLEFIELD PUBLISHERS, INC.
Lanham • Boulder • New York • Oxford

ROWMAN & LITTLEFIELD PUBLISHERS, INC.

Published in the United States of America
by Rowman & Littlefield Publishers, Inc.
4720 Boston Way, Lanham, Maryland 20706

12 Hid's Copse Road
Cummor Hill, Oxford OX2 9JJ, England

British Library Cataloguing in Publication Information Available

Library of Congress Cataloging-in-Publication Data

Hunt, Lester H., 1946–
     Character and culture / Lester H. Hunt.
          p.   cm. — (Studies in social, political, and legal philosophy)
     Includes bibliographical references and index.
     ISBN 0-8476-8474-1 (cloth : alk. paper). — ISBN 0-8476-8475-X (pbk. : alk.
paper)
     1. Character. 2. Character—Social aspects. I. Title. II. Series.
     BJ1521.H87   1997
     170—dc21   97-20977

ISBN 0-8476-8474-1 (cloth : alk. paper)
ISBN 0-8476-8475-X (pbk. : alk. paper)

Printed in the United States of America

⊖™ The paper used in this publication meets the minimum requirements of American
National Standard for Information Sciences—Permanence of Paper for Printed Library
Materials, ANSI Z39.48–1984.

For Deborah and Natty, again.

v

To insist on knowing right from wrong while ignoring your mind is like saying, "I left for Yűeh today, and got there yesterday."

—Chuang Tsu

Contents

Preface

Readers of this book might be glad to know that, depending on their interests, I can suggest various ways in which they might omit reading parts of it (or delay reading them until later) without damaging their understanding of what they do read. Chapters I through V would be of greatest interest to readers who are mainly concerned with ethical theory, while chapters VI through XI are most relevant to those concerned with social and political philosophy. The former group of readers can understand the first five chapters without reading those that follow. The latter group of readers is not quite so lucky. To understand chapters VI through XI they must read chapter I, but could afford to skip various parts of chapters II through V. There are a number of passages in VI through XI that rely on sections of these earlier chapters, but these sections are mentioned in the later passages when they become relevant, and a reader in a hurry could in principle read them at that time.

When I refer to other parts of this book I generally do so within parentheses, and usually in the body of the text rather than in footnotes. Reference to other sections in the same chapter are made by representing the number of the section with an Arabic numeral. If the section is in another chapter, the chapter is identified with a Roman numeral: for instance, (III.4) would mean the fourth section of chapter III.

***

I have been persistently thinking and writing on the topics treated in this book since 1972. Over the years, a great many people have commented on one or more of the chapters that follow, and I have no hope of remembering and thanking them all. Those I do remember, either because they made comments in writing or because I know of some definite change in the text that was inspired by their remarks, are the following: Kurt Baier, James M. Buchanan, Claudia Card, Antony Flew, Philippa Foot, David Friedman, Allan Gotthelf, Gilbert Harman, Deborah Katz Hunt, John Kekes, Charles King, Marc Kummel, Jerome Levi, Loren Lomasky, Eric Mack, Fred D. Miller, Jr., Christopher Morris, Ellen Frankel Paul, Lloyd Reinhardt, Robert

C. Roberts, Amelie Rorty, Ivan Soll, Michael Stocker, Gordon Tullock, James D. Wallace, and Morton Winston. The comments of Bob Roberts, with what amounted to a commentary on the first three chapters, were especially enlightening. To all these people, and to all the others who shared their reactions with me, I give my heartfelt thanks. This book would have been very different and certainly worse without them.

I owe another sort of debt to the people who gave me financial assistance that made it possible to take several periods of time away from teaching and devote them entirely to writing. This assistance included two summer grants from the Graduate School of the University of Wisconsin—Madison, and a large grant from the Earhart Foundation that made it possible to spend nine months at the Social Philosophy and Policy Center in Bowling Green, Ohio, during 1989-90. This last, in particular, allowed the project to begin to take something like its final shape.

Much of chapter I of this book appeared, in somewhat different form, as "Character and Thought" in *American Philosophical Quarterly* 15, 1978. Portions of chapters II and V appeared in "Courage and Principle" in *The Canadian Journal of Philosophy* 10, 1980. Parts of chapter III appeared in "Generosity" in *American Philosophical Quarterly* 12, 1975. A part of chapter VII was published in "On Improving Mankind by Political Means" in *Reason Papers* 10, 1985. Chapter IX was originally published as "Punishment, Revenge, and the Minimal Functions of the State" in *Bowling Green Studies in Applied Philosophy* 1, 1979. Chapter X was originally published as *The Politics of Envy* in *Social Philosophy and Policy Center Original Papers* 2, 1983. Permission to use this material is gratefully acknowledged.

I should also thank Mary Dilsaver of the center for suggesting that she do the typing necessary to put an early draft on computer disk. She enabled me to enter the Information Age at last. In addition, I gratefully acknowledge Charlie Starkey for preparing the index, and Nancy Graham for doing the typesetting.

I

Character and Thought

If man is superior to other living beings in dignity because of his powers of
speech and reason, what is more universally efficacious and more likely to win
distinction, than to surpass one's fellows, who possess the same human nature,
and are members of the same human race, in those sole respects wherein man
surpasses other beings?

—John of Salisbury, *The Metalogicon*

1. Introductory

We know that human beings are capable of possessing behavioral traits of
several different kinds. Some, such as right-handedness and stuttering, may be
good or bad but have no necessary connection with the matter of whether the
person who possesses them is good or bad. Others, such as the inability to
prove theorems in number theory or the ability to extract human teeth without
breaking them into pieces, are in a certain way necessarily relevant to whether
their possessors are good or bad in some role that they happen to serve:
someone who can draw out teeth without doing unnecessary damage is, with
respect to that ability, a good dentist. Someone who cannot prove theorems in
number theory is so far a bad mathematician. Still other traits are necessarily
connected in the same way to a person's merits, not as a player of some limited
role, but as a person. This is true, for instance, of generosity, obedience,
ruthlessness, gluttony, courage, stinginess, laziness, gentleness, temperance,
tolerance, and impulsiveness. They are directly relevant to the matter of
whether those who possess them are admirable human beings. This third group
of traits constitutes what I will call traits of character.

It is obvious from the list I have just given that these traits form a rather
heterogeneous group. Some of them seem cold and intelligent, like temperance; some, like impulsiveness, seem hot and stupid. Courage seems to
include acting against or in spite of feeling and desire; laziness seems to
include capitulating to them. Traits of character, as I have already described
them, obviously include both the virtues and the vices. A virtue would seem

to be a meritorious trait of character, one that indicates that its possessor is, with respect to that trait, a good person. A vice would in that case have the opposite sort of significance. Courage and generosity seem to be virtues, while cowardice and stinginess seem to be vices. Some of the traits I have mentioned, however, do not appear clearly to belong to either of these categories. Some seem to function as virtues or vices depending on the individual or the circumstances in which they are found. Obedience, for instance, is arguably a virtue in small children and a dangerous and degrading vice in adults.

Admittedly, it is no easy task to say something about all traits of character that is both interesting and true, but that is what I will try to do in this chapter. My object will be to identify one important feature they all have in common.

One might wonder, even aside from its difficulty, why this project is worth attempting. We will eventually see that there are all sorts of reasons why it is, but I hope that one fairly simple one will suffice, at the outset, to make this subject seem interesting. I have said that virtues are evidently traits of character. This claim is a platitude and therefore cannot properly be called a theory, but it has the same form as certain claims philosophers have made that are indeed theories about the nature of virtue. Such claims, like this one, sometimes take the form of identifying the virtues as a species of some other, more general class of attributes: Socrates and the Sophists apparently thought they are *skills*. Descartes held them to be *passions*, and some translators of Aristotle and Aquinas attribute to them the claim that they are *habits*. If my account of traits of character is sound, it will show that the platitudinous claim is an *alternative* to these theoretical ones, because my account will describe traits of character as fundamentally different from skills, passions, and habits, and if virtues are traits of character it will show by implication that the virtues are none of these things.

In carrying out my analysis of traits of character, I will employ the following strategy: In section 2, I will contrast traits of character with habits and certain passionate states which I will call "temperamental dispositions" in ways that suggest what character is like. Then, in sections 3 through 7, I will sketch a view of traits of character in which the points of contrast I will have described are held to be partly a result of the unique relationship that holds between character and thought. The same relationship will enable us to see how traits of character differ from skills.[1] Finally, in section 8, I will comment on what

---

[1] The idea that traits of character are not habits, temperamental dispositions, or skills will already be familiar to those who have read chapter 7 of G. H. von Wright's *The Varieties of*

the foregoing discussion indicates about the importance of character.

Before I do any of this, however, I should distinguish the problem of the nature of traits of character from another, closely related issue. The words that are the names of traits of character have at least two applications: sometimes we say that a person is courageous or obedient, and sometimes someone's acts are said to be courageous or obedient acts. In the one case the word ascribes to the person a trait of character; in the other it ascribes to his act what I will call an *act-character*, or *the character of an act*. So, in addition to asking what traits or character are like, we can ask the same question about the characters of acts. In this book I will only make a sustained attempt at treating the first of these two problems. The attention I will give to act-characters will take the form of making more of less isolated remarks, and I will not attempt to give a general account of them.

2. Habit and Temperament

The claim that traits of character are habits is an attractive one if only because, roughly speaking, they appear to have the same ontological status: both are spoken of as though they were qualities of a person by which he or she comes to do certain things. Neither is cited as a thing that we do but rather as an explanation of the things we do. Yet there are obviously important differences between traits of character and habits. I will briefly discuss three of them.

First, in the case of habits, the act involved seems to be more readily detachable from the trait than is the case with traits of character. A person with a certain trait of character does acts that have the corresponding character: a gluttonous or ruthless individual does gluttonous or ruthless things. Similarly, a person who has a certain habit also does acts of a certain sort, such as drinking tea at three o'clock or biting one's nails. Further, in both cases the acts involved may be done without the corresponding trait: someone who is not a ruthless person can do a ruthless thing; it is possible, in this sense of the words, to "act out of character." And of course we all frequently do things that we are not in the habit of doing. But there is a large difference here.

Acting out of character is always odd: if we find a man who is not ruthless acting ruthlessly, or a person who is not brave acting courageously, we are apt to want an explanation. Further, the explanations we are given for such actions

---

Goodness (London: Routledge and Kegan Paul, 1963). See especially pp. 143-45.

often undermine the claim that the act has to the character in question. When people who are not brave do brave things it may well turn out that they somewhat underestimated the danger they were in, or that although they did know about the dangers involved they were not quite "alive to" them because they were drunk or in a rage. On the other hand, there is nothing odd—as such—about doing something one is not in the habit of doing. Today I drank tea at three o'clock, though I am not in the habit of doing so, and no one found it odd at all (I have no habits as to when to drink tea). Though it is possible to act out of character, the character of an act tends to depend in some way on the character of the agent; this sort of dependence is not found in the case of habits as such.

The second difference between traits of character and habits is the most intuitively obvious, and yet the most difficult to formulate. I think there is a tendency to feel a slight shock on the first reading in translations of Aristotle and Aquinas that such traits as courage, stinginess, and magnanimity are "habits." Surely part of the reason for this is that to have such traits includes performing actions that in many cases are subtle responses to complex and problematic situations, so that these traits would seem to involve our intelligence in some important way, while habits seem to be unintelligent by nature.

Such intuitions prove nothing by themselves, but a little reflection suggests that there is some truth in this one. To answer the question, "Why did you do that?" with "It's a habit" is not to tell one's reason for doing it; it is rather to *deny* that one has a reason. On the other hand, to say that a certain act is stingy is precisely to say what the agent's reason for doing it was: it is to say that the agent meant to preserve his or her wealth. Of course, it is possible for an act to be done "by habit" and also for a particular reason: most of us brush our teeth habitually, but we also brush our teeth because we know it preserves our health. But the relation between habits and reasons for acting is external: habitually brushing one's teeth for no reason at all would be the same habit as habitually doing it for this reason. The relation between traits of character and reason seems to be stronger than this: no act that is not done to preserve one's wealth would be done from the same trait as the act of a stingy person.

The third point of contrast between traits of character and habits is one that has already been indicated with admirable simplicity by von Wright.[2] If you were to ask me what I am doing and I were to reply with a remark like

---

[2] von Wright, *The Varieties of Goodness*, p. 139.

"something courageous" or "I'm acting courageously," I would not be answering your question. Such replies can of course make sense (as jokes, etc.), but they leave this particular request for information unsatisfied, and the questioner would want to know *what* is being done courageously. If we replace "courageous" and "courageously" with any other character words the same result is obtained. In this respect, such words do not behave like names for things that people do.[3] On the other hand, as von Wright says, all the acts that can be done habitually—walking, chopping wood, playing cards, and so forth—*can* supply answers to the question, "What are you doing?"

Traits of character, like habits, are examples of what Aristotle calls *hexeis*: that is, both are relatively enduring states of a person. One may have precisely the same habit or trait of character, continuously, for a period of many years. For this reason, traits of character cannot be occurrences of some emotion or feeling, such as we have when we feel contented or angry. However, as far as this consideration is concerned, they could be *dispositions* to have certain emotions rather than others. I will call such states "temperamental dispositions" or, more traditionally, "temperaments." The four classic examples are of course the choleric, the phlegmatic, the melancholic, and the sanguine.

The notion that traits of character are temperamental dispositions has at least one advantage over the notion that they are habits. While most habits are dispositions to do certain "outward" actions, such traits as courage and laziness seem, intuitively, to have a great deal to do with what is happening "inside" the person who has them. Since temperaments are by definition dispositions toward something that is entirely "inner," the notion that traits of character are really temperaments can be an attractive one.

Aside from its initial plausibility, this notion is interesting for raising a very important issue. Animals have emotions just as we do, and a particular animal can have an aptness for a certain mood which is as enduring as any of ours: some dogs have cheerful dispositions all their lives while others seem to have depressed ones. The possibility that character traits are temperaments suggests they are *natural*, in the sense that they do not belong to the part of human life that is a product of culture. "The brutes"—beings without culture—can have temperamental dispositions just as well as we can.

---

[3] However, what seem to be character words do supply answers to questions such as "How is Johnny behaving?" Johnny can behave considerately, cooperatively, selfishly. Notice that this question asks for "how" and not "what" and that, unlike "what" questions, "how" questions can always be answered with an adverb.

We can see that not all character traits are temperaments by considering an example. A moment's thought will show that there is a difference in kind between being gentle (gentleness being a trait of character) and having a mild disposition (which I take to be temperament). If Mary is a gentle person and finds that she must tell Martha some bad news, she will do so gently, while a mild-tempered person would merely do it blandly: that is, Mary will *take care* that the news not hurt Martha as much as it could, while if she were mild-tempered she would simply not be as horrified by the news as others would be, and her behavior would show it. The fact that an act is generated by a disposition of the sort that mildness is, is the fact that it evinces a certain sort of emotional state (namely, a state that the agent is especially apt to be in), while the gentleness of an act is not exhausted by the fact that it evinces an emotional state. Its character is not its expressiveness.

The difference between gentleness and mildness is actually greater than this, since gentleness does not include any particular emotional state: we can act gently without feeling any one particular way about the situation we are addressing. This suggests the possibility that all traits of character are like gentleness in this respect; it seems obvious at any rate that some of them are. Laziness, for instance, can go with a feeling of complacent satisfaction with one's lot, but it can just as easily coexist with despondency instead. Laziness and the phlegmatic temperament are different sorts of things.

3. Kant's Account

To see that traits of character are like and unlike habits and temperamental dispositions is not yet to understand what they are. I will now sketch a view of what traits of character have in common, making it as plausible as I can. It will, I hope, show how the various similarities and differences we have examined are connected with one another. I will launch my account with a criticism of a very different view of these traits, one set forth by Immanuel Kant.

Kant presents an account of such characteristics as timidity, insolence, sympathy, courage, discretion, and obedience. Most of these seem to be clear examples of what I have called traits of character, but, interestingly, that is not what he calls them. He insists, rather, that they are "a matter of temperament."[4]

---

[4] Immanuel Kant, *Education* (Ann Arbor: University of Michigan Press, 1960), pp. 96 and 97. See also *Groundwork of the Metaphysic of Morals*, trans. H. J. Paton, (New York: Harper, 1964), p. 61.

The issue of what we should call them is not a mere question of usage; it is attached to matters of considerable weight. In calling them "a matter of temperament" Kant means to deny that such things can have the sort of ethical importance I have assigned to them.

For Kant, "moral culture," the phase of education in which a child is made a morally responsible person, has for its "first endeavor" the formation of what he calls character. Character is the "readiness to act in accord with 'maxims.'" A maxim is "a principle on which the subject acts." He does not place the formation of what I have called traits of character under the heading of "moral culture," but locates it instead in that part of education that deals with human beings as animals rather than as moral beings—the part in which the child is taught how to walk. This phase of education creates habits by drill and rote.[5]

Kant places the formation of these traits in this phase because he holds that they are not generated by maxims, that to do something out of sympathy or obedience is not to do it on the basis of principle. As he says, such traits are first acquired at a very early age, when the child cannot yet think in terms of moral rules and consequently cannot understand such remarks as "Fie, for shame! You shouldn't do that!" He remarks that saying such things to children at that stage of their development can only impart to them a certain bad trait: not understanding anything beyond the fact that they are being disapproved of, they will become timid. These traits are instilled, when they are not the result of chance, by a process more primitive than moral education, which he calls discipline. This process requires no intelligent attention from the child and consists solely in "restraining unruliness."[6]

Kant recognized only three sources from which action can spring: the a priori commands of morality, empirical maxims that enable us to get what we want, and, as one of his commentators put it, "completely irrational desire or inclination."[7] His account of the formation of the traits I have been discussing means that the acts that arise from these traits have the third sort of source. This might at first seem to clash with his idea that the traits involved can be the result of "discipline." The notion of disciplined behavior seems on the face of it to be incompatible with completely irrational inclination. For Kant, however,

---

[5] Kant, *Education,* pp. 84 and 88 fn., and chap. 2, *passim.*

[6] Kant, *Education*, pp. 83, 49, 50, and 18.

[7] H. B. Acton, *Kant's Moral Philosophy* (New York: St. Martin's Press, 1970), pp. 10 and 11.

discipline is merely a sort of drill that curbs blind impulse by forming habits. This of course does not make the impulses any the less blind. The sources of acts that result from Kantian discipline alone are irrational in the nonpejorative sense that these acts are not guided by the agent's mind: they are not done on the basis of any sort of maxim. This is the force of his calling the traits that can be formed in this way "a matter of temperament."

From these considerations, Kant very reasonably draws the conclusion that such traits cannot comprise a high sort of human worth, that—to put it another way—virtue cannot be constituted by the qualities that I have called traits of character. As he understands them, such things are not *human* at all; they are the same in kind as the characteristics of a well-behaved horse or dog.

I began this discussion by defining traits of character through the primitive means of giving a list, and I pointed out that the virtues all seem to belong on this list. Kant seems to be speaking of the class of traits defined by this list, but he denies that these traits constitute character and clearly disbelieves that the virtues are among them. The reason for this denial and disbelief is his conviction that these traits are utterly unintelligent. This last is the root of the difference between Kant's position and my own. I have already suggested that, on the contrary, such traits do involve our intelligence in some important way, and I will now attempt to reinforce, extend, and clarify that suggestion.

One passage in Kant that is particularly illuminating in this connection is the one in which he discusses the trait that distinguishes a spoiled child. This, I think, is a fairly plausible example of a character trait, as I have used that term. His explanation of how children come to be spoiled is rather simple. Some parents, he says, spend too much time trying to please their children, "singing to them, caressing, kissing, and dancing with them." Among other things, they are eager to comfort them when they cry, and so they encourage them to cry more often. "Once a child has become accustomed to having all his whims gratified, it is afterwards too late to begin to cross his will." Children consistently brought up this way become "veritable despots." Given this diagnosis, the prescription must be that "the child's sensibility be not spoilt by overindulgence"; specifically, Kant recommends that they not be allowed to "pick and choose" what pleases them. The idea seems to be that the mistake the parents make lies in the *extent* to which they please their children (not the *manner* in which they do so) and that the resulting trait consists of two qualities: that of being accustomed to having many of one's desires gratified, together with the simple inability to tolerate not having them gratified.

The trouble with this is that it does not do justice to the disparity between this trait and others that appear to be very different from it. Kant's implied analysis of the trait also fits the condition of a small infant who is healthy and well cared for: it would also be used to having its desires satisfied and would bawl furiously when they were not. Of course, Kant's description of how children are spoiled does suggest a difference between a healthy baby and a spoiled child; spoiled children are the way they are because of a sort of unconscious training, whereas in the other case this is not true. But it is far from clear that a difference in the genesis is enough to show that there are two different traits here; and, at any rate, on Kant's understanding of the traits that he calls "a matter of temperament," it does not seem to be necessary for any one of them either that it be learned or that it be unlearned. And yet it seems obvious that there are two different traits here, and even that they belong to different *kinds* of traits.

Further, Kant's implied analysis also fits the condition of children who have had such sheltered lives that they do not know that life is as frustrating as it naturally is. It is said that Tolstoy's childhood was so Edenic that he did not realize until he went away to school that not everyone in the world loved him. Such people will be acutely disappointed if their desires are not gratified in large measure, but they are not spoiled; they are simply innocent. Of course, such disappointment would not find expression in stamping and raging, as it would in the case of a spoiled child, but this behavioral difference suggests that there must be a deeper difference that explains it, and Kant's account does not indicate what this difference would be.

4. Thought

Kant makes a remark that plays no role in his discussion of the traits that he says are a matter of temperament, but which seems to me to be very much to the point. He says that, after a certain phase of a child's development, whenever the child cries "*there is always some reasoning*, however vague it may be, *connected with his crying*. He cries with the idea that some harm has been done him." From that time, he says, the child can cry not just as a result of "mere bodily hurt" but also from "a sense of grievance."[8] I think that, without our indulging in amateur psychology, this remark can serve as a clue to the nature of traits such as that of the spoiled child. The fact that a bawling infant is not spoken of in at all the same way as a spoiled child, even though their behavior looks much the same, must surely have to do with the infant's

---

[8] Kant, *Education*, p. 48. The emphasis is Kant's own.

incapacity for "some reasoning" (in this immensely broad sense of these words).

To be more definite, I submit that what distinguishes spoiled children is the fact that they regard their wanting something as *good enough reason why they should have it*, so that other considerations—such as wants of others, one's own true good, convenience, and fairness—can't count at all when they clash with this one. On this view, it is at least plausible to suppose that parents spoil their children, not simply by the extent to which they try to please them, but by the fact that in doing so they treat their children's desires as good enough reason why they should give them what they give them, thus giving them the impression that their wants do have royal status. At any rate, spoiled children must get this impression in one way or another. Their outward acts are also distinctive, but what is special about them is not the fact that they consist of such things as stamping and raging: It is the fact that *by* stamping and raging they are *laying claim to something*; they are *demanding* it. What is distinctive about their outward actions depends on something distinctive about the way they see things: they can lay claim to something simply by expressing their frustrated desire for it because they regard their desire as the reason why they should have it.[9]

This account suggests crucial differences between this trait and those of the infant and the "innocent." Babies cannot have this trait because they cannot have any notion—not even a primitive one—of there being reasons why things should or should not be done. By that fact, any trait they can have will be fundamentally different in kind from that of a spoiled child. Innocents do not have this trait either, because their mistaken impression is about, not what is good or justifiable, but what is *possible*. Such people would not rage when the facts conflict with their impression because they would not see those facts as an injustice, so they would have no cause for anger.

All traits of character can be understood in ways that are crucially similar to the way I have understood the trait of a spoiled child. Impulsiveness is not simply a propensity to act even when it is unreasonable to do so: it also involves regarding those features of situations that inspire caution as relatively unimportant. This distinguishes impulsiveness from, for instance, hyperkinesis. Similarly, carelessness, as a state of character, includes regarding things that normally inspire care as unimportant—so that it is different from

---

[9] I hope it is plain enough that I am not attributing to children any thoughts that are too sophisticated for a child to have. Later in this section, I will try to remove any doubts one might have about this.

distractibility, for example. Laziness is different from a mere lack of energy because a lazy person is one who sees a relatively large number of things as not worth spending any effort on. Gluttony is not the same thing as having a large appetite, nor are people gluttons simply because they have gotten into the habit of stuffing themselves whether they are hungry or not: a glutton is someone who places more importance on food than on certain other things.

Of course, to succeed in proving that this is what impulsiveness, carelessness, laziness, and gluttony are like would require a substantial discussion of each one of them. I think these observations are plausible as they stand, however, since they do serve to distinguish between these traits and others that are genuinely different from them. I have deliberately used as examples only traits that include some sort of irrationality: each one seems to differ from something else by including a certain *thought*, and if that holds true of them, then it must be true of the more intelligent traits of character as well. On this showing, these traits are not the brute propensities that Kant takes them to be.

5. Qualifications and Caveats

I have said that in possessing a trait of character the agent thinks that certain things are so. By this I do not mean that the "thinking" involved is something that the agent necessarily puts into words. I also do not mean that the thinking is something of which the agent is necessarily aware. This is important because acting on the basis of a trait of character does not necessarily involve conscious calculation as to what to do. In this way, they are no different from other behavioral traits, including habits, temperamental dispositions, and skills. To have one of these traits means, in part, that some issues are settled in advance for the agent: it means not needing to consciously think out all the issues involved in what one does. Consequently, if some of these traits necessarily involve thought, it must be a kind of thought that need not be conscious or put into words.

Though speaking of nonverbal and nonconscious thinking might sound a little odd at first, it does not depart from common usage. Critics sometimes say that the work of a certain artist shows that he thinks, for instance, that sex is evil, and they may say so in spite of the fact that the artist disowns such beliefs and without implying that the artist is a liar. Since what we think is one source of our actions, our actions and their products are sources of information as to what we think; and we sometimes treat them as more reliable indicators than the thoughts that actually run through a person's head in internal soliloquy.

"Thinks," as I have used it here, simply means "believes," and beliefs are ascribed to a person as though they were states of which the person is not necessarily aware.

Despite its consistency with common usage, some people might still be inclined to deny the idea that we can have beliefs of which we are not conscious.[10] Unless we have some reason to repress or evade them, beliefs are necessarily conscious. I would say, on the contrary, that whenever human beings do anything, there are always, among the factors that influence their conduct, beliefs that lie outside their consciousness, and that this is so for reasons that have no apparent connection with repression or evasion. The Spanish phenomenologist José Ortega y Gasset gives an argument to this effect that is simple but, I think, quite persuasive.

Ortega asks his readers to consider exactly what lies before their conscious awareness as they perform a simple action: namely, going from one's house out into the street. The reader, he says, will have noticed such elements of the action as "his motives, the decision taken, the execution of the movements by means of which he has walked, opened the door, descended the staircase." This list could go on, but, however long one makes it, the reader will have made one interesting omission: however much he searches in his consciousness, he will not find in it any thought in which one registers that there is a street. The reader has not for a moment called into question whether it is there.

This, however, does not mean that the existence of the street did not in any way "intervene in" the reader's behavior:

> One would have the proof [of this] if, upon arriving at the door of one's house, one should discover that the street had disappeared, that the world ends at the threshold of the house, or that an abyss had opened before it. Then there would be produced in the consciousness of the reader a most clear and violent surprise. About what? About the street's not being there. But hadn't we agreed that there had earlier been no thought about its being there, had been no questioning it? This surprise makes plain to what extent the existence of the street functioned in one's earlier state. . . . This manner in which something

---

[10] Others might hesitate to apply the word "belief" to the phenomena I am trying to describe here, thinking that some other way of saying what I mean would be more perspicuous and less misleading. Perhaps I should say, for instance, that in possessing a trait of character the agent sees life in a certain way. To the extent that this alternative turn of phrase would say what I mean, this sort of "seeing" is also a sort of believing.

intervenes in our life . . . is the manner which is proper to our effective beliefs.[11]

The argument, to put it rather differently, seems to be this: The nonexistence of the street in this case would be surprising. But things are only surprising if they contradict one's beliefs. Consequently, one must have believed that the street does exist, despite one's not having consciously thought about it. Since all actions contain elements that are relevantly similar to this one, human conduct always rests on beliefs of which we are not aware.

This argument, despite its simplicity, is not easy to answer. It is true, of course, that we are sometimes surprised by an event because it differs from our past experience, but such past experience itself is never sufficient to produce the additional experience of surprise. Unless such past experiences produce a belief that things will go on in the same way (something they occasionally fail to do), one is not set up to be surprised when they do not. Again, we are sometimes surprised that things do not go as we had wished, but if we do not believe that things will go as we wish, there will be no surprise when things go against us. The presence of surprise is conclusive evidence of the presence of belief, and a surprise as violent as the one in Ortega's imagined case is particularly striking evidence.

It is also true that we do tend to reserve the use of the word "belief" to describe states of mind of which we are lucidly aware, as in the case of one's religious or political beliefs. This habit is apt to make Ortega's conclusion sound somewhat odd. But what good reason is there to think that the difference between these two sets of phenomena is so deep that we should distinguish between them by calling one of them beliefs and denying that name to the other? Both play the same sort of role in guiding conduct, can contradict states of mind that everyone calls beliefs, can be refuted by the same sorts of evidence, and so forth.

The only reason I can find for discriminating between them in this way is what Ortega would call the "intellectualist" prejudice of considering the most efficacious aspects of human conduct to be the most conscious.[12] One version of this prejudice is the notion that what people really stand for, what reveals the sense and direction of their lives, is a matter of what *credo* they will swear to. Any adequate account of traits of character—including, I hope, the one I

---

[11] José Ortega y Gasset, "*Ideas y Creencias*," in *Obras Completas: Tomo V (1933-1941)*, 6th ed. (Madrid: Revista de Occidente, n.d.), p. 386.

[12] Ortega, "*Ideas y Creencias*," p. 387.

will be elaborating in this book—will show that this is not true. I will return to this subject in the final section of this chapter.[13]

Having said this, there are three other points I have at most only suggested in the preceding sections of this chapter but which I should make explicit:

First, one need not be what Kant would regard as a fully developed moral being to possess traits of character. As far as we have seen, for instance, one need not be able to understand what someone means when they say, "You should be ashamed!" and one need not be able to make such judgments about the worth of a whole person. The only necessity we have uncovered is that of being able to make more primitive sorts of judgments, as that thus-and-such is a reason to do a certain thing, or that certain sorts of things are important or worthwhile. Kant's position seems to rest on the assumption that only a full-fledged moral agent can have character. There is no obvious reason to think that his assumption is true. It is also worth noting that the thoughts that lie behind traits of character need not be moral judgments; most of the judgments I have used as examples are not, nor do they contradict any moral judgments. This suggests that virtues and vices need not be *moral* virtues and vices. They have to do with whether one is a good person, and there may be many ways in which a person can be good that have little to do with morality.

Second, as the examples I have given suggest, these beliefs are always beliefs about what is in some sense right or good. This explains an important difference between traits of character and traits such as innocence. Due to the fact that the innocent's distinguishing belief is about how the world works, innocence can be destroyed by a single experience, such as the young hero of Nathaniel Hawthorne's "My Kinsman, Major Molineux" has when he sees his distinguished relative carried "in tar-and-feather dignity" by a jeering mob. One need only see an instance in which the world manifestly does *not* work that way. Traits of character on the other hand are very hard to bend, and experience cannot destroy them in such a simple way; on my view of traits of

---

[13] Perhaps I should point out that, although the phenomena I am trying to describe here are unconscious, they are quite different from the "unconscious" as described in psychoanalytic theory. Freud's unconscious, as I understand it, is mainly the garbage dump of consciousness, a place where unwelcome beliefs and drives are buried. They are shoved there because the agent regards them as bad. It should be clear from Ortega's description that the beliefs he is treating are often not only of great value to the agent but also indispensable for life and conduct. It *would* be bad, however, to handle all these valuable beliefs entirely within the field of consciousness. They belong in the "tacit dimension" discussed in the works of Michael Polanyi. See his *The Tacit Dimension* (New York: Doubleday, 1966), chap. 1, and *Knowing and Being* (Chicago: University of Chicago Press, 1969), part 3.

character, this would be so because experience alone cannot contradict beliefs about what is right and good (in the relevant ways).

Finally, the examples I have given suggest that none of the beliefs that distinguish traits of character are beliefs about what is a good means for a certain end or the right way to bring about a certain result, that this is not the sort of rightness and goodness they are about. In other words, they cannot be adequately represented by what Kant calls "hypothetical imperatives." This would seem to mean that having a trait of character does not consist of having mastered a certain technique, and accordingly that virtues are not skills. For if mastery of a technique is distinguished by a certain sort of belief (and it seems likely that it is), such beliefs *would* be expressed adequately by hypothetical imperatives: they would amount to believing that a certain act is a way of securing a certain sort of good. If traits of character were the possession of techniques, they would be as easily destroyed by experience as innocence is: people often abandon a technique from seeing one instance in which technique definitely does not work. If I abandon justice because I see one just person being harmed then the justice I am abandoning was not a virtue (that seems obvious enough); beyond that, it was not even a trait of character: it was only a technique for making my way through the world.

6. Principle

I have said that both traits of character and skills include beliefs of some sort. Let us call such a belief a "principle" when one does what one does because one holds that belief (when it is *principium actuum*).[14] Given this, we can say that people have a given trait of character insofar as they hold the corresponding belief and hold it as a principle: insofar, that is, as they believe it and act on it consistently (for both these things admit of degrees). On this view, a trait of character is not something that is simply internal, like a belief or a feeling that a person may or may not express; nor yet is it external in the manner of a habit, which may indicate nothing about what the agent believes or feels. It includes an entrenchment of something internal in our outward behavior. Moreover, *which* trait of character a given pattern of behavior evinces apparently depends on which principle generates the pattern. This is

---

[14] "Principle," as I use the word, is a technical term. For instance, it does not mean quite the same thing that it means in the title of Henry David Thoreau's essay "Life without Principle." The principles of a Thoreauvian "man of principle" are one kind of principle in this technical sense.

suggested by the fact that the principles I formulated for impulsiveness, carelessness, and other traits earlier on in section 4 of this chapter seem to clearly distinguish each of these traits from all others.

The principles that produce character traits are never beliefs about particular things, and, in fact, they tend to be about very general kinds of things (such as knowledge, public esteem, pleasure, and effort). From the fact that I buy a chocolate eclair because I think it would be more pleasant to eat than the dish of yogurt sitting beside it, it does not follow that my act has any particular character. But if I am overweight and on a diet and buy the eclair because I think that health does not really matter more than the pleasure of the table, then what I do is gluttonous. I will limit my use of "principle" to beliefs that are about kinds of things rather than particulars.

The case of gluttony suggests that, if an act is done on the basis of a belief which is the principle of some trait of character, then it has the act-character that corresponds to the trait. This seems to be true, but I should point out that this will not provide us with an account of *what it is* for an act to have some character or other: as far as this point is concerned, it might still be possible for an act to have a definite character although it is not done on the basis of principle.

7. Habits Again

The theory of traits of character set forth here gains additional support from the fact that it is consistent with the disparities listed in section 2 between such traits and habits, and even helps to explain them.

There I pointed out that, although acting out of character is possible, it is treated as odd and calling for an explanation (whereas, for instance, pulling one's ear when one is not in the habit of doing so is not). What I have said here suggests a possible explanation for this fact. I have said that a trait of character includes a certain perhaps inarticulate view about what is right or good. Such views are apt by nature to influence our conduct, and the fact that a person lacks a certain trait of character is therefore evidence that the person lacks the corresponding view. Thus, acting out of character suggests that an act-character has occurred without the cognitive backdrop included in the trait. This itself may be difficult to understand. If someone does some particular act that is courageous or gluttonous or has some other definite character, the most immediately forthcoming explanations for what they do will ascribe to the agent a view of life that makes sense of their behavior. These explanations will ascribe to the agent the principle that lies behind the corresponding trait of character. But if the act we are explaining is out of character for the agent, the rest of the agent's behavior—the way of life in which the corresponding trait of character is obviously lacking—is most easily explained by *denying* that they hold the relevant principle.

Given this sort of explanation, the oddity of acting out of character is like the oddity of appearing to contradict oneself. As a matter of fact, some of the explanations we give for acting out of character are also appropriate when people contradict themselves: in both cases we can explain the aberration in terms of such things as inattention, exhaustion, vested interests, and the influence of passion. Of course, to fully develop and substantiate an explanation of the oddness of acting out of character one must have an account of act-characters, and I have not offered one here.

The account of traits of character I have sketched supports the impression, indicated in section 2, that traits of character depend on the intellect in some important way: to have such traits is to *have reasons* for what one does, and the reasons involved are of a sort that "the brutes" cannot have. Perhaps a dog can "think" that it is about to be fed, but surely it cannot "think" anything about the importance of food in relation to other goods, nor about what sorts of behavior are justified by the necessity of eating something. And surely part of the reason why we can think such thoughts while dogs cannot is that we have at our disposal the powers that culture (as contrasted with raw nature) makes possible, including most especially the use of language.

The unique way in which traits of character involve the intellect can be made more vivid by considering the way in which they are related to education. We can come to be able to do many kinds of acts—including courageous and temperate ones—by being taught to do them, but precisely what is being taught is different for different cases. In the case of being taught to walk, one is simply shown or told how to perform certain bodily movements, the movements of which the act consists. It is obvious that teaching someone to act courageously is different from teaching someone to do acts of this sort. In the case of another sort of act, of which cutting wood is an example, the difference is less obvious although it is no less profound. Cutting wood is not identical to certain movements but rather mainly consists of producing certain results, and there is probably always more than one set of movements that would produce any particular result. Accordingly, teaching someone to cut wood would seem to mean transmitting certain notions that amount to a method for bringing certain things about.

This would mean that what is being transmitted is a principle on which the student is to act, which on my view is a large part of what would be transmitted when someone is being taught to act courageously. But the status of what is being transmitted is entirely different. People who have been taught to cut wood will be able to alter or discard the notions they have received and go on doing the acts they were taught to do: if there is more than one set of movements that will secure the result, there is more than one method, and the act is done whenever the result is secured by *some* method (no matter which one). Since the principle only gives *a* way of doing something, one can abandon it and yet retain the capacity for action that one acquired by learning it. Like a standardized part for a mass-produced machine, the principle is interchangeable with indefinitely many other things of the same sort.

On the other hand, when teaching imparts a trait of character the case is entirely different: the notion that the teachers must somehow impress on the students' minds is what makes the trait what it is, so that the students cannot alter or discard it without losing the capacity to act as they were taught to act. They would not be continuing the work of their teachers; they would simply be turning their backs on them. In the case of traits of character, teaching someone *to do something* is (partly) teaching someone that *something is so*, and exactly what one is taught is so is the heart of the matter.

8. The Importance of Character

Why is it important what one's character is, or whether one has a character at all? The account of traits of character I have set forth here suggests the elements of an answer to this question. To grasp what these are, it is necessary, first, to see what it is that is important if character is important.

When we use concepts of traits of character, we are thinking of individual human beings and the lives they live as admirable or in some way the reverse of admirable. In either case, the status of the life involved is partly constituted by certain traits of character. I have said that traits of character are generated by principles; without them, there could be no such thing. Further, these principles on which a way of life is based—when indeed it is based on principles—are part of what is admirable (or despicable) about it. An admirable life is partly *constituted by* the virtuous principles from which it springs. The principles that lie behind the virtues are important, not merely because they are productive of good, but because they are constitutive of the good.

This way of evaluating a way of life will be reasonable if certain other things are true. First, it must be the case that there are some general truths about what is right or good in human conduct. On the supposition that no such truths exist, the only proper way to make decisions would be to do so on an absolutely case-by-case basis, in a sort of vacuum. Such a decision-making procedure would, of course, represent a way of *lacking* character. On this supposition, there might be traits of character, but they would all represent improper ways of making decisions: they would be vices.

Second, supposing on the contrary that there are such general truths, it would be better to possess them than to be ignorant of them, and it would be better to act well because one possesses them than to do so by coincidence. In that case, the achievement of being in possession of these truths would lie at the basis of one's actions. It would constitute a deep truth about who it is that is doing these actions.[15] They would justify us in evaluating, not just individual acts, but the agent who is doing them. The same is true if the general notions acted on are wrong rather than right, except that the implications for the worth of the person would be negative rather than positive.[16]

---

[15] This might also help to explain why, as I observed earlier (section 2), the actions that spring from traits of character are not treated as "things that we do" in the same way that actions that are done out of habit are. The importance and value of such actions lie not only, perhaps not primarily, in what the individual is actually doing, but also in the enduring state of the agent from which they arise. This is not true of habitual behavior. The fact that I am doing something by habit tells you nothing, by itself, about what my values are. If you are interested in whether I do something habitually, that is simply because you are interested in what I am doing: you are interested, for instance, in whether I do it frequently and reliably.

[16] Here I think we find the basis for part of an answer to an objection that many people would raise to the conception of character I have outlined in this chapter. This is the charge that it is arbitrarily narrow. Edmund Pincoffs put it this way: "It is not clear what is to be gained by a definition that rules out such qualities as cheerfulness, imaginativeness, civility, gracefulness, and resourcefulness as qualities of character. For these qualities and very many others, it is difficult to see that any special belief need be had in order for the quality to be present." *Quandaries and Virtues: Against Reductivism in Ethics* (Lawrence, Kans.: University Press of Kansas, 1986), p. 95. Except for civility, which seems to me to include many beliefs about how one should behave, I agree that none of these qualities are clearly traits of character in my sense. A complete answer to this objection would show that these qualities are different from what I am calling traits of character in ways that are important enough to justify me in not attaching that name to them. In particular, I would argue that none of these qualities is as clearly or directly relevant to whether one is an admirable person as traits of character are. Cheerfulness and gracefulness make one an attractive person but not, of themselves, an admirable one. Imaginativeness and resourcefulness, on the other hand, *do* seem to be relevant to whether a person is admirable, but I would explain this on the supposition that they are not brute, unanalyzable abilities (as I.Q. is often thought to be) but rest on traits that are qualities of character, including a cognitive sort of courage and a kind of ambitiousness. I hope that, for those who do find my distinction between character and everything else arbitrary, it will seem much less so as I develop it further in the chapters that follow.

There is, however, one plausible reason to hesitate in accepting these conclusions: it seems clearly impossible to keep all the notions one would need to live an admirable life in one's consciousness. Performing all the calculations that would be have to be carried out in deploying such an arsenal of notions would seem to be beyond the capacity of the human mind. Even if it were possible, it would probably be neither pleasant nor attractive—nor indeed particularly admirable.

This means that, if evaluation of individuals on the basis of traits of character is to be reasonable, a third proposition must be true: that it is possible to apply such notions and act on them without being consciously aware of doing so. As I have already argued, this is indeed possible. In fact, as I have also suggested, it seems to be a large part of the function of traits of character to put conduct under the control of our knowledge without subjecting it to the meddling of consciousness. One could say that character is an essential part of the solution to what would otherwise be a fundamental problem faced by human beings: how to subject life to the guidance of ideas without turning it entirely over to the control of explicit consciousness.

So far, I have sketched my account of traits of character in rather broad strokes. The primary element in the sketch so far is, of course, the notion of a principle, but I have so far said rather little about what the principles are like that generate traits of character. In the next three chapters I will look at a number of traits of character, ones that I think it is fair to assume are virtues. My purpose will be to understand something about the principles that lie behind them and how these principles differ from one another. In chapter 5 I will make some general observations about the nature of virtue itself, and about other states of character (including vice). In the same chapter, I will also add something to my account of character that up to that point will be noticeably lacking: a general account of how character is related to the passions.

II

The Limits of the Good:
Courage, Temperance, and Self-Respect

A great and golden rule of art, as well as life, is this: that the more distinct,
sharp, and wiry the bounding line, the more perfect the work of art.
                                                    —William Blake, *Descriptive Catalogue*

1. The Problem of Courage

As I have just suggested, my account of traits of character as I have so far
presented it relies rather heavily on the concept of a principle. My account
should gain some plausibility if I can identify and discuss in some detail the
principles that lie behind various traits of character.

There is at least one good reason why courage is a good trait to look at
with this end in view. Courageous acts are responses to situations that
present the agent with a certain sort of problem, with problems that can be
characterized in a general way, and a courageous act often clearly constitutes
the agent's solution to his problem. It so happens that people often solve
problems precisely by applying principles of one sort or another (such as the
principles of engineering and the principles of strategy in war), and if
someone has solved a problem in this way, we have a method for seeking out
what principle that person was applying: we ask what principles would solve
the problem and look for one that would explain the behavior that was the
agent's solution to it. Since the problems that courage confronts can be
characterized in a general way and courageous actions also seem to have
something in common, one can hope to apply this method to such actions
generally and find some principle involved in them all.[1] Eventually, we will

---

[1] This method can be used here in spite of the fact that a courageous people need not *see*
their situations as problematic (i.e., they may not see any need to deliberate about their
present circumstances when they are acting courageously): the same fact holds in the case

see that the principle that is involved in courage has the same structure as the principles that lie behind various other traits of character, so that the analysis of courage can be used to define a whole family of traits.

Situations that are occasions for courage are, very broadly, ones in which goods that are ends of action for the agent come into conflict. Consider the following example: Peter is a lawyer who, because of his professional position, has found an opportunity to further the career of a woman who is an old friend of his.[2] The friend's husband, a colleague of Peter's, is a jealous and rather violent man who has been suspicious of their friendship for some time and is in a position to harm Peter if he wants to. Peter wants to take the opportunity to help his friend, but he knows he would be exposing himself to some danger if he did so; he also knows, however, that the husband's chivalrous code of ethics would prevent him from harming his own wife. It is clear to him that no one else can do this particular favor for his friend. Here there is a conflict of goods that are ends of action for Peter: in this situation, the good of his friend and his own safety are *alternatives*, to pursue one is to some extent to take leave of the other. Circumstances are such that he has sufficient time to reflect on this, but he hasn't enough time to discover any new facts that would show that these goods do not conflict in this way after all: he must decide soon or the opportunity will be lost. How might principle move him to act in spite of this conflict?

This question is somewhat broader than "How shall he figure out what to do?" Peter is in a situation that is capable of creating an impasse, and the question is, What could prevent it from doing so? Obviously, he could act, and even "act on principle" (in my sense of those words), without any conscious thought on his part. However, the difficulties involved in a situation like this will become clearer if we assume that Peter does deliberate

---

of the engineer and the strategist.

[2] I will be making a serious effort here to give an example that is more or less the sort of thing that my readers can imagine happening to themselves. Following an unfortunate precedent set by Aristotle, discussions of courage often focus on extreme cases involve terrifying dangers, usually in a military setting. Fixation on such cases tends to give the impression that courage involves acting contrary to powerful emotions, mainly ones that are inspired by crudely physical hazards, and doing so from idealistic reasons. Probably, most of the real courage we see in the world around us is not like that at all. Worse yet, attending mainly to such extreme cases inevitably gives the impression that courage is something most of us will never need and are just as well off without. For a treatment of courage that follows this approach to its ultimate conclusion, see Douglas Walton, *Courage: A Philosophical Investigation* (Berkeley: University of California Press, 1985).

and try to decide between two courses of action—either benefiting his friend or "playing it safe" and forgetting about it—and ask, What principles, in that case, could he use to solve his problem?

There is a broad class of principles that, at any rate, he cannot use. For instance, he cannot use any principle that tells him that, given plans of action that realize the same end, he is to choose the plan that best realizes that end.[3] Such a principle is clearly irrelevant to Peter's situation because the choice facing him is not between two ways of bringing about a single end; each of the two plans of action serves a quite different end. For the same reason, he could have no use for a principle that says that one is to choose the plan that secures all the desired ends of the alternative plans, and one or more further ends in addition. Nor, again for the same reason, could he use a principle that tells him that if two plans serve the same ends but one has a greater likelihood of achieving them one should choose that one. More generally, those principles are of no use to him that merely aid him in evaluating courses of action as good means or methods for achieving whatever ends they aim at. The alternatives before him lead to different ends, and he cannot act unless he chooses between these ends.

But can we conceive of a principled way to make such a choice? This task is complicated by the fact that the ends proposed by Peter's two alternatives are, as I will put it, incommensurable. Two ends are commensurable when and only when there is some characteristic that is such that, if one end possesses more of it than the other, the former end will be preferable. The soup on the menu tastes very different from the salad, but one may be more delicious than the other and so preferable. Only if two particular ends are commensurable can we choose between them simply by comparing them in this way.

Often, goods that are incommensurable when they are ends in themselves become commensurable when at least one of them is pursued to secure some further end. This would happen in Peter's case if he were only concerned about his own safety because it is beneficial to his friend. If that were so he might be able simply to calculate the results of his two alternative plans of action and find one to be preferable on the ground that it would be more beneficial—although not if he realized that the two plans would produce two different benefits for his friend (like peace of mind and wealth) that are themselves incommensurable. The same difficulties would crop up all over

---

[3] The three principles I discuss in this paragraph are drawn from John Rawls, *A Theory of Justice* (Cambridge, Mass.: Harvard University Press, 1971), pp. 411-13.

again. But suppose—as seems most likely—that he would not pursue either of the conflicting goods simply as ways of securing some further result. In that case, merely measuring the ends of the two plans and comparing them would fail to establish one as preferable to the other: as ends in themselves they are incommensurable. There is no relevant characteristic that safety and the good of others share, apart from consequences, such that, if one possessed more of it, it would be preferable. However, until some means are found to rank the alternative ends, it will do Peter no good to calculate how effective either of his alternative courses of action is as a means to its own end.[4]

Intuitively, conflicts between incommensurable goods seem to be typical of the sort of problem that calls a person's character into play. If the only difference between the soup and the salad that I have any reason to think is relevant is that one tastes better than the other, the choice between them has nothing to do with my character. But if I think that the entree sauteed in clarified butter is the tastier one while the one that has been grilled is better for my health, then, given the right circumstances, the choice between them obviously can involve an exercise of character on my part. But how does one's character settle conflicts between incommensurable goods? Principles of the form "An A should always be chosen over a B" are useless in such cases. It would be foolish to say that healthier foods should, no matter how slight their advantage in that respect, always be preferred to tastier ones, no matter how delicious they are. Again, although there are reasons for thinking that discussing metaphysics is in some sense a "higher" human activity than eating steak, there is no reason to think that the one should always be chosen over the other when there is a choice. Classes of incommensurable goods can never reasonably be ordered in this way.[5]

---

[4] I am assuming throughout this discussion that it is not the case that all things are pursued only because they secure some single end, such as pleasure or happiness; if that were so there would be no such thing as incommensurable ends.

[5] Some conflicts that involve moral issues seem to provide counterexamples to this. Justice and wealth are generally incommensurable, but it is hardly absurd to think that, whenever a person can acquire a certain piece of property only by doing something unjust, he should choose justice over wealth. This is only a counterexample if we suppose that justice in such contexts is an end. According to an account of the matter I will present in chapter IV, justice is not an end but a limit on the means which agents should permit themselves in pursuing their ends, whatever they may be. See also Robert Nozick, *Anarchy, State, and Utopia* (New York: Basic Books, 1974), pp. 28-35.

2. Solutions

Perhaps it is not surprising that at least one philosopher has claimed that "the role of subjectivity" in forming valuations lies precisely in the choices we must make between incommensurable goods, that "only subjective preference can guide us" in such cases.[6] I argue that, whatever the ultimate role of subjectivity in choice might be, a preference that cannot be established simply by comparing two goods can nonetheless be backed by a reason. In one sense of the word, it is not "subjective," in that it is not utterly arbitrary. It is possible to order incommensurable ends, and in reasonable ways, on the basis of certain principles.

We can find one sort of principle that could perform this function by considering two ways in which Peter might proceed to act: First, he might calculate the probable consequences of the act he is considering and worry about whether it is worth the risks involved, until at last he might think something like, "Of course it's a little risky, but being safe isn't that important" and then *make* himself do it. If he is a moralistic sort of person, he may scold himself for being so weak and small-minded as to have considered doing otherwise. On the other hand, he might barely notice the risks and, without having to deliberate and make a decision, simply go ahead and do what he was thinking of doing, because safety is not that important to him.

These two ways of acting are obviously quite different—in one he makes a decision; in the other he does not have to decide; one sounds "Kantian" and the other sounds "Aristotelian"—but, just as obviously, they have something in common. In both cases the agent acts in spite of danger because he believes that his safety is not as important as the alternative course of action would imply. That is, he is acting on the basis of some general although perhaps very vague notion of the importance of his safety. This is a case of what I have called acting from a principle. Further, I suggest that in both cases, if Peter's estimate of the importance of safety is not wrong, then his act will be a courageous one. Of course, given its somewhat trivial circumstances, the amount of courage in his act would perhaps not be great, but it does seem to show what courageous acts in general are like: they are ones that are done on the basis of the principle that one's own safety, in general, has no more than a certain measure of importance.

---

[6] Ronald de Sousa, "The Good and True," *Mind* 83, (October 1974): p. 551.

My statement of this principle is obviously incomplete: by failing to say what this measure of importance is I have left a hole in it. How might the statement be finished? One method of supplying the missing quantity is plainly inadequate: it cannot be done by stating how often one may prefer safety over other ends. We can perhaps form an idea of how important safety is to Peter by finding out how hazardous his life is generally and then determining how often he pursues safety and comparing it with how often he pursues ends that conflict with safety. But while our understanding of his principles might be partly statistical in nature, Peter, if he is rational, cannot be following a rule like "Pursue safety in no more than 40% of the cases in which you have a choice." When we act, the question is, In which cases is safety something to seek? and such statistical formulas will not answer that question.

In discussing Peter's case, however, I have already given a glimpse of the importance safety might have for him by describing him in a specific situation and saying that he might act because he believes that his safety is not as important as the alternative (i.e., inaction) would suggest. This gives an impression, although an incomplete and murky one, of how important safety is to him. One could give a quite vivid one by describing many actions, with their circumstances and the alternatives and temptations that were avoided, supplying the abundance of detail one finds in a novel or biography. This would be an adequate way to formulate the principle of courage (that is, to put it into words), and it may well be the only way. Although, like all principles, it is a belief that is general in nature,[7] it might only be possible to formulate it by describing particular actions and circumstances. The writings in which living ethical traditions are embodied, writings such as the Bible for instance, are written far more often in the language of narrative than in that of casuistry. This could be partly due to the fact that they aim at teaching us principles like this one.[8]

---

[7] I have described it as belief about one's own safety, and my safety does not seem to be a particular, as my dog and my computer are. At any rate, this belief about one's own safety is a belief about indefinitely many actual and possible situations, just as beliefs about typewriters in general and dogs in general are about indefinitely many actual and possible objects.

[8] Here my account of the role of practical reasoning in virtue contrasts sharply with that given by John McDowell in his "Virtue and Reason," *The Monist* 62, (July 1979): pp. 331-50. He claims that virtuous conduct is rather loosely related to the thoughts that virtuous people have about what is right or good (or, as he puts it, their conception of how to live). Such people do not act by "applying universal principles" (p. 347). He concedes that "if the

There are many broad classes of goods to which nearly all human beings are attached in one degree or another, including not only safety but also wealth, pleasure, the esteem of one's neighbors, knowledge, and so on. It is possible for these classes of goods to be weighted with different degrees of importance as they intervene in an individual's thoughts, feelings, and actions. If the individual has a coherent vision of human life then, to some extent, the various goods to which he or she is attached will be articulated in this way. What one's hierarchy of values—as it might be called—is can only be shown in one's actions in concrete situations such as the one in which Peter has found himself. If what you have done is courageous, your action reveals one fact about your hierarchy of values—in it, safety is not overvalued; there is a certain limit to the importance that this good has for you.

I will call principles that consist in recognizing a limit on the importance of some end "limiting principles." It is an important feature of such principles that they can only move us to act when we are faced with conflicts between incommensurable ends. We will have more evidence of this later in this chapter, when I will discuss other traits that are generated by limiting principles, but for the moment we can see that this is true of the principle of courage. Consider the case of a soldier who is of two minds as to whether to go into battle or run away, but only because his superior officer has threatened to shoot him if he does run away. Fear of the enemy and his fear of his sergeant's wrath push him in opposite directions. The principle of courage has no work to do in this situation because the problem here is not how important safety is, but only which course of action would yield more

---

conception of how to live involved a ranking of concerns . . . the explanation of why one concern was operative rather than another would be straightforward" (p. 344), apparently meaning that, in that case, one's conception of how to live would explain why one action was done rather than another. Nonetheless, he maintains—apparently as an alternative to the idea that one's conception of how to live involves a ranking of concerns—that it "shows itself . . . in" the way one perceives the concrete situation one is in (*ibid.*), and that it therefore "cannot be definitively written down" (p. 343). I think we have seen here that a "ranking of concerns" is precisely the sort of thing that can "show itself" in the way one sees one's options and chooses among them. In fact, it may only be possible to describe and contemplate such rankings in terms of concrete situations. More important, and contrary to McDowell's frequent suggestions to the contrary, the fact that a notion cannot be fully written out does not entail that it cannot require the individual who holds it to act in certain ways. Though Peter cannot definitively explain his notion of how important safety is, it can nonetheless be very obvious to him that if he were to fail to help his friend out of fear of her husband, that would be inconsistent with the notion he does hold.

of it. If he acts because he has a solution to this problem, his act will not be courageous no matter which way he goes.[9]

3. Fortitude

Courage is a complex psychological fact that must include more than simply a principle and the acts that are generated by it. The account I have given of the principle of courage suggests something about what more is included.

I have presented limiting principles as ones that settle conflicts between goods by subordinating one good to another. Such conflicts can only exist between goods that the agent *sees as* good. People who could never regard their safety as a good, who could not see injury to themselves as something to be avoided, would have no use for the principle of courage and could not be brave. Further, things seen as good are apt to exercise a sort of emotional "pull" on the one who sees them as good, and in such conflicts we may very well be more emotionally attached to the good that according to the principle is the subordinate one: thus passion may lure us away from the end that the principle selects. In fact, this is more than a mere possibility because, as I hope will be evident by the end of this chapter, limiting principles tend to subordinate goods that have an especially primitive sort of appeal.

The existence of this emotional pull indicates that the character traits that proceed from limiting principles require a capacity that might be called *fortitude*: the ability to act in spite of passion and desire when they conflict with principle. Having such a character trait means acting on the principle consistently, and sooner or later in the course of one's life—perhaps very often—passion and desire *will* conflict with principle; in such cases we need the ability to disregard them. This ability is distinct from the principle it assists and does not itself seem to be a principle (in my sense of the word) at all.

I have focused on the idea of principle because it seems important for understanding what courage and character in general are and how they work.

---

[9] Robert C. Roberts has asked, in a personal communication, how this affects the question of whether Christian martyrs were being courageous in allowing themselves to be fed to the lions, supposing the reason they did so was that they thought disobeying God is actually a more hazardous course of action than facing these wild beasts. I believe I have to say that if this really was their attitude, if they were literally playing it safe, then what they did was not courageous. Of course, this is not to deny that they were evincing other valuable traits, including genuine virtues.

From a practical point of view, however, there are times when other conditions of courage, such as fortitude, are more important.

One can lose one's courage from a variety of causes, and the condition of courage that the destroying cause removes is at least sometimes and perhaps often fortitude rather than principle. A person's courage can be exhausted by having faced too many dangers or too serious ones, and it may be broken by a devastating defeat or extreme physical injury. People who live through such shocks may lose their ability to respond to any dangers, real or imagined, with any courage at all.

It seems that this could happen without their having lost the relevant principle and without changing their other beliefs on a large scale (for instance, they need not come to believe, seriously, that the dangers they face are greater than they really are). The shocks they have suffered may so have shaken their sense of their own efficacy that they can never form a clear, definite estimate of how much danger they are in: forming such an estimate includes estimating one's ability to deal with the danger, and people with no firm sense of their own power cannot do that. To the extent that such damage has occurred, the role that the principle of courage plays in generating action would be cut back. To that extent, fear would be given a free hand; one would lose one's ability to resist it. The result would be the loss of one's courage, but one would have lost it by losing fortitude, not by changing one's principles.

Nearly all of the facts about courage that I have surveyed here—including the fact that the situations in which it is called for are instances of conflicts between goods, that these goods are incommensurable, that the conflicts between them are often the occasion for strife between one's emotions, and the fact that this trait consequently requires fortitude—have some connection with the additional fact that the trait derives from a limiting principle. Traits of character that are produced by other sorts of principles—and we shall soon see that they exist—could be quite different from courage as I have described it. Virtually none of the things I have said about courage can be translated a priori into an account of any other trait of character: we must at least know whether it proceeds from a limiting principle.

On the other hand, supposing that there are other traits that are related to limiting principles in the way that courage is, we can expect them to have certain broad features in common. This should lead us to suspect that we can give some sort of generalized account of all the traits of which this is true.

A discussion of two more traits of character that are derived from limiting principles will bear this suspicion out.[10]

4. Temperance

The virtue that Aristotle calls temperance (*sophrosyne*) has been given little or no attention by recent writers on virtue and character.[11] This is no doubt partly due to the fact that it does not seem to be a very interesting virtue. Indeed, one can easily wonder why it should be regarded as a virtue at all. Temperance, as Aristotle tells us, is concerned with the pleasures of the body, especially those of eating and sex.[12] It is opposed to vices like gluttony. As such, one can doubt that its subject matter is the sort of thing that could be important from an ethical point of view. How much one eats,

---

[10] Robert C. Roberts has argued that there is a group of virtues that are "in an important aspect skills or skill-like powers." "Will Power and the Virtues," *The Philosophical Review* 93, (April 1984): p. 246. These virtues, "the virtues of will-power," include courage and, evidently, temperance. The skills involved are "skills of self-management" (p. 238), and seem to be forms of what I have been calling fortitude. He is saying that courage and temperance either are fortitude or behave very much as if they were. I agree that fortitude is a skill, or skill-like, and that it is a necessary condition for possessing the virtues I am discussing in this chapter, but I must deny that these virtues are identical to or resemble them very much. Consider the following story. Suppose my wife decides that she is fed up with my abandoned overindulgence in food and drink: I must learn the virtue of temperance. She has me kidnapped by "deprogrammers" who force me to undergo a series of exercises in which I endure pain and delay gratification. Realizing that my only chance of escape lies in cooperating, I do so. Eventually, I learn to do something I have never been able to do: control my appetites. I do so scrupulously, and am released. As soon as I am free, I do what I was planning to do all along: stuff myself with rich food and stay drunk for days on end. Though I gained a certain skill of self-management, and though it is applied to the subject matter of temperance, what I have gained is not the virtue of temperance. Temperance cannot be turned on and off so suddenly. One way to explain the difference would seem to be this: whether one has temperance depends on what one's values are and how one values them, while this is never true of a skill. But here I am anticipating the argument of the next section of this chapter.

[11] Virtually all the sustained discussions of it I have found are, like Alasdair MacIntyre's contribution to *Midwest Studies in Philosophy*, vol. 13 (Notre Dame: University of Notre Dame Press, 1988), discussions of the writings of the ancients. The only exception is chapter 5 of N. J. H. Dent's *The Moral Psychology of the Virtues* (Cambridge, Mass.: Cambridge University Press, 1984), pp. 130-51. Dent's discussion is an attempt to show how it is possible to "regulate" one's desire for sensory pleasure.

[12] Aristotle, *Nicomachean Ethics*, 1118a2 and 1118a25.

or how often one has sex, does not seem to be the sort of thing that can tell us what sort of person one is, at least as far as this is relevant to one's merits as a human being. It seems to have no more relevance, in itself, to people's character than their sexual preferences, whether they are heterosexual or homosexual. Perhaps we should see excessive eating and sexual activity in the way that some people claim to see homosexuality, as behavioral disorders requiring therapy, and not as flaws in one's character.

Further, it does not seem, at least at first glance, that the difference between temperance and gluttony is so profound as to justify us in seeing the one as a virtue even if the other is a vice. Genuine gluttons are distinguished from other people not merely by what they do, but by their reasons for doing it: they are moved to act as they do by the very high value they place on the pleasures of eating and drinking. It is these reasons that justify us, if anything does, in passing judgment on the sort of person they are, rather than merely judging their behavior as something that had best not be done. But what reasons do temperate people have for restraining themselves in their pursuit of these same pleasures? My self-restraint might be motivated by the thought that I will enjoy my food more in the long run if I don't glut myself now and ruin my health. In that case, however, my goals and values, so far as this trait of mine is concerned, are fundamentally the same as those of the glutton: I am simply more skilled at seeking them than the glutton and will be more successful in the long run. A trait that differs from vice only in being more skillful does not seem to be a virtue and might not be a trait of character at all.

Finally, it seems that temperance is too easy, or at least too common, to be a virtue. In recent years, the notion that we should indulge ourselves more moderately in food, drink, drugs, and sex has been circulated more and more widely and with ever greater intensity in the mass media. Sex is to be safe and our lives are to be smoke free and lower in alcohol, fat, and sodium. This idea has clearly had a massive effect on the behavior of the middle class. Is this increased moderation an instance of temperance? If it is, one can certainly doubt that something that can be achieved so quickly, and simply by means of vigorous public relations campaigns, could be what moral philosophers call a virtue.

I believe we can resolve all of these problems by explaining temperate behavior in broadly the same way I have explained courage. According to this explanation, temperate people behave as they do in part because there is a certain limit on the importance certain pleasures have for them. This immediately implies that people who eat moderately simply as a strategy for increasing their eating pleasure in the long run are not temperate at all. If this is their reason for acting as they do, they may be showing good sense, but it is also quite possible that they are controlled by an overweening concern for food and drink. They may indeed be no more than skillful gluttons. The difference between temperance and vices like gluttony is more fundamental than this.

This explanation of temperate behavior also suggests how such seemingly mean and trivial matters as how much one eats or drinks can raise issues that call for an exercise of one's character. The pleasures of the body can conflict with other goods that are ends of action for us—conspicuously including the good of health—and these conflicts can be resolved by the limits the individual places on the importance of these pleasures.

As was also true in the case of courage, these conflicts are only an occasion for the exercise of temperance if the goods involved are incommensurable. Consider the following case. I often find that the foods I like most are ones that I cannot enjoy nearly as often as I would wish without gravely damaging my health in the long run. I steel myself and exercise restraint because my health matters to me. However, the only reason my health matters to me is that if I were suffering from gout and chronic gastritis I wouldn't appreciate my food as much, which is the only thing I really care about. I value my health, but only as a means to certain further ends—which are precisely the ends a glutton seeks. This would make me an *in*temperate person: gluttony does not necessarily include overeating.[13]

This, however, presents us with a certain problem in understanding what a virtue of temperance must be like: how is it possible to pursue the pleasures of the body as goods that are incommensurable with the goods that conflict with it? Such pleasures can be incommensurable with health (to focus on the most conspicuous relevant conflict) if both are pursued as ends in themselves, but it does not seem rational or virtuous to pursue them in that way. Admittedly, everyone seems to pursue pleasure as an end in itself, but what would it mean to give health that sort of status? It is difficult, at least for me, to understand such an attitude without imagining something more or less absurd, a hygienic fanaticism in which people treat their bodies as

---

[13] In a less extreme form, this is what the current fashion for healthy eating might often amount to: one indulges oneself less in the short run in order to live longer and enjoy more of the same pleasures in the long run. Such timid and calculating epicureanism would not be true temperance.

sacred objects of which they are mere caretakers.[14] Even if this can be rational, it does not seem to be something that virtue could require.

I think we can secure some valuable help in framing a solution to this problem by turning momentarily to Aristotle's discussion of temperance. Aristotle denies that the temperate person practices self-denial, abstaining from things he or she wants; such a person "takes no pleasure at all in the things the intemperate enjoy most, on the contrary, he finds them offensive."[15] In a way, it seems reasonable enough to find such things as gluttony and unrestrained sexual promiscuity offensive: probably, most people are repelled by them to some degree or other. But why *does* this seem reasonable?

The answer to this question cannot lie, simply, in our knowledge that such things are unhealthy. If I see someone eating something I know is unhealthy—for instance, if I know that the food they are eating is colored with a red dye that causes cancer—I do not find this offensive, even if I find out that they know this, too, nor do I feel what I would feel on seeing the behavior of a genuine glutton. Unhealthiness is either irrelevant to the revulsion one feels at the pleasures of the intemperate or it is only part of the story. What is the explanation, or the rest of it?

The explanation that Aristotle would most likely give is suggested by a further remark he makes about the temperate person's attitude toward the pleasures of the body:

---

[14] This is another possible interpretation, in addition to the one I have just suggested in footnote 13, of what the current fashion of healthy living sometimes amounts to. One sometimes hears, directed against some dietary or recreational practice, arguments that obviously assume that nothing that is detrimental to one's health, even slightly and in the short run only, could possibly be a good idea. This implies that we must not, under any circumstances, do anything that conflicts with the hygienic needs of our bodies. This in turn would mean that the body's well-being is not a means to anything. After all, if something is a means to an end there can, in principle, be competing means to the same end. In that case, it can be a good idea to sacrifice for it, in some degree, to a competing means that for the moment presents a more effective method for achieving their common end.

[15] Aristotle, *The Nicomachean Ethics*, trans. H. Rackham (Cambridge, Mass.: Harvard University Press, 1926), 1119a12-13. I have altered Rackham's wording somewhat. I render *akolastos* as "intemperate" rather than as "profligate" to make it consistent with my own usage. Also, in this context Aristotle's *dyscherainei* suggests, to me, something a bit stronger and more specific than Rackham's "positively dislikes," which I have tried to catch with "finds . . . offensive." For other cases in which Aristotle clearly uses this word in this stronger sense, see 1166b15 and *Politics* 1306b4. In both cases, he uses it to describe the way people perceive the doings of bad or evil human beings.

> But such pleasures as conduce to health and fitness he will try to obtain in
> a moderate and right degree; as also other pleasure so far as they are not
> detrimental to health and fitness, and not ignoble, nor beyond his means. [16]

In explaining why such a person avoids certain pleasures he uses not only
the concept of health but, in addition, the very different category of the noble
or, more precisely, the ignoble. This category clearly provides us with an
appropriate answer to the present question: we *are* offended by things we
find ignoble.

But why is it reasonable to find certain pleasures ignoble? Here Aristotle's
likely answer is in part rather quaint and archaic, but it contains an idea that,
for our purposes, is powerfully useful.

He claims, first of all, that temperance and intemperance are not concerned
equally with all the pleasures of the senses. People are never called
intemperate, he tells us, because they love things that delight the eye, such
as paintings, even if they love them too much. The same is true of someone
who is inordinately fond of music. [17] Here Aristotle is appealing to intuitions
that roughly correspond to ones that we have today. If we see excessive
fondness for things such as music and painting as character flaws at all (and
this itself is far from obvious), we treat them as flaws of an entirely different
order from the sort of behavior I have been calling intemperance. We might
think that fanatical film buffs are worthy of some sort of criticism, but they
do not offend or disgust us, as the glutton or Don Juan does.

How could it be reasonable to discriminate between pleasures in this way?
According to Aristotle, the answer is, simply, that the pleasures of the
intemperate are those of taste and touch. These are pleasures "which man
shares with the lower animals, and which consequently appear slavish and
bestial."[18] This seems to be Aristotle's account of why it is reasonable to be
offended by the pleasures of the intemperate and find them ignoble. While
the excesses of the inordinate lover of music represent errors within the
realm of recognizably human motives and choices, those of the intemperate
represent a degradation of one's humanity itself, in that such behavior is
proper to an animal and not to a human being.

---

[16] 1119a15-18.

[17] 1118a1-9.

[18] 1118a24-26.

This idea has an obvious intuitive appeal, but Aristotle seems to base it on two others that are at best debatable. One is the idea that animals enjoy the pleasures of touch and taste but not those of vision and hearing.[19] The other is the idea—apparently implicit in the passage I have just quoted—that the pleasures of a given sense modality are less human when we experience them just in case that sense modality is *also* a source of pleasure for the lower animals.

Fortunately, I think that what is most valuable in Aristotle's account can stand without either of these ideas. In fact, he makes one remark almost in passing that promises to put it on a much more secure footing than they do. He qualifies his claim that temperance and intemperance are concerned with the pleasures of touch and taste in the following way:

> But even taste appears to play but a small part, if any, in temperance. For taste is concerned with discriminating flavors, as is done by wine-tasters, and cooks preparing savory dishes.[20]

This suggests a plausible and fruitful line of reasoning, which may or may not be exactly what Aristotle has in mind here. What renders a given sensory pleasure less human, so to speak, is not simply and solely the fact that it appears in a given sense modality, but the extent to which it includes, as an essential part of itself, relatively complex states of awareness of actual events and objects. If some senses are more human than others it is because, as humans experience them, they have greater potential for such states of awareness. Vision and hearing yield immense possibilities for noting similarities, differences, and complex harmonies and dissonances among the qualities they reveal, while taste and smell are poorer in this respect, and touch is much poorer still. One cannot imagine, for instance, smells that are related to one another in ways as complex and full of intelligible meaning as are the sounds in a piece of music. If the pleasures of the lowest sense modality in this hierarchy should come to dominate my attention at the expense of the higher ones, it would constitute a change in my awareness of the world around me that could be a very important one. I know that such domination could be great enough to clash with my conception of the sort of mental life that is properly human and indeed the source of much of what I value in human life. It would simplify human consciousness in a way that would constitute a mutilation of it.

---

[19] 1118a16-24.

[20] 1118a27-29.

The reason why some people are not dominated by such pleasures is precisely that they sense this clash. Sometimes they express their sense of deviation from proper behavior by referring to some class of beings who are thought to symbolize such deviations, saying things like "I don't want to act like a pig" or "that is how animals live."[21] Ultimately, the idea that guides them, however, is not the questionable zoological theory that animals live this way; it is the ethical notion that such a way of life does violence to things that make a distinctively human way of life possible and worthy of respect. There is a limit to the importance such pleasures have for them because of their respect for their own humanity.

The difference between the conduct of such a person and that of a glutton is obviously very deep, deep enough to call one the virtue of temperance and the other a form of the vice of intemperance. This difference has to do with a fundamental distinction between ways in which conflicting goods can be weighed in deliberation. True gluttons are not people with compulsive "eating disorders." They act from a view of life in which the pleasures of the table are inordinately important. In the context of this sort of life, choices between goods can become very simple. In the extreme case, all goods are commensurable: things are more or less preferable depending on whether they possess more or less of a single characteristic, which is their serviceability in the pursuit of the relevant sort of pleasure. This is what their choices will be like precisely to the extent that they are intemperate.

The effect of the idea that animates the temperate person is to prevent choices from being simple in this way. The concerns that absorb the attention of the intemperate person are limited in the temperate one by an ideal of human conduct in which they have a subordinate sort of importance. This has the effect of freeing up the goods that compete with them, so that such goods can have their own importance, quite independently of these concerns. Health may be a means to an end, but it is not simply a means to physical pleasure and is not commensurable with it.

---

[21] There are classist versions of this practice: Aristotle is guilty of this when he says, in a passage I have already quoted, that these pleasures seem "slavish," taking slaves as paradigms of subhuman behavior. There are also racist versions, as when some neighboring tribe is given the same sort of symbolic role. The practice I am endorsing here is obviously separable from these primitive and oppressive ways of expressing it. You can have a conception of deviating from a standard without stigmatizing some group as suffering from a natural inclination to deviate in that way.

If the account of temperance I have sketched out here is correct, it is obvious that the seemingly mean and trivial matter of how much I eat or how often I have sex can reveal something important about the sort of person I am, something that is clearly relevant to whether others should find my way of life offensive or worthy of respect. On the basis of what I have said so far, we can also expect that temperance will be neither very common nor very easy to acquire if one does not already possess it. This point can perhaps be made more vivid by seeing the close connection that holds between temperance and another trait of character, which I will discuss next.

5. Self-Respect

I will approach the problem of the nature of self-respect by briefly describing a series of examples, two of which are well known and frequently discussed in the literature on self-respect.[22] Each is an instance of a person whose conduct clearly shows a lack of self-respect. I will first ask what all these cases have in common and, on the basis of my answer to that question, make a general statement about what the trait is that this sort of conduct lacks. This statement will then serve as a basis for understanding what a virtue of self-respect might be like.

The Self-Deprecator. This is a man whose accomplishments—moral, professional, and otherwise—are negligible, and he is painfully aware of this fact. In consequence, he thinks he is not entitled to decent treatment from others. He never complains when he is treated unfairly or contemptuously. He never offers his opinion, even if asked. He is content to be ignored, mistreated, or exploited by others.

The Deferential Wife. She devotedly serves her husband by doing virtually whatever he wishes. The clothes she wears, the guests she invites to dinner, the city she lives in, are all dictated by his preferences and not hers. She tends not to form preferences of her own, and when she does, she thinks of them as less important than his, simply because they *are* her preferences and not his.

---

[22] These two examples, and a third one in addition, are drawn from the influential work of Thomas E. Hill, Jr. See especially his "Servility and Self-Respect," in his *Autonomy and Self-Respect* (New York: Cambridge University Press, 1991), pp. 4-18. The first two examples I will describe are from pp. 5 and 6 of this essay. The third example is from p. 19 of Hill's later essay, "Self-Respect Reconsidered," which is reprinted in the same volume, pp. 19-24. The title I give for this case is my own and titles of the others are taken from Hill.

The Sellout. A brilliant artist creates a great painting and finds that no one seems to want or even appreciate it. He makes another version of it, altering it enough to make it popular and eliminate what makes it great. He then paints copy after copy of what is essentially the same vulgarized painting. He is somewhat disgusted at himself for what he is doing, but he wants to be rich and famous, and that is why he is doing it.

The Reckless Youth.[23] This is a young native American woman who, having grown up surrounded by the grinding poverty and hopelessness of the reservation, drops out of high school and pursues a life of petty crime and dissipation. She dangerously overindulges in alcohol and other drugs, shoplifts, goes to rough bars in the hope of getting into a fight, and sleeps with a series of young men she has no reason to respect. She thinks it is neither admirable nor good for her to live this way, but she also thinks it does not matter much what she does or what happens to her.

I hope it is plausible enough that each of these four people shows a lack of self-respect, and that in each case this lack constitutes a flaw in their characters. It is perhaps also obvious that some of these cases are quite different from others. In fact, some ethical theorists would want to say that the differences are so deep that what we see in these cases is not a single character flaw at all: the self-respect that these people lack is really two quite different traits. On one version of this view, the sellout and the reckless youth fail to show self-respect in that they fail to live up to certain personal standards of conduct, while the self-deprecator and the deferential wife fail to show self-respect in that they fail to appreciate the fact that they have certain basic rights that make them the moral equals of the people around them.[24]

---

[23] This case was suggested to me by Mary Crow Dog's account of her adolescence in her autobiography, written with Richard Erdoes, *Lakota Woman* (New York: Harper Collins, 1991). See chapter 5, "Aimlessness." The portion of her narrative that follows that chapter can be read as the story of her attempt to gain self-respect through political action. She continues the story, less persuasively I think, in her *Ohitika Woman* (New York: Grove Press, 1993).

[24] This is Thomas Hill's view of the matter. See "Self-Respect Reconsidered," p. 22. Most of the authors influenced by Hill's earlier piece, "Servility and Self-Respect," make the assumption, as he did at the time he wrote it, that the first sort of self-respect is the only sort there is. See, for instance, Laurence Thomas, *Living Morally: A Psychology of Moral Character* (Philadelphia: Temple University Press, 1989), p. 161 ff. and David Sachs, "How to Distinguish Self-Respect from Self-Esteem," *Philosophy and Public Affairs* 10 (Fall 1981): pp. 346-60. Sachs explicitly denies (p. 358) that the latter sort of self-respect is a sort of self-respect at all. See also Bernard Boxill, "Self-Respect and Protest," *Philosophy and*

This would obviously mean that there are at least two different sorts of self-respect: one in which we live up to standards and another in which we claim and secure rights for ourselves. Given the great differences between conforming to standards on the one hand and asserting rights on the other, the difference between these two sorts of self-respect would seem to be profound.

In the rest of this section and in the one that follows I will argue that the four stories I have told have more in common than this view of the subject admits, and that there is a conception of self-respect that applies unequivocally to all of them. This conception is, I maintain, the commonsense view of self-respect, the one that we actually adopt when we are not theorizing about it. I believe we will see that this conception is a coherent and interesting one, and does seem to represent a virtue. Before I can try to show any of this, however, I must pass in review a few obvious facts about the way we ordinarily understand self-respect.

People often speak of self-respect as something that prevents its possessors from doing things they might otherwise do. They say, for instance, "No self-respecting mechanic could charge money for such sloppy work" or "No self-respecting girl would go out with a boy like him." They also speak of it as a resource that helps its possessor to do things that would otherwise be difficult, as when someone says, "If you had any self-respect at all, you'd stop seeing her." Further, they treat self-respect as something that can be destroyed, preserved, or enhanced by human behavior, including their own behavior, and they sometimes claim that preserving or enhancing it is the goal of what they do. "I finally decided I had to quit that miserable job while I still had a shred of self-respect left."

Apparently, self-respect is both active and passive in its relation to human behavior: my self-respect can be both the cause and the effect of what I do. Why is this so? I think we can best get at the correct answer to this question by first unraveling another mystery.

Perhaps the most obvious feature that all four of the cases I have recounted have in common is this: in all of them, the protagonists are doing something we see as degrading or demeaning to them. In some cases, though not in all, there is also degrading treatment that they suffer at the hands of others. The notion of being degraded or demeaned carries with it an undeniable

---

Public Affairs 6 (Fall 1976): pp. 58-69. Steven J. Massey criticizes the assumption this body of literature is based on, and defends a position substantially similar to the one that Hill takes in his later treatment of self-respect, in "Is Self-Respect a Moral or a Psychological Concept?", *Ethics* 93 (January 1983): pp. 246-61.

implication of suffering a diminution of one's worth, of having one's grade lowered or being made more mean. Undeniable though it is, this implication is at times rather mysterious. What is it to be "degraded?"

I think we can find a clue to the answer to this question by considering one more example, one that involves degradation in a more strikingly obvious way than the four I have described so far. It occurs at the end of the celebrated Josef Sternberg film, *The Blue Angel*.[25] Professor Rath, who in a manner of speaking is the hero of the story, was once a stodgy but respected schoolteacher, but he left his position to marry the burlesque queen Lola Lola and travel with her road show. Eventually, he is assigned the job of the burlesque show's clown. In the climactic scene, he appears on stage in his hometown, serving as the butt of the jokes of the burlesque troupe's magician. The magician pretends to pull eggs out of the professor's nose and breaks them on his head while verbally insulting him. The audience, full of former colleagues and students, responds with jeers and laughter. Obviously, we perceive this treatment as very degrading to him. Why do we see it that way?

In a way, what the magician does to the professor does not diminish him at all. He takes nothing from him, inflicts no injuries. What he does to him, at least as I have told of it, is purely symbolic or expressive in nature. Yet this very fact seems to hold the answer to my question: it is precisely in this symbolic or expressive character of the magician's conduct that the degradation would seem to lie. Such treatment would only be *appropriate* toward someone who really is a mere figure of fun, who is indeed nothing more than a clown.

Partly because this fact is so obvious, it indicates that the person who is treating him this way does indeed think of him as a mere clown. Human beings generally, including even the magician and Lola Lola, base their opinions on reasons of some sort or other. For that reason, we almost inevitably perceive the fact that somebody holds a particular opinion, at least if it is about a matter of which the holder has direct experience, as evidence that things are indeed as the opinion maintains they are. In the present case, this would mean that the magician's opinion of the professor, and by extension his degrading treatment of him, are seen as evidence that the unfortunate man really is nothing but a clown. That is why treating him like a clown makes him, as we often say in such situations, "look like" a clown.

---

[25] Thomas Hill discusses the same film in "Self-Respect Reconsidered," but the use he makes of it is quite different from the way I employ it here.

The perceptions that human beings have of their own worth are deeply embedded in the world in which they live. Though we treat our worth as something that is real, we cannot perceive it directly, either by sense perception or by introspection. What we *can* directly perceive is only evidence, and this evidence includes both our own behavior and that of others. Conduct—whether one's own or that of another—is degrading if and only if it significantly worsens the perceived evidence of one's own worth.

These considerations suggest a hypothesis that can explain why our self-respect is, as I have suggested, passive in relation to our own behavior. The hypothesis is that self-respect includes something that is threatened by the experience of degradation: it includes a perception of one's own worth as being to some extent adequate and intact. This would mean that self-respect includes, as an essential part of itself, some degree or kind of self-esteem.[26] To have self-esteem one must have positive evidence of one's own worth, and what we do, obviously, is evidence of our own worth. Self-esteem can be destroyed, preserved, or enhanced by what we do, and that is why the same thing is true of self-respect. In other words, self-respect depends on our own behavior because self-esteem does.

The same considerations also explain why self-respect functions as a motive for things we do and as a resource that makes difficult things less difficult. Since an awareness of one's own worth is something that is deeply valuable to human beings in general, the fact that this awareness depends on one's own behavior can be the source of powerful reasons for acting or for avoiding actions one might otherwise do.

There are several different ways in which self-respect can provide us with reasons for acting. One of them often results in actions that appear irrational at first glance. It is said that during the nine-hundred-day siege of their city during World War II, the residents of Leningrad never cut down the trees in their gardens or parks for fuel, though they dismantled many wooden buildings and razed forests outside of the city. This was at a time when fuel was so scarce that it was largely reserved for heating factories rather than homes, and thousands were dying from exposure to the cold. People had been driven by hunger to eat their pet dogs and cats. There were rumors, widely believed, of

---

[26] Note that I am not saying that self-respect is identical to self-esteem, or a species of it. For that reason, the arguments presented by Sachs in "How to Distinguish Self-Respect from Self-Esteem," cited above in footnote 23, do not constitute objections to the position I am taking here.

parents who had been driven mad by their suffering and had killed and eaten their own children.

Under such terrible circumstances, sparing ornamental trees can seem a strange thing to do, but we can begin to see it as rational if we understand it as an expression of self-respect and an attempt to preserve it. The terrors of war often drive people to do things that make it difficult for them to go on believing that they are the sort of people they thought they were. After doing a series of humiliating things, each worse than the last, I can arrive at a point at which it appears—at least to me—that if I go any further I will no longer be a good person struggling in a bad situation but something worse than that: someone who has allowed his situation to ruin him. Appearances can be very important, especially when they are a matter of how one appears to oneself. In that case, I would have a good reason to draw a line, as if to say, "Here is something I will not do." The drawing of this line may be costly and have little "practical" significance at all but, of course, that is not the point. I want to avoid creating the worst sort of evidence against myself. At times, this can be a weighty reason for enduring cold or hunger.

Such conduct, then, is not entirely mysterious. It is a response to a dissonance between, on the one hand, a certain course of action that the people involved could take and, on the other, the view they have of themselves and would like to preserve. The things we do that are done out of self-respect are done on the basis of a concern for what I will call dignity. One's dignity is the fact that one appears, in one's own eyes, to be a worthy human being. As such, dignity is what is threatened by the experience of degradation. It is one's perception of one's own positive worth. When we act out of self-respect we act in order to protect our dignity, in this sense, from being lessened or spoiled. Self-respect is a trait that enables us to protect and enhance our dignity in the only way in which it can rationally be done: by producing actual evidence of our worth and preventing the creation of evidence against it.

It might be important to realize that this way of characterizing acting from self-respect does not imply that the individual involved is uncertain of his or her own worth. We can imagine the sellout, in a different version of his story, conceiving of his plan to vulgarize his own masterpiece and then realizing, with complete certainty, that he is an artist and not a hack, and that artists do not do such things. This could give him a weighty reason for not considering his plan seriously at all. Turning out popularized versions of his earlier work *feels wrong* to him, simply because it seems like the sort of thing someone else would do, someone for whom he would have contempt. That is, he regards it as something that is beneath him. If this consideration moves him to reject the plan, he would be rejecting it because, if it were carried out, his own conduct would create a certain appearance—in his own eyes—of his having less worth than he feels certain he has. He is rejecting the prospect of appearing that way in part *because* he is certain that that is not what he is really like.

6. Two Kinds of Self-Respect?

The claim I have made about the nature of self-respecting conduct is a fairly modest one: that it aims at preserving or enhancing the agent's dignity, which in this context is understood as the agent's perception of his or her own worth. This is not meant as a complete definition of self-respect as a trait of character. We will soon see that there is at least one other feature that is essential to it, besides the one just mentioned. However, as I have already suggested, there is room for doubting even the modest claim I have made here. On one plausible view of the matter, it could be argued that, although my claim might apply well enough to some cases involving self-respect, it is nonetheless a gross overgeneralization.

The view I have in mind is the one I stated briefly near the beginning of section 5. According to it, the trait that is lacking in the third and fourth of the examples I described there—namely, the sellout and the reckless youth—consists in a failure to live up to certain personal standards of conduct. On my own view, the trait that the reckless youth and the sellout conspicuously lack includes acting in order to preserve a certain sense of one's own worth. Stated as an account of the third and fourth cases, these two views are compatible. Indeed, it is very plausible to say that the actions that would preserve the sense of one's own worth involved in my view are precisely what in the other view is referred to as living up to standards. So far, my account simply adds something to the other one.

In fact, this addition is probably an improvement, since it enables us to explain the difference between self-respect and other, quite different ways of trying to live up to standards. Suppose, for example, that the reckless youth decides to abandon her pointlessly dangerous and violent way of life, and that she does it for certain purely religious reasons. She does not do it because she thinks that living decently will make her a better person. She thinks that, like everyone else but even more so, she is irremediably wicked and deserves nothing but everlasting punishment. The only way she can avoid the fate she merits is to submit to especially strict standards of personal conduct, ones that are quite incompatible with a life of promiscuity and crime. Obviously, her behavior would not be self-respecting, despite the fact that she would be living up to personal standards. As long as we view this sort of self-respect, simply, as consisting in the observance of such standards, we cannot explain this fact. Things are different, though, if we amend this view in the way I just suggested. Then we can say that she would be observing her exacting standards for a reason that makes her conduct irrelevant to self-respect. She is not acting out of concern for her dignity.

I can accommodate what the alternative theory maintains about the cases of the sellout and the reckless youth because there is obviously a very close relationship between the elements that our respective theories pick out in these cases as essential to self-respect: personal standards on the one hand and concern for dignity on the other. However, the same sort of thing cannot so easily be done in the cases of the self-deprecator and the deferential wife. According to the other view as I have already briefly characterized it, the sort of self-respect that is lacking in their cases consists simply of showing an adequate appreciation for the fact that one has the same rights that other people have, or that the same moral principles that apply to others also apply to oneself. Such considerations do not seem to be necessarily related to questions of individual merit. Why should we think that the sort of self-respect in which one stands up for one's rights requires a concern for, in my sense of the word, one's dignity?

Consider the following two stories. First, suppose that I am standing in line at the supermarket. I have been waiting for a while and there are several people behind me. A man I have never seen before approaches and after briefly looking me straight in the eye steps in front of me in line. Feeling angry and intimidated, I debate with myself whether I should say something to him, and I find that maintaining what feels to me like a cowardly silence is too much to bear. After all, it couldn't be more obvious that he is in the wrong. I say a few sharp words to him and tell him he should start at the end of the line like everyone else. The woman standing behind me energetically agrees, and the man sullenly moves to the end of the line. It seems obvious that what I would be doing here is just the sort of behavior than can be said—in its own small way, and at least if we were to add some more details to the story I have told—to show self-respect.

Again, suppose instead that, when I come to the supermarket cash register and make my purchase, the man at the checkout counter absentmindedly shortchanges me by five dollars. Angry at this obvious violation of my rights, I speak sharply to him and suggest that he pay attention to what he is doing. Flustered and apologetic, he gives me the correct change. It seems obvious that my conduct in this case is not the sort of behavior that can be said to show self-respect. It does not matter whether we add more details or not, since what I have already said is incompatible with such an interpretation.

Why is this so? The reason is not that what I do here is unjust, since what I do in the case of the man who breaks into line might have been unjust and yet still have been an expression of self-respect on my part. We could change the story, for instance, so that my comment to the interloper is something of an overreaction without changing the character of that reaction as a show of self-respect. Conduct that displays self-respect in the face of a violation of one's rights might often be unjust in one way or another.

The most immediately obvious reason why this story is so different from the preceding one is that, in it, the violation of my rights is clearly an honest mistake, while in the other one it clearly is nothing of the kind. To be the victim of an honest mistake, unless it is flagrantly negligent, is normally not degrading (though it may be very annoying), nor is it degrading to acquiesce to such treatment. On the other hand, the treatment I suffer in the first story is degrading (in its own small way) and to capitulate to it would be more so.

The reason why the one sort of treatment is degrading while the other is not would seem to have something to do with the attitudes of the individuals who are doing it. As Adam Smith says, "What chiefly enrages us against the man who injures . . . us, is the little account which he seems to make of us."[27] The man's breaking into the line seems to be an expression of contempt for me, while the checkout clerk's behavior does not.

It is not utterly obvious, though, wherein the contempt in the first story consists. It cannot consist in the man's believing that I do not possess the right he has violated. Though it is obvious that he is expressing some sort of contempt, it is very unlikely that he thinks that I lack this right. It is much more likely that he does not care about my rights, and does not think he needs to care. More generally, people who deliberately violate my rights, unless they do it out of desperation, thereby give evidence that this is the sort of thing they think they *can* do. Except in cases of desperation (or, of course, inadvertence), they must believe there is a good chance that I can neither stop them from doing what they are doing nor make them try to avoid doing it again. This means that, although they do not intend to represent me in an unflattering light, they are implicitly denying that I have a characteristic that is vital to everyone's perception of their own worth. This characteristic is efficacy, the ability to make events turn out as one wants them to. By doing something to me that I

---

[27] Adam Smith, *The Theory of Moral Sentiments* (Oxford: Oxford University Press, 1976), p. 96.

obviously have every reason to prevent, they are implying that I lack this ability. If I take this implication to heart, I will thereby be lowered in my own eyes.

My standing up to mistreatment by others can, however, only show self-respect if I have some reason to take this implication to heart: I must have some reason to take it as evidence of my actual worth.[28] This means that there are deliberate violations of rights that, even when not done out of desperation, are not occasions for self-respect. One cannot show self-respect, for instance, by "standing up to" the misbehavior of a small child or a severely retarded and physically handicapped adult. If you are my slave, I am not showing self-respect by having you whipped for stealing from me, even assuming that you really did steal from me and that your theft violated my rights. Self-respect is the scourge of tyrants, not of slaves. The actions of slaves are not normally occasions for self-respect because, like children and retarded adults, slaves have so little efficacy that they cannot normally present a threat to an ordinary adult's self-esteem.

Clearly, then, self-respecting conduct does not consist simply in showing an appreciation for one's moral status or rights. Self-respect is *self*-respect: it is an intentional state of which the self is the object. My self-respect, if I have any, is about me, and not about moral principles or rights in general, nor even about my rights.[29] Violations of my rights, or of rightlike claims I have against

---

[28] Of course it sometimes happens that, in contrast to the story I have just been discussing, people who violate the rights of others really do believe that their victims do not possess the rights that they are transgressing. If I knew that my skin color marks me as a likely victim of prejudice, I might often believe that an individual who treats me badly thinks I have no right to be treated in any other way, and in that case I would find such treatment particularly degrading.

[29] I think this point is missed in the argument of Thomas Hill's "Servility and Self-Respect." What that argument purports to show is that the particular way of lacking self-respect that Hill finds in the self-deprecator and the deferential wife is a "moral" flaw, without question—beggingly assuming a duty to defend one's rights. It can be roughly paraphrased like this: (1) people who do not defend their rights do not adequately appreciate their rights; (2) morality, whatever its contents might be, requires that one adequately appreciate rights as such; and (3) whoever does not do what morality requires is morally flawed; but (4) those who do not adequately appreciate their own rights do not adequately appreciate rights as such; so (5) people who do not defend their rights are morally flawed. But what exactly is the flaw that is alleged in (5)? The only premise that states a moral duty is (2), which says that we must care about rights, no matter who possesses them. On the basis of this principle, the only thing, precisely, that we can say is wrong with what the self-deprecator and the deferential wife are doing is that they are failing to appreciate *someone's* rights—the fact that

someone, are sometimes relevant to my self-respect, but only because they sometimes really are about me. When such violations do have this sort of relevance, it is partly because there is reason to believe that the violation expresses an opinion that in some way clashes with my self-esteem.

Confronted with such treatment, I can easily feel that this sort of treatment constitutes evidence that I am not the sort of person who is worthy of my esteem, and that my accepting or tolerating it would be further, more devastating evidence. If I act out of self-respect in refusing to accept or tolerate it, then I am acting in order to protect my perceived worth from the appearance of being lessened or spoiled.

This, of course, would mean that the modest claim I earlier made about the nature of self-respect fits the cases of the self-deprecator and the deferential wife just as it does those of the sellout and the reckless youth. What makes the lack of self-respect in the former two cases so clear is the fact that they are about people who have obviously capitulated to the opinions expressed in the treatment to which they are subjected. In my telling of the story of the self-deprecator I have made this capitulation explicit. In the case of the deferential wife it is evident, by an obvious inference, as the only plausible explanation of her behavior. Any plausible explanation that would show why she subordinates her will so completely to that of her husband, to the point of tending to not form preferences of her own, will imply that she thinks that she is inferior to him in her ability to make and carry out decisions that are fully her own.[30]

---

these are their rights is no part, so far, of what is wrong with what they are doing. However, as I say, self-respect is *self*-respect. People who act out of self-respect, or struggle to preserve it, are concerned with their rights *because* they are theirs and no one else's. If they are really only concerned because someone's rights have been violated, so that it makes no difference to them that the rights happen to be theirs, then the trait involved is not self-respect but something else. It seems to be simply a respect for rights. Hill's argument fails to show that a clearly essential feature of self-respect is a moral duty and, consequently, failure to show self-respect is no part of the moral lapse of which Hill has convicted the self-deprecator and the deferential wife.

[30] Hill seems to doubt that this is true of the sort of behavior we see in the case of the deferential wife. In his version of her story, he says: "She readily responds to appeals from Women's Liberation that she agree that women are mentally and physically equal, if not superior to men. She just believes that the proper role for a woman is to serve her family." "Servility and Self-Respect," p. 178. We can imagine—though just barely—that she can believe that her proper role is simply to "serve her family" while disbelieving her own inferiority, at least if serving one's family means promoting their well-being. But this is not really an accurate description of the role she has reserved for herself. She has simply

7. Limits

Though still in his early twenties, an age at which many in his profession have years of obscurity and semistarvation to look forward to, Andrew seems to be standing at the beginning of a brilliant career as a movie actor during the reign of the old Hollywood studio system. He has achieved something he has wanted for a long time: a small part in a high-prestige picture. Though the director reduces the importance of his part somewhat, prompted by persistent arguments over what the press would call "artistic differences," Andrew's striking presence and obvious talent catch the attention of studio executives and he is given a contract. He is soon assigned the leading role in a vulgar entertainment aimed at a teenage audience and he refuses it, despite the fact that the assignment is an order and not an offer.

His friends remonstrate with him, but he says, "I won't make an ass of myself" and complains that the project to which he has been assigned is shallow and phony. His friends cannot deny the truth of his complaint, nor can they say he underestimates his talent and potential achievement, but they point out that virtually all fine actors had to take work that really wasn't worthy of them at the beginning of their careers. "Right now the main thing is to be seen," they say. But he is only really interested in avoiding the threat of degradation that confronts him. After a few more minor quarrels over artistic differences, the studio ends his contract when his current option is up. He gets a few more minor roles, but his reputation for being "difficult to work with" pursues him from one studio to another and his attempts at correcting it are half-hearted and too late. Eventually, the offers stop coming and he is forced to abandon a career he had loved.

---

absorbed her husband's interests and preferences, acting on them instead of her own. We can only explain *that* sort of behavior by either attributing beliefs to her that imply her own inferior worth, or by imagining something that is extremely unrealistic. Further, if we take the latter course we take away the basis for claiming that she lacks self-respect. For instance, we might suppose that she thinks that a family cannot exist for long unless one of the parents submits unconditionally to the other, and that the reason she should be the one to submit to despotic rule is something that does not reflect in a negative way on her worth at all. Perhaps she thinks that men are physically incapable of performing this essential function, or that they lack the bullet-biting strength it takes to mortify one's petty vanity by accepting the whims of another human being as if they were laws of nature. If we were convinced that this is really how she thinks then, though we would believe her behavior is foolish and harmful, we could not say that what it shows is a lack of self-respect on her part.

Obviously, Andrew's conduct appears to betray a flaw in his character. This flaw does not seem to involve his overestimating his own merits, nor is he clearly wrong in feeling that the behavior that he refuses to accept or tolerate on the part of others is demeaning to him. Nonetheless, he does seem to be wrong in refusing to tolerate or accept this behavior.

His refusal is based on a tension he feels between his own worth and what he is repeatedly asked to do. This tension may be real enough and, if it is, it is certainly important, but just as certainly its importance is finite. It is quite possible to be too concerned about what is degrading and demeaning to oneself, as indeed it is possible to be too concerned about the insults that are often implied in violations of one's rights.

We can put this point more generally as follows: It is quite possible to rate too highly the importance of the things that are the concerns of self-respect. Such things are important to us because they constitute evidence regarding our worth: certain sorts of behavior (both our own and that of others) can make us feel low and mean because they are evidence that low and mean is just what we are. How we appear to ourselves is important to us, and rightly so, but this is mainly because what we are *really like* is a matter of still greater importance. The sense of one's own worth that self-respect jealously guards is important because it is a powerful incitement to becoming and remaining a worthy individual, and while it is conceivable that there is no limit to the importance I should place on being the sort of person who is worthy of being admired and taken seriously, that is certainly not true of the importance I should place on *appearing*—even in my own eyes—to be that sort of person. In other words, there is a limit to the importance of dignity. As we can see in Andrew's case, there are times when it will crowd out things that, for the moment, are more important.[31]

---

[31] In contrast to what I have said here, it seems to be an implication of Hill's "Servility and Self-Respect" and the literature that has followed its lead that the things that are the concerns of self-respect are things that cannot be rated too highly. Values like human rights and the status of human beings as moral equals are, at any rate, not *obviously* the sorts of things that can be overvalued, and these are precisely the things that, according to this literature, self-respect is about. It is not clear how, on such a view, one would go about distinguishing between self-respect and, for instance, petty quarrelsomeness. One cannot do it by saying that the latter trait involves doing things that are unfair because, as I have pointed out, self-respect is also compatible with doing such things. Besides, petty quarrelsomeness itself is not necessarily unfair, only petty. That is, it consists in treating things of small value as if they were great.

Some people will want to say that what all this shows is that, as in the story of Andrew's brief career, self-respect can be a bad thing if carried too far, but I doubt it would ever occur to someone actually observing behavior like his to say something like, "He carried self-respect too far," or "He has too much self-respect." Andrew suffers from what we call "vanity" or, perhaps more accurately, "arrogance." Similar distinctions seem to be called for whenever someone is taking the concerns of self-respect too far. People who are too sensitive to insults that are expressed in violations of their rights are displaying quarrelsomeness or petty resentment and not self-respect. In general, one cannot show self-respect consistently, as a trait of character, unless there is a certain upper limit to the importance one attaches to the need to protect one's dignity from being lessened or spoiled. If there is no such limit, whatever trait one displays is something quite different from self-respect.

Self-respect, then, includes a limiting principle of the same sort we saw at work in courage and temperance: a recognition of an upper limit to the importance of some good that is an end of action for us. More obviously it includes as well a recognition of a lower limit to the importance of the same good. One cannot be said to show self-respect unless there are certain things that, from considerations of self-esteem, one will not permit oneself to do or will not tolerate on the part of others. Although, as we have just seen, this does not require us to give such considerations infinite weight, it does require us to take them seriously, and it is incompatible with sacrificing them to alternative ends of action that are comparatively unimportant. We cannot say that the deferential wife fails to show self-respect if the reason she submits so completely to her husband is that to do otherwise might give him a fatal heart attack or would expose her to the danger of death by starvation, but it is a very different matter if she does so merely to avoid slight risks to herself or to avoid hurting her husband's feelings.[32]

Self-respect has a characteristic that Aristotle attributed to all virtues. According to his "doctrine of the mean," each virtue is opposed not merely to one vice, which is its opposite, but to two, "one of excess and one of defect."[33] There are two directions in which one can wrongly deviate from self-respect. Andrew takes one of these ways, while the four characters whose cases I recounted at the beginning of section 5 err in the other direction. Self-respect

---

[32] This point is due to Hill, "Servility and Self-Respect," p. 11, though he puts it rather differently and would probably explain it differently as well.

[33] Aristotle, *Nicomachean Ethics*, 1117a3.

lies, just as Aristotle's doctrine would have it, in "observing the mean" between these extremes.[34]

Each of these two errors takes various forms or, at least, is called by various different names. In one direction one wanders from self-respect into arrogance, vanity, quarrelsomeness, and petty resentment. These are some of the names we have for the errors of excess, in which dignity is overvalued. For the errors that lie in the other direction we have, for some reason, fewer names. "Servility" is perhaps the most appropriate word for the error we found in the cases of the deferential wife and the self-deprecator,[35] but there seems to be no single word in English for the corresponding vice (or vices) of defect that do not consist in submitting to ill treatment on the part of others. "Self-contempt" applies only to some cases, and even then only refers to the way individuals perceive themselves and not to their behavior. It is obvious enough, though, that self-respect is as it were bordered by vices on both sides.

The same thing is true of courage and temperance. In fact, it is true of all virtues that are based on limiting principles. To understand why this is so, we can begin by considering courage as an example. If we are to call an act courageous we obviously must assume that it is done because the agent does not overvalue safety. But we must assume more than that. For this assumption would be true just in case the individual places no value on safety whatsoever. This would not be an instance of the virtue of courage, nor of any other virtue, because safety does have value for human beings. It would be an the extreme case of a vice that might be called recklessness. People who act this way, if they exist, would be avoiding the error that the coward makes, but *only* because they are committing another error.

If we are to call an act courageous we must assume, then, that the agent values safety rightly, neither more nor less than it should be valued. If one does value it either more or less one is, of course, in the realm of vice rather than virtue.

This argument can be generalized. If a given end of action is good and—like the ends that are regulated by temperance, courage, and self-respect—is not good without limit, then it is also something that can be either overvalued or undervalued. If I avoid overvaluing it simply by *under*valuing it (or vice versa) I am merely deluded about what its value is. There is no merit at all in that. A principle that regulates how much one values such a good cannot be a

---

[34] *Nicomachean Ethics*, see 1104a12-18.

[35] Hill, "Servility and Self-Respect," *passim.*

foundation of virtuous action unless it avoids both sorts of errors, for otherwise it would in some cases merely be a consequence of an error about the subject it is supposed to regulate.

Aristotle's doctrine of the mean is true of virtues that are based on limiting principles. Assuming that the goods that these virtues regulate are goods with less than infinite value, each of these virtues consists in getting something right. In this context, "getting it right" means pursuing the good neither deficiently nor excessively. The corresponding deficiency and the contrasting excess constitute getting it wrong and are vices. Indeed, so long as we are looking at virtues like the ones I have discussed in this chapter, Aristotle's celebrated doctrine seems almost to be a truism. We shall see in the next chapter, however, that it is not true of all the virtues.

8. Temperance Again

Before I go on to a new subject, I should make more explicit a hint I made about temperance at the end of section 4. I said that one problem that confronts us as we try to understand what a virtue of temperance could be like is that it is not easy to see how it could be a virtue—given, among other reasons, that it is concerned with rather petty things and seems to be a very widespread trait and easy to acquire. We can now see that, at least if we add a plausible assumption about temperance to the account I have given of it, it is closely connected with another trait of character, one that deals with a much broader range of problems.

The idea that animates temperate people consists, in part, in the notion that certain ways of acting do violence to things that make a distinctively human way of life possible and worthy of respect. Wherein, exactly, does this violence consist? Part of the answer, at least for some temperate people, would most likely be that such ways of acting would simply feel wrong to them because they would seem to be the sort of thing some other agent would do, one that is not human and does not live the human sort of life. More generally, part of the what bothers temperate individuals about the conduct that they avoid is that, if they were to indulge in it, it would create a certain appearance—in their own eyes—of their not having the value that they feel that human beings have. If that is so, then part of what lies behind temperate behavior is a concern with dignity: not simply with one's dignity as an individual but with one's dignity as a human being.

Insofar as they act and abstain from action to maintain their dignity, their concerns are much the same as those that motivate people with self-respect.

We have seen ample reason in the course of my treatment of self-respect to think that these concerns are not easy to live up to, are not very likely to become commonplace, and are far from trivial. To the extent that both traits aim at preserving dignity, the reasons for thinking of temperance as a virtue are identical to those that favor self-respect.

III

The Unity and Diversity of the Virtues: Generosity and Related Matters

1. What Generosity Is Not

Thinking about the virtues has often brought out the Eleatic tendencies of philosophers. Socrates, the Sophists, Plato, Aristotle, and Kant all believed, in one way or another, in what is sometimes called "the unity of the virtues," the idea that the virtues are all one thing, either because they are really the same trait or because they are somehow inseparable from one another.

In sections 3 through 5 of this chapter, I will argue that the relations among the virtues are more complicated, and perhaps more interesting, than this idea suggests. Though it is true that, as the philosophers have often suggested, there are hidden and sometimes surprising connections among the virtues, they are also related by contrast and mutual tension. The virtues are divided into fundamentally different *types* of character traits, and foreign relations among the types are not always friendly.

To some extent, this argument will rest on the foundations I have already set down in Chapter II. In the first two sections of this chapter I will lay the rest of its foundations by giving an account of the virtue of generosity. I will begin, in this section, by contrasting this virtue with other ways of acting that are generally thought to have ethical merit.

It is very natural to want to say that, whatever else might be true of them, ethically meritorious acts are always done "in order to fulfill our obligations" or "for the sake of duty." Such remarks can mean various things. For the moment, I will use "obligation" and "duty" in what I take to be their ordinary language meanings. Obligations, in this sense of the word, are generally incurred by previous committing actions (such as signing one's name), while a person is generally said to have duties by virtue of one's special status or position relative to other people (for instance, one's profession).[1] It is easy to see that in this sense it is not true that generous acts are done in order to fulfill one's duties or obligations. In itself, this fact is perhaps not very interesting, but when it is understood it will suggest why, in a more theoretically loaded sense of those words, this statement is still not true.

Consider an example of an obligation in the ordinary sense of the word. If I were to take a bottle of wine next door and give it to my neighbor my act would not be generous if, for instance, I borrowed a similar one from her last week and am giving her one today in order to set matters straight. This is not a generous act but an attempt to pay a debt. I say "attempt" because it is not by virtue of the fact that it *is* the payment of the debt but rather because it is *intended* to be, that an act fails to be generous. For example, suppose that I have forgotten that I had borrowed the wine from my neighbor and give her some today as a friendly favor; afterward she reminds me of the debt and we agree that it is settled. In that case the act would be both a generous deed and the payment of a debt. But if I do it *in order to* pay the debt what I do will not ordinarily be generous at all. In general, to the extent that acts are done to fulfill one's obligations—to pay one's bills, keep one's promises, and live up to one's contracts, for instance—they cannot be generous. The same is also true of acting to fulfill the duties of one's station in life: father, janitor, citizen, and so forth. Peter is not being generous in sweeping Paul's floor if he is Paul's janitor and is supposed to sweep his floor and does it for that reason.

Though the actions that are interesting for ethics are not often done for a single reason, we can see by considering reasons for acting in isolation from one another that some fail to distinguish a deed as generous because of the kind of reason they are and make it a different sort of action. Early in Thucydides' *History* a group of representatives from the city of Corcyra come to Athens to ask the Athenians to fight with them in their present conflict with Corinth. At the beginning of their plea they make a frank admission:

> We have come to ask for help, but cannot claim that this is due us because of any great services we have done you in the past or on the basis of any existing alliance.[2]

---

[1] Here I am following a precedent set by E. J. Lemmon in "Moral Dilemmas," *The Philosophical Review* 71 (1962): pp. 140-42.

[2] Thucydides, *The Peloponnesian War*, trans. Rex Warner (Baltimore: Penguin, 1954), p. 30.

That is, Athens has neither an obligation to help by virtue of favors it has accepted in the past nor a duty to do so as a member of a league. But the Corcyrean embassy goes on to say that their request is actually "an extraordinary stroke of good luck" for Athens, because under the circumstances helping them would be a noble thing to do: "the world in general will admire you for your generosity."[3] It would be a generous thing for them to do *because* it is not due them in these ways. On the basis of what we have seen so far it is at least plausible to say that if the Corcyreans had argued for assistance on the ground that it was owed them in any way, that it was theirs by right, they would be recommending it as something other than a generous act. I will return to this point shortly.

There is another sort of act, similar to the two just considered, that can easily be distinguished from generosity. It includes those actions in which something is given to someone because the recipient is thought to deserve it. It is just, and not generous, to give a student an "A" for having done excellent work, or to give a soldier a medal for unusual bravery.

Each of these three sorts of action—those I have associated with obligation, duty, and desert—is one in which something is given to someone, and in each one the recipient of the act has some characteristic (this person has loaned me a certain thing; this person is my employer; this person is a student who has done outstanding work) by virtue of which the giving is *called for*, and the thing given is *the person's due*. In the case of duties and obligations, this means that the person who has the duty or obligation *must* do the giving (unless there are counteracting considerations involved), that it is a fault to omit it (a failure to do one's duties, etc.). The case of desert is somewhat different, in that the fact that people deserve something, such as praise, does not by itself mean that any particular individual should give it to them; that would depend on further facts about the particular person. If you are a filmmaker who has produced a brilliant film and I am a film critic writing a review of it, then it would be a fault of mine if I were to fail to praise it. But still, the fact that people deserve something means that it would be bad if they were not to get it, that someone (if not anyone in particular) should give it to them; so there is a sort of necessity in this case, too.

The contrast between generosity and these other ways of acting reinforces the suggestion I made earlier in this section that in generous acts what is given is not given because it is owed to the recipient in *any* way. However,

---

[3] Ibid., p. 31.

this suggestion is somewhat too broad to be adequately supported by the evidence I have given so far. A philosopher who believes that the intention to fulfill one's obligations or duties is what makes an act ethically meritorious might well want to object to it as it stands.

When it occurs in philosophical theories, the word "obligation" is often used to mean something rather different from what I have used it to mean here. As the word is often used, a person can be said to have an obligation just in case there is a valid rule that enjoins one to do a certain thing, so that to follow the rule is to do the right thing and to deviate from it is a fault. In this sense, I can have an obligation I did not incur by some previous committing action. Thus, one might want to say that if it would be admirable of the Athenians in the episode from Thucydides to agree to the Corcyreans' request, there must be a rule that requires them to do so, and they must be acting on the basis of it. Their assistance could then be said to be something they owe to the Corcyreans, though it is also generous of them to give it.

In that case, one would be interpreting this episode in terms of a general theory of what all virtue is like, which in turn derives from a notion of what all the principles of virtue are like: they are rules that enjoin actions (including, presumably, omissions), and they do so by declaring which act must be done (or omitted) in the circumstances to which the rule applies. I will call such rules "act-necessitating rules." It is undeniable that such rules are part of morality as we know it. Moral principles that prohibit theft and fraud, for instance, are act-necessitating rules. In addition, I will argue in chapter IV that there are virtues in which such rules do play the sort of role claimed for them by this theory. But is this what all virtues are like? In particular, is this what generosity is like?

We should notice, first of all, that this description of the incident from Thucydides merely assumes this is what generosity is like; the story does not support this idea by itself. The Corcyreans neither say nor suggest that the Athenians would be at fault if they didn't come to their aid, and it is not obvious that they must think so. They appear to be requesting help, not demanding it.

There is actually a rather simple reason why generous acts *cannot* be observances of act-necessitating rules. As I have suggested, failure to act as an act-necessitating rule enjoins is (assuming the soundness of the rule and the absence of a valid excuse) a fault, conduct worthy of criticism or censure. For instance, the omission of an act enjoined by a rule of etiquette is generally an impropriety: a slip, a blunder, or a piece of rude or crude behavior. But there does not seem to be any generous act the omission of which would be a fault. Admittedly, it might be wrong of me to omit helping someone whom I know is in serious need and whom I can easily help, but—to introduce what seems to me a useful and natural distinction—the act that I would be omitting would be an act of charity rather than generosity. In this sense, a charitable act is a response to conditions of need, such as poverty, by virtue of which the act is called for, while a generous act is not.[4] Charitable acts appear to be observances of act-necessitating rules, but that would not mean that generous acts are.

Again, it is natural to suppose that, since stinginess is the opposite of generosity, the omission of any generous act is stingy and therefore worthy of censure. But this is not so. Stinginess is never simply the omission of a generous act; stinginess is a trait of character and must include its own underlying motivational source just as generosity does, which means that a stingy act (or omission) is one that is done for certain reasons and is not the mere omission of some other sort of act. Generosity and stinginess are contraries, and not contradictories, as observances and breaches of etiquette are.

I will soon give another reason why generous acts cannot be observances of act-necessitating rules, but first I must press the analysis of generosity a bit further.

2. What Generosity Is

So far, I have distinguished generosity from other ways of acting by indicating reasons for action that do not produce generous action. I will eventually try to show what generosity itself is by showing what reasons do lie behind it. As first step toward this end, I will focus on a somewhat simpler and easier task: that of showing with what intention generous acts are done. "The generous intention," as it might be called, is crucial for understanding what it is to act generously. By saying what sort of intention it is, I will have distinguished generosity from nearly every other way of acting. I can then distinguish it from the rest by making a small addition to my account of the reasons for which generous things are done. When this is done, we will have an account of what generosity is.

One fact about the generous intention is quite obvious. In acting generously, one always intends to benefit someone other than oneself. But

---

[4] In Christian literature, "charity" is often used to signify (something like) benevolence in general; here I am using it in the narrower sense in which it means almsgiving.

this fact does not distinguish generous acts from ones done to fulfill one's duties or obligations or to give people what they deserve. Sometimes the duties of a person's station in life include not only specific actions, like the janitor's sweeping the floor, but also a requirement to benefit someone in some general way, to protect and advance their real interests. A father stands in such a relation toward his children, and the same is true of what the law calls a trustee and the person in whose behalf the trust is managed. In such cases, an action may be done in order to benefit someone and by that fact be an action done in fulfillment of duty. And, in similar ways, acts in which something is given because one has an obligation to do so or because the recipient deserves it can be done with the intention of benefiting the recipient.

But in generous acts the *way* the benefit is intended is different from the way it is intended in the other cases. If we ask a man with a worthless son why he persists in helping him out of trouble the answer will be something like, "Because he's my son," insofar as he is doing it because it is his paternal duty. That is, so far he is benefiting him in order to fulfill the requirements of being a father, and what he does is to that extent not generous. The same result obtains with acts in which we benefit someone in order to give them what they deserve or in order to return a favor. In the case of generous acts there is no such "because" or "in order to" beyond the intention of benefiting someone: we do not do *that* in order to do something else. In this way, the intention in such acts is gratuitous.

This provides us with an explanation of some facts mentioned in section 1: that it is sometimes impossible for an act to be done in order to fulfill a duty or an obligation, or in order to give someone what they deserve, and also be generous; in fact, we can see that these phenomena have something necessary about them. The contrast between generosity and these other ways of acting is not a matter of having two different sorts of intention in doing what one does; it is a contrast between having certain intentions and *not* having them. There are cases in which an act can be characterized as generous and also as belonging to one of the types I discussed in section 1, but such cases don't seem to be the sort that show this principle to be false. An act can be both generous and done in order to fulfill a duty if the duty is one that the agent does not find clearly binding (a "duty" to give gifts to relatives at Christmas could be like this). Just as a vague statement can be said to be both true and false, so an intention that is vague in this way can be said to be in a way dutiful and in a way not. We find something similar in the case of some supererogatory acts, as when I repay cheap wine with excellent wine. Here part of what I do is something required of me (giving back what I have borrowed) and part of it is not (giving more than I received). In both sorts of cases a person may be said both to have and not to have the sort of intention that cancels the generosity of the act.

For many generous acts, if we ask the agent why it was done—"Why did you give your neighbor a bottle of wine?"—we are liable to get an answer like "I just thought I would" or "It was an impulse." At any rate, such answers to such questions would always make perfect sense. Answers like these, however, do not make sense with many other transactions in which something is given to someone. If you ask a man why he gave a dollar bill to his grocer and he replies, "I just thought I would," that means he was not trying to buy something. If a teacher is asked why he or she gave certain students high grades and responds, "It was an impulse," it means that the teacher was not trying to give them what they deserve. If I told you that I sent ten dollars to the telephone company "on impulse" you would probably suppose that, whatever I was doing, I was not trying to pay my bill. When people give something and then claim that it was given on impulse, they thereby exclude what they do from these three classes of actions: attempts to purchase something, attempts to reward personal desert, and attempts to pay one's debts. And, what is most important, such claims have the same significance in relation to observances of act-necessitating rules. If a man at a dinner party truthfully claims that he has just eaten mashed potatoes with his spoon (rather than his hands) "on impulse" it means that he is not doing so because he believes that this is what one should do in these circumstances —because, that is, he subscribes to a rule of etiquette. Generous acts are different in kind from such observances because such claims do not exclude an act from being generous.

This fact raises a problem about the rationality of generous acts, or at least impulsively generous ones. In one sense of "rational," an act can be said to be rational if the agent had some reason (perhaps a bad one) for what he or she did. A clue to the nature of the problem can be found in a remark Elizabeth Anscombe has made, to the effect that such claims as "It was an impulse" and "I just thought I would" signify that the speaker *had no reason* for what he or she did.[5] This suggests that the generosity of an act is always compatible with a claim that would indicate that the act was irrational. However, this suggestion somewhat exaggerates the nature of the problem.

---

[5] G. E. M. Anscombe, *Intention* (Ithaca, N.Y.: Cornell University Press, 1963), sections 17 and 18.

While many acts that are done "on impulse" are done for no reason at all, this is not true, without qualification, of all of them. If you generously give a book to someone else and we ask you why, there are *some* things you might truthfully say that could be called giving a reason: you might say, "Because it's an interesting one" for instance, or "I thought she would enjoy it," or "It explains some things very well." And it seems that, even if someone had acted for reasons like these, they might instead have truthfully said, "It was an impulse" or "I just thought I would." However, although acting on impulse and the like is compatible with acting for such reasons, it is not compatible with acting on the basis of certain types of *principles*:

A. Many kinds of acts have what might be called a constitutive aim: that is, there is some state of affairs that must be mentioned in the definition of that *kind* of act as the one the agent intends, by the act, to bring about. Every generous act is an attempt to bring it about that someone other than the agent possesses some good. All other effects of the act might be called its consequences. In this sense, although an act that is done on impulse may have a constitutive aim, such acts are never done for their consequences. Everyone who opens a window on impulse intends to get the window open, but if I open the window on impulse, I do not do *that* to cool the room down, signal someone across the street, etc. The same thing is true of impulsively generous acts, and, indeed, of generous acts in general. This implies that impulsive acts and generous ones as well are not done on the basis of rules that cite some consequence of the act as a reason for doing it. That is, they are not done on the basis of a "hypothetical imperative."

B. Impulsive acts and generous acts are not done on the basis of act-necessitating rules.

Together, (A) and (B) suggest that Miss Anscombe's remark about acting on impulse may be substantially correct, and that it might with the same force apply to generous acts as such. The fact that generous acts—to concentrate on the case that concerns us directly—have a constitutive aim makes possible such answers to the question, "Why did you do that?" as "Because it's an interesting one," "I thought she would like it," and so forth. Such claims simply assert the efficiency of the act as a route to its constitutive aim. But (A) and (B) cut off two classic ways of giving one's reason for *doing the act at all*. In fact, it rather looks as though all ways have been cut off. The answers in my example all make sense as answers to the question, "Why give this person this book (instead of something else)?" But suppose we were to ask the person who has given the book, "Why give him something (anything)?" The answers given are not answers to *this* question, and indeed it seems that any answer that might be given to this one would signify that the act was so far not generous—for instance, "I owe him a favor," "I promised I would," "It's his reward for being a good boy," "She's in a position to help me out later on." It looks as though, to put the point another way, the *way* a generous act is done can have a reason, but *that* it is done cannot.

Kant seems to have believed, at the time he wrote the *Groundwork of the Metaphysic of Morals*, that actions that do not proceed from either hypothetical imperatives or act-necessitating rules do not proceed from reason at all, but merely from the blind stirrings of inclination or impulse. This idea has a certain intuitive appeal. It means that the only way that reason can guide conduct, other than by indicating how our actions can lead to some ulterior end, is by imposing requirements on us. Given what I have said so far, however, this idea would seem to have rather strange implications concerning the nature of generosity. Since generous actions are ones in which we seek the good of others as an end in itself, and in circumstances in which such is not required of us, it would seem to imply that generosity arises from some irrational source. In what follows I will try to show that generosity does, in a sense, proceed "from reason." In doing so, though, I must do justice to the antinomian physiognomy of generosity, which gives it at least a superficial similarity to things done on blind impulse. This can be done if one realizes that hypothetical imperatives and act-necessitating rules are not the only sorts of principles that move human beings to act.

In the preceding section I distinguished generosity from many other ways of acting by referring solely to the agent's intention to bring about a certain state of affairs. But different intentions relate to the agent's beliefs and desires in radically different ways. One can realistically imagine intending to bring about a state of affairs that one does not believe is really worthwhile. John, who is alcoholic, buys a bottle of whiskey with the intention of drinking it in spite of the fact that he believes on religious and hygienic grounds that drinking, as he does it, is bad, and in spite of the fact that he has in good faith made promises to his wife and his clergyman never to drink again. Of course, there is pleasure in his drinking, as there would be pain in his abstaining—that is why he intends to drink—but he regards the pleasure as worthless and the pain as salubrious. There is evidently a difference between believing that something is good on the one hand and such things as finding it pleasant or liking it on the other; and just as the akratic behavior of this alcoholic is possible, so is it possible to attempt to bring some state of affairs about because one believes it is important or worthwhile.

Generous acts are plainly of the latter sort. That is, such acts are done at least partly because one believes *that the good of others is important or worthwhile.* But we have seen that insofar as acts are generous, those who do them do not benefit someone else in order to accomplish some further result. Consequently, if they were to believe that the good of others is only worth pursuing when one thereby accomplishes something else, they would believe that the end they seek is not worth pursuing in the way they pursue it. If we call ends that do not need this further support ones that are important or worthwhile in themselves, we must add that one who acts generously believes that the good of others is important or worthwhile *in itself.* One acts generously *because* one holds this belief. This means that, in spite of the similarity generosity bears to acting on impulse, it does proceed from what I have called a principle.

However, the way in which it is generated by principle is different from the way in which an act proceeds from an act-necessitating rule. Although to hold the principle of generosity, as I will call it, is to act in certain ways, the principle itself does not require that any *particular* act be done. For instance, at this moment I know that I would be benefiting my neighbor if I went next door and gave a certain book to her. But even though I know this, and would lose nothing of importance by doing so, I am not at all inclined to do it. Such a consideration does not ordinarily function as a reason to do something, all by itself. There are further considerations, however, that could *make* it a reason: if my neighbor had recently done me a favor and I believed that favors should always be returned, that could make the fact that doing this would benefit my neighbor a reason for going out and doing it (perhaps not a sufficient reason, but a reason all the same); the belief that I could advance some particular interest of mine by doing it would have the same sort of significance. But the notion that the good of others is a worthwhile end of action does not have this significance: it does not imply (even vaguely) that one should (now, in these circumstances) give something to a certain person; it does not answer the question, "Why give this person something?" Granting that this notion is true, the question of whether I should now give my neighbor a certain book is still wide open. To answer a question like this, one needs other kinds of principles. This principle can move me to act, but it would not do so by implying what I should do. It can only do so by enabling me to see certain possible courses of action as *opportunities.*

3. There Are at Least Two Kinds of Virtue

This last point can easily be generalized. Generous acts are not done because circumstances require them but because the agent, quite apart from such requirements, *seeks* to do such things. In this sense, generosity is spontaneous. It has this characteristic because of the type of principle on which it is based. The principle of generosity is what I will call an "axiological principle," one that identifies some good as a worthwhile end of action in itself. Such principles have a definite function in the life of the individual who holds them. They do not enable us to solve problems or do what is appropriate to our circumstances; they simply turn us and direct us toward the good.

We should expect other traits that are based on principles of this kind to be spontaneous in the same way generosity is. For instance, this is true of what I would call "industriousness." This is the trait that is generated by an axiological principle to the effect that productive effort, effort that produces something of value, is worthwhile as such. Although one's effort can be required by one's circumstances, an act is never industrious in this sense if it is done simply for that reason. In fact, the most distinctive sign of a person who has this trait is precisely his or her aptness to look for opportunities for productive effort, and to press activity further than circumstance requires— even, sometimes, further than it properly allows.[6] Like generosity, industriousness suits very well the view of virtue expressed in Ferdinand Galiani's ambivalent aphorism, "Virtue is enthusiasm."

Traits that arise from principles that are relevantly different from those of generosity and industriousness are not characterized by spontaneity. It does not belong to the nature of courage as such to spontaneously seek to do courageous things. If brave people do sometimes seek to do such things, it is not simply because they are courageous, but because (for instance) they are aggressive or love adventure or honor. Nor is temperance spontaneous. The very idea that temperance leads people to seek out pleasures of the flesh

---

[6] I should acknowledge that I am departing from ordinary language in calling this trait industriousness. In ordinary usage, a person who, because he thinks it his duty, drags himself through the motions of a job that means nothing to him can also be called industrious, provided that the dragging is sufficiently energetic and reliable. Of course, this is quite a different trait from the one I am describing here. I should also point out that, precisely because of the sort of principle on which it is based, this industriousness of duty utterly lacks spontaneity.

in order to exercise their iron wills in resisting them has something absurd about it.

These facts are not hard to explain if we suppose, as I argued in the last chapter, that courage and temperance are based on what I have called limiting principles, principles that consist in the agent's recognizing the limits of the importance of some end of action. In the case of courage and temperance, the relevant ends are safety and physical pleasure, respectively. While axiological principles commit the agent to seek certain goods, limiting principles do not. They commit the agent to *letting go* of certain goods in certain circumstances. Traits like courage and temperance are revealed, not in what the agent seeks, but in what the agent can do without or put up with. Such traits exemplify the Stoic maxim, "Bear and forbear."

There is another important difference between these two classes of traits that, from what I have said so far, is rather less obvious than the ones I have just named. I have argued that generous acts are not irrational, in that they do not proceed from a blind stirring of the will, but rather from the agent's beliefs about what is good. This does not by any means imply that such acts are essentially intelligent, as we ordinarily use that word. As we ordinarily understand it, generosity is not necessarily intelligent at all. In ordinary language, there is no contradiction at all in saying something like, "He shouldn't have given that much money away because he can't afford to, but you can't doubt his generosity," or "She shouldn't have given him that money because he will only use it to harm himself, but you can't fault her for her generosity." One can say that an act is done generously and deny that it was done intelligently.

This, in fact, is an implication of the account of generosity I have presented here. An act can only be intelligent because of what the agent thinks about the particulars involved, such as the appropriateness of the act to its recipient or to the agent's own circumstances. The belief that makes an act generous is general in nature; it is not a belief about the agent, the recipient, or their circumstances. Nor does it necessarily require one to have insight about such things. A generous person regards a certain end of action as worth pursuing in itself. One can pursue an end in this way without knowing anything about any particular aspect of the circumstances of one's pursuit. Consequently, the fact that someone did not think rightly about such things does not mean that what he or she did failed to be generous.

Of course, if an action shows a gross sort of negligence, that would lead us quite rightly to doubt that it was a generous one, but only because it would lead us to doubt the genuineness of the agent's intention to benefit someone, and not because intelligence in the ordinary sense is part of the concept of generosity. It is the negligence—that is, the lack of concern for the good of another—and not the errors themselves that is incompatible with generosity. The fact remains that a fully generous act may be utterly misguided and miscarried.

According to the account I have given of them, this is not true of virtues that are generated by limiting principles. The function I have assigned to traits like courage, temperance, and self-respect is relevantly different from that of generosity. One follows the principle of generosity simply by pursuing a certain objective as an end in itself, but one can only follow the principle of self-respect by making judgments about particulars and by doing so correctly.

Suppose that I am offered a job that I find attractive but, as was the case with Andrew's assignment in the preceding chapter (II.6), rather degrading as well, and I must decide whether to take it. To make a decision in which avoiding degradation is, as the virtue of self-respect requires, not overvalued, I must know how seriously demeaning the job would be to me were I to accept it. Suppose I turn down the offer because I exaggerate the seriousness of this aspect of the job, not because of some purely factual error but because I am too concerned about the possibility of being demeaned. In that case, people would be likely to say that my decision showed, not self-respect, but some other trait, such as vanity. This is just the sort of thing my account of self-respect implies one should say. The fact that I set proper limits to the importance of some good consists, in large part, in my intelligently appraising the particular instances of this good that I meet in the concrete situations in which I find myself. The virtue of self-respect requires me to correctly determine whether, in a certain respect, my action is appropriate to my circumstances.

If the account I have given of them is correct, we have here two quite different kinds of virtue. But this conclusion, and the account on which it rests, is liable to an objection, or a family of objections, that I have so far not addressed. So far, I have tried to understand what these traits are like mainly by unearthing the structure that underlies the way we ordinarily think about these traits: I have assumed that the way we ordinarily think on this matter is correct. But there is at least one reason why one might doubt that we should keep and use our ordinary conceptions of these traits, a reason for replacing these conceptions with other ones with very different implications.

Consider, as an example, the virtue of generosity. The good of others is certainly something that one can undervalue, and it is probably something one can overvalue as well. If such is indeed the case, both of these errors would seem to be character flaws, and the trait that lies in the mean between them would be a virtue. Why not say that this virtue is generosity, that part of what generosity is, is valuing the good of others in this way?

More generally, why not say the same sort of thing about all the virtues that have to do with ends that are to be pursued as worthwhile in themselves? Perhaps we should say that for each of the ends of action that are worth pursuing in this way there is one virtue that governs its pursuit, and that the function of the virtue would be, simply, to ensure that the good is pursued properly. This would mean that each virtue consists both in pursuing that good as an end in itself *and* in setting proper limits to its value. This view would collapse the two radically different kinds of virtue I have treated in this chapter and the last into one homogeneous species. According to this alternative way of understanding these virtues, while it may be that we ordinarily think about traits like generosity and courage in a way that makes them quite different types of traits, as I have said we do, this is merely a matter of folk psychology and not ethical theory. We are only entitled to think of these traits *as virtues* if we see them as fundamentally alike.

Though it is undeniably plausible, I think there is good reason for rejecting this alternative way of thinking. The reason has to do with the nature of the goods that these virtues govern and with the nature of virtue itself. I think it can be best understood by considering, briefly, the difference between two virtues that have to do with closely related goods.

I believe I can take it as obvious that being a good person, and becoming a better one, is in itself a worthwhile goal for human beings to pursue and that, while some people recognize this and act accordingly, others do not. Further, it also seems obvious that, though we have no name for it, the trait possessed by those who do act in this way is a virtue. For lack of a better name, we can call it "self-perfection." As I have just described it, this trait is based on an axiological principle, since it includes acting on the recognition that a certain end of action is worth pursuing in itself. In a way, it resembles the virtue of self-respect, which, according to my account, also includes acting on a certain concern for one's own worth. However, self-respect includes, crucially, acting on a recognition of the limits of the good that is its area of concern while, as I have described it, self-perfection does not.

Why should we regard these as two different traits, and as differing in this way? A plausible answer to this question is suggested by something that is more or less immediately implied by the way I have described them: namely, that these traits are not concerned with precisely the same goods. Self-perfection aims at achieving the status of actually being a worthy person while self-respect, as I described it in chapter II, aims at maintaining the appearance (in one's own eyes) of being that sort of person. It seems likely that these two goods really should be valued and pursued quite differently. But wherein should the differences lie?

One possible response to this question could go like this: While appearances can be very important, they have (as I have said in II.6) only a limited importance. To pursue such a good in the proper spirit is (in part, but crucially) to recognize these limits. On the other hand, there seems to be no limit to how important it is to really be a good person. Pursuing this goal in the proper spirit cannot include recognizing its limits, since they do not exist. It could consist only in an enthusiastic pursuit of the goal as good in itself. But this answer to my question rests on an idea that is at best debatable: the idea that there is no limit to the importance of the goal of self-perfection. This would seem to mean, if it means anything, that it is impossible to overvalue it. But it is arguable that such a thing *is* possible. One can think of people—the life of Vincent van Gogh seems to me to be an example—in whom the mania for ethical perfection seems to go too far.[7] One can probably pursue even this good in such a way that it crowds out too many other things of value.

However, there is one difference between the goods with which these two virtues are concerned that is obviously real and is relevant to the question at hand. As I indicated early on (I.1), a virtue is a meritorious trait of character; it is one that indicates that its possessor is, with respect to that trait, a good person. This would mean that, if the fact that one values and pursues a particular good in a certain way can by itself indicate some merit on the part of the person who does it, this fact will be constitutive of some virtue.

If one's valuing and pursuing these two goods is to have this sort of significance, they must be valued and pursued in quite different ways. Merely valuing and pursuing the end of self-respect, even as good in itself,

---

[7] I might add that, if we were to rest our case on this debatable idea, it would force on us a conclusion that is much stronger than the principle I have identified as the one that underlies self-perfection. If some good really has unlimited value, the only appropriate way to pursue it would seem to be that of dedicating oneself to it as the highest good, to which every other good should be sacrificed in the event of a choice between them. Even if this is true of the good that is the goal of self-perfection, it makes no sense for that of generosity (the good of others is not *that* important) nor, probably, for the goods with which any other virtue is concerned.

is no indication of merit at all. It seems to be impossible *not* to value this good as something worth pursuing in itself. Even evil people try to see themselves as worthy individuals, and typically manage to think that they differ from people who act decently in ways that are really to their credit: that they are, for instance, more clever than others or more realistic. Moreover, they do not seem to seek this end merely as a means to producing some further result. The desire to see oneself as in some way good seems to belong to human nature itself.[8]

On the other hand, it is not in the same way natural to desire the end of self-perfection. Though it is virtually impossible to be indifferent about whether one feels worthless, it is evidently quite possible to be indifferent about whether one really *is* worthless. After all, caring about how something seems is quite a different thing from caring about whether it really is that way. As far as one's own worth is concerned, the former seems to be a more or less indispensable part of the way the human mind works, while the latter is the result of learning and wisdom. But this means that valuing and pursuing the end of self-perfection, as such, does indicate merit by itself: it shows that one has some insight into what is important or worthwhile, and that one has whatever other inner resources are needed for this insight to guide one's conduct.

Nothing like this is true of valuing and pursuing the end of self-respect. However, partly because it is so natural to value it, it is quite possible to overvalue it, and because it evidently is something that is good for us, it is also possible to undervalue it. Clearly, to avoid these errors, to recognize the limits of the value of this good and act accordingly, is something that requires wisdom and consequently does indicate merit. They constitute the sort of trait that, on the face of it, may legitimately be regarded as a virtue.

In some contexts, it may be important to realize that what I have just said about the end of self-respect may also be true of the end of self-perfection: it might well be possible to overvalue it as well. This would imply, by the same sort of reasoning I have just used, that it is virtuous to recognize the

---

[8] There is, I think, a plausible explanation of this fact. Whatever I wish to do or to have, the experience I have if my wish comes true is that of *my* doing or *my* having whatever it is. If I really see myself as worthless, the experience I will have when my wish is fulfilled is that of something done by someone who is incapable of doing anything of value, or who is at best unworthy of possessing anything good. My conception of myself colors every experience I have, and an unfavorable one would contaminate them all. Thus, no matter what one wishes to do or have, one has every reason to want to have a favorable conception of oneself.

limits of this end. In the present context, however, the important point is that valuing and pursuing it is nonetheless something that indicates merit by itself. People who carry the quest for personal perfection to self-destructive extremes still have something admirable about them: we might pity or criticize them for lacking the wisdom it takes to put their goal in proper perspective, but it is nonetheless true that they have the sort of insight it takes to see it as good and pursue it. Though we may see them as lacking one virtue, we should also see them as possessing another. Their ruined lives are not merely bad; they are tragic.

The remarks I have just made about self-respect and self-perfection can be generalized to show that there are (at least) two kinds of virtue, with each kind having more than one exemplar. There are a number of ends of action that are worth pursuing as ends in themselves, and a number of these are such that it is virtually impossible not to value and pursue them as good in themselves. Ignoring certain obviously pathological exceptions, everyone values and pursues safety and physical pleasure, and not merely as a means to some further end. On the other hand, some things that are worth pursuing as ends in themselves are not necessarily pursued in that way by everyone. Not everyone shows an interest, for instance, in productive effort as an end in itself. It may always be possible to overvalue or undervalue such goods—as is certainly the case with productive effort—but valuing and pursuing them is nonetheless something that is meritorious by itself.

It might be virtuous to recognize the limits of the value of goods of the latter sort, but the traits in which one does so are different virtues from the ones in which one values them as ends in themselves. The reason is that seeking such goods as ends in themselves, if one does so with some consistency, is something that by itself shows that, in one respect, the agent is a good person.

It is perhaps obvious how the generalized version of my remarks on self-respect and self-perfection would apply to the virtue of generosity. At the risk of being tedious, I will make these implications more explicit, but will delay doing so until the end of the next section of this chapter.

4. Can One Be Generous to a Fault?

Is it possible to be too generous, to be generous to a fault? Indirectly, I have already suggested that the answer to this question is yes. As I have said, I can give, out of generosity, more than I can afford, or to people who will use what I give them to harm themselves. It seems obvious that in such cases

I will have been altogether too generous. But this seemingly obvious fact poses a problem that, in the context of some of the other things I have said in this chapter, takes the form of a dilemma. I believe I can make some of the implications of the view of virtue to which I have committed myself a bit more clear by spelling this dilemma out and showing that, as a matter of fact, a way of resolving it can also be found among the things I have said in this chapter.

The first horn to this dilemma is a simple argument leading to the conclusion that, contrary to one's first impression of the matter, one cannot be generous to a fault. It goes like this. Suppose that one *can* be generous to a fault. If that were true, then generosity would sometimes be a bad thing. But generosity is a virtue, and a virtue cannot be bad. So it is not possible to be generous to a fault. If we accept the idea that it is possible, we seem to fall into the self-contradiction of holding that there can be bad virtues.[9]

The other horn of the dilemma is also fairly simple. Suppose, to begin, that we decide that one cannot be generous to a fault after all: if one goes too far in pursuing the object of generous conduct, one's conduct does not show the virtue of generosity. This would mean that, at least insofar as it functions as a virtue, generosity does not consist merely in valuing and pursuing a certain goal but in doing so properly. Generosity would include a certain due regard for the good of others and, as such, would have to include a recognition of the limits of the importance of this end.[10] Obviously, this conclusion would require me to accept the position I have just argued against in section 3 of this chapter.

In fact, the second horn of this dilemma has some rather radical implications, for it can easily be generalized. The reasoning I have just presented against the possibility of being generous to a fault will apply equally well to any virtue: virtues, after all, cannot be faults. If we suppose that generosity could never result in our doing anything but what is proper, then we must also suppose that it depends on other virtues in complex and potentially far-reaching ways. We cannot consistently avoid giving to unworthy people or giving more than we can afford unless we have other

---

[9] This appearance of paradox in the idea of being generous (or more generally, virtuous) to a fault has been pointed out by Gary Watson, "Virtues in Excess," *Philosophical Studies* 46 (July 1984); pp. 57-74, especially pp. 57-59.

[10] This is more or less the conclusion that Gary Watson reaches, starting from the assumption that one cannot be generous to a fault. Ibid., pp. 57-59.

virtues in addition to generosity. By this sort of reasoning, generosity, as a virtue, might well require a large number of other virtues. But the generalized version of the argument would seem to require us to say the same thing of all the traits that are supposed to be virtues. This would require us to accept a position that is at least very similar to the doctrine of the unity of the virtues—which, as I said at the beginning of this chapter, is an idea I shall be arguing against.[11]

It seems, then, that the idea that one can be generous to a fault saddles me with the dilemma of either accepting its apparently self-contradictory implications or, if I reject the idea in order to avoid the contradiction, rejecting my account of generosity and accepting something like the unity of the virtues. Both horns of the dilemma, though, include the notion that the idea that one can be generous to a fault involves a contradiction. I can escape the dilemma if I can plausibly avoid accepting this notion. But how might I do that?

Suppose that, acting on a genuinely generous impulse, I have given someone more than I can afford to give, leaving myself without enough money to do things that I need to do. I have been generous to a fault, but wherein, exactly, does the fault lie? We can say that what I did was faulty without embracing the paradoxical idea that the fault in my act was its generosity. Instead, we can say that the fault involved was a certain lack of intelligence or prudence, that what I did was good in that it was generous and bad in that it was imprudent.

In a similar context, in section 3 of this chapter, I suggested that this is what we *would* say. Why shouldn't we? One argument against doing so might be stated like this: In the case we are supposing, I should not have been generous. In general, if there is some act one should not do, that act is a bad one. It would follow that being generous is itself, in this case, a bad thing to do.

My response to this argument is to deny that acts that one should not do are necessarily bad. If I say that you should (or ought to) have ordered the sauteed shrimp instead of the stuffed chicken breast, I might only mean that ordering the chicken would have been better, not that ordering the shrimp was bad. I might only be saying that it was not the best alternative. Similarly,

---

[11] John McDowell argues for the unity of the virtues in this way in his influential paper, "Virtue and Reason," *The Monist*, vol. 62 no. 3 (July 1979), pp. 332-33. Watson claims, correctly I think, that this sort of argument does not really support the unity of the virtues itself, but a weaker version of the same doctrine, in "Virtues in Excess," pp. 59-62.

the obvious truth that I shouldn't have been generous might only mean that, in the circumstances we have supposed, doing what is prudent would have been better than doing what is generous, and not that doing what is generous was (in itself, *qua* generous) bad.

If we interpret the phenomenon of being generous to a fault in this way, it does not commit us to the notion that generosity can, in itself, be faulty. It would only mean that generosity is sometimes not the highest virtue available to us. The plausibility of seeing things this way is evident from the obvious fact that people can say of me something like, "He shouldn't have given that much money away because he can't afford to, but he deserves credit for his generosity." I can only think of one way of arguing that it would nonetheless be wrong to interpret the matter in this way. One could add some details to the case we have been assuming here that would indicate that people would indeed be wrong to see anything good in what I have done. The peculiar recklessness of my giving might indicate that I was giving out of a neurotic compulsion that springs merely from chronic feelings of guilt, or a desperate desire for approval from others. In that case, it could be wrong to see anything good in what I have done, apart from its consequences for my beneficiaries. Similarly, it can be wrong to praise people for their industriousness when their excessively hard word takes the form of mere "workaholism."

But in such cases the traits we are talking about are not generosity or industriousness as I have defined them, but something else. To the extent that my "generosity" is motivated by guilt, it is something I am doing in order to escape from a situation I recognize as evil. In this way, it is quite different from genuine generosity, in which one pursues an end one sees as *good*. To the extent that my giving is driven by a desire for the approval of others, I am only aiming at the good of others in order to accomplish some further result. This, even more obviously, is also different from generous giving, in which one pursues an end because one sees it as important or worthwhile *in itself.*

Relevantly similar things can be said of neurotically compulsive workaholism. One who works compulsively is acting either from the mere mindless inability to do otherwise or from one or another of several different motives, such as: to punish oneself for real or imagined sins, to retroactively win the approval of a cruel childhood taskmaster, to dull one's awareness of unpleasant facts about oneself or the world. In any case, the forces that drive a compulsive person seem to be radically different from the motive that moves an industrious one, which is to pursue productive effort as something that is important or worthwhile as such.

In general, it seems that when we look closely at cases in which apparently excessive generosity or industriousness really are bad in themselves, they turn out not to be instances of these traits at all. We see why they are bad when we look into the motives from which they spring, and these motives indicate that the traits involved do not fit the definitions of generosity or industriousness. If this is so, there is no apparent reason to refuse to interpret the phenomenon of being generous to a fault as I have done here.

Indeed, this interpretation follows from the generalized version, with which I ended section 3 of this chapter, of my remarks on self-respect and self-perfection. An excessively generous act is nonetheless a generous one and, as such, indicates that the agent values the good of others as something worth pursuing as good in itself. Human beings do not inevitably pursue this good in this way, by a sort of natural tropism: some seem to take no such interest in it at all. People who do value the good of others as something worth pursuing in itself thereby show that they have some insight into what is important or worthwhile, some fragment—however confused it might be—of wisdom about what is good. That is why a generous act, in itself, is a good thing, even when there is some alternative act that would have been better.

Following a line of reasoning I discussed and rejected in section 3, one might want to avoid these conclusions by rejecting the ordinary conception of generosity and offering an alternative, philosophical conception in its place. One could say that generosity essentially includes *properly* valuing the good of others as an end in itself, neither overvaluing it nor undervaluing it. It would consist, in part, in recognizing the limits of the value of this good in any context in which one might give something to someone else. This, of course, would mean that there is simply no such thing as being too generous, and my way of understanding it would fall to the ground.

Such a line of reasoning would amount to claiming that one has discovered a new virtue. Even if this claim is true, however, it does not provide an alternative to the conclusions I have reached here. I have said that pursuing the good of others as something worthwhile in itself is—by itself, provided that the pursuit is genuine—something that reflects favorably on the merits of the person who does it. If that is so, then such pursuit is worth mentioning and praising. Indeed, it is a virtue. There might be some point in framing a concept of a new virtue that is like generosity as we know it except that it never goes wrong, but it would not relieve us of the need to mention and praise generosity, and, for that reason, it could only cause confusion to call this supervirtue "generosity." The same things can be said, and with equal force, about all the virtues that are based on what I have called axiological principles.

5. The Diversity of the Virtues

If we accept what I have said about the nature of various virtues in this chapter and the last, the old idea of the unity of the virtues begins to lose its principal traditional means of support. The main traditional argument for it, as formulated by Aristotle (under the influence of Plato), is this: Virtue, or *true* virtue, is produced by wisdom; people act virtuously because they are wise. But if someone is wise, they will possess all the virtues. Wisdom brings all the virtues with it. Consequently, either we possess all the virtues together, or the supposedly virtuous traits one does have are not truly virtuous. They simply are more or less mindless tendencies to act in what happens to be the right way.[12]

I have claimed, in effect, that the virtues I have discussed do rest on wisdom in a way. But nothing I have said implies that they require the individual to possess wisdom as a totality, or a generalized ability to reason practically and do it well. Rather, each virtue, one might say, requires that one be wise *about something*. One must possess a fragment of wisdom. For certain virtues, such as generosity, one must see that a certain end of action is worth pursuing in itself, but one need have no particular insight into the proper limits of the value of this end. This sort of insight is necessary for an entirely different class of virtues, of which courage is an instance. Further, though it is true that one cannot have insight into the limits of the value of an end of action without also recognizing that it is worth pursuing, all these virtues seem to be concerned with goods that—unlike the goods that are the focus of virtues like generosity—can be recognized without any wisdom at all. So far, then, neither of these two kinds of virtue require the sort of insight that is presupposed by the other. There is, so far, no reason to deny that they can exist separately.

Nonetheless, it is conceivable that the virtues might be connected by means of some characteristic of the agent other than wisdom in general. It seems rather likely, in fact, that there is at least one virtue that requires a

---

[12] See Aristotle, *Nicomachean Ethics*, bk. 6, chap. 13.

certain psychological power or disposition that is also presupposed by some other virtue. We have already seen evidence that this is so. As I have described it, temperance requires a concern for one's self-image which is at least very similar to the concern that is involved in self-respect. Temperate people do not live as the glutton lives because (this is at least one way to put it) it does not fit the image they have of themselves as human beings, and the nature of this discrepancy is such that they would feel degraded by living that way. Part of what bothers us about people who are gluttonous or extremely promiscuous is that they have an inadequate regard for their own dignity, that in some sense they have no self-respect.

If the concern for one's self-image we see in these two virtues is in both cases the very same trait, this fact has some interesting implications. For present purposes it makes no difference whether we think of it as a principle the individual holds or as an emotional commitment of some sort. What would follow in either event is that, if one has one of these virtues, then one has at least a good part of what it takes to achieve the other. Either one of them will bring the other with it or it will make it easier to attain. If all the virtues are related in just this way, then something like the old doctrine of the unity of the virtues will be true.

However, we have seen no evidence that the sort of self-concern that we have seen lurking behind these virtues is in the same way essential to others, such as generosity or courage. It could be, and has been, claimed that some such trait is essential to courage.[13] For instance, the pilots of the last months of World War II deliberately went to their deaths in the service of their cause. In an obvious way, this resembles things that courageous people do. But their horrifying exploits stemmed from a conviction, drawn from a totalitarian version of the Shinto religion, that their lives had no value except as instruments in the service of the emperor and the Japanese state, and this means that what they did was not an instance of courage. True courage is incompatible with throwing one's life away as if it were a thing with no intrinsic value. Thus, courage seems to require some sort of respect for oneself.

As a matter of fact, the analysis of courage I have given in chapter II does imply that the kamikaze pilots' behavior was not courageous, but not for the reason suggested by this argument. Courage is a solution to a conflict

---

[13] See Marcia L. Homiak, "Virtue and Self-Love in Aristotle's Ethics," *Canadian Journal of Philosophy* 11 (December 1981): pp. 633-51. The brief argument that follows, concerning the kamikaze pilot, is adapted from Homiak, pp. 642-43.

between goods: between the agent's safety and some other good that, for the agent, is also an end of action. Courageous people do things that they have a reason, and a good one, not to do. This is what gives to the problem for which courage is the solution its peculiar poignancy, and it is what makes a courageous act the peculiar sort of victory that it is. But the principle on which the kamikaze pilot acts indicates that his safety is not a good at all. Indeed, it is an evil, insofar as it would be a catastrophic failure if he were to survive his suicidal flight, just as it would be a failure if his bombs were to fail to destroy themselves by exploding. The only problem is how he will get the strength to live up to his principle.

Thus, the trait of the kamikaze pilot fails to be courage for the same reason that hygienic abstinence fails to be temperance (see II.4): we might say that it displaces the ethical problem of how fundamental ends are to be ranked with the technical problem of how best to employ available means to achieve a single end. Anything that brings about this same sort of displacement would have the same result: for instance, as I have pointed out (II.2), an action that involves facing danger fails to be courageous if the agent is only doing it to escape a still greater danger. In that case, one is only employing one's available wherewithal to achieve the single goal of safety. On the other hand, self-contempt on my part would not seem to prevent me from being courageous, provided only that it is not that degree and kind of self-contempt that prevents me from seeing my own safety as an intrinsic good.

This means that courage is incompatible with a certain kind of self-contempt or, alternatively, that it presupposes a certain recognition of one's own value. But in the present context it is most important to notice how minimal the required recognition is. It is not the sort that leads one to refuse to tolerate being demeaned or degraded. The self-regard that my courage, if I have any, requires of me is only the sort that would lead me to think that what becomes of me is something that matters in itself. This is a trait that is not nearly so rare and difficult as the one we find in self-respect. It is one that almost everyone already has. As such, it is not something that, for most of us, would make courage any easier to attain than it already is. In some contexts, the fact that courage requires this sort of self-regard might well be important and interesting, but it does not indicate that the ancient doctrine of the unity of the virtues, or anything much like it, is true.

On the basis of what I have said so far, the Eleatic moral psychology of the philosophers was quite right, in a way, in positing subterranean connections among the virtues, but it erred in overestimating the strength and pervasiveness of these connections. They are real enough, but they differ in power and importance, and, moreover, they are trait specific: if two virtues presuppose the same psychological power or disposition, it is because of the nature of those particular traits, and not simply because they are virtues.

If we were to let the matter rest here, however, the notion that the virtues form a unity would seem closer to the truth than it actually is. We would be left with the impression that the virtues do form a kind of unity, though their unity is, so to speak, intermittent and, consequently, comparatively weak. But this impression would be profoundly wrong. Various things I have said already suggest that relations among the virtues are also characterized by various trait-specific tensions. If there are forces that draw virtues together, there are others that drive them apart.[14] Generosity, in particular, if the things I have said about it are true, is apt to be somewhat difficult to combine with certain of the other virtues. The same thing is true of a virtue I will discuss in the next chapter, the trait that is traditionally called justice.

Consider, as perhaps the clearest case, a kind of justice that I have referred to several times in this chapter: that in which one rewards personal desert.

To say that it was generous to give a certain student an "A," or a certain soldier a medal is to say that they did *not* deserve it, or that it is not clear whether they did, at least in the giver's estimation. The same relationship holds between generosity and every kind of justice. If I promised to repay you today ten dollars I borrowed from you, then I would, under ordinary circumstances, be perpetrating an injustice if I were to fail voluntarily to give you the money today. This is not because you are a deserving sort of person but because, even if you are a very bad sort of person, I should, ordinarily, pay all my legitimate debts to you as promised. The justice I would be doing in paying my you debt thus is not the sort in which one rewards personal desert. But there is at least one thing it has in common with that sort of justice, and with justice of every kind: in paying my debt, I am giving someone his or her *due*. To say that it was generous of Peter to give Paul twenty dollars is to deny that it (at any rate, the whole amount) was Paul's due.

Generosity includes a certain disregard for desert and, more generally, for the issue of what is or is not anyone's due. Moreover, it is relevant to the way in which generosity and justice are related that it is a sort of disregard that can be liable to criticism at times. To focus again on the case of personal

---

[14] For an insightful discussion of tensions among the virtues, see Amelie O. Rorty, "Virtues and Their Vicissitudes," *Midwest Studies in Philosophy* 13 (Notre Dame: University of Notre Dame Press, 1988), pp. 136-48.

desert: Suppose I believe that an essay by Peter is obviously superior to one on the same subject by Paul, and I discover that Peter has included Paul's essay but not his own in an anthology he has edited. I could either criticize Peter for being unfair to himself and for giving Paul more than he deserves—or I could praise him for his generosity.

In this case, two responses are open to me, and, in an obvious way, they clash with one another: one is favorable and the other is unfavorable. This immediately suggests that there is some sort of tension between the two virtues involved, but wherein does this tension lie? It cannot consist in the fact that the principles of generosity and justice have logically contradictory implications in this case, for they do not. The principle of generosity does not require Peter to include Paul's essay rather than his own, because it does not require anybody to do any particular action. Nor do the relevant principles of justice seem to prohibit him from being generous to Paul in this way, at least if we accept the plausible notion that it is not unjust to benefit others more than they deserve, nor to benefit oneself less than one deserves, but only the reverse.[15] None of the relevant principles seem to compel me either to criticize or to praise Peter for what he has done.

Supposing I am, to some extent, both a generous person and a just one, whether I will criticize Peter or praise him does not seem to depend, directly, on the principles of these two traits of mine. It depends, rather, on certain other things I will tend to think. Nonetheless, which of these other thoughts will come into my head depends, in significant part, on the relative dominance of these principles as parts of my character.

To the extent that, as a dominant feature of my character, I act on the principle of generosity, I will look out for opportunities to benefit others, and this would mean that I tend to notice them and find them important whenever they occur. This would tend to lead me, in the absence of conflicting influences, to notice the fact that Peter has taken such an opportunity and to find that fact important.

On the other hand, to the extent that I am moved by considerations of personal desert, rather different sorts of things will matter to me. If my way of life is characterized by this sort of justice to any great degree, I must take great pains to see that people get what they deserve, and it would be difficult to see such pains as anything but wasted unless I see the fact that people do get what they have coming to them as a good thing. In situations in which some scarce good is being distributed and the merits of the recipients

---

[15] See Aristotle, *Nicomachean Ethics*, 1134a1-7 and 1138a4-28.

constitute an obviously relevant consideration—in situations like grading examinations, hiring people, selecting students for admission to school, or selecting authors for inclusion in an anthology—I will take those merits very seriously and view flagrant disregard of them with suspicion. Even when such disregard does not involve treating anyone unjustly, I will tend to see it as sloppy and frivolous at best. In such situations, people's merits will seem to call for certain responses, and Peter's response is accordingly uncalled for—is perhaps even contrary to what is called for. If it is generous, it looks excessively generous.

In obvious ways, my thoughts about Peter's conduct are equally relevant to my own. Considerations that suggest that what he does is either praiseworthy or dubious are with equal force reasons why I should either do or not do what he has done in similar circumstances. If the thoughts that are brought about by a powerful concern for personal desert cast doubt on generous actions, they will also have a certain tendency to crowd out considerations that would lead one to act generously oneself. This would mean that there is a tension between generosity and a certain sort of justice. An important part of this tension consists in the fact that the very nature of these two virtues place difficulties in our way if we are to acquire both of them.

Though there seems to be no logical contradiction between the principles of these virtues, the reason for the tension between them does have to do with their respective principles and is partly a matter of logic. First, the principles of this sort of justice, however they might be stated, govern the very same type of situations that the principle of generosity governs: ones in which something is given to someone. That is, the situations to which these principles of justice apply are precisely the sort that provide opportunities for generosity. Second, one cannot act on both virtues at once. Finally, this incompatibility, which is partly a logical consequence of the principles involved, brings into conflict the habits of thought that come with each of them when they form the core of a trait of character that dominates the thoughts, feelings, and conduct of the individuals who possess them.

Much the same thing is true, and for related reasons, of the relations between generosity and any sort of justice, and not merely the sort that deals with personal desert. Of course, we can expect the relations between generosity and justice in general to be relevantly different because showing a disregard for what is someone's due seems relevantly different from the more specific phenomenon of giving them more than they deserve. In particular, it is not, on the face of it, as likely to arouse suspicion. Paying someone more money than one promised to pay does not strike people as intrinsically dubious, in the way that giving someone an undeserved grade or job does. However, the two phenomena have a certain structural similarity that has deep psychological and ethical implications. If there is something that is in any sense your due, that thing is always a single action, or a comparatively narrow class of actions, and in either case it is as it were surrounded by infinitely many possible actions that are not your due. If I promised to return ten dollars to you, then that ten dollars is exactly what I owe you, neither more nor less. Essentially the same thing is true if my task is to give you what you deserve by, for instance, grading a performance of yours.

If I am to do what is just, I must correctly determine what is your due, distinguishing it from the infinite multitude of things that are not. If the only issue is whether to give you the ten dollars I have promised you, this task presents me with no serious difficulties, but issues about justice are often not so simple. As we try to discern what we really owe to people, we are crossing potentially treacherous terrain in which, as an old saying has it, *malum est multiplex*. Errors are more than possible; in the long run they are likely—and many of these errors would destroy the justice of what we do. No one can be persistently just unless they are mindful of this fact, which means maintaining the appropriate stance of sometimes anxious caution and care. Anything less than this would mean not caring whether what one does is just. The intellectual discipline of the judge who decides a case after days of conflicting testimony is merely the paradigm and logical extreme of all just acts. To be just to an exemplary degree, one must be *scrupulously* just.

On the other hand, generosity is not a constitutionally scrupulous virtue. As I have argued in section 3, error is not the enemy of generous acts. This means that, although scrupulousness—the exercise of caution and care to avoid making mistakes—is a trait that can make me better at giving things to others (it can help me to avoid being excessively generous, for instance), it does not enhance the generosity of what I do.

In fact, persistent generosity requires a trait that is in some respects the opposite of this one. As I have suggested several times in this chapter, beginning in section 2, the principle of generosity does not move us to act by narrowing down the many acts we might do to a single necessary act, or to a narrow band of possible acts one of which should be done. Rather, it enables us to see various possible courses of action as opportunities to do good.

We cannot understand what this idea implies unless we understand two important facts. The first is that these possible courses of action are necessarily plural. There is always more than one generous thing we might do, and the possibilities we notice increase with the power of our imaginations. When we undertake to do what generous people do, *bonum est multiplex*.

Second, these possibilities do not simply come to our notice, as if they were active and our awareness of them were passive. Opportunity is often at the door, but it never knocks. An opportunity that is obvious to you might never occur to me, or, if it does, it might occur as a bare possibility with no practical interest whatever. To see an opportunity, and see it *as* an opportunity, requires a certain mental stance. Obviously, one can only regard a possibility as an opportunity if one sees as good the end toward which the opportunity aims. Beyond that, one will not be likely to think of such possibilities unless one really *cares* about the end, which is rather more than simply seeing it as good. To care about the end of generosity is, among other things, to have a certain openness to a multitude of possibilities together with a desire to search them for yet better ones. There is no name for this trait as far as I know, but it is an easily recognizable one. In an obvious way, it is the opposite of scrupulousness. They are as different as a submission to necessity is from an openness to possibility.

We could say that, while justice is managerial, generosity is entrepreneurial. We can expect that exemplary justice will be supported by a spirit of rigor and an aversion to making mistakes. Outstanding generosity, on the other hand, would be based on a spirit of openness and exploration. These are obviously very different personality types, not easy to combine in the same person. One could only have the adventuresome spirit that supports outstanding generosity if one does *not* see error as something that is unacceptably terrible. On the other hand, to someone in the grip of rigor and caution, such a spirit will be apt to look very much like irresponsible recklessness. The mental traits that make it easier to possess one of these virtues to an exemplary degree tend to make it difficult to acquire the other.[16]

---

[16] Amelie Rorty, in "Virtues and Their Vicissitudes," p. 143, names four ways in which virtues can "check" one another. The arguments I have just given provide examples of three of them: (1) The "cognitive components" of the traits, she says, may be contradictories or contraries. (The principles of the pairs of traits I have described could be said to be contraries in the somewhat tenuous sense that, in the situations described above, one cannot act on both principles in the pair at once, though of course one might act on neither of them.) (2) The actions that evince the traits might undermine each other's success in some way. (3)

Matters would be very different if generosity and justice were mere habits that could be built up by repeatedly performing the same actions. Overeating and taking strenuous exercise are, like generous and just conduct, very different sorts of actions, and they are almost impossible to perform at the same time. But I can form a habit of overeating every day and another of exercising to exhaustion every day by the simple expedient of doing these actions at different times of the day. But generosity and justice, unlike habits, are distinguished by the reasons for which the individual that possesses them acts. Persistently acting for these reasons is greatly facilitated by certain more fundamental psychological dispositions, and, because occasions for generosity or justice can arise at virtually any time, these dispositions cannot be taken up or abandoned at will. They function, in part, by enabling us to notice the occasions for action when they next occur and to see them in the appropriate way. They probably must be more or less perpetually active, and this means they can interfere with one another.

Roughly the same sort of tension that we find between generosity and justice can also be found between generosity and self-respect, and for more or less the same reasons. Consider, for instance, a situation similar to one I considered earlier (II.5), in which I have been waiting in line for a while at the supermarket and a strange man boldly cuts in front of me. Suppose, to simplify the issues involved, that there is no one behind me in the line. Suppose, further, that I do not speak sharply to him at all. Instead, after reflecting momentarily that, while I am not in a hurry, he evidently is, I say (without a hint of irony): "That's alright, friend—go right ahead!" It is easy to imagine someone either praising me for generously giving up what is rightfully mine or criticizing me for failing to assert my dignity.[17]

"The development of one set of traits can typically inhibit the development of the other."

[17] A biographer of Booker T. Washington tells a story that, in obviously relevant ways, is parallel to the one we have just imagined: "On another occasion he was going down a hotel hallway in Des Moines when a woman guest, mistaking him for a porter, asked him for water. Completely unruffled, he went to the desk and had water sent up to her." Samuel R. Spencer, Jr., *Booker T. Washington and the Negro's Place in American Life* (Boston: Little, Brown and Company, 1955), p. 187. This story opens Washington to the charge, which one sometimes hears from black intellectuals, that he was something of an "Uncle Tom," a charge that is meant to imply a culpable want of self-respecting behavior in his relations with whites. On the other hand, if one considers this anecdote in the context of the many others that tell of Washington's inexhaustible generosity to people of all races and classes, a different response becomes available. Of course, his critics are aware of such stories and need not admit that, by themselves, they prove that their criticism is wrong.

The latter response is available even to someone who does not believe that my yielding my place in line actually shows servility, as was the case with the conduct of the self-deprecator and the deferential wife. One could think that behavior is only servile if it indicates a certain capitulation to the low opinion of one's own worth that is suggested by bad treatment from others, and that one only "capitulates," in this sense, if one *shares* that low opinion to some extent. In that case, if my yielding is not motivated by considerations of this sort, it is not servile. It could be that I was moved by the sorts of considerations that move people to act generously, and not by those that lie behind either self-respect *or* servility. Still, someone might well say that, in these circumstances, the goal at which generosity aims is less important than the one that is the concern of self-respect. That is, I was undervaluing the concerns of self-respect in relation to those of generosity: if I was being generous, I was being generous to a fault. This, in fact, seems to be just the sort of thing that an especially self-respecting person would say.

One sort of self-respect—the sort that in the cases of the self-deprecator and the deferential wife was so conspicuous by its absence—involves asserting one's dignity against ill-treatment by others. The response to which it prompts us is always to some extent or other adverse to the interests of those who have ill-treated us. The responses vary on the scale of severity from, at the mildest, a few sharp words or a refusal to cooperate with someone to such ultimate acts of resistance as revolution and tyrannicide, but they are always something that our malefactors have reason to wish us not to do. Moreover, these responses are always things that the individual who acts out of self-respect believes, at least at the moment, he or she has a right to do.

To refrain from doing something harmful or annoying to another person, when one has a right to do it, is to confer a benefit on them. To take the most extreme case: if you have a perfect right to kill me, your not killing me confers on me the great gift of life, and the same is true of any other merited harm or annoyance. This means that any situation that seems to call for an assertion of self-respect against one's ill-users is also an opportunity to act generously, and the generous act would be, precisely, to *not* assert one's self-respect.

Partly for this reason, we can expect an individual who possesses the relevant sort of self-respect to a conspicuous degree to view people who act generously in such situations with disapproval or, at best, suspicion. Such people seem to be acting contrary to what is called for or, at least, in flagrant disregard of those features of the situation that are most salient to the conspicuously self-respecting person. Such a view of the matter will have a powerful tendency to crowd out thoughts of the sort that one must have if one is to act generously in situations of this kind.

6. Conclusion

The existence of tensions between virtues raises a very interesting problem, one that a non-Eleatic account of virtue should try to solve.

Friedrich Nietzsche imagined a disturbing scenario in which each of the virtues tends by nature to destroy all of the others:

> Behold how each of your virtues covets what is highest: each wants your whole spirit that it might become *her* herald; each wants your whole strength in wrath, hatred, and love. Each virtue is jealous of the others, and jealousy is a terrible thing. Virtues too can perish of jealousy.[18]

I have argued in the preceding section that, at least on a smaller scale than Nietzsche envisions, something like the process he describes here does tend to happen: when some virtues approach "what is highest," they tend to crowd certain others out of the soul. This is clearly not a desirable state of affairs. If what I have said here is true, a generosity that is not checked by the competing influence of other virtues is still generosity and is still a virtue, but it would nonetheless be *better* if it were thus checked and confined. The problem, however, is to show what could prevent or discourage this from happening. What sorts of factors can render the virtues mutually compatible?

One possible solution to this problem would be to place one's entire trust in the trait-specific connections between virtues that give the doctrine of the unity of the virtues its plausibility: we might hope that these connections somehow compensate for the tensions between virtues. Perhaps further investigations into the moral psychology of individual virtues will reveal a pervasive web of positive relations among them, so that the picture we see as we look at the virtues as a whole is somehow one of unity.

In the next chapter, we will indeed find further trait-specific connections among the virtues (IV.4), but we will also turn up further trait-specific

---

[18] Friedrich Nietzsche, *Thus Spoke Zarathustra*, in *The Portable Nietzsche*, trans. and ed. by Walter Kaufmann (New York: Viking Press, 1954), p. 149. For a discussion of Nietzsche's version of this idea—which is more extreme than the one I have been defending here—and of the shortcomings of his version, see my *Nietzsche and the Origin of Virtue* (New York: Routledge, 1991), pp. 81-84.

tensions as well (IV.5). There will not be, anymore than there is now, any obvious reason to expect the entire picture of the virtues, if we could assemble one, would somehow present us with a vision of unity after all. In particular, we have no reason to expect that the connections between the virtues that are connected can remedy the specific problems raised by tensions between the virtues that are in tension.

In the final chapters (VI-XI) I will try to show that an important part of the solution to this problem can be found by looking, not at the states of the individual soul that lie deep within virtuous conduct, but at the social context that surrounds it. In various ways, social and (to some extent) political institutions help to keep various virtues alive and facilitate their formation.

Before I turn to this subject, however, I will need to say more about the individual virtues and, in addition, more about the moral psychology of character in general.

IV

JUSTICE AND BEYOND

1. Conscientiousness

Some virtues are derived from principles that are different in kind from the types on which I have focused in chapters II and III, which are what I have called axiological and limiting principles. These other principles are the ones I call act-necessitating rules (III.1). Such rules have received a great deal of attention from philosophers.[1] Accordingly, there is no need to discuss them at length here. I assume that I do not need to convince anyone that they do sometimes serve as principles of human action. I limit myself instead to indicating how they fit into the conceptual scheme I have built up so far; as a first step I must show that, like limiting and axiological principles, they generate character traits.

Let us assume—plausibly, I hope—that conscientiousness is a trait of character. Suppose that Mary borrowed a substantial amount of money from Martha on the condition that she return it on a certain day, when Martha knew she would need it back. When the day arrived, Mary returned the money in

---

[1] There was a period during this century when moral philosophers wrote as if they did not recognize the existence of any other sort of principles that are legitimate guides for conduct as far as ethics is concerned. This habit is no longer widespread. I suspect that it began gradually to die out with the publication of J. O. Urmson's "Saints and Heroes," in *Essays in Moral Philosophy*, ed. A. I. Melden (Seattle: University of Washington Press, 1959). The reason I suspect this is that Urmson's argument obviously (to me, at least) implies that this view is too narrow. On the issue of what the ethical status of a given act might be, only three stances are possible for an act-necessitating rule: it can enjoin the act, enjoin its omission, or fail to indicate that either the act or its omission is enjoined. It can do nothing else. If such rules were the only guides to ethical conduct, there could only be three sorts of ethical status that an act could have. It would have to be either obligatory, forbidden, or merely permissible. Urmson points out that this three-way division is incomplete. The supererogatory actions of saints and heroes are not obligatory and yet, being admirable, they are not *merely* permissible. Thus, human actions are capable of a fourth sort of ethical status. I only need to point out that it is one to which act-necessitating rules could never lead us.

spite of the fact that her financial difficulties were not over and she was still very much in need of it herself. Whether what she did was conscientious depends partly on what her reason was for doing it. It was not conscientious of her to return the money on time if she did so only in order to establish credit with Martha, so that, had Mary had no further use for her, she would have just kept the money or returned it late. Again, imagine that Mary is asked why she returned the money when she promised she would and she gives the strange but, let us suppose, perfectly sincere answer: "Oh, just to see if I could scrape the money together on time—just for the hell of it." This rather bizarre statement makes it clear that, whatever else might be true of it, her act was certainly not done conscientiously.

If it was done conscientiously, her reason for doing it was *that she promised.* That is obvious enough. But this fact is not sufficient to distinguish acting conscientiously from the other two ways of acting with which I have just contrasted it: in one case keeping a promise is used as a means of creating confidence, in the other it is viewed (rather surreally) as an amusing challenge, and in both cases the fact that she promised is a part of Mary's reason for doing what she did. The difference seems to lie in the fact that, in a conscientious act, the fact that one promised has a status different from those it has in the other instances. If Mary returns the money conscientiously, she returns it because she sees the promise (in her present context, given whatever other obligations impinge on her at the moment) as *necessitating* repayment: because she believes that, due to the fact that she promised, omitting payment would be a fault of some sort; it would be conduct worthy of criticism. Further, she must believe that the promise necessitates payment by itself, in the sense that she does not believe that it does so only when payment would lead to some further good—at least it need not lead to some benefit for herself. This is enough to distinguish paying conscientiously from doing so only to establish credit.

In addition, if a promise is kept conscientiously, it is not kept just because this promise strikes the agent's fancy (for the moment and for no reason at all) as somehow worth keeping; it is done because one regards the fact that one has promised as per se a good reason for doing what one has promised to do. That is, wherever one has promised, one has such a reason. Of course, conscientious people need not think that such a reason is always a sufficient reason, but they always act on the basis of a general notion that a certain factor is capable of necessitating a certain course of action. When they act on the basis of such a general notion, they do so because they think that, in the present context, it does require them to do what they do. This means that they do what they do because it is necessary according to a rule.[2]

If this analysis is correct, some act-necessitating rules are principles of conscientious acts.

2. Justice and Virtue

A number of character traits are derived from such principles. They evidently include a family of traits that I have already discussed in a piecemeal fashion in the preceding chapter. I am referring to the traits to which the ancient and medieval philosophers attached the name of justice (*dikaiosune, justitia*), a general heading that covered such particular qualities as gratitude, fairness, truthfulness, and considerateness. In acting from any of these four particular traits we do what we do because we think that in some respects it is necessary—we do it because we believe that in some respect it is "the right thing to do."[3]

Traits of character that are derived from act-necessitating rules can be divided into two quite different kinds. The division is mirrored in two uses of the words "conscientious" and "conscientiously." We can say, "She is conscientious in everything she does" or "He conscientiously honors all his commitments," meaning simply that the individual involved consistently observes certain standards as to what is fitting and proper. However, when we apply these words not to patterns of action but to particular acts, something more than mere observance of standards is meant. Suppose I borrow a dictionary from someone nearby and return it after a few minutes because I said I would; it would ordinarily be wrong to say that this is a conscientious thing to do. This is not because the reason behind the act is different from the reasons for which conscientious acts are done. So far, the reason is the same

---

[2] Recall that, as I have defined it, the necessity of the act is distinct from the exceptionless universality of a rule. Failure to untangle these two things led Kant to believe that (to put it in my terminology) to think that lying is usually wrong but sometimes right is to misunderstand what an act-necessitating rule is.

[3] An example should indicate why I say "in some respect." Martha is generously giving cookies to some children. It is necessary to distribute the cookies equally because any other way would be unfair. If she does so and does it so that each child gets his or her fair share, then what she does is fair. In one respect, however, what she does is not necessary at all, since there is no necessity in giving the children something in the first place (that is why the act can be generous); but *if* she does it, then doing it in a certain way is necessary.

as the one that would enable us to say that Mary's repaying Martha *was* conscientious. Beyond that, the reason in the present case could even have, as I have put it, the same status as in the previous one (that is, the principle could be the same) and yet the act still could not be called a conscientious one. The mere fact that I am observing the relevant standards is not enough.

The difference between my returning the dictionary on the one hand and an act that is genuinely conscientious on the other does not lie in the reason for which the agent acts; rather, it lies in the conditions, if any, *in spite of which* the act is done. I have no special reason for *not* returning my neighbor's dictionary, aside from the reason anyone has to refrain from returning any borrowed object: the simple fact that I would thereby gain possession of it. In the other case, Mary has a much more powerful reason for not returning what she has borrowed: it would help her out of financial difficulty, and by returning it she only makes her financial problems worse. Generally, the difference between conscientious acts and those that are done from the same principles but are not conscientious seems to be this: conscientious acts are done in spite of some condition that could lead a reasonable, psychologically normal, and *more or less decent* person to do otherwise. The deed must be done in the context of an "understandably tempting condition," as I will call them. Although the agent need not actually feel tempted by them, these conditions must be such that they *could* prevent a person who is not simply corrupt from doing the deed.

Conscientiousness typifies one of the two different kinds of traits that are derived from act-necessitating rules. To grasp the difference between this type of trait and the other, we need to rely on a distinction I made earlier (I.2) between traits of character on the one hand and character as it applies to isolated acts, or act-characters, on the other: between being a courageous or obedient person and courageous or obedient acts.

The difference between the two kinds of traits is this: in one of them, the corresponding act-character can only be present when circumstance brings the rule into conflict with an understandably tempting condition, while for others there is no such requirement. An act is said to be "fair" or "an expression of gratitude" whether the agent has any substantial reason to behave otherwise or not. As we have seen, this is not true of conscientiousness. Nor does it apply to truthfulness (or, more colloquially, honesty)[4] or considerateness: I am not being truthful every time I give someone the correct time of day rather than enjoy a sense of power by deceiving them, nor is it considerate to avoid

---

[4] I owe this point to James D. Wallace, *Virtues and Vices* (Ithaca, N. Y.: Cornell University Press, 1978), p. 56.

bumping into people on the sidewalk when my only reason for walking blindly straight ahead would be to avoid a small amount of effort; such acts must be done in spite of some understandably tempting condition.

In a certain respect, these two kinds of act-character differ sharply with regard to whether we find them admirable. People can sometimes be commended for acting fairly, but only when they do so in spite of some live temptation. It seems obvious that, as a teacher, I am not doing something admirable every time I grade a student's work impartially and every time I respond to a student's ideas without ridiculing or distorting them or subjecting them to sophistical objections: acting fairly is not something that is admirable every single time it occurs. However, teachers *can* be commended for behaving in these ways when (for instance) they do so in spite of some strong and understandable prejudice against a student. We can commend someone by saying generally and simply, "He is a fair person," but only, it would seem, because we know that in being consistently fair one must sooner or later face temptations like these. However, fairness, as an act-character, is not always commendable. The same is true of gratitude. Indeed, it is difficult even to imagine commending someone for expressing gratitude, and no one would commend someone by saying, "He is a grateful person."

On the other hand, the acts having the characters that require understandably tempting conditions are ones that we always find admirable, insofar as they have those characters. To say that an act is truthful (or honest) is to commend it, and the same is true of calling an action considerate.

In a way, these two types of traits differ with respect to whether the cognate acts reflect favorably on the merits of the person who does them. Yet in another way they are really the same. It is true that in one type—which includes fairness and gratitude—the corresponding act-character is not always seen as admirable, while in the other—including truthfulness, considerateness, and conscientiousness—it is. But it is also true that in the former instance the acts are always done in spite of some understandably tempting condition, while in the latter we reserve our admiration until they are. What they have in common is that in both cases the acts are only seen as admirable when circumstances bring the rule into conflict with some understandably tempting condition.

Two things make this fact interesting. First, this is one instance in which our ordinary moral intuitions are very difficult to doubt. I submit that we cannot realistically imagine an argument that should convince you that you ought to admire me when I return your dictionary and have no solid reason to do otherwise. Second, these firmly rooted intuitions seem to distinguish these traits from the traits that I treated as virtues throughout chapters II and III. Those traits seem to have a certain characteristic that, as I have argued earlier (III.4), is possessed by generosity: the cognate actions always reflect positively on the merits of the individuals who do them. Admittedly, to do something that is courageous or temperate or industrious may not in every case be the best and highest thing one could have done in just those circumstances. It is also true that an action that is good in one of these ways might also be bad in some way, so that a generous act might be imprudent and a courageous one might be done partly to serve an unjust cause. In such cases, it might even happen that the thing done was more bad than it was good; that it was, all things considered, worthy of condemnation. Nonetheless, as long as the act really does have some character that corresponds to a trait that is clearly a virtue, there is always at least one thing that was admirable about what was done: namely, the fact that it did have that character.

At least one of the two classes of traits I have been treating in this section does not seem to be like this. The fact that I grade a student paper fairly when I had no grounds for prejudice does not seem to be good, in the sense of admirable, at all. And, clearly, the reason it does not seem so is not that we have in mind some other, more admirable act I should have done instead of grading the paper fairly. The reason seems to be that mere fairness does not have enough of whatever it is that we admire in virtuous conduct. Ordinarily it is, we might say, merely decent. Exactly the same thing can be said of gratitude.

In fact, it can be said about a good deal more than these two traits. Many of the traits that the ancients and medievals called justice are like fairness and gratitude in this way, including the traits—which seem to have no accepted and prevalent names in English—that enable us to keep promises, pay debts, and observe the other property and contractual rights of our fellow human beings. Such conduct, though indispensable if we are to live with our fellow human beings, does not ordinarily inspire us with admiration, nor does it seem that it should.

There is a problem here. These traits, comprising a significant portion of what has traditionally been regarded as the virtue of justice, are fundamentally different from the traits that I have been taking as more or less clear instances of virtue until this chapter. This raises the possibility that the traits I am presently considering are not, strictly speaking, virtues. Perhaps we should call them "elements of decency" instead, since they seem necessary if we are to be decent human beings. Ultimately, the issue at stake here is what our conception of virtue will be like. If we take this view of the matter, we would be deciding that a virtue is a trait of character that is such that, when one acts on it, what one does is always in that respect admirable. This would have the advantage, for me, that it is obviously consistent with the provisional characterization of virtue I offered at the very beginning of this book (I.1): that it is a meritorious trait of character, one that indicates that its possessor is, with respect to that trait, a good person.

Alternatively, we might dispense with this simple characterization of virtue and embrace tradition by saying that these traits do belong among the virtues. This, however, would still seem to commit us to departing from tradition to some extent, as long as we admit that the actions that flow from the traits presently under consideration might not be admirable but merely decent. In that case, these traits apparently would constitute an inferior category of the virtues.

What I would like to attempt in what remains of this section is a third alternative to these two approaches, one that is fully compatible with my initial characterization of virtue. I will try to show that justice, including suitably redescribed versions of these troublesome traits, can be regarded as a virtue in just the way we can regard generosity and courage: as something that is always admirable.

One way to try to accomplish this end would be to do with these traits the same thing that ordinary language does with truthfulness, considerateness, and conscientiousness. That is, we could redefine these traits so that they only refer to action in the face of understandably tempting conditions: those are the conditions in which they strike us as admirable in just the way that clearly virtuous conduct does. In that way we could carve out some new traits that behave just like virtues do. Alternatively, we could declare that these traits, as we presently understand them and without any such attempts at redefinition, only *function as* virtues, or only constitute part of the virtue of justice, when such conditions are present.

Actually, I do not think such measures would really succeed in putting these traits on the same footing as generosity and courage. As I have already had occasion to remark (III.4), what seems to allow us to think of a generous act as, in itself, a good thing is the fact that people who see that the good of others is something worth pursuing in itself thereby show that they have some fragment of wisdom. The same thing can be said, with even more confidence, about traits like courage: grasping the limits of the value that fundamental goods have is obviously one of the most important functions of wisdom and one of the clearest proofs that one does possess it in some measure.

I do not think that the same sort of thing can be said of someone who accepts the idea that, for instance, it is ordinarily wrong to make a promise that one does not intend to keep. As long as such ideas are understood as I have presented them so far, as *rules*, it is not by any means obvious that such acceptance is a part of what we call wisdom. If I firmly accept the notion that a certain class of actions is wrong, then I might be a wise person, but on the other hand, I might not be wise at all. As far as my accepting such a notion is concerned, I might simply be a mindless rule worshiper who accepts the rule solely because my parents taught me to do so. I might have no understanding at all as to why the action is wrong or what the point and value of the rule is. In such matters, it seems, wisdom only begins with such additional understanding. Without *something* in addition to the rule, it is not clear why following it in the face of understandably tempting conditions would be admirable.

To this it might be objected that rule following looks more like wisdom, and hence more admirable, if we keep in mind what it is really like. The relevant sorts of act-necessitating rules are extremely complex, so laden with exceptions and qualifications that many if not all of them could never be stated or written down, at least in brief compass. Applying such principles cannot be a matter of following memorized maxims; it is an intellectual process that requires a great deal of mature judgment, including the abilities to make distinctions and attend to facts that are relevant while refusing to be distracted by those that are not.

I agree that the activity of applying the relevant rules really does have something like the sort of intellectual complexity alleged in the foregoing objection. What I deny is that, by itself, such complexity constitutes an instance of wisdom and, consequently, that it is sufficient to explain why the traits involved are virtues. The admiration we give to virtue is not the sort of admiration we give to the subtle person, the intelligent person, or the person we believe has complex ideas. Such skills, worthy as they might be in themselves, do not answer to our concept of good character.

Admittedly, it seems true that we cannot become wise without achieving *some* sort of mental subtlety, including at least the ability to make certain sorts of distinctions. However, the place that such subtlety has as a part of wisdom and, consequently, as a part of virtue requires an explanation. If we follow tradition and consider all of the traits that I have been discussing in this section in terms of what they have in common, we would be regarding them, as I have said more than once, as aspects of justice. In this sense, justice is a trait of character that enables us to give others their *due*. In general, we do regard certain kinds of crude and sloppy thinking as disqualifying some one from possessing this trait. Failure to make the right sorts of distinctions destroys justice. How can this be explained?

The brief description I have just given of the character trait of justice suggests an answer to this question. It indicates that justice, unlike generosity, is not a matter of good intentions. Justice, it says, enables us to bring about a state of affairs in which someone has what is their due. An act can only be said to be just if it would actually bring about such a state of affairs, unless something extraneous to the agent prevents it (as when a judge renders a just decision and the police fail to enforce it). This implies that justice requires, in some measure, a certain sort of intelligence. If I grade a student paper and, in doing so, fail to make certain distinctions between higher and lower levels of achievement, or fail to make them with sufficient clarity and accuracy to respond to the student's deserts, then I have not graded the paper fairly, even if I sincerely intended to do the right thing by the student. Without such lucidity, it will be an accident if the student gets what he or she deserves. Where fairness is concerned, what matters is not our intentions but whether, so far as it is within our power, the recipients of our actions get what is coming to them. The same thing can be said of the other traits that traditionally comprise the elements of justice.

This enables us to explain the fact that, as we ordinarily see them, these traits require a certain intelligence of some sort. The explanation rests on a certain more fundamental and more important requirement: that people get what is their due, so far as it is within our power.

This more fundamental requirement suggests, further, how and under what circumstances these traits can be virtues. Applying act-necessitating rules can be virtuous, but only if the individual who does it cares about whether people get what is coming to them. Without this, the virtue of justice degenerates into an arid rule fetishism. When that happens, as it sometimes does, the rules and the making of subtle distinctions become sacred ends in themselves. One who falls into this trap misses the point of the rules. The point of the rules is that they protect people. If we apply the rules and act on them because we understand this, the sometimes subtle discriminations involved in applying them come to have an ethical status they would otherwise lack. They come to serve as an important part of wisdom.

The understanding that is needed if this is to happen—the understanding, that is, of the point of the rules—rests in turn on something even more fundamental. It requires that we view our fellow human beings in a certain way: as beings toward whom it is appropriate to observe certain limits, whose presence in our world imposes necessities on us. If we see people this way and act accordingly, we do not merely *observe* the rights of others, we *respect* them. Thus, it seems fitting to call such a view of our fellow human beings "respect for others."[5]

We will learn more about what this sort of respect is like when I discuss how we can acquire it (in IV.4, VII.6, and VIII.5). For the time being, at any rate, I think it is plausible enough to say that conduct in which our applying the principles of justice is animated by such respect is the sort of trait that we can regard as a virtue: such respect, being a species of caring, seems to be admirable. Having said that, we can also say that conduct that is fair or that observes the rights of our fellow human beings, and all the sorts of conduct I have focused on in this section, are virtuous to the extent that they are informed by the same spirit. Saying so, we would be entirely consistent with the brief characterization of virtue I suggested at the outset of chapter I.

3. Beyond Justice

When confronted with someone's bad conduct, especially when violations of certain act-necessitating rules are involved, we generally believe that certain responses are appropriate. We blame them and criticize what they have done, we sometimes express resentment or indignation, and in extreme cases we may feel that we can no longer have anything to do with people who act as they have. For convenience, these activities may be collected under the label "censure." If one is a parent or a representative of the state, one may be responsible for performing a function even more grim than censure: that of punishing the malefactor. Clearly, a sensitive person has ample cause to find such activities distasteful: as one philosopher has said, they are all "rather repugnant."[6] They also present difficulties that are not merely matters of taste.

As an instance of such difficulties, consider the following situation. I am confronted with a friend who has probably done something bad, but I am not

---

[5] Here I am adopting language used by Kant and his followers. My use of this term could confuse some readers because respect for others, in this sense, is not analogous to the *self*-respect I discussed in chapter II, where I took a noticeably non-Kantian position. In both cases, though, the way I have used these terms seems at least very close to usages that are sanctioned either by philosophical tradition or ordinary language, and I could find no substitutes but ones that would have been either more confusing or more awkward.

[6] Kurt Baier, *The Moral Point of View* (New York: Random House, 1965), p. 3.

quite sure of it; I know in some sense "what he did" but, despite my best efforts to find out what happened, I am not certain enough of the circumstances or the intentions involved to be sure that he really has behaved badly. Supposing there is no workable remedy for the incompleteness of my information, I have a choice: on the one hand I can censure him in some way; on the other hand I can simply let it go.

It is possible, at least with some forcing, to see this choice as a dilemma. In one option, I resolve to censure my friend while knowing that there is a possibility that I am doing this to an innocent man, that precisely in the name of justice I am doing an injustice. While such a resolution, in the context of such knowledge, may not imply a genuine logical contradiction, it is for moral reasons not an easy one to hold. It is *morally* repugnant. In the other option, as I refrain from censure I know that I may be letting a culprit "get away with it." Of course, the thought of letting wickedness "get off scot-free" can also be morally repugnant. For some people justice means, as Nietzsche puts it, "Everything is dischargeable, everything must be discharged."[7]

For most of us, though, such situations do not ordinarily present any dilemma at all because we believe that bad conduct in others does not necessitate censure on our part, that we do not *have to* attack every wrongdoer in some way. For lack of a better name, I will call this belief "the principle of forbearance." It, together with the belief that it *is* necessary to avoid censuring the innocent, enables us to give possible wrongdoers the benefit of the doubt in spite of the perhaps repugnant consequence that some culprit may be "getting away with it." These beliefs make possible the practice of mercy, "this self-overcoming of justice," as Nietzsche calls it.[8]

As I have described it so far, mercy might appear to be merely a mechanism for realizing a certain policy: "To avoid accumulating guilt for myself I will avoid censuring people when I am not sure they deserve it. Of course, occasionally a real scoundrel will get off scot-free, but that is nothing to me. I cannot be blamed for it."[9] This would be a distorted picture of mercy if only because a paradigm instance of mercy is that in which we show mercy even though we are sure the object of our mercy has behaved badly, and we believe

---

[7] Friedrich Nietzsche, *On the Genealogy of Morals,* in *Basic Writings of Nietzsche*, trans. and ed. Walter Kaufmann (New York: The Modern Library, 1968), pp. 508 and 509.

[8] Ibid., p. 509.

[9] Alwynne Smart, "Mercy," *Philosophy* 43 (October, 1968): p. 349.

we have a right to punish or censure him. In such cases, there is no guilt to be avoided by practicing mercy: the principle that it is necessary to avoid punishing and censuring the innocent has no application in a case like this.

What reason do we have for showing mercy in such cases? The principle of forbearance, the mere notion that we *may* refrain from censure and punishment, does not imply that we should do so, nor can it by itself enable us to see such situations as opportunities to bring about some good. An adequate answer to this question may be found in the notion that the good of others, even that of wrongdoers, is worthwhile in itself and needs no further justification as an end of action. This suggests that mercy is based, not on the principle of forbearance alone, but on the principle of generosity as well. This is an additional reason why the policy of guilt avoidance I described a moment ago is not a full description of the thought that lies behind mercy.

Roughly the same two basic claims that I have just made about this trait —that it comes from the principle of forbearance and that it comes from the principle of generosity—can be applied to another one, a trait that bears an obvious resemblance to mercy: namely, forgiveness. To see that forgiveness is an instance of a sort of forbearance, in case it is not obvious already, imagine the following situation. Paul has been quarreling with his daughter, Veronica, because she intends to marry a man who is not a member of their religion and who will obviously not convert. For various reasons, Paul is firmly opposed to marrying outside the faith. Veronica believes, with equal firmness, that his position is pure and simple bigotry. He eventually tries to patch things up with her by saying: "I've thought it over and I realized that you are much more important to me than this religious issue. I want to put all this behind us. I've decided to forgive you." Obviously, Veronica might well be more upset than mollified by this declaration of Paul's big-heartedness. Why? There are various ways to answer this question, but they would all include, at a minimum something that amounts to this: Paul is clearly implying that he still thinks she is doing something wrong.

More generally, we can only forgive those who we believe have wronged us. To forgive is to forswear censure and retribution in circumstances in which we believe we have some reason to carry out precisely the responses we are forswearing. In forgiveness, however, we do not forgo these responses out of timidity or laziness but, in part, because we realize that such responses are not morally necessary. This means that it is based, at least in part, on the principle of forbearance.

Further, we do not forswear conduct that seems reasonable to us unless there is some point in doing so. One motive for forgiveness is particularly prominent in cases in which we are connected with the person who has offended us by certain relationships—most notably friendships and love relationships—that are based on mutual affection. We wish to protect the relationship from the damaging effects of censure and retribution: despite their indispensable social function as enforcers of the moral rules, they tend to have a poisonous effect on such relationships, damaging the bonds of sentiment on which the relationships depend.

In such cases, one of the factors that motivates forgiveness is our concern for the good of the offender. This is partly due to the nature of the relationships themselves: they are based on mutual benevolence. More generally, though, this same factor seems to be involved even when forgiveness occurs outside such relationships. Some concern for the good of the person who has wronged us must be involved if what we are doing is properly to be called forgiveness. Accordingly, it does not seem possible to practice forgiveness as a trait of character unless one holds the principle of generosity.[10]

A third trait, obviously similar to both mercy and forgiveness, also seems to be generated by the principle of generosity and something like the principle of forbearance: namely, tolerance. People show their tolerance by living on terms of peace and civility with people whose opinions and ways of life they think are wrong in some important way. Baptists who behave with genuine cordiality toward Methodists are not being tolerant, but if they do the same with Jews and atheists then perhaps they are.

This is why finding out that someone is tolerating you can be offensive. The reason is roughly the same as the one that might prompt Veronica to be offended at Paul's forgiving her. Someone tolerates you when they think there is something about the way you think or what you are that could reasonably be thought to justify some sort of negative response, at least some sort of coolness or shunning. Tolerance is possible for them if they nonetheless think that such

---

[10] This raises the possibility, as a hypothesis that is worth pursuing, that acts of forgiveness have a characteristic that I have attributed to generous acts: namely, spontaneity (III.3). This evidently is the view of Hannah Arendt: "forgiveness" she says ". . . does not merely re-act but acts anew and unexpectedly, unconditioned by the act which provoked it." *The Human Condition* (Garden City, N.Y.: Doubleday Anchor Books, 1959), p. 216. The same thing might be said, with roughly the same intuitive plausibility, of mercy. I am not sure either claim is true, however. Punishment and censure raise very serious issues of justice, and for all I have said here there may be circumstances in which it would be unjust *not* to forgive or show mercy, and this may be part of the reason why a particular forgiving or merciful act is done.

responses are not necessary. That is, it is based on something very much like the principle of forbearance that lies behind mercy and forgiveness.

Of course, this cannot explain, by itself, why someone would continue to deal with you in an amiable way. If they do, some other force must, as it were, overcome the resistance to amiability. If they do it solely in order to manipulate you into giving them money, that might only mean that their desire for money is stronger than whatever ideological or religious principles they might have. They must do it because they are concerned about the effect that coolness or shunning would have on your well-being. Part of what separates tolerance from mere indifference is the attitude that, though ideological and religious differences are important, people are also important as beings whose well-being is worth supporting. That is, genuine tolerance rests in part on the principle of generosity.[11]

4. Benevolence and Respect

There is an obvious similarity between the traits I have been discussing in section 3 and those I discussed earlier, in section 2. The members of the latter group, those that comprise the traditional virtue of justice, have one thing in common. They are all based on a certain more fundamental feature of the individual who possesses them: what I call respect for others. The former group of traits—mercy, forgiveness, and tolerance—also seem to rest, and in just the same way, on another characteristic more elementary than themselves. This other characteristic is the view, which also lies at the heart of generosity, that the good of others is worth pursuing in itself. For obvious reasons, I will call this vision of our fellow human beings "benevolence."

To find such connections underlying different traits—traits, moreover, that seem to be obvious examples of virtues—recalls an argument for the unity of the virtues I discussed earlier (III.5). This is the venerable line of reasoning that is based on the idea that all the virtues can be traced back to a single faculty, which is wisdom. Wisdom, the argument contends, brings all the virtues with

---

[11] Here I must say about tolerance the same thing that I said about forgiveness and mercy in footnote 10: tolerance might not in all cases be spontaneous. Indeed, in a liberal democracy, it is assumed that in a wide category of contexts, tolerance in some sense of the word is a duty and should be practiced as such. In chapter XI I will discuss the serious consequences that would follow if enough people should decide (as many already have) on the contrary that, within the same category of contexts, tolerant forbearance is an optional expression of generosity.

it. Thus, one must either possess all the virtues or none at all, depending on whether one is wise or not. Here the connections I claim to have found within each of two groups of virtues seem to be forms of wisdom and, further, they seem to be aspects of the same thing: the attribution of value to human beings. Do my claims lend some support to this ancient argument? What they indicate, I think, is that it is not utterly without merit. However, the strength they attribute to it, when they are understood and elaborated as they ought to be, is of a rather limited sort.

It is clear, first of all, that respect and benevolence are quite different things. The intuitive difference between them was captured with admirable simplicity by Kant: "The principle of mutual love [what I am calling benevolence] admonishes men constantly to *come nearer* to each other; that of the respect that they owe to each other, to keep themselves at a *distance* from one another."[12] What respect for others requires of me is that, whatever my purposes might be, I do not pursue them by doing certain things to others. In relation to other people, it recognizes that there are lines I must not cross. Benevolence, on the contrary, specifies what one of my purposes should be. You might say that it does require me to cross a certain line: the one that separates mere neutrality toward the well-being of others from actively promoting their good.

More important, it seems that one can possess a considerable amount of respect without any benevolence at all. It seems possible, for instance, to have an enormous respect for the privacy of others without seeing any point in helping them to put their privacy to good use. Such indifference to the good of others, it seems to me, would not necessarily show that the respect involved is unreal. It could consist in a genuine recognition of what Justice Louis Brandeis called "the right to be let alone." I can imagine someone who thinks that elimination of benevolence is necessary on the ground that a strong concern for what is good for others can only interfere with this righteous leaving alone: people will grow and develop more effectively, or do whatever they are supposed to do with their privacy, if left entirely free of interference. Someone has respect for others in my sense if they adhere to certain rules that protect others, provided that they do so because they have some understanding of the point of the rules. They have the required sort of understanding if they see that

---

[12] Immanuel Kant, *The Doctrine of Virtue: Part II of The Metaphysic of Morals*, trans. Mary Gregor (New York: Harper, 1964), p. 116. As will be obvious to some readers, the way I understand this distinction owes much to Kant. See his discussion of it in *The Doctrine of Virtue*, pp. 115-17.

their self-restraint does serve this protecting function. It seems to be possible to have this sort of insight, however, without taking on the good of others as an end of one's own action—without, that is, being benevolent. This would mean that it is possible to utterly lack the virtues that rest on benevolence and yet to possess the elements of justice and possess them *as virtues*.

If respect and benevolence are independent in this way, it certainly counts against the argument for the unity of the virtues. It would be hasty, though, to conclude from this that the argument is entirely without merit. We may only draw that conclusion if it can also be shown that the relationship I have just tried to establish is symmetrical. I have just made the claim that we can have the virtues of respect without those of benevolence. Does this independence of respect and benevolence go, so to speak, the other way? Can we have the virtues of benevolence without already having those of respect? The argument for unity may be wrong in asserting that the virtues are one enormous package deal but, if *some* of the virtues require certain other virtues, then virtue in general does display some of the unity that the argument alleges.

One thing is reasonably clear, or will be after we have given a little more thought to the matter: it is possible to have great benevolence while having, in my sense of the words, no respect at all. I would achieve this dubious status, for instance, if I were to promote the good of others as an end in itself while at the same time recognizing no limits to what I may do to them to achieve this purpose, provided only that my actions on balance do tend to achieve it.

There is one sort of person who at least arguably does have this status: namely, the paternalist. People who treat us paternalistically treat us benevolently but, at least in certain important respects, without respect. They violate certain rights we think we have against coercion or manipulation but, of course, "for our own good." Benevolence in the absence of respect would also characterize people who live by the doctrine of act-utilitarianism. Such people would aim to increase, as an end in itself, the well-being of all the people affected by their actions, on the whole or on the average, as much as possible. This purpose would be the only principle by which they would determine what they should do. This would mean that they would be unable to reject any action that promises to achieve their goal as beyond the limits of what they may do.

Perhaps the clearest evidence that benevolence without respect is possible is the fact that it characterizes the way that many of us, including myself, try to treat our pets. If my dog had an incurable disease that caused her considerable pain, I would probably have her painlessly "put to sleep," even if she were fully conscious and despite the fact that she had expressed no desire to die. Of course, I would not think of treating an ailing relative that way. For whatever reason, I do not give my dog the peculiar sort of inviolability that I associate with human beings. Yet the reason I would have her killed is "her own good." In addition, though I would not be pursuing this good to realize some other objective of mine, my efforts in pursuing this good show that absence of constraint that is characteristic of benevolence in the absence of respect. It would be morally evil to treat a normal adult human being that way, but there is unfortunately nothing contradictory or impossible about it.[13]

This last fact suggests that there is merit in the argument for the unity of the virtues after all. Though benevolence can exist without respect, it then becomes compatible with moral evil. What this means is something that is at least very much in the spirit of that argument: though benevolence can be present without respect, *virtues* such as generosity and its close relatives cannot. Either they cannot be practiced without it or they cannot be practiced as virtues. This might appear at first glance to be false because—to focus momentarily on the case of generosity—if I generously give you something, that cannot be because I think I would violate some constraint on my behavior if I omitted giving it. The sort of thinking that evinces respect cannot provide me with my reason for giving you whatever it is that I am giving. But you may not be the only person affected by what I am doing, nor is providing reasons for action the only role that thinking can play in human conduct.

If I give you the shirt off my back, that may be a generous thing to do. If I give you the shirt off my neighbor's back, it couldn't have been generous—not unless my neighbor had somehow transferred to me beforehand the right to give it away.[14] I can only be generous with what is mine to give. In a world in

---

[13] I imagine someone might want to object here that such behavior counts as benevolence when it is done to animals but not when it is done to human beings because it can be good for animals to be manipulated and disposed of in this way but it could not be good for human beings. The good of human beings is indissolubly linked to their power of free choice and cannot be served by violating that freedom. I believe some version of this doctrine is true, but it quite is irrelevant to the point I am making here. As I have defined it, the benevolence of an action does not stand or fall with what is actually good for the recipient but with what the agent believes or intends. In this sense, I can benevolently seek what is good for you while actually—as it so happens—doing you no good at all, or even doing you harm.

[14] This point seems obvious enough to me, but certain voters forget it when election time comes around. I have in mind those who vote for a program that transfers public funds to some group to which they do not belong, and think of themselves as obviously more generous than those who voted against the program. Only that portion of the funds that

which there are no property rights, in which physical goods really do not belong to one person more than anyone else, no one could generously give such goods to anyone. It would still be possible to generously donate one's own time and effort to another—I might be able to generously harvest some of the communal nuts and berries for you to eat, for instance—but this would only be true if my own time and my own actions are mine to use and dispose of. If the community somehow really had exclusive rights to plan and direct my conduct, then any time *I* chose to donate to you would be stolen from the community, and could no more be generously given than could a stolen shirt.

Generosity presupposes certain rights to liberty of choice that are at least similar to property rights: they are rights to decide whether and how one will use or dispose of various entities and processes, including one's own actions. There seem to be two reasons why it must require such rights. First, we can only give something generously if the thing given constitutes a cost we undergo for the sake of the other person, and it can only have this sort of significance if it was in some sense ours in the first place. For instance, if I cannot freely dispose of my time and effort on some other purpose, my donating it to you costs me nothing and cannot be generous. Further, where the giving of physical goods is concerned, part of the point of the act of giving them is to make them belong to the recipient: in this context, that is what "give" means. If the shirt I hand you is stolen, I do not succeed in making it yours and I haven't given it to you in the relevant sense. In relation to physical goods, then, generous giving presupposes property rights because, in general, giving such goods presupposes them.[15] What this means is that, to a being who had no regard for property rights or anything like them, generosity would be quite impossible. It is a trait of character that requires, as a foundation, the sort of thinking that is characteristic of respect for others: thinking that responds to considerations of justice, including especially thoughts about what rights people have.

The same thing is true, perhaps more obviously, of the other virtues that require benevolence. That they rest on the ability to think in terms of

---

comes from the voter's own income can possibly support the claim that he or she is being generous, and it is often insignificant or non-existent.

[15] For the sake of simplicity, I will ignore the fact that, in addition to generously giving something to someone, it is also possible to generously loan it or generously give someone the use of it for a while. In such cases, it would be possible, though tedious, to say things that are relevantly similar to what I am saying here.

considerations of justice is directly implied by my discussion of them in section 3. As I have said, we can only forgive those whom we believe have wronged us. This means that forgiveness would not be possible for a thoroughgoing immoralist. For someone who is utterly unable to think in terms of right and wrong, perhaps the closest one could ever come to forgiveness would be to achieve a certain interesting trait that Nietzsche attributes to Mirabeau, "who had no memory for insults and vile actions done him and was unable to forgive because he—forgot."[16]

By parity of reasoning, a thoroughgoing relativist would be incapable of tolerance. Someone for whom the ideological or religious views of others can never be wrong could have nothing to tolerate, just as an immoralist could have nothing to forgive.[17] More generally, all the virtues that I described in section 3 as resting on benevolence also rest on the sort of thinking that is characteristic of respect for others. All involve the principle of forbearance, and in each case what the agent forbears from is behavior toward another person that, according to the agent's own views, could to one degree or another appear to be justified. Historically, these virtues have been associated in one way or another with liberal values, in part perhaps because they protect individuals from an encroaching body of rules. But if they are liberal virtues they are at any rate not anarchist ones: they do not involve rejecting the rules or denying their importance.

There is, then, this much merit in the argument for the unity of the virtues. The independence of respect and benevolence I argued for earlier is not quite symmetrical: the virtues of benevolence are not entirely independent of respect, in the way that I have argued that the virtues of respect are independent of benevolence. But how much aid does this give the cause of the unity of the virtues? I think the correct answer to this question is not much.

What the doctrine of unity asserts is that the virtues require one another. We have seen here that the virtues of benevolence require some degree of respect or, at least, the sort of thinking that is characteristic of it. This, however, does

---

[16] Nietzsche, *On the Genealogy of Morals*, p. 475.

[17] "This struggle with an enemy who is understood is true tolerance, the proper attitude of every robust soul. Why is it so rare in our race? José de Campos . . . wrote: 'The virtues of tolerance are rare in poor peoples'; that is to say, weak people." José Ortega y Gasset, *Meditations on Quixote*, trans. Evelyn Rugg (New York: Norton, 1961), p. 36. The individual who is the object of tolerance remains an "enemy" in that he or she is "understood" in terms of categories that are more or less moral in nature, categories that *could* justify an intolerant response if it were not for a greater force that overcomes them.

not mean that they require the *virtues* that are associated with respect, the ones that are elements of justice. What the virtue of generosity requires, roughly, is this: that I care enough about the property rights of others not to give away stolen goods. Unless we drop our standards as to what is to count as a virtue to absurdly low levels, we cannot call this an instance of the virtue of justice. I cannot become virtuous merely by abstaining from theft, even if I do so out of respect for the rights of others. Yet this is as close as generosity comes to requiring that I also be just.

The requirements of the other virtues of benevolence that I have discussed in this chapter are similarly lax. Forgiveness, for instance, requires that we care about the difference between right and wrong, at least when we are the victims of conduct that is wrong. Generally, what these virtues require is that we think in terms of the sorts of concepts that are distinctive of the way just people see the world, or at least that we do so in certain contexts. But thinking in such terms is not the same thing as having any of the traits of character that comprise the ancient virtue of justice. The sort of justice, if we may call it that, that the virtues of benevolence require is at most a matter of decency rather than virtue.

5. Forgiveness and Self-Respect

In the last chapter we saw a problem for the unity of the virtues that seems much more serious than this mutual independence that exists between some of the virtues: namely, the mutual tension that exists between certain others. One of the traits we have discussed in this chapter raises this additional sort of problem, and does so in a way that is important both for the theory of character and the practice of everyday life.

The trait I have in mind is forgiveness, which conflicts with self-respect in precisely the same way that I have said generosity does (III.5). The basic reason for this is not difficult to see. As I have said, one can only forgive wrongs against oneself. This is precisely the subject matter of one sort of self-respect, the sort that involves asserting one's dignity against ill-treatment by others. Any possible occasion for showing this sort of self-respect is also a possible occasion for forgiveness. Further, on such occasions, these two traits could only be exercised by incompatible and, indeed, opposite sorts of actions. The acts in which this sort of self-respect is shown always involve active censure or retribution against the person who has wronged us. To forgive, however, means to forswear precisely such actions as these. We should expect an individual who excels in the relevant sort of self-respect to view people who forgive those who transgress against them with suspicion at best.

Indeed, it is not hard to imagine a plausible scenario in which this trait manages very nearly to drive forgiveness out of the life of a self-respecting person. Such an individual is concerned to defend his or her rights, and this concern is a moral one, based on our understanding of moral principle and our personal attachment to the distinction between right and wrong. Forgiveness always involves setting aside such considerations for the sake of something else that, in the present context, one values more highly than exposing and penalizing moral infractions. Usually, the good that the forgiver seeks to preserve is a relationship with the offender, one that would be damaged or destroyed by continued censure and retribution. This often means valuing concerns that crucially involve moral rights less highly than ones in which rights are not involved in any important way at all. To one who values the concerns of self-respect highly, it might well appear that someone who acts this way does not adequately appreciate rights or, indeed, morality itself. It might also appear to show inadequate self-esteem, and an insufficient willingness to look out for oneself.[18]

In a similar way, we can easily imagine forgiveness driving out the relevant sort of self-respect. Though the forgiver can seldom if ever think that the offender has a right to be forgiven, forgiveness is based on a concern that has a power over the ethical imagination at least as great as that possessed by the

---

[18] Some philosophers have come close to arguing that self-respect, something much like it, *should* crowd forgiveness out in more or less this way. What I take to be a moderate (and, in fact, challenging and profound) version of this thesis is put forth by Aurel Kolnai in his "Forgiveness," in his *Ethics, Value, and Reality: Selected Papers of Aurel Kolnai* (Indianapolis: Hackett, 1978), pp. 211-24. A more extreme version is defended by Joram Graf Haber in his *Forgiveness: A Philosophical Study* (Lanham, Md.: Rowman & Littlefield, 1991), chaps. 4 and 5. Arguing on the basis of a conception of self-respect that is drawn from Thomas Hill's early work (see above, chap. II, footnotes 22, 24, 29, 30 and 31), he argues that this trait requires that, when we are wronged, we feel (and, presumably, act on) all of the resentment that would be "warranted" by the wrong (p. 85). He then argues (correctly, I think) that, if this is true, then almost every reason for forgiving someone that one might have is simply illegitimate. The only legitimate reason would be one that cancels out all justification for resentment and positively supports the forgiver's self-respect. There is, he thinks, only one reason that qualifies: that the wrongdoer has undergone a complete change of heart, so that the forgiver "can join" the wrongdoer "in condemning her evil deed" (pp. 104-5). If Haber were right, justified forgiveness would seem to be an instance of mere decency and not virtue: *not* forgiving, in such cases, would be an instance of gross injustice, and the forgiver's entire achievement would consist in not perpetrating it.

notion of rights. This is the notion, which also lies behind the other virtues of benevolence, that the good of others is worth pursuing in itself. Notions such as rights are important, but they are not as important as people and relations between them, especially relations that are grounded in a mutual concern for the good of the other. To someone in the grips of this idea, protecting one's hurt dignity by blaming the offender can seem to be a foolish course of action at best, since it always gives the appearance of sacrificing things that more important for the sake of things that are less important.

In the case of forgiveness and the related sort of self-respect, the danger that Nietzsche imagined of the virtues crowding one another out of the soul (see III.6) seems close to a realistic possibility. Having said this, I should hasten to point out that, of course, I do not mean that this process is inevitable. In particular, we have seen no evidence that there is anything like a logical contradiction between the principles of these two traits. We have no reason to think, for instance, that, taken together, they require us to do two mutually incompatible acts. As I have described it, forgiveness is based on the notion that the good of others is worth pursuing in itself and on the principle of forbearance, which indicates that we need not do certain things that are contrary to the interests of others. In general, this is quite consistent with sometimes doing such things, just as the principle of generosity is consistent with sometimes refraining from giving things away. On the other hand, although the good that is promoted by self-respect often conflicts to some extent with those promoted by forgiveness, it is also true that, if it is practiced as a virtue, self-respect includes a recognition of an upper limit on the importance of its good (II.7).[19]

---

[19] The error that lies behind Haber's argument is to assume, on the contrary, that the concerns of self-respect are infinitely important. See footnote 18, above. Perhaps it is not too far afield to comment further on the main thesis I attributed to him there, particularly as it is closely relevant to issues that I will discuss in chapter XI. This is the thesis that we should refuse to forgive those who offend against us unless they undergo a complete change of heart, so that they come to agree with us in condemning what they did. To place such a condition on forgiveness would have very serious consequences. In the case of Paul and Veronica, described above in section 3, it would mean that Paul should not forgive Veronica for marrying the man of her choice, since she is obviously not going to agree with him about whether his act is right. Disagreement of this sort is by no means a rare occurrence. Both in the large issues of life and in the many small ones that cause cumulative troubles between friends and lovers, there is often disagreement over whether an offending act is wrong. There is also much disagreement about whether an offense was *as* wrong as the offended person thinks it was, raising the issue of whether the offender is sufficiently contrite. Haber's doctrine would seem to require that in such cases the offended party should hold on

As far as the principles of these two traits are concerned, there is no reason to think that it is impossible to practice both of them as important virtues. Nonetheless, each does seem to have a certain potentially dangerous tendency to inhibit the development of the other. A sufficiently strong regard for the concerns of either trait brings with it habits of thought that could easily crowd out one's attention to the concerns of the other. We shall see later (in chapter XI) that there is at times a similar sort of tension between self-respect and tolerance, one that has important political consequence). My suggested solutions to these problems will have to wait until later chapters (VII-XI). As I have already indicated, I will look for them in the social context that surrounds our attempts to act virtuously. In the case of forgiveness, I will say (in chapter IX) that certain legal institutions help to make room for it by making retributive conduct less relevant to issues of self-respect than it would otherwise be.

Before I can turn to these subjects, though, there are others I will need to discuss.

---

to some residue of resentment regarding the original offending act. If differences of opinion are common and difficult to eliminate, this narrowly restrictive view of forgiveness would obviously have devastating effects on personal relations. If we could say that liberal societies are based on the assumption that ineliminable differences of opinion are indeed common, that would be another reason (in addition to the one cited in section 4) why forgiveness, in a form that is not restricted in this way, is a liberal virtue.

V

Virtue, Vice, and Passion

1. Two Problems

In this chapter I will begin to remedy two omissions in my account of character as I have presented it so far.

The first of these is my omission of any sustained discussion of the relations between traits of character and the emotions. Except for some brief remarks in discussions of specific traits (as in II.3), the only claim I have made about the emotions is the purely negative one that traits of character are *not* temperamental dispositions (I.3). Indeed, the definition of traits of character I gave in chapter I pointedly omitted any mention of what the agent feels, appealing instead to things that are (in a certain wide sense of the word) believed.

My account of character would certainly be misleading and one-sided if it were left in this state. Intuitively, it seems obvious that traits of character must have *something* to do with emotion, and that this is an important fact about them. This fact should, at any rate, become obvious if we contrast such traits with other human characteristics—such as productive skills, habits, and purely theoretical or speculative states of mind such as mathematical knowledge—that seem to have no necessary relations with the emotions. After all, no one would say that an act is a display of skill in carpentry just because it originates from a certain emotion, and yet such claims *have* been made about virtues and vices. I have said that they are not true, but the fact that these claims are initially plausible suggests that there must be some systematic connections between character and the passions of the soul.

As a matter of fact, the account of traits of character I have given so far suggests one good reason—as contrasted with the purely intuitive sort of consideration I just pointed out—for suspecting that there must be connections of this sort. In the opening chapters of this book we have seen enough to realize that the principles of traits of character are about things that are especially liable to inspire emotions: such things as danger, effort, ease, authority, the good of others, and physical pleasure. Some of these are typically the object of a single emotion, as danger is most often the object of fear. Others, such as the good of others and authority, are apt to inspire different passions in different people. Again, some principles are about things that usually have no emotional significance at all, except in situations in which the principle is called to do its work. The pleasures of the table do not normally inspire me with emotion but, when I am on a diet and my temperance is put to the test, a slab of cheesecake swimming in raspberry sauce might fill me with an intense yearning followed, in rapid succession, by anguish and shame. Nothing like this is true of the subject matters of geometrical theorems or the rules of carpentry.[1]

My account of character has appealed almost entirely to the thoughts that are part of it. However, the very nature of these thoughts indicates that they cannot be the whole picture: they are precisely the kind of thoughts with which our emotions can be expected to reverberate, and we can also expect the relations between character and emotion to be complex and interesting. In this chapter I will begin to fill in this missing part of the picture.

Another part of my picture of character that I have so far omitted to fill in is the part that depicts the nature of vice. Though I have discussed several different vices in the preceding three chapters, these discussions were mainly incidental to my treatment of one virtue or another, and I have said rather little about vices as such.

It seems natural to treat these two subjects—emotion and vice—together, if only because there is an old and plausible theory that holds that they are connected in a very simple way.

I have said that it is not ultimately very plausible to say that an action displays some virtue just because it is done on the basis of some emotion. However, the same claim could *very* plausibly be made concerning vice. What could be more obvious than that cowardice is very closely associated with fear? Beyond that, it is obvious that acting in a cowardly way includes *acting out of fear*. Generalizing from this, one might think that acts that display vices are simply ones that are done on the basis of certain emotions, as opposed to being done on the basis of the agent's principles. In honor of the first philosophers to defend this generalization, one might call it "the stoic conception of vice."[2]

---

[1] See Aristotle's *Poetics*, 1450b5-10, where a closely related point is made.

[2] Versions of the stoic conception can be attributed to at least two contemporary writers on traits of character. G. H. von Wright, in *The Varieties of Goodness* (London: Routledge and Kegan Paul, 1963), chap. 7, section 7, says that a virtuous act is one that results from a

As plausible as this idea is, it is also incompatible with the account of character I have been defending here and with various comments I have made along the way about vices such as arrogance, lack of self-respect, laziness, and gluttony. Clearly, I am as committed to thinking that this conception of vice is not true as I am to rejecting the corresponding claim about virtue, but I do not think it is adequately answered by anything I have said so far. Actually, I do not think it is entirely wrong. At least, it is right in maintaining that we can only understand vice by understanding how it is connected with the passions. What is wrong with it, I will argue, is that it obliterates the distinction between vice and another sort of character flaw, one that has complex relations to both vice and virtue.

2. Akrasia

Aristotle used the term *akrasia*—usually though unsatisfactorily translated as incontinence or moral weakness—to refer to a specific character flaw. It is a trait that seems to resemble both virtue and vice. The intuitive idea, very roughly, is that the akratic person acts badly but "knows better." The akratic person's behavior resembles that of the vicious one, while the attitude toward life and conduct involved is to some extent like that of the virtuous person. The behavior of akratic individuals, however, conflicts with their distinctive attitudes, where in the case of virtue there is harmony instead of conflict.

What is the attitude of akrasia like? Here is one plausible answer to this question:[3] Akrasia is characterized by a conflict between different sorts of ends. Some of the ends we seek (such as being a decent person) include other ends as parts (e.g., paying a certain debt) and these include other ends (withdrawing money from the bank, and so forth). The akratic person is attached to some end (such as seducing a friend's lover) but is not at all attached to a certain more inclusive end of which it would be a part (such as

---

contest between reason and the obscuring effects that passion has on our judgment, a contest that reason wins: "the brave man has learnt to conquer his fear." Though he does not say what he thinks vice is, this statement suggests that vicious acts are what results when passion wins, either by opposing reason or without a contest. What James D. Wallace says in *Virtues and Vices* (Ithaca, N.Y.: Cornell University Press, 1978), pp. 65-76, can be regarded as a complex adaptation of the stoic conception to the vice of cowardice.

[3] This is similar to a view tentatively ascribed to Aristotle by Elizabeth Anscombe at the beginning of "Thought and Action in Aristotle," in *Aristotle's Ethics*, ed. J. Walsh and L Shapiro (Belmont, Calif.: Wadsworth, 1967), pp. 56 and 57.

a life of pleasure). Rather, the akratic individual desires some other more inclusive end that is incompatible with both of these (in this case, perhaps, a life in which pleasure is not very important). The desired more inclusive end is that of a virtuous person, while the more special end is that of a vicious one, and the more special end is the one that the individual actually seeks. On this view, akrasia is nothing but a certain conflict between more inclusive and more special ends: the akratic person has some more inclusive end, which is incompatible with it.

This view is a plausible one, but it will not stand up to a certain familiar fact: that it is possible to akratically seek a whole way of life. It is possible, for instance, to live the life of an alcoholic and want to do so, while despising oneself for wanting it. This would mean that one's pursuit of this end is akratic. In that case, however, the end one seeks akratically is precisely the most inclusive end one desires. To despise oneself for seeking this way of life, it would seem to be necessary to also desire some alternative way of life, but that end would not differ from this one by being more inclusive.

This suggests a second view of the attitude behind akrasia. We might just say that the akratic person has divided loyalties: such a person is attached to two incompatible ends and that's all there is to it. The individual is as it were split into two parts: a "bad" part that, for instance, wants and seeks the life of an alcoholic, and a "good" one that wants something else.

This view is at best seriously incomplete. Akrasia is a state of character in which people do certain things and pass judgment against themselves for doing them. This indicates that if akrasia is a conflict between different parts of a person then these parts are asymmetrically related and there must be some generic difference between them. On this view of akrasia, the agent's passing judgment would apparently amount to something like this: if John akratically lives the life of an alcoholic, then the wicked part of him wants to be an alcoholic, while his good side not only wants something else but also despises the bad part for its bad desires. What is interesting here is that this condemnation in fact goes all in one direction: given that John's drinking is akratic, the side of his character that prefers drunkenness does not despise the other side for its attachment to a different way of life. Why is his makeup asymmetrical in this way?[4] This view of akrasia cannot provide an answer to

---

[4] Akrasia can be distinguished from a more deeply confused state of mind that does show the sort of symmetry that is lacking here. On weekends, James gambles his money away and despises the hardworking, rent-paying man he is on weekdays. Taking a chance, living on the edge of disaster—that is what life is all about! On weekdays he bitterly regrets the fool he is on weekends and vows to change his ways, but each Friday night he is at the tables

this question. The most it can suggest is that one part of John despises the other part because the other is attached to ends that are incompatible with its own. But the despised part has precisely the same reason for returning the compliment, so the fact that it doesn't remains a mystery.

There is a rather obvious and, I think, adequate answer to this question. Human beings are capable of being attached to different ends in very different ways. If John is an akratic alcoholic, he will want to be a nonalcoholic because he has some notion of what is the right way to live. On the other hand, he will pursue his present way of life for some other reason: for instance, because it is the path of least resistance, because it is pleasant or painless in certain ways, or because some sufficiently powerful emotion pulls him that way. Such motives do not imply, by themselves, that this is the right way or that any of its alternatives are wrong. To revert to the conceit of a split into parts, this means that John's bad side does not have a vocabulary with which it can upbraid its competitor; thus, the passing of judgment can only go in one direction.

Most of us have some notions about the worth or worthlessness of various things that we might seek, and about the rightness or wrongness of various sorts of conduct. Such notions, when one does what one does because one believes them, are examples of what I call principles. To act akratically is, at least in part, to hold a belief that *would* be a principle of one's action, except that one fails to act on it.

3. The Vices and Their Doubles

In ordinary language, "cowardice" refers to at least two different traits, which correspond to two different ways in which one can act out of or because of an emotion. There are people who *would* enter a dangerous situation to achieve something they regard as important enough to justify taking the risks involved, except that the terrors of the situation prove too much for them and pull them back. Such is the case of young Henry Fleming in the early parts of Stephen Crane's *The Red Badge of Courage*. To him, the glories of battle are worth its perils and he thinks it is disgraceful of him to run away. Yet he does run because he is frightened. If we say that he did what he did out of fear, we mean that he acted out of fear *as opposed to* acting on the basis of what he holds to be worthwhile or right. A very different sort of case is that of

---

again. This deeply divided state of character can be called "moral weakness," as akrasia is also sometimes called, but it is not akratic. This is part of the reason why I am using "akrasia" rather than "moral weakness" to name the trait I am discussing here.

Shakespeare's Falstaff, who avoids danger because he thinks that whatever good can come out of fighting is not worth the sacrifice of his personal safety. Those who act differently lack what he chooses to call "discretion." It might be true that Falstaff avoids the scene of battle because he is afraid, but it would be a deeper explanation of his conduct to say that he does so because of what he thinks to be worthwhile or right. It is precisely because of his beliefs that his fears function as good reasons to run away. It is not at all true that he is acting out of emotion as opposed to acting on the basis of principle.

Both these traits would ordinarily be called instances of cowardice. This means that, according to what I have said so far, this word is not (simply) the name of a vice. The cowardice of which Falstaff is an extreme example is indeed a vice, but that of Henry Fleming is not a vice because it is not a trait of character. Because young Fleming holds a principle and fails to act on it, his conduct is a form of akrasia, which in my view would mean that it is a way of lacking character. The stoic conception of vice is not true of Falstaffian cowardice, because such cowardice does not involve acting on the basis of an emotion in the way that the theory requires, and it is not true of Fleming's sort of cowardice because it is not a vice.

If we accept this distinction between kinds of cowardice we are probably committed to making the same distinction for the vices in general. The words that are the names of vices all seem to have the same sort of ambiguous reference that I have attributed to "cowardice." They sometimes refer to traits in which the conduct of those who possess them proceeds from their views of what is worthwhile, justifiable, or necessary, in such a way that such people are able to embrace their behavior as a good way to conduct oneself (as "practical," "sensible," "realistic," and so forth). But they can also refer to quite different traits, ones in which the conduct of the bearers has no such source and can receive no such sanction from them. All of the vices have akratic doubles. Once we have made this broad distinction, we are committed to thinking that the stoic conception of vice is not true.

At this point, one might well suspect that there is a certain element of arbitrariness in what I have just said. In the present context, the main interest of the stoic conception is that it picks out an enormous class of cases that do not seem to fit the conception of vice I have adopted as my own. It seems arbitrary to keep my conception of vice by refusing to admit that these troublesome cases are instances of vice. Why not admit that both these traits are vices and that, while the stoic conception only fits one of them, mine only fits the other? Both views, in that case, would be overgeneralizations. What reason is there, other than the desire to keep my theory, for using this word as I have used it?

Actually, the idea that the traits I call akratic deserve to be called vices is sometimes a very plausible one. Consider, for example, the case of a married man who repeatedly has extramarital affairs despite repeated promises that he will stop. Every time he breaks his promises, he confesses to his wife and begs her forgiveness. His contrition is intense and each time he is resolved not to do it again, but eventually he does just what he did before. Probably, his wife would eventually feel that he gets no credit for his episodes of contrition. Wouldn't she be justified in thinking that his weakness is bad in the same way and to the same degree as cold-blooded profligacy? If the answer is yes, then what important ethical difference is there, really, between what have I call vice and what I call akrasia?

I will answer this question by a rather indirect route. I begin (in sections 4 through 7) by presenting an account of what an emotion is, which I eventually apply (in section 8) to explaining the ethical difference between vice and akrasia. Before I can make this application, I need to get around (also in section 8) to the first issue I raised at the beginning of this chapter: building on my account of emotion, I will attempt to show why the passions of the soul are ethically important. Finally (in section 9), I will draw some conclusions from all this that I can then apply to understanding the peculiar value that virtue has.

4. Theories of the Emotions

Emotions are very familiar phenomena. Indeed, people with stoic tendencies suspect they are altogether too familiar. Nonetheless, competent and distinguished theorists have set forth starkly different theories about what emotions are. Three specimen theories can serve as an illustration of the surprising variety of ideas on this subject and as a basis for further discussion.

The first one is suggested by certain seemingly obvious facts. It does not seem possible for me to be angry unless I judge that someone has committed an offense against me or someone I care about. I cannot be afraid unless I have some reason to believe that something is menacing me, or might do so. Some theorists have been sufficiently impressed by such facts to come forth with the idea that the emotions not only require beliefs or judgments, but that they *are* beliefs or judgments of some sort.[5]

---

[5] One of the most frequently discussed theories of this sort is that of Robert C. Solomon. See *The Passions* (Garden City, N.Y.: Doubleday, 1976). He identifies emotions as "self-involved and relatively intense evaluative judgements." See p. 187. See also Joel Marks, "A Theory of Emotion," *Philosophical Studies* 42 (1982): pp. 227-42. Robert Gordon argues

Other theorists have pointed out that emotions, unlike judgments, *feel like* something when we undergo them, and that in ordinary language "emotions" and "feelings" are in fact often synonymous. William James claimed that a certain particular sort of feeling is essential for the occurrence of an emotion:

> Can one fancy the state of rage and picture no ebullition of the chest, no flushing of the face, no dilation of the nostrils, . . . but in their stead limp muscles, calm breathing, and a placid face? The present writer, for one, cannot.

More generally, James argued, if we subtract from any strong emotion the feelings of its so-called bodily symptoms, all that is left behind is "a cold and neutral state of intellectual perception."[6] Such a neutral state clearly is *not* an emotion. From this James drew the conclusion that, when we perceive something that excites an emotion in us, "the bodily changes follow directly the perception of the exciting fact, and . . . our feeling of the same changes as they occur *is* the emotion."[7]

In different ways, each of these two theories reduces the emotions to some other, seemingly distinct element of human life. A certain important fact about the emotions makes it possible to accomplish the same result in yet another way. Emotions serve very well to explain what people do. Behavior that seemed unintelligible a moment ago can become crystal clear when somebody says something like, "He didn't follow us up here because he's afraid of

---

for what amounts to a complex variation of this sort of theory in *The Structure of Emotion* (Cambridge, Mass.: Cambridge University Press, 1987), esp. chaps. 2-4. One addition that Gordon contributes is the idea that the belief involved is one that either satisfies or frustrates the wishes of the person who holds it. Robert C. Roberts puts forth what could be regarded as a heterodox variation of this sort of theory: he identifies emotion with a cognitive state, but these states are not beliefs. See footnote 10, below. "What an Emotion Is: A Sketch," *The Philosophical Review* 97 (April 1988): pp. 183-209.

[6] William James, The Principles of Psychology, vol. 2 (New York: Dover Publications, 1950), pp. 151 and 451.

[7] Ibid., p. 449. In the original, the quoted passage is in italics. Another frequently discussed view of this same general type is that of social psychologists Stanley Schachter and Jerome Singer. In their view, an emotion is a feeling of a certain sort of bodily change, which feeling has been "labeled" by the person who experiences it under the influence of social clues. See Schachter and Singer, "From 'Cognitive, Social, and Physiological Determinants of Emotional States,'" in *What is an Emotion* (Oxford: Oxford University Press, 1984), pp. 173-83.

heights." Accordingly, some have tried to understand what an emotion is mainly by identifying its relations to human behavior. The simplest way to do this is to adopt the thesis that many of the states that we call emotions are simply inclinations to do certain things in certain situations. If adhered to more or less faithfully, such an approach yields behaviorism or one of its variants.[8]

When these three views are stated as briefly and baldly as I have put them here, they all might sound more or less obviously false. After all, each identifies emotion with something that, as I have said, seems to be quite distinct from it. What could be more obvious than that an emotion such as grief or terror is not the very same thing as a belief, or a bodily sensation, or a mere inclination to do something?

What I will eventually try to show is true, however, is in a way almost the opposite of this plausible first impression. The problem, I will maintain, is not so much that each of these views is false as it is that each states no more than part of the truth. What is needed is to combine them, or perhaps suitably altered versions of them, into a single conception of the passions of the soul.

As a sort of initial indication that this is the right approach to take, consider a fact about these three theories that I have already hinted at in the way I have worded them. With the necessary changes, William James's argument for his own view can be used in defense of the other two as well. It is plausible to say that we cannot imagine rage without certain sensations that are caused by such things as accelerated breathing and tensed muscles. But the same sort of thing can be said, with as much plausibility, regarding cognitive states such as beliefs or judgments. It is at least as difficult to imagine my being enraged without imagining any sort of evidence that some serious wrong has been done to me or mine. On the face of it, it is very doubtful that any collection of physical sensations—of altered pulse rate, muscle tone, perspiration rate, and so forth—could possibly amount to the state of mind we call rage unless the too-familiar sense of being *aggrieved* were also present.

---

[8] Certainly one of the best known variants is that of Gilbert Ryle, who formulated a linguistic version of this thesis. He held that, at least part of the time, the word "emotion" simply refers to some motive or other. To explain an action by ascribing a motive to it is to say that this is just the sort of thing the agent does in circumstances of a specified sort. To say that I boasted out of vanity, for instance, is to say that I boasted and, moreover, I always boast in circumstances of this sort. *The Concept of Mind* (New York: Barnes and Noble, 1949) pp. 83-93. Basically the same view of the emotions can be found in the later works of Ludwig Wittgenstein, especially *Philosophical Investigations* (Oxford: Oxford University Press, 1956).

If James's sort of reasoning proves what he thinks it proves, then it proves altogether too much. If it shows that emotions are identical to bodily sensations, it also proves the incompatible conclusion that they are identical to something like a belief. It would also show that emotions are identical to inclinations to act. Imagine, for example, that you have some reason to think that I am angry at someone. Suppose, however, that you find out, by some method you find absolutely convincing, that I have no inclination at all to do anything unpleasant to the person you suspect I am angry at. It is not that I have suppressed this inclination because I think it would be wrong to act on it, nor that there are simply other things I would much rather do. There is no such tendency to be suppressed or outweighed at all. The possibility of harassing or annoying this person simply leaves me utterly indifferent. Whatever state of mind you can fancy me to be in, could it be what we call anger? I do not think so.

Obviously, this does not show that anger is simply a tendency to do certain things. Nor do analogous arguments prove that it is identical to a belief or a bodily sensation. The fact that we cannot imagine one thing without imagining another is not evidence—is not even *weak* evidence—that the two things are identical. It does, however, provide some sort of evidence to the effect that one of them is a necessary accompaniment, or perhaps a necessary part, of the other. More exactly, it provides evidence that we ordinarily see the two things as being related in one of these ways.

The way emotions appear, in unguarded moments, to ordinary human consciousness is rather different from the way they look when we entertain any of the three theories I have described here. Each of them takes some element that seems to be closely associated with emotion and simply identifies the emotion with that element. In each case, we get the impression that the emotion is only accidentally related to its other associated elements. An emotion could still be an emotion, it seems, though these other elements were entirely absent. When we are not actually contemplating some such theory, however, there are several quite different things that seem to have a more-than-accidental relation to emotion. Either they appear to be merely aspects of a single entity, which is the emotion, or they seem to stand in some other necessary relation to it.

If I am right about this—if ordinary awareness of emotions and these theories about them do differ in this way—that would suggest an approach to the problem of what emotions are that might represent a viable alternative to theories such as these. We can take a closer look at what, exactly, emotions seem to be like when we approach them without any particularly sophisticated preconceptions. In particular, we can ask how they impress us when we are actually experiencing them. If we can come away from this inquiry with a coherent picture of what emotions are, we can then ask whether there is any good reason to reject the accuracy this picture. If no such reasons present themselves, we will have a plausible account of what an emotion is.

This is the approach I will take in the next section of this chapter. It will tend to show, among other things, that the theories I have discussed in this section all reveal some part of the truth about what an emotion is.

5. What Emotion Seems to Be

Consider what is happening when someone experiences fear. I am taking a walk late at night, deep in thought. Suddenly my neighbor's enormous dog lunges at me, snarling and baring its teeth. It leaps all the way to the end of the heavy chain attached to the front porch of my neighbor's house and barks furiously. The sudden noise catches me off guard. My immediate reaction is one of intense fear. Some of the things that I am aware of could, in principle, provide me with evidence that I am really in no danger at all: I could hear the dog's stout chain jingling as it leapt, followed by a distinct thud as it came to the end of it. But that is not what captures my attention. In the dark all that really gets through to me is the beast's white, fang-like teeth and its loud bellowing. The overall impression it makes on me is terrifying. It looks and sounds dangerous to me.

Of course, what is going on here is not *merely* a matter of how something looks and sounds to me. The experience I am having is deeper than that. It seems to involve my whole body somehow. I feel my scalp tighten; there is a watery sensation in the pit of my stomach. I feel a powerful urge to back away; my left hand reaches awkwardly toward the angry animal, as if in an half-hearted attempt to shield me. Even after I realize that I really am in no danger, I feel uneasy about being where I am; I feel that I am shaking, and a certain inescapable impression of the presence of menace lingers on. It does not merely *seem* that the dog was dangerous, it *feels like* it was.

I think I have just given an immediately recognizable description of a familiar experience. In it, we can distinguish these three elements: (1) a certain state of mind in which one of the objects in my world seems to be bad for me, (2) certain bodily sensations, and (3) certain felt desires to act. Further, though I have described these three elements as if they were distinct and in some sense separate, that is not really how they seem while I am actually experiencing fear. While it is happening, it hits me as a single experience.

What I would like to suggest is that, at least with some modification or qualification, everything I have just said about fear is true of all the emotions: When I experience grief, I see something or someone I have lost as profoundly good (at least for me) and consequently I see the loss as profoundly bad for me. When I experience joy, I see some something as being very good (again, at least for me). More generally, whenever we experience any emotion, we are in a state of mind that seems to be cognitive in nature. In it, something appears to be good or bad, or right or wrong. In most cases the thing seems to be good or bad, right or wrong, in some specific way. When we experience fear or terror, we see something as not merely bad but as *menacing*. According to one author, when we undergo the peculiar sort of horror we experience when viewing a horror movie, we see some being (e.g., Dracula) as both menacing and "impure."[9] We can summarize most of what I just said by saying that when we experience an emotion, we are *interpreting* certain facts (real or imagined) in terms of the categories of good and evil or right and wrong.[10]

Of course, the fact that I am experiencing terror does not consist, merely, in the fact that I am interpreting something as being bad in some specific way. As William James said, such a state of mind would not be an emotion but a "cold and neutral state of intellectual perception."[11] Emotions, as I have said, *feel like* something, in a way that mere intellectual perception does not. Is there any general way to describe what an emotion feels like? Actually, I think the

---

[9] Noël Carroll, *The Philosophy of Horror: Or Paradoxes of the Heart* (New York: Routledge, 1990), p. 27.

[10] What I am calling interpretations here are almost identical to what Robert C. Roberts calls "construals" in "What an Emotion Is: A Sketch," cited above in footnote 5. I am using a different term to avoid confusing readers who are familiar with Prof. Roberts's views: there is an important difference between the way he is using *construals* to illuminate emotions and the way I am using *interpretations* to the same end. His construals are states of mind "in which one thing is grasped in terms of something else" (p. 190). So far, the same could be said of my interpretations. However, in his view the thing in terms of which something is grasped when we experience it emotionally can be almost any mental event, including a "perception, a thought, an image, a concept" (ibid.). In my view, on the other hand, there are narrower limits: in the state of mind that is necessary for emotion, the something that is experienced emotionally must (perhaps in some specific way) be grasped as (in terms of the notions of) good and bad or right and wrong. For an idea that is very similar to both *interpretation* and *construal*, see Cheshire Calhoun's use of "seeing-as" in *What is an Emotion?* ed. Cheshire Calhoun and Robert C. Solomon (Oxford: Oxford University Press, 1984), pp. 327-42.

[11] James, *The Principles of Psychology*, vol. 2, p. 451.

feelings involved are of more than one kind. Roughly, it is possible to distinguish two different sorts:

People often describe what their emotions feel like by using strongly physical language, such as "my blood runs cold when I think of it," "my heart stood still," or "I could feel myself starting to shake all over." Among the feelings that are typically, perhaps always involved in our experience of emotion are ones that actually seem to be physical sensations. They appear to consist in a certain direct awareness of things that are happening in our own bodies, such as racing heartbeat, erecting hair follicles, damp palms, rapid or labored breathing, and so on.

Another sort of feeling that is involved in emotion has a very direct relation to behavior. In the case of certain emotions, such as terror, this relation can be described very simply: when we are in the grips of the passion, we feel like doing something.[12] What we feel like doing will differ, but, so far as these feelings are an aspect of terror, they will be appropriate to the fact that we interpret the object as menacing: we may feel like desperately striking out at it, or shielding ourselves, or running away.

On the other hand, there are other emotions in which we do not seem to feel like doing anything in particular. If we may assume that depression and contentment are emotions, then some emotions seem to be states of mind in which we feel like doing nothing. But these cases are still similar to emotions like terror in certain respects. In both depression and contentment, the felt inclination to do nothing is just that: a positive feeling, not merely the absence of a felt inclination to do something. Further, in each of them, the felt indisposition to act is of a sort that is appropriate to the way things seem. In both depression and contentment things seem a certain way to us: in one of them, things seem drained of value, while, in the other, there seems to be a surfeit of the good. In depression we feel disinclined to act because nothing seems worth doing, while in contentment it is because nothing seems to *need* doing. To generalize: in every emotion there seems to be some felt disposition regarding action, either to act or not to act, which disposition is a consequence of and appropriate to the interpretation involved in the emotion.

When we experience an emotion, we always experience a certain sort of cognitive state (1) and certain sorts of feelings, including always a felt tendency regarding action (3) and—at least typically—certain bodily sensations (2). Further, when we experience any of the phenomena I have

---

[12] This point is made persuasively by Magda Arnold in her *Emotion and Personality*, vol. 1 (New York: Columbia University Press, 1960), chap. 9, especially p. 172.

described under (1) through (3) as elements of an emotion, we experience them as if they were very closely connected and, indeed, as if they were aspects of a single experience.

6. Emotion and Interpretation

Such, as I have said, is what emotions seem to be when we experience them. But why should we think that this indeed is what they are? Admittedly, the fact that something seems a certain way to us does not, by itself, mean that this is how it really is. It is not in general a good idea to suppose that things really are the way they seem to be when we approach them without any sophisticated preconceptions.

However, when we are dealing with a subject with which we are in intimate contact every day, our pretheoretical impressions at least give us a position from which to begin thinking about what the subject is really like. In such matters, the burden of proof would seem to fall on the theories that are supposed to supplant our naive impressions. The proponents of these theories need to show why the impressions of ordinary experience are illusory. This would mean that they have to show that it is not the case that all three of the factors I have discussed are necessary elements of emotion.

Arguments for this thesis usually take the form, in effect, of rebuttals to my initial response to William James's argument for his theory in section 4. I claimed that we cannot imagine an emotion and at the same time imagine that one of these other elements is absent. Here the rebuttals are attempts to show that in fact we can imagine such things.

James himself advances an argument of this kind against the general sort of idea I have described under (1) in the preceding section. What I am calling the interpretation is not a brute perception of some physical fact, but a state of mind in which, at least while we are in the throes of it, the value of some fact—whether it is good or bad, right or wrong—seems to be revealed. James insists that no such state of mind is necessary for an emotion to occur: an emotion can arise from a perception alone, without an intervening "emotional idea." His arguments for this claim take the form of a series of convincingly described examples, such as this one:

> If our friend goes near the edge of a precipice, we get the well-known feeling of "all-overishness," and we shrink back, although we positively *know* him to be safe, and have no distinct imagination of his fall.

That is, it is possible to experience fear even when we actually *disbelieve* the idea that we would expect to be associated with it. A similar notion lies behind what James calls "the best proof" of his claim that ideas are not necessary conditions of emotions, which is to be found in "those pathological cases in which the emotion is objectless." An individual who is struck by pathological anxiety experiences "intense fear" but "is not afraid of anything; he is simply afraid." In such episodes, "the *intellect* may, in fact, be so little affected as to play the cold-blooded spectator all the while, and note the absence of a real object for the emotion."[13]

The notion behind James's "best proof" seems to be something like this: in the case of pathological anxiety, as in the case of seeing one's friend approaching the edge of a precipice, we have the experience of fear without an accompanying idea that something is dangerous. If there *were* an idea that is a necessary condition of fear, this would be it. So there is no such idea.

I think such arguments do prove something: that at least some "ideas," to use James's word, are separable from emotion. But I do not think they are a telling case against the sorts of ideas I have said are necessary conditions of emotion. Consider the case of the friend near the precipice. If I feel fear as I see you walk deliberately up to the edge of a cliff, it might well happen that I do not believe you are in any danger. But then it is also true that, as I glance over the edge, there is something about the sight of that sheer drop into nothingness that clashes with what I believe and, indeed, with what I know to be true. In spite of me, the damn thing *seems*, almost with the immediacy of direct perception, to be a menace to you.[14] It *feels like* the gaping void at your feet might kill you somehow. Without this experience, whatever else I am feeling would not be the emotion of fear. The involuntary stiffening of my midriff would be a mere

---

[13] James, *The Principles of Psychology*, vol. 2, pp. 457, 458, 460, and 461.

[14] I am tempted to say that it *looks* menacing and, of course, the seeming menace usually will be a matter of visual appearance. However, the point I am making here would still apply to me even if I were blind. The point is that things appear to be a certain way to me and this appearance is experienced *as if* it were something I perceived: that is, it is experienced independently of my wanting to, provided only that I pay attention to the object involved, whether I actually accept this appearance as real or not. Probably, this appearance is commonly experienced in some sense modality or other (the fact that something seems dangerous is the fact that it looks dangerous, sounds dangerous, etc.), but this is not necessary. If the trip I have just agreed to take on the space shuttle presently fills me with fear, it is necessarily true that it strikes me as perilous; it is not necessary that it looks or sounds any particular way to me now. My trip, after all, is still in the future and not present to any of my senses.

spasm. The urge to clench my fists, as if grasping for support, would be compulsive behavior with no meaning at all.

The same sorts of things can be said about the person suffering from an attack of pathological anxiety. If I am suffering from such an attack, what is it that makes me so certain that my violent heartbeat, trembling, and dry mouth constitute a sort of fear, and are not simply facts about my physical organs? Here is an autobiographical description of a case of objectless anxiety:

> One day, . . . having eaten a comfortable dinner, I remained sitting at the table after the family had dispersed, . . . when, suddenly in a lightning-flash as it were—"fear came upon me, and trembling, which made all my bones to shake." . . . The only self-control I was capable of exerting was to keep my seat. I felt the greatest desire to run incontinently to the foot of the stairs and shout for help to my wife—to run to the roadside even, and appeal to the public to protect me; but by an immense effort I controlled these frenzied impulses, and determined not to budge from my chair till I had recovered my lost self-possession. [15]

What is it that distinguishes the trembling described by the author (who happens to have been William James's father) from a meaningless physical event, such as the trembling we might experience at the sudden onset of a disease of the nervous system? A good part of the answer lies in the fact that he feels a need for protection from something. Admittedly, it is a need he believes and knows he does not actually possess; it is moreover true that he does not know *what* he would be seeking protection from if he were to run incontinently into the street. These are facts that enable us to regard this emotion as a case of pathological fear. It is nonetheless true that what enables us to think of it as a case of fear in the first place is the fact that he sees the world as if it were a place in which something, somehow is menacing him.

Both of James's arguments are based on emotions that in obvious ways are irrational and abnormal. Some authors have claimed that such deviant emotions cannot show us anything about the nature of emotion in general.[16] If my responses to these arguments are sound, they suggest that this claim is not entirely right. The sorts of emotions James cites do lend support to an interesting conclusion about the nature of emotion in general. They show that the idea that is essential to an emotion experienced by a particular individual

---

[15] Henry James, Sr., *The Literary Remains of the Late Henry James*, ed. by William James (Boston: Osgood, 1885), pp. 59-60. Quoted in Nathaniel Branden, *The Psychology of Self-Esteem* (New York: Bantam Books, 1971) pp. 155-56.

[16] See Magda Arnold, *Emotion and Personality*, p. 170.

need not be one that the individual believes. This is interesting because it conflicts with the first of the three theories of emotion I discussed in section 4, which at the time seemed to express at least part of the truth about emotion.

It also suggests that a certain modification is called for in the account of emotion I have given so far: it indicates an important constraint on what my notion of an interpretation ought to mean. I have said that the interpretation that is essential to emotion consists in the fact that something appears to be good or bad, right or wrong. James's arguments show that this appearance need not be believed. I interpret your standing next to the cliff in the way that is essential to the emotion of fear if I find—perhaps in spite of myself—that the void at your feet *looks* menacing. However, James's arguments do *not* show that an emotion can occur in the absence of an "emotional idea."

7. Emotion and Feeling

Let us suppose, then, that an interpretation *is* necessary for the existence of emotion. Is the same thing true of the other two elements I identified as essential to emotion under (2) and (3) in section 5 of this chapter?

As in the case of emotional ideas, perhaps the most obvious argument against my claim that we have here an essential element of emotion is the very simple one that there seem to be cases of emotion in which this particular element is entirely absent. A plausible version of the argument would go like this: Emotions include such states as fear, hope, and sorrow. I can truthfully tell you that I fear that the present drought will continue a while—or that I hope that it will not, or that I am sorry that your crops have already begun to fail—without feeling any of the pangs or urges I discussed above under (2) or (3). To say that I fear that the drought will continue is merely to say that I believe the drought might continue and that I wish it wouldn't. It has nothing *necessarily* to do with feelings of any kind. Similar things can be said about hoping and being sorry.[17]

As a matter of fact, I admit that everything stated in this plausible argument is true. The only thing I would deny is the unstated but indispensable assumption that the state of mind I am reporting when I say, for instance, that I fear that such and such is the case is the *emotion* of fear. Suppose that General Pickett had replied to the orders that General Lee gave him at

---

[17] This, if I understand him, is essentially how Robert M. Gordon argues in his *The Structure of Emotions*, cited in footnote 5 above. See, especially, his general discussion of the nature of emotion in chapter 2 and his claim, on p. 105, that the way one feels when one is angry is simply an *effect of* one's anger.

Gettysburg by saying, "I fear that, were I to charge as you have ordered, our assault would fail disastrously." Would he be confessing to *being afraid* to charge? Of course, he might indeed be afraid, but that is not what he is talking about if he says that he fears that the charge will fail. And only if he *is* saying that he is afraid is he reporting the emotion of fear.[18] Obviously, the same sorts of things can be said of the emotions of hope and sorrow.

Of course, if Pickett says what I have imagined him saying, he would indeed be reporting a mental state of a sort that bears a more-than-accidental relationship to the emotion of fear. Typically, and not coincidentally, people who fear a certain object also fear that something (something having to do with that object) will happen. I fear bats and (not coincidentally) I fear that a bat might get tangled in my hair: that is why I fear bats. However, though these two phenomena are closely related, they are genuinely different. Admittedly, one of them does not necessarily include feelings of any kind, but it is the other one that is an emotion. As long as I only *fear that* a bat will get tangled in my hair—and I am not in any other mental state about bats—then it is true that so far I feel nothing about bats, but it is also true that so far I am not emotionally involved with bats, that they are not yet an emotional issue for me.

Another argument to show that emotions do not necessarily include feelings—of any sort, including bodily sensations and felt dispositions regarding action—could go like this: We are quite capable of undergoing an emotion without feeling it at all. That is, some emotions are unconscious. The fact that I can undergo unconscious anger, jealousy, fear, or grief indicates several things. First, it shows that the emotions themselves are not feelings. I cannot have a feeling without being aware of it. Beyond that, it also constitutes evidence that emotions must not even include feelings as essential elements of themselves. After all, if emotions did include feelings in this way, this would mean that, whenever I undergo an emotion, I am at least aware of an essential part of it: I am aware of some feeling that the emotion brings with it. But in that case, why am I not aware that I am afflicted by the emotion itself?[19]

---

[18] Here I am indebted to J. P. Day, who made the same point, in somewhat different language, as follows: "For one must distinguish '*A* fears death' (and, generally, '*A* fears *X*') from, '*A* fears that he is dying' (and, generally, '*A* fears that *P*'). It is . . . '*A* fears *X*' which ascribes an emotion to *A*." "Hope," *American Philosophical Quarterly* 6 (April 1969): p. 90.

[19] I adapt this argument from one given by Robert C. Roberts in "What an Emotion Is: A Sketch," p. 189. Roberts's argument is mainly directed against the idea that the emotion is simply identical to the feeling, but as I read him he also aims his argument at the position I am defending here, that the feelings involved are not merely "concomitants of the emotion" but essential parts of it. See Roberts, fn. 13.

Again, I do not deny everything that this argument purports to show. In particular, I think it does establish that emotions are not feelings. This is true despite the fact that, as I have already had occasion to point out, "emotions" and "feelings" are often used to mean more or less the same thing. One undeniable difference between them is the fact that unconscious emotions do exist while unconscious feelings do not. If emotions were simply a sort of feeling, we could no more have unconscious emotions than we could have an unconscious itch.

However, the view of emotion I am defending in this chapter does commit me to the idea that—contrary to the above argument—genuine emotions always include feelings of some sort as elements of themselves. Accordingly, I need to show how, given my view of the matter, an emotion can be unconscious even though, according to an admission I have just made, a certain essential element of emotion is always consciously experienced.

To see how this can be, consider the following example. Paul and Priscilla are giving a party. Paul is busily preparing food and performing the other duties of a host when he notices Stephen enter. He notices that, as usual, Stephen is pretentiously overdressed. Paul feels a pang of annoyance, as he often does on seeing Stephen. He sees that Stephen goes directly to Priscilla and takes up a good deal of her time chatting with her, while Paul is wishing that she would help him set the appetizers out. She seems to enjoy talking to Stephen—again, as usual. When Stephen finally greets Paul, Paul can barely keep a snarl out of his voice as he replies. He feels vaguely like making some barbed comment, though he is not sure what it would be. When he later complains to Priscilla that she pays too much attention to Stephen, she asks him—as she has before—if he is jealous of her friendship with him. Paul denies that he is jealous. He simply doesn't like the man. Stephen, he says, is just the sort of person he can't stand: pompous and inconsiderate. We can easily imagine that none of what Paul says is a lie. But we can also think, at the same time, that he *is* jealous. Indeed, both things can be true. How is this possible?

According to our ordinary conception of emotion as I have sketched it here, an emotion consists of several, quite disparate elements. The emotion is not, according to this conception, identical to any one of these elements. Suppose, for the sake of illustration, that Paul really is jealous, in spite of what he says and believes. This would mean that his jealousy is not the very same thing as the pang he feels on seeing Stephen, and that it is not the same thing as the urge he feels to say something rude. If this conception of emotion is true, he will not be aware that this pang is a pang *of jealousy* unless he is also aware that he is interpreting Stephen in a certain way. This feeling, we are supposing, is in fact a pang of jealousy, but it can only have that status if it is due to Paul's regarding Stephen as an interloper who is wrongly alienating Priscilla's affection for him.

If the feeling were due to another sort of interpretation, it would be a pang of something else, such as righteous indignation. If Paul does have the sorts of ideas that are constitutive of such indignation, in addition to having jealous ones, he can easily misidentify his own emotion. All he needs to do is to misidentify the thought in which the relevant bodily sensation or felt disposition originates. This is made easier by the fact that, though he cannot have a pang without being aware of it, he can regard Stephen in a certain way without being aware of it. Though feelings are necessarily conscious, interpretations are not.

An emotion that is experienced by someone who is not aware of it is, of course, an unconscious emotion. The above explanation, then, would show how jealousy can be unconscious even though a certain essential element of emotion is consciously experienced. I hope it is obvious that it can easily be generalized to reveal one good reason why it is possible for any emotion, in principle, to be unconscious. We are not automatically aware of our emotions, precisely because they consist of widely disparate elements. If I am aware that I am experiencing something that happens to be an essential element of a particular emotion, I am not necessarily aware of the emotion itself. By itself, that element may not serve as an arresting and infallible clue to the presence of the other elements. My awareness of the emotion represents an achievement of some sort.

This line of reasoning, however, raises one more argument against the conception of emotion I am defending here. So far, I have considered arguments that are supposed to show that at least one of the elements I claim are necessary for the existence of an emotion is not necessary at all. Indirectly, I have just raised the perhaps more deeply worrying possibility that these elements in fact *cannot* all be elements of one thing. If the supposed parts of an emotion are widely disparate—so much so that I can be vividly aware of experiencing one part and remain completely unaware of the whole—then perhaps an emotion is not a whole at all, but a mere collection. One of the parts, as I have described it, is cognitive in nature, a sort of thought. The two sorts of feelings that I have also said are involved are very different from thoughts, and from each other. One is a perception of one's own bodily states, while the other seems to be a way in which we perceive our desires. Why isn't our commonsense impression that the members of this diverse collection are actually aspects of a single experience simply an illusion, one that theories of emotion should not attempt to rationalize?

I realize that this question sounds as if whatever interest it might have is entirely metaphysical, but I think the answer to it can shed light on the ethical significance of the emotions. As I will argue, one of the reasons the emotions are very important to us lies, contrary to what the present objection might suggest, precisely in their power to bring wholeness and unity into our mental lives.

Actually, there are many entities in the world that we resolutely persist in thinking of as single, unified things even though we know that they consist of many parts with widely differing natures. General Motors and the government of Mexico consist of individual human beings, physical objects such as industrial machinery and weapons, written documents, and thoughts and intentions that certain people have. One perfectly good way to explain why we are justified in thinking of these as aspects of a single thing is to point out that they are *related* in ways that make such thinking appropriate. Accordingly, we can find the answer to the question presently before us by asking what relations hold between the parts of an emotion that might justify us in thinking of it as a single thing.

We have already encountered one such relation. I have said that what makes the pang that Paul feels on seeing Stephen a pang of jealousy is the fact that it is due to Paul's seeing Stephen as wrongly alienating Priscilla's affections. When I stumble upon a fierce dog in the middle of the night, the bodily sensations I then experience—the tightening of the scalp, the watery sensation in the pit of my stomach—are part of the emotion of fear because they are caused by my seeing the white fangs snapping in the darkness as menacing. The interpretation and the bodily sensation, when both are parts of an emotion, are not mere elements of an arbitrary collection but are united by the relation of causality. Obviously, the same is true of the connection between the interpretation and the other sort of feeling I have identified as involved in emotion, the felt tendency regarding action. The interpretation *gives rise to* the tendency. An emotion, we might say, is a causal system.

The elements of this system are also connected by relations of meaning. When the dog barks at me, the feelings in my scalp and stomach are not experienced by me as meaningless physical events, as if they were the result of my taking an overdose of vitamins or diet pills. They are *about* the apparently dangerous dog. The same is more obviously true of the urge to get away from the beast. When I am in the grips of a powerful emotion, it is as if my body and my mind are functioning together as a single organ of perception. Moreover, what they perceive is not a brute physical fact, such as a dog or a cliff, but *the menace* of the dog or cliff. That is, they are experienced as perceiving the facts in terms of the categories of good and evil or right and wrong, which means that they perceive the facts as *interpreted* by the individual who is experiencing the passion.

More generally, in all emotions, including ones that are not overwhelmingly strong, the individual's experience is powerfully unified: from a cognitive state, through the conative and, at least typically, the affective parts of experience. As Aristotle said, the passions of the soul are *logoi ennuloi*, they are embodied ideas.[20] In them, the cognitive side of life has a certain immediate and sometimes powerful effect on the purely physical and sensual side.

The power that emotion has to unify our experience is a particularly striking fact about it. I will soon try to show why this is also an important fact, that it sheds light on the function emotion plays in life. For the moment, I would like to point out another sort of unity emotion tends to introduce into our lives, one that is valuable in a somewhat more obvious way. Passion tends to encourage the persistence of conscious thoughts in the face of influences that would otherwise cause them to change. I will keep thinking about the dog that has frightened me even after I realize that I never was in any danger. For a few moments at least, my feelings of uneasiness and shakiness will make it difficult to think about anything else, even though I believe I have more important things to think about.

In this way, the emotions introduce a sort of temporal unity into our lives: they strengthen the connections between the succeeding moments of our experience. Admittedly, the persistence of thoughts due to the influence of emotion can amount to an unhealthy obsession. Indeed, there is a certain tendency in all emotional interpretations to become somewhat obsessive.[21] We should realize, though, that in a general sort of way the inertia that the emotions bring into our conscious lives probably also helps us in our efforts to stay alive and to live well. Things that impress us as good or evil, right or wrong, are typically—unless our impressions are false—things that require action of some sort, and things that require action are often things that require persistent attention and, thus, immunity from distraction. If the dog really is dangerous to me, it is very important that I *not* think about anything else for a while. When we experience an emotion, some conscious impression of ours

---

[20] Aristotle, *On the Soul*, 403a24.

[21] One author has pointed out that jealousy tends to be "highly obsessional." See Leila Tov-Ruach, "Jealousy, Attention, and Loss," in *Explaining Emotions,* ed. Amelie O. Rorty (Berkeley: University of California Press, 1980), p. 472. In this respect, I think jealousy represents, in an extreme and sometimes destructive form, what all emotions are like.

sends roots into our bodily feelings, and these roots anchor the impression in place for a while. They transform a cognitive state into a more powerful and more likely basis for action.

8. Akrasia and Vice Contrasted

I am almost ready to return to the problem I left at the end of section 3: that of explaining the ethical difference between vice and akrasia. Before I can do more with that problem, though, I have to add something to the account of emotion—and that of akrasia—that I have given here so far.

I have said that the interpretation involved in an emotion need not be one that the emoting individual believes. We should also realize that it is nonetheless true that emotions are typically based on *some* belief or other. When I experience an emotion, something (perhaps the world as a whole) seems good or evil, right or wrong. I may vehemently reject the idea that the thing in question really has the value thus assigned to it, but the fact that it *seems* to have that value typically results from some standard of value that I do accept. This is true even of a comparatively primitive emotion such as fear. If the dog lunging against its chain looks dangerous to me now, despite the fact that I believe it is harmless, that is because I do believe that, generally, dog bites tend to cause painful injuries. The same sort of thing is true, and more obviously true, of the many emotions that are more closely related than fear is to the subject matter of ethics. If I resent a man who steps in front of me as I stand in line at the supermarket, I see him as committing an offense against me. This is because I think that one's place in line—what he has, in effect, taken from me—belongs to one by right and that, in general, people who do what he has done are doing something that is more or less like stealing.

Wherever there is resentment or indignation there is some notion of what rights people have, or at least of some right that some person has. Emotions typically rely on some standards of value held by the individual that experiences the emotion.[22] Does some such relation also obtain in reverse? That is, does our holding standards of value somehow require us to feel certain things?

There is reason to think that this reverse relation does not hold. For instance, there seem to be people who claim—honestly and without self-deception—that human beings have rights and that it is wrong to violate them, but who *almost* never feel resentment or indignation, and then only mildly and under the

---

[22] The same point is made by Robert C. Solomon in *The Passions*, pp. 262-63.

strongest provocation. Consider, though, what one can say about such people. Whatever their behavior might be like, and they would obviously behave differently from other people in some important way or other, we can say something about what sort of people they are. More exactly, we can say something about what sort of people they are not. What we know is that either it seldom strikes them that someone is violating someone else's rights, so that they seldom see anyone as an offender of this sort, or, if this is not so, these impressions fail to have a certain sort of uptake in the way they experience themselves and the world.

There could be many reasons for this failure. Perhaps they think that people are seldom to blame for the wrong they do, or that it is generally wrong for some other reason to blame them. Again, they might simply not care about the rights of human beings. Whatever the reason might be, we know that, to one extent or another, they are not the sort of people for whom the belief that people have rights plays an important role in determining what their experience will be like. That is, this belief of theirs tells us relatively little about what sort of people they are.

The emotions, one might say, are a way in which certain sorts of beliefs are integrated into the rest of the self. This fact enables me to make an important addition to the account of akrasia I outlined in section 2 of this chapter. I said that the behavior of an akratic person conflicts with his or her attitude, and that this attitude otherwise resembles that of the virtuous person. The aspect of this attitude that my account picked out as crucial was a certain belief, one that can be a principle of action but that in the akratic person fails to function in that way.

That is the account of akrasia I have given so far, and it is clearly not a complete one. The akratic conflict between belief and action admits of differences of degree. People in whom the akratic conflict is notably strong and important, including Stephen Crane's Henry Fleming for instance, are people in whom the belief that is not acted on has a certain seriousness and depth. The fact that Fleming does hold the beliefs he fails to act on is a very important fact about him, deeply connected with the rest of his inner life, and a major determinant of his experience of the world in which he finds himself. They are just the sort of beliefs that he *would* act on if it were not for the fact that something powerful stops him from doing so.

This means that Fleming also experiences a certain, perhaps very complicated, array of emotions and, most noticeably, that he experiences remorse, guilt, or shame when he fails to act on these beliefs. That is why his ethical status is entirely different from that of a vicious coward, such as Shakespeare's Falstaff. Certain of young Fleming's beliefs are those that a courageous person would have, and this is not a mere matter of his giving his assent to the better course of action (while doing the worse). These beliefs tell us something important about the sort of person he is: in a certain way, he is the same sort of person that the courageous person is.

Actually, the ethical status of akrasia is more ambiguous than this might suggest. In a certain way, akratic individuals are also the opposite of virtuous. As I have said, akratic behavior resembles the behavior of a vicious person. But the similarity goes deeper than mere behavior. Akratic people always have some reason for what they do, and the reason is one that could have prompted someone with the relevant vice to do the same thing in the same circumstances. This is perhaps obviously true when an akratic individual does something just because it is easy or pleasant. The fact that something is easy or pleasant is just the sort of reason that would have prompted someone with some vice or other to do the same thing. The same thing is true in those cases in which akratic individuals are moved to action on the basis of some emotion, such as overwhelming fear, rather than any sort of self-conscious reasoning.

It may not be obvious that acting on the basis of an emotion is acting on the basis of a reason but, if the view of emotion I have sketched here is true, that is indeed the case. If Henry Fleming runs away from battle out of fear, this means (in part) that he does so because the battle seems very dangerous to him at the moment. That is his reason for doing what he does. Of course, it is also an important part of the reason why a vicious coward would also have run away. The crucial difference between vice and akrasia lies in the fact that vice includes principles that enable one to think that one's reason was in fact a good enough reason for doing what one did, whereas akrasia does not. This, of course, is a deep difference. As a result of their principles, vicious people will feel an array of emotions (such as satisfaction at having done the smart thing, contempt for those who do not realize what the smart thing is, and so forth) that involve approval of their own conduct. Their principles do not enable them to feel any remorse, guilt, or shame. Their behavior, insofar as it proceeds from vice, will give the impression of an integrated personality, a psyche unified by a central falsehood. Their behavior indicates what sort of people they really are. The reasons that prompt akratic individuals to act are isolated fragments, and not integral parts of a system. Such behavior does not indicate the sort of person involved in the same unambiguously representative way that vicious behavior does.

But the fact remains that the reason that leads to akratic behavior is partly the same as the reason for which some vicious person would have done the same thing in the same circumstances. This is why the ethical status of akrasia is, to a certain extent, the same as that of vice. The similarity between them is not simply one of outward behavior. Both do what they do for reasons that are bad.

This has one rather obvious implication concerning the story of the angry wife I told at the end of section 3. If we make the plausible assumption that the behavior of her philandering husband is indeed wrong, and if we assume that his conduct is genuinely akratic, what I have said so far in this section implies that she would be justified in condemning her husband. That is, she would be justified, not merely in thinking ill of his behavior, but also in thinking ill of the person from whom the behavior comes. She can think that he is a flawed person. The reason is that what is bad about the way he is living his life is not his actions alone, but the reasons for which he does them as well. This is what separates him from someone who might do the same thing involuntarily, perhaps because they were suffering under some sort of psychotic delusion, and establishes his similarity to the vicious person. The reasons are part, not merely of what he does, but of who he is.

Beyond that, what is the answer to the question I raised at the end of section 3? Would the man's wife be justified in thinking that his akrasia is bad in the same way and to the same degree as what I would call vicious behavior? I think we are in a position to say that the answer is no, at least if his behavior is genuinely akratic.

First, it is important to realize that, at least as I have described his behavior so far, it may not be akratic at all. Vice and akrasia, as I have been using these terms, represent extremes. Probably many of the ethically objectionable traits we see in the world around us fall short of the purity of either one of them. If my conduct seems *persistently* to display the akratic double of cowardice or intemperance, for instance, that fact would suggest that there is something more than akrasia behind what I am doing. It would be evidence that, to some extent and possibly in some confused way, I hold the view of life of a coward or an intemperate person.

There is an obvious possibility that this sort of thing is true of the philandering husband in my story. This would seem to be why we eventually are not inclined to give him much credit for his episodes of contrition. After repeated offenses, they look like *mere* episodes, in spite of their intensity. We get the impression that there is more to his view of the world and his place in it than is revealed to us at these moments, something more fundamental and enduring that enables him at other times to view his misconduct with moral indifference or with wholehearted approval. To the extent that this is indeed the case, his behavior is not akratic and his story would not undermine the distinction I have made between akrasia and vice.[23] His wife might disapprove of his conduct in just the way that one can disapprove of vice, but that would not mean that akrasia can be disapproved of in that way.

On the other hand, we can suppose that his behavior *is* genuinely akratic. In that case, there is still a certain surface plausibility in the claim that what the husband does is bad in just the same way that cold-blooded profligacy is. The reason for this is that what is bad in what he does is not a mere matter of his outward behavior: the badness characterizes, so to speak, *more of him* than that. But how much more of him is involved? It includes the reasons for which this conduct is done. But the very fact that the behavior is akratic means that these reasons are not indicative of the conative and affective parts of his experience in the same way and to the same degree that vicious behavior would be. It does not justify the same sorts of judgments about the worth of the whole person. What we have here are states of character of two quite different kinds. It seems just the sort of difference in kind that can appropriately be marked by some verbal distinction or other, such as the one I have drawn between vice and akrasia.

This, then, is my response to the challenge presented by the stoic conception of vice. It implicitly obliterates a genuine ethical distinction. Actions that are done on the basis of emotion, as opposed to being done on the basis of the agent's principles, are deeply different from ones that represent what I call vice. On the other hand, there is, as I have suggested, a certain amount of truth in the stoic conception. Certain ways of acting on emotion are bad in somewhat the same way that vicious actions are: in both, we do something bad and do it for bad reasons.

I think there is in fact more truth to this ancient theory than that. There is at times a close relationship between vice and certain ways of acting on emotion, one that can shed light on how genuinely vicious conduct sometimes is born and grows. The relationship I have in mind is marked in some cases by a close linguistic connection. There are a number of instances in which an emotion and a vice are signified by the very same word, or by obviously cognate ones. "Revenge" often refers to a state of mind that is clearly only an emotional episode, a disturbing interruption in a life that does not have anything particularly vengeful about it. Sometimes, however, it (or "vengefulness" or "vindictiveness") refers to a chronic condition, or to something deeper and

---

[23] His behavior would be an instance of the sort of moral weakness I describe in footnote 4, above.

worse: a trait of character and a vice. The same things can be said of "envy" and "jealousy."[24]

In each case, the relationship between the emotion and the vice is obviously not an accidental one. The notion that Paul, in the story I told in section 7, responds with a pang of jealousy to seeing Priscilla speak to Stephen does not necessarily mean that Paul is a jealous person. It is also true, however, that some forms of emotional jealousy create for the person who experiences them problems that can all too easily be solved by developing a distinctively jealous character. If Paul is experiencing jealousy, this means that he is interpreting Stephen's conduct in a certain way. At least for the moment, he sees Stephen as an intruder who is wrongly alienating Priscilla's affection for him. There can be good reasons for seeing someone this way, and it may sometimes be due to a healthy impulse that this thought causes a painful pang when it strikes someone in Paul's position.[25]

Suppose, however, that none of these reasons apply in this case and that Paul's interpretation is due only to a certain sort of irrational insecurity. Imagine that Paul reacts with this malevolent pang simply because he feels the attention of any man Priscilla likes to be a threat to his own relationship with her. He views Stephen as committing some sort of injustice simply because, since Stephen's conduct is painful to him, it *feels* like a threat of some sort. He does not know why it feels painful and threatening, nor does he know the precise nature of this threat. He prefers not to think about that. The answers to these questions would not be very flattering to him. On the other hand, harboring what seems to be a nakedly irrational hostility would not reflect on him in a positive way either. But he need not see his hostility as lacking any basis in reason. What Stephen is doing *feels* to Paul as if he were trying to rob him. Paul thinks something like: "Leave her alone, she's mine!" He never explores the implications of what he is thinking, but he thinks it many times,

---

[24] The same is arguably true, as well, of a term I will use in chapter XI: "hypersensitivity."

[25] Here I am going against the common view that every episode of jealousy is irrational, immoral, or in some other way bad. For an argument to the effect that this view is in fact wrong, see Tov-Ruach's "Jealousy, Attention, and Loss," cited above in footnote 21. For related arguments, see also Jerome Neu's "Jealous Thoughts," which appears in the same volume as the Tov-Ruach essay. It would take me too far afield to discuss this issue fully here, but I should say I believe that jealous feelings may be rational and healthy, though being a jealous *person* is bad. For a contrasting view, see Hugh LaFollette, *Personal Relationships: Love, Identity, and Morality* (Cambridge, Mass.: Blackwell's, 1996), pp. 171-73.

and to him it has the ring of truth. The truth he dimly hears in it, never giving it the clarity of verbal expression, is that his lover is his property, that unapproved contact with her is an offense against him and an approach to worse offenses. This is not exactly what is really bothering him, but it is close enough: it justifies the same behavior and explains the same pangs and urges. It is, moreover, a view of Priscilla that he fully accepts. To the extent that this notion persistently dominates his feelings and his conduct, his jealousy is a trait of character and a vice.

In the story I have just imagined, a certain emotion has developed into a vice, one that (not coincidentally) shares the name of the emotion. This is a story that can be generalized into an account of how any emotions of a certain kind can develop in the same adverse way. The kind of emotion I have in mind consists of all episodic emotions that embody an interpretation about what is right or wrong, or what is good or bad, where this interpretation untrue.

People who experience such emotions are apt to need to justify them. The fact that it is only an episode indicates that the person who experiences it probably does not have a belief that would imply that the emotion is actually based on an interpretation that is true. If they do not have such a belief, they are liable to have the uneasy feeling that what they are experiencing is irrational, unfair, or inappropriate in some other way. An eruption of anger, for instance, might seem to them misdirected, a twinge of regret may feel utterly baseless, or a spasm of hostility might seem a gross overreaction.

These uncomfortable impressions can be avoided if the emotion can be justified somehow. Often, the easiest way to provide such a justification is to form a belief about what is right or wrong, good or bad, a principle that implies that the interpretation involved in the emotion is actually true. It might consist, for instance, in thinking that all actions that crucially resemble certain ones, which happen to provoke one's anger, are actually despicably unjust. Given that the interpretation was false, this belief would itself have to be untrue. Its introduction takes the original error and expands it to an indefinitely wider subject area.

It also, so to speak, relocates the error. It moves it to a deeper part of the individual who makes it. Before, the individual who experienced the emotion saw the facts in light of the interpretation that underlay it, but did so without accepting this interpretation. Such an experience is as if it were something that one undergoes, that happens to one, and is not really one of the things one stands for. Of course, once one has accepted a principle that justifies the interpretation, this is no longer true. The error has been embraced. This interpretation, however, was the reason the emotion was bad in the first place:

it is what made it irrational, inappropriate, or unfair. Now what is bad about the emotion is also something that is bad about the character of the person who was undergoing it. The emotion now characterizes the person in a much deeper and more complete way than before.

9. What Virtue Is

How is virtue related to the emotions? The connection between them, whatever it might be, must be different from the ones we have just seen between passion and vice. The stoic conception, which contains some truth as it is applied to vice, would seem to have no truth at all if it were converted into a conception of virtue. The virtues do not seem to have akratic doubles.[26] There is, for instance, no trait that is otherwise like Henry Fleming's cowardice, except that it results in courageous behavior. As far as the emotions are concerned, virtue is not the mirror image of vice. This means that I cannot apply the conclusions of the preceding section of this chapter to the analysis of virtue simply by making a literal translation—that is, I cannot simply transform it into an account of two traits that are just like vice and akrasia except that they are both good.

The element in my discussion of those traits that does promise to be helpful in understanding the nature and value of virtue is the general role that the emotions played in my account of vice and akrasia. There the emotions served to integrate certain beliefs into the rest of one's experience, determining the

---

[26] An apparent exception to this is a well-known incident from *The Adventures of Huckleberry Finn*, discussed by Jonathan Bennett in "The Conscience of Huckleberry Finn," *Philosophy* 49 (April 1974): pp. 223-33. Huck's friend Jim is trying to escape from slavery. Huck believes that Jim is rightfully the property of the Widow Douglas and that he has an obligation to turn him in to the sheriff, but he cannot bring himself to do it. Instead, he helps Jim to escape and feels guilt stricken about it. One might suspect that what we have here is the akratic counterpart of some virtue, such as compassion or a certain sort of justice. It is certain that, as isolated episodes, such things do happen. Really evil principles are sometimes difficult to live up to and one can fail to do so out of pure squeamishness. What I doubt is that a trait like squeamishness can consistently mimic the effects of a *trait* that is virtuous, as distinct from doing so in isolated episodes. Actually, I do not think that we should see what Huck is doing as an isolated episode of virtuous akrasia. In the context of Mark Twain's novel, the episode conveys the strong impression that Huck is acting on the basis of deeply held but unformulated notions about the obligations of friendship. That is, he is caught in a contradiction between these notions and other, more conscious ones, which he has absorbed from the institutions around him. In that case, what he does is not a case of akrasia at all, but of conflict between principles.

extent to which those beliefs indicate what sort of person one is. We should probably expect them to play the same role in virtue as well. To see that they actually do so, I think it will help to have an example of virtue to reflect on.

In 1917, a company in Sidney, Ohio, was considering offering the architect Louis Sullivan a commission to design a small bank for them. He had once been one of the most successful architects in America, but his revolutionary style had been pushed aside by a revival of neoclassicism in the 1890s and his career had never recovered. He refused to change his style to suit shifting fashions and in consequence he had designed less than one building a year in some twenty years. Poverty had forced him to close his office, release all his draftsmen, and sell his library and many of his personal possessions at a public auction. At the time he had not designed a single building for several years. This is how an early biographer of Sullivan tells the story:

> Sullivan was called to Sidney, and the directors outlined for him in informal conference their requirements for a new building. The site was then an empty corner lot. Sullivan retired to the opposite corner, sat on a curbstone for the better part of two whole days, smoking innumerable cigarettes. At the end of this time he announced to the directors that the design was made—in his head, proceeded to draw a rapid sketch before them, and announced an estimate of the cost. One of the directors was somewhat disturbed by the unfamiliarity of the style, and suggested that he had rather fancied some classic columns and pilasters for the facade. Sullivan very brusquely rolled up his sketch and started to depart, saying that the directors could get a thousand architects to design a classic bank but only one to design them this kind of bank, and that as far as he was concerned, it was either the one thing or the other.

Luckily, Sullivan's abrupt refusal did not produce the tragic results that could easily have followed it. After conferring again, the directors agreed to build the bank as he designed it.[27]

His refusal to compromise, as described by his biographer, presents a striking image of certain virtues, including courage and a heroic sort of integrity. What makes the image so striking is not the bare behavior itself but the *way* it is done. Sullivan brusquely takes up his papers, as if to leave, before he has even finished rejecting the conservative director's suggestion about the building's design. It is as if he turns and runs from the possibility of betraying his ideals as readily, as unthinkingly, as others turn and run from the prospect of poverty and disgrace. In fact, he has voluntarily accepted poverty and

---

[27] Hugh Morrison, *Louis Sullivan: Prophet of Modern Architecture* (New York: W. W. Norton, 1935), pp. 180-81.

disgrace because they seemed to be the price of adhering to his principles. Escaping them by betraying his ideals is something toward which he seems to feel no attraction at all.

Intuitively, this sort of conduct seems to be of an entirely different order from another one, one that might nonetheless have all the same practical consequences. Suppose that the bank's board had given someone in Sullivan's position an ultimatum like the offer that the conservative director seems willing to make. We can easily imagine someone so circumstanced responding by saying, with furrowed brow and clenched fist, after a pause to struggle with himself, that he is unable to do what they propose. Such a response would be admirable, even heroic. What Sullivan's biographer describes him as doing, on the other hand, seems to be something beyond that: it is awe-inspiring.

This intuitive impression is supported and, I think, explained by some of my comments on vice and akrasia in the preceding section of this chapter. In one respect, the sort of conduct Sullivan's biographer attributes to him bears a striking resemblance to vice as I have described it. One thing that impresses us about his conduct is the appearance it gives of a soul at peace with itself, however fiercely it may battle the world around it. We seem to catch a glimpse of a psyche that is integrated by a central idea—which in this case is an insight and not, as in the case of vice, an error. There is a deep certainty about the importance of his ideals and the relative importance of the other things the world can offer. It is clear to him, however dubious it might seem to others, that having a decent chance to buy food and pay the rent is not a good reason to design a building in a way that he believes is wrong.

In the contrasting sort of conduct, the sort that we have merely imagined someone in Sullivan's circumstances doing, the inner peace is missing. There we were imagining someone who, as in the present instance, is faced with a choice, one in which there are reasons to take either one of two different options. What makes the contrasting case different is the fact that, even after the individual has decided which option he should take, the reasons for taking the other option still exert an emotional pull on him. He feels a pang of regret at having to take the course he takes. It is as if part of him feels a desire to pursue the option he has discarded. In a certain way, the state he is in is strikingly similar to akrasia: he is as it were split into two parts, one of which wants to do what he has decided to do, the other of which does not.

More generally, there are at least two ways to act admirably and in a way that reflects favorably on one's character. In one of these ways, one acts on principle, and the interpretations involved in all of one's occurrent emotional interpretations are consistent with the principle on which one acts. In the other, this consistency is incomplete. Some of one's emotions involve interpretations that clash with the principle acted on. One's act reflects less favorably on one's character. We might say that it represents a smaller part of one's constitution.

As in the preceding section of this chapter, we seem to be dealing with states of character of two quite different kinds, and, as before, it seems appropriate to mark the difference between them with verbal distinction of some sort. As my more learned readers will have noticed a while back, my mentor throughout this chapter has been Aristotle. I will follow his lead once more. I propose to call the state of character exemplified by the story about Sullivan "virtue," which is the traditional translation of Aristotle's *arētē*. I will call the other of these two ways in which character can be qualified "strength of character," which is one possible way of rendering his *enkrateia*.[28]

At this point, I suspect that someone will be eager to raise a certain objection. It is this. It seems arbitrary to reserve the name of virtue for something as rare and difficult to attain as the trait evinced by Louis Sullivan. That is not mere virtue but, one might say, heroic greatness, one that few people can hope to achieve. Most people, if they were to do something that outwardly resembles what Sullivan did, would do it with teeth-gritting reluctance. It seems counterintuitive and, in a way, cruel to deny that most people can achieve virtue. In addition, the cruelty seems gratuitous, since such reluctant conduct often seems admirable in spite of its reluctance.

As to this last point—whether such conduct is admirable—I do not deny that such conduct reflects on one's character in a positive way. As far as that is concerned, I am only saying that it does not reveal an admirable sort of character in the same way or to the same extent that true virtue does. Reserving the name of virtue for another sort of conduct is only gratuitous if the difference between these two ways of acting lacks the depth that is suggested by such a linguistic practice. I have given reason to think it does not.

The fact remains, however, that to most of us it does not seem true that virtue is out of the reach of most people. We live in a world that, unlike that of Aristotle, has been deeply influenced by democracy. People living in a culture as egalitarian as ours tend to be slightly uncomfortable with distinctions of value between different human beings, and any distinction that seems to deny to most people any hope of achieving genuine excellence of character may well be intolerable to us.

It would be very interesting to discuss the merits of this ethical egalitarianism, but I doubt that it is necessary to do so here. I do not think that

---

[28] For Aristotle's use of this term, see especially *Nicomachean Ethics*, bk 7, chaps. 1-10.

my distinction between virtue and strength of character expels most of the human race from the field of human excellence. The anecdote about Sullivan—which reveals heroic virtue in desperate circumstances—at first conveys the impression that it does, but a closer look at it will show that it does not really have any such depressing implications.

What is it in the anecdote that makes the action of its protagonist stand out, above the imaginary conduct with which I contrasted it, as an instance of exemplary virtue? It is not that Sullivan, unlike the other person, has no desire for financial security. Nor is it that he is emotionally unattached to such things, that he would, for instance, experience no fear at an imminent and believable threat of having no income at all. Admittedly, most human beings are not capable of such conative and affective detachment, but that is because it would be psychologically abnormal, and not because it is a difficult achievement. I think we can understand Sullivan's conduct without supposing that there is anything in it that is abnormal in this way.

What seems to make his behavior stand out is his apparent serenity about the *course of action* that he has decided on. The alternative option, the one he has discarded, does not seem to tug at him. This is clearly a different matter from being emotionally attached to goods such as wealth and fame. If one is certain enough about *how* important such things are, then it is possible to care about them in a general sort of way—even to care about them very much—while nonetheless being sure that, in certain particular circumstances, they do not constitute a good reason for rejecting a course of action in which they must be forfeited. This would explain the impression of inner peace that the story conveys.

I do not think this sort of certainty is, as such and in general, beyond the reach of most people. Within the peculiar circumstances of the Sullivan anecdote, it probably is unattainable for most of us, but that is because the circumstances are very unusual. When the cost of a course of action is extraordinarily high, it may indeed be very difficult to be certain that it is worth the cost. Matters are quite different in the case of actions that are placed in more normal circumstances, where good conduct has costs that fall short of the catastrophic.

Consider the following more commonplace sort of story. Martha tells her friend, Lydia, that the ride to the airport that she had been counting on for this afternoon did not materialize and she cannot find another way to get there, other than a cab ride she can ill afford. Without hesitating, Lydia tells her that she will take her. She makes a mental note of the fact that she will not be able to go to the concert in the park she was hoping to attend. The orchestra will be playing the first suite from *Carmen*, a favorite of hers, but there is no doubt that helping Martha is more important to her than going to the concert. When they get to her parking place, they discover that her car is gone, and Lydia remembers that her roommate had been talking about borrowing it for the afternoon. She feels frustrated, as she would at any obstacle to her doing something she wants to do, and searches for another inexpensive way to get Martha to the airport on time.

Obviously, this story does not present Lydia as a saint, merely as a genuinely kind person. As such, though, it depicts her as good and as better than some people. There are those who, on finding the car gone, would have breathed a sigh of relief, perhaps thinking something like, "Good! Now Martha will have to take that cab and I can catch the concert after all!" Such a person might even be called kind if, after a brief struggle, and the thought that, after all, that is rather mean-minded of me and helping your friends is more important, they went ahead and helped their friend. Both sorts of kindness seem to be within the reach of many people. Moreover, they are obviously instances of the distinction I have urged between virtue and strength of character.

With all the words that are the names of virtues it is possible to make the same distinction between two traits of character, one of which qualifies as a virtue in my sense of the word while the other, though it is also a trait of character and a good one, does not qualify. Every virtue will be one that we can expect to see in people who are not outlandishly heroic, provided only that the trait is one that, in the world as it exists, can be practiced in a substantially consistent way without shouldering the burden of outlandishly heroic costs.

VI

Character and the Social World

1. The Question

In the remaining chapters of this book I will build on the discussion I have presented so far in an attempt to treat a somewhat different problem. The new problem I wish to treat is, stated in its most general form, the problem of how character is formed and, especially, how it is changed for the better.

Stated in this general way, this subject includes most of the problems of what is called moral education, a field that already has a fairly voluminous literature.[1] Moral education, as it is generally understood, includes a constellation of problems that are somewhat different from the ones I wish to treat here. Generally, it concerns the activity of a moral instructor who is trying, with benevolence aforethought, to guide someone (who is almost always assumed to be a child) into certain ways of thinking, feeling, or acting. Strictly speaking, however, there is more to moral education than such moral instruction. The character of adults and children alike is influenced by a multitude of social forces that are not controlled by any instructor's intentions. This, I think, is a familiar fact of everyday life. Parents who try to discourage their children from becoming obsessed with their clothing, their weight, and their general appearance often realize with disturbing clarity that children in our culture receive very different messages from the world around them. They are subject to omnipresent and intangible influences from commercials, television shows, movies, and the convention—governed behavior of other people—including the behavior of the parents themselves. The messages they receive tell them that being thin and beautiful is the main avenue to success, happiness, and personal worth. They are often messages that no one actually intends to send; they are often simply by-products of the social conventions

---

[1] Two contributions to this literature that focus on the formation of character are Edmund Pincoffs, *Quandaries and Virtues* (Lawrence, Kans.: University of Kansas Press, 1986), and Betty Sichel, *Moral Education* (Philadelphia: Temple University Press, 1988).

and other institutional arrangements that dominate our highly commercialized society. Nonetheless, their influence can be strong and frustrating. It is probably important to take a reasonable pride in one's own appearance, but it is at least as important that this pride not grow into a mania. There are aspects of our culture that can make this difficult to avoid, for adults as well as for children.

On the other hand, it is likely, though less obvious, that there are some virtues that it is comparatively easy to acquire and instill in the context of American institutions. At any rate, parents who are trying to get their children to respect the property of others or keep their promises probably do not so often have the feeling that they have the whole world working against them. Our institutions do seem to be arranged so that they facilitate the acquisition of some good traits of character. Indeed, we have good reason to hope that something like this is often the case. We have seen in the earlier chapters of this book that virtues and traits of character in general are complex and multifarious things, and that they are deeply imbedded in the personalities of those who have them. We therefore have reason to suspect, even before inquiring closely into the nature of moral education, that inculcating them in someone (whether it is a child or one's own self) would be a dauntingly complex and difficult task, if one had to do it entirely alone, unaided by the social world one lives in. If the world is indifferent or hostile to the formation of virtue, it may be foolish to have much hope that it can exist.

For better or worse, human character is formed, in part, by the institutions in which we live and, to that extent, not by the intentions of a moral instructor. It would obviously be worthwhile to understand something about this aspect of moral education. It clearly would help us to understand the process of moral instruction itself if we could place it in the social context in which it actually occurs. We may find, for instance, that some of the limits to the powers that moral instructors possess are not due to the immutable facts of human nature but to institutions that we have the power to change. Perhaps people are no more generous or just than they are, no less envious and vengeful than they are, because of the institutions that influence their behavior, and not because the guardians of virtue—whoever they may be—have failed to be sufficiently vigilant or skillful.

We all want, to varying degrees, to become better people. If we could understand more fully how social institutions influence character for better or worse, we would know something important about which institutions we should want to have.

2. Some Difficulties

Philosophers have from time to time—apparently not often—discussed the ways in which social and political institutions, as distinguished from the efforts of moral instructors, can influence human character. But I know of no sustained discussion by a philosopher of ways in which such institutions can make us better.[2] Such silence—if indeed it is real and not a mere artifact of ignorance on my part—is unlikely to be a mere oversight, an indication merely of absentmindedness on the part of the people who have thought most deeply about the problems of conduct and character. Perhaps there is some reason, even good reason, why to such people this subject does not seem to be worth discussing. There could be weighty objections to the idea that social institutions can instill or support genuine virtue. Again, there could be objections to the idea that there could be a philosophical theory showing how institutions can influence character at all.

I can think of possible objections of both sorts, ones that are at least plausible. I will spend the rest of this chapter stating these objections and trying to show their force. I will spend the next one trying to overcome them.

Regarding the possibility of philosophical theories of character, the objection I have in mind is relatively simple. It begins with the plausible notion that the question of how a given institution affects character is a straightforwardly empirical matter. The only way to answer questions of this sort, it seems, is by comparing the actual behavior of people whom fate has placed in different institutional settings—say, capitalist and socialist—in terms of how often they give to charity, how often they commit violent crimes, the amount of time they spend in the pursuit of personal gain, how often they award valued positions to their relatives, and so forth. This, and nothing else, would tell us something important about the tendencies that these institutions have to make people charitable or stingy, gentle or cruel, greedy or not greedy, fair or unfair. Whatever one's view of philosophical methodology might be, it clearly rests

---

[2] The greatest discussion of the relations between character and society is surely Plato's *Republic*. But the ideal society he describes there promotes virtue only because it is ruled by philosophers who, by various means (including their control of what we would call the mass media), educate all the people and lead them into virtue (or as close to virtue as they can come). This is simply moral instruction on a colossal scale. When he discusses the effects on character that are produced by various societies that are not ruled by moral teachers, it is simply to show that they produce vices, such as greed and power lust. This strongly suggests that the effect that society and the state have on character, apart from the efforts of moral instructors, is to make us worse.

on some sort of ratiocination, and not on gathering facts of this kind. Philosophical thinking about such questions would be sheer speculation. It would not provide us with anything like knowledge.

The problem I have in mind regarding the power of social institutions to foster virtue is rather more complicated than the foregoing one. To make the problem as concrete and vivid as I can, I will further complicate matters by first discussing a somewhat crude version of the idea that institutions *can* have this sort of power, together with a classic counterargument to this version of the idea. I will then argue that the counterargument can plausibly be generalized into an argument to the effect that no social institutions could ever instill genuine virtue. We will also see, finally, that the same argument can be used to attack the idea that the social environment can influence character at all.

I will begin by discussing an idea that was widely held during the eighteenth century.[3] This period saw a considerable expansion of market-based economic relations in which the foundations of the commercial society we now live in were being laid. The intellectuals of the time were well aware that fundamental changes were taking place, and their attitude toward the expected new order was almost unanimously one of approval. One major reason for their approval, according to Albert O. Hirschman's account, was one that might sound strange today. They thought that the spread of commerce inevitably produces *douceur*: gentle manners and cordiality. Hirschman calls this idea "the *doux-commerce* thesis." The most interesting feature of this idea was expressed clearly by Thomas Paine, one of its many proponents, in *The Rights of Man*:

> [Commerce] is a pacific system, operating to cordialize mankind. . . . The invention of commerce . . . is the greatest approach toward universal civilization that has yet been made by any means not immediately flowing from moral principles.[4]

Paine is saying that there is at least one virtuous trait—cordiality—the existence of which does not rest entirely on the rather shaky foundation of individual insight. It is also supported, he believes, by a social institution that

---

[3] Albert O. Hirschman, "Rival Views of Market Society," in *Rival Views of Market Society* (New York: Viking, 1986), pp. 106-9. Relevant material can also be found in his *The Passions and the Interests: Political Arguments for Capitalism Before Its Triumph* (Princeton: Princeton University Press, 1977), to which this chapter is in some ways a sequel.

[4] Hirschman, *Rival Views of Market Society*, p. 108.

is obviously an enduring one. This would be a most welcome truth, if indeed it is true.

Paine, however, does not tell us why he thinks it is true. To find an argument for the *doux-commerce* thesis we must turn to a technical treatise on business by a now-forgotten author, Samuel Ricard, who lived a generation before Paine. Ricard's interesting statement deserves to be quoted at length:

> Commerce attaches [people] to one another through mutual utility. Through commerce the moral and physical passions are superseded by interest. . . . Commerce has a special character which distinguishes it from all other professions. It affects the feelings of men so strongly that it makes him who was proud and haughty suddenly turn supple, bending and serviceable. Through commerce, man learns to deliberate, to be honest, to acquire manners, to be prudent and reserved in both talk and action. Sensing the necessity to be wise and honest in order to succeed, he flees vice. . . ; he would not dare make a spectacle of himself for fear of damaging his credit standing and thus society may well avoid a scandal which it might otherwise have to deplore.[5]

The main idea here seems to be that commerce makes people more useful to one another and, at the same time, fosters habits of mind that make people better at recognizing their interests and more apt to act on them once they are recognized. Thus, it increases excellences that have to do with a certain kind of deliberative rationality and, through them, it increases the desire to please other people and to refrain from displeasing them.

Despite its flaws, which are at least partly obvious, there is some truth in what Ricard is saying. This becomes most evident, perhaps, if one bears in mind the sort of social system that he must have had in mind as the alternative to commercial society: an aristocracy based on land ownership and some form of servitude such as serfdom. In its extreme form, such a society is one in which the individuals who are most respected are men who, more or less independently of one another, can expect to have their needs satisfied by people who are obligated to satisfy their needs. One can readily imagine that the people who occupy the positions of privilege in this sort of system will not feel strongly that they need to do things that will secure the favor and help of others. The people whose help they do need cannot do otherwise, and they are relatively free to quarrel and fight with the others. Among the members of this

---

[5] Ibid. Hirschman tells us that this brief passage is the closest thing to a formal argument for this idea that he was able to find. Though it seems rather counterintuitive today, it apparently struck those who first conceived of it as nearly self-evident.

class, it seems that the noble and warlike traits of daring and haughtiness can flourish—as, indeed, they did among the aristocrats of the Middle Ages.

On the other hand, to the extent that a society is characterized by the commercial relations that Paine and Ricard are defending, people are related to one another as traders. Traders, as such, gain from others only by giving something in return. In the trade relation, we get things from others only by offering something of value to them and by presenting this offer as a good enough reason why they should give us a certain thing back. The making of such an offer includes a recognition that the other person is free to refuse the exchange. This distinguishes trade from many other ways in which we can try to gain from others—including stealing from them and taking advantage of alleged obligations that they did not choose. It is a system of exchange within which one only gains from others with their free consent and in which this consent never arises except on the basis of some indication that one will give them something of value in return for it. Strictly speaking, all other ways of gaining from people fall outside the commercial system.

Obviously, this is a system that will reward us for having certain traits and punish us for having others. First, trade will only exist to the extent that individuals are not producing by themselves everything that they need and cannot expect their needs to be fulfilled as a free gift from others. Getting what they want from one another by means of trade requires some sort of planned, purposeful effort. The system therefore offers a premium for the ability to frame goals and discover the means to achieving them. Further, since the goals one must pursue effectively to get what one wants must include supplying others with things that will please them, it obviously rewards certain other traits as well. One will only do well in this system if one has the ability to discover the wants and needs of others and if one is interested in doing so. In addition, since trade relations are commonly based to some extent on trust, trade will tend to come, other things being equal, to those who have traits that inspire trust. This would include manners that are pleasant and cordial. It would also include the ability to gain a reputation for honesty and for honoring one's commitments.

Ricard's argument for the *doux-commerce* thesis, as I have fleshed it out, rests on the idea that social systems tend to elicit those forms of behavior that they systematically tend to reward. More generally, it assumes that people tend to have behavioral *traits* that they are systematically rewarded for having. It seems to underlie methods we often use, for instance, in raising our children. Many of the things we do to mold the character of our children assume that they do respond to incentives, and these include rewards as well as punishments. If this is true of people in general and not just children—and it is certainly plausible to say that it is—then there may well be some truth in Ricard's argument.

But how much truth does it contain, and does it serve our present purposes? Those who follow this way of reasoning are surely right in holding that the incentive structures that are built into different forms of society promote, in some way or other, the development of different traits in the people who are subjected to their influence. But for our purposes, not just any traits will do. Ricard's argument is only helpful in the context of the present discussion if the traits that are promoted by the mechanism he describes are traits *of character*, and, if they are, it will miss its mark unless they are virtues as well. Unfortunately, there are good reasons to doubt that the traits involved can be either of these things. I will begin by discussing the difficulty involving virtue. I will return to the problem involving character in general immediately afterward.

The difficulty I have in mind regarding virtue is raised in rather stark terms in an early manuscript by Karl Marx, the so-called *Excerpt-Notes of 1844*. There, Marx has the following to say about the way in which traders respond to incentives offered by commercial relations:

> Of course as a man you have a human relationship to my product; you have a need for my product. Therefore, it is present to you as an object of your desires and will. But your need, your desires, your will are powerless with regard to my product.[6]

What Marx is pointing out here, I think, is that one who responds to the incentives offered by trade is—to the extent that this is what one is doing—only regarding certain things as important or worthwhile. The positive incentive (the reward) that trade offers is, simply, possession of the product that one's potential trading partner offers in trade. The negative incentive (the punishment) is the absence of such possession. Such possession is the purpose with which the trader acts. But to be interested in the product of another person is not to be interested in that person's desires or will in themselves.

Certainly, one is interested in one's trading partners, but only in a certain way:

---

[6] "On James Mill," in *Karl Marx: Selected Writings*, ed. David McClellan (Oxford: Oxford University Press, 1977), p. 120.

> Of course in your eyes your product is an instrument, a means to be able to control my product and thus to satisfy your needs. But in my eyes it is the aim of our exchange. For me you are only an instrumental means for the production of this object, that is an end for me while you yourself conversely have the same relationship to my object.[7]

If one is interested in one's trading partners in this way, one is viewing them as means to an end. Marx takes this to mean that, to the extent that one is involved in trade, there is a severe limit to the value one is placing on one's fellow human beings. He states this limit in hyperbolic: "Our mutual value," he says, "is for us the value of our mutual products. Thus, man himself is for us mutually worthless."[8] Of course, this is not literally true. Marx is saying that as participants in commercial relations we value man only as a means to man's product. This is plausible enough, but it does not entail that we see human beings as worthless. What it does mean is that we see human beings as having precisely the value that useful instruments do have.

And this, no doubt, is really his point: as traders we fail to see our fellow humans as valuable in themselves. Any such recognition falls outside the commercial part of one's life. Further, Marx is obviously assuming, as we all probably do, that human beings do and should have the sort of value that the trader, as such, apparently cannot recognize.

The issue Marx is handling here is whether the traits that a commercial society is liable to produce are virtuous. By way of making his case, it is clear from the bitterness of his language that he makes the rather strong assumption that regarding people as means to an end is itself vicious, and not merely nonvirtuous. This, I think, is a good deal more than most of us are willing to assume, or should be. Employers regard employees as sources of labor, employees use employers as sources of income, and students see teachers as sources of knowledge (at least we teachers hope so). There seems to be nothing necessarily wrong with any of this. What is vicious is regarding and treating people as means, and doing so *in a certain way*.

On the other hand, the fact remains that, while seeing others as means to an end is not per se vicious, it is not admirable either. It is not virtuous. This, by itself, is enough to make Marx's point, or the part of it that is relevant in the present context. Ricard's argument for the *doux-commerce* thesis appealed to the idea—which I have said is plausible enough—that incentives, including the

---

[7] Ibid., p. 121.

[8] Ibid.

ones that are built into social systems, can systematically and consistently alter the behavior of people who are subjected to them. But, according to any theory of virtue one may care to choose, a behavioral trait is never virtuous solely because of the behavior that flows from that trait. The virtuousness of the trait depends (or also depends) on something that is, so to speak, internal to the agent. If the fact that Martha tells the truth means that she is honest, that is because of some motive, belief, desire, feeling, or other element of her psychological makeup that provides the basis for what she does. Saying what one believes is true might otherwise be merely cruel or venal and not honest at all. Of course, the idea that virtue depends crucially on factors that are internal to the agent follows from the view that I have defended here. But it also follows, though in different forms, from the views of Plato, Aristotle, the Stoics, Aquinas, Nietzsche, and all the major theorists of virtue.

What Marx's argument asks us to do, in effect, is to look at what might be called the internal aspect of the mechanism Ricard describes. To respond to an incentive is always to act with a certain motive, the motive of seeking the reward or avoiding the penalty involved. Having the motive also always involves seeing the world or some part of it in a particular way. If one looks at the motive that is elicited by commercial incentives—the motive of seeking the rewards that it offers and avoiding the penalties that it threatens—and if one looks at the way of seeing the world that is necessarily a part of these motives, what one sees is not virtuous. What one seeks in trade is always some sort of material gain, and what one seeks to avoid is some sort of material loss. This motive requires us to see our fellow human beings as means to material gain. Even if one does not follow Marx in thinking that there is necessarily something bad in this, it does not seem to be particularly admirable either.

As I have said, there is an element of truth in what Ricard is saying. The owner of a store I visit is particularly liable to greet me with a friendly smile when I come in, and wish me a good day when I leave. Such behavior contrasts with the behavior of, say, an employee of the Department of Motor Vehicles who curtly informs me that I should have gone to window ten first and all too obviously does not care if I ever come back. Such behavior, it seems to me, is typical of people who, in contrast to the store owner, are in the position of providing a service in which they gain nothing from the individual people whom they are serving, so that it does them no good when the people they serve come to them and no harm when they stay away. They may well have no strongly felt reason to be pleasant.

Nonetheless, Marx's argument presents us with a simple and powerful reason for denying that the "friendly" behavior of the shopkeeper represents the *virtue* of friendliness. Insofar as it is produced by commercial incentives, it is motivated by a concern for what the shopkeeper can gain from me; it is not motivated by an interest in my happiness as an end in itself, or by the idea that I am somehow intrinsically valuable. Some such recognition of the value of others seems to be required by friendliness if it is to be something more than pleasant behavior—if, that is, it is to be a virtue. I argued in chapter IV that this sort of recognition is also required by the virtues that fall under the general heading of justice. This would mean that, insofar as an act is a response to commercial incentives, it does not evince any one of a broad range of virtues that show a regard for the interests and rights of other people. This would also seem to mean that there is a broad range of virtues that the mechanism that Ricard describes cannot instill in the individuals who are subject to its influence. There is reason to think that this mechanism can influence us to act in a way that mimics the behavioral effects of these virtues, but, as far as Ricard's argument is concerned, there seems to be no reason to think that it can bring us to have the virtues themselves.

Ricard, however, also claims that commerce instills certain virtues that do not necessarily rest on a concern for the value of others and consequently are not directly affected by Marx's argument. These include prudence and the ability to deliberate. David Hume and his friend Adam Smith made similar claims about various non-other-regarding virtues. Among the virtues they mention as being instilled by commerce are industriousness, frugality, and punctuality.[9] Historically, the *doux-commerce* thesis was about various virtues that are not covered by Marx's argument, in addition to the ones that are. Nonetheless, I think this argument can easily be generalized to show that the mechanism Ricard describes cannot instill these other virtues either. More interestingly, or more disastrously, it can also be generalized in another direction as well. With some plausible additions, it can be applied in a certain way to all social systems whatsoever, and not merely to commercial society, or "capitalism."[10]

---

[9] Hirschman, "Rival Interpretations of Market Society," p. 1465.

[10] Note that I refrain from using this term throughout this discussion, except in scare quotes. The word "capitalism" was invented by critics of capitalism, and like most words that were invented for polemical purposes, it has no very clear meaning. The definition of commercial society I am using is the one that was given by Adam Smith: a society is a commercial society insofar as the individuals in it live by trade. Adam Smith, *The Wealth of Nations: Books I-III* (Baltimore: Penguin Books, 1976), p. 126.

3. The Difficulties Generalized

Consider, first, some facts I have already discussed. The social and psychological mechanism that Ricard describes consists very simply in the fact that a certain social system offers incentives for certain sorts of behavior. Marx's argument relies on the insight that one who responds to an incentive with the relevant sort of behavior acts with a certain motive: namely, the motive of seeking the reward or avoiding the penalty of which the incentive consists.

Consider in addition the sorts of incentives that social systems in general, and not merely commercial ones, are routinely able to offer. It is obvious that social systems can consistently offer wealth and income as rewards for certain sorts of behavior. We have just been discussing a system that seems to do just that. Just as obviously, such systems can offer power as an incentive as well.

Though it is less obvious, it is also true that systems can reward or penalize types of behavior by awarding or withholding the admiration of others. We admire one another to the extent that they live up to standards that we accept. To a considerable extent, these standards are not ones we have invented ourselves or even examined very critically. They are, to that extent, social conventions that we have absorbed from the culture around us. They are part of the structure of the society we live in. In this way, society distributes esteem just as it does wealth and power, and, insofar as it does, people who do things to win the esteem of others are responding to incentives that are built into the social system. In the case of certain forms of human behavior, this mechanism is very well known. We are all aware that people struggle to look thin or tall or wealthy in order to live up to standards that are widely accepted in their social world, and that these standards are often ones that few people have really thought about very much at all. To a significant extent, this must also be true of the efforts people make to be thought of as honest, loyal, charitable, and so forth.[11]

---

[11] I have argued elsewhere that the esteem and disesteem produced by social conventions are not mere side effects they happen to have; they are essential and inevitable aspects of the way they function. Social conventions, at least of the sort I am concerned with here, are certain shared beliefs about the way people ought to behave. Thus, those who contemplate violating the conventions know that they will be disapproved of automatically if others know that they have done so. Since nearly everyone is averse to the disapproval of others, this provides an incentive to observe the conventions. Thus, social conventions are enforced simply by existing as conventions, even without any further effort on anyone's part. See "Some Advantages of Social Control: An Individualist Defense," *Public Choice* 36 (1981):

These seem to be the incentives that social systems are most obviously able to offer in a consistent and reliable way: wealth and income, power, and the esteem of others. One who responds to these incentives acts with the motive of seeking them (or avoiding their loss). To offer these incentives is also to produce these motives: desire for wealth and income, desire for power, and desire for the approval of others.

However, there are no theories of virtue according to which any of these motives make an act virtuous. According to Kant, an act is virtuous if, and only if, it is done because it is one's duty.[12]According to Aristotle, a virtuous action must be done for the nobility of the act itself (*tou kalou heneka*).[13] In these theories, an act is held to be virtuous at least partly because of the motive that lies behind it, but the motive involved is in each case profoundly different from the desires for material goods, power, and approval. These three motives do not seem to be the sort that any sensible theory could possibly say can make an act virtuous.

Indeed, these motives are especially liable to degenerate into vices: namely, the vices of greed, power lust, and servility. Unless there are incentives that social systems can offer that are relevantly different from these, it is at least plausible to maintain that nothing the social world can offer us can make us better. Thus, there seems to be a problem with the mechanism that Ricard describes that is much more general than its application to commercial society: it looks as if the offering of incentives of whatever kind for good behavior is, in itself, incapable of instilling genuine virtue.[14]

---

pp. 3-16. There I argue that this means that there is a surprising efficiency in the way social conventions function as ways of controlling human behavior. Here, of course, I am concerned with a somewhat different issue: the nature and ethical status of the behavior that they produce.

[12] Kant, *Groundwork of the Metaphysic of Morals*, chap. 1.

[13] Aristotle, *Nicomachean Ethics*, 1115b13.

[14] In 1888, Edward Bellamy published a utopian novel, *Looking Backwards* (New York: Signet, 1960), in which the corrupting influences of the profit motive are eliminated from the world by paying everyone the same income and making it impossible to accumulate wealth. The author tells us that people are given an "incitement" to be productive and to otherwise behave well by organizing society into a system with military-style distinctions of rank, with promotions depending on good behavior. This gives people a powerful incentive to behave themselves because they know that others will admire and respect them more if their rank is higher. Bellamy thought that the commercial motive of material gain

Such is the conclusion one is inclined to draw from one's intuitions about the nature of virtue and from a cursory glance at the traditional theories about it. The same conclusion can be reinforced by a brief consideration the account of virtue that I presented in the opening chapters of this book. The motives that a system of socially presented incentives brings about are desires or intentions to bring about a state of affairs. This is the one effect of such a system that seems potentially relevant to the production of virtue. On my account, however, motives in this sense are not at all sufficient to make an act or a person virtuous.

First, most of the virtues I have discussed do not involve pursuing any particular goal at all. I have only found one family of virtues that necessarily involve acting for the sake of some particular end of action, and those are the ones that are based on what I call axiological principles. But in these traits it is crucial that the end is pursued in a certain *way*: namely, as something worth pursuing in itself. Obviously, if a social system offers incentives for pursuing such ends, it does nothing to encourage us to pursue them in this particular way. If anything, it would seem to have the opposite effect. If the political system awards political power to people who promote the good of others, it would seem to encourage office seekers to pursue that end for the sake of political power. More generally, to offer incentives for pursuing a given goal would seem to accomplish no more than to produce a new motive: that of pursuing this goal for the sake of some further result that one thereby brings about. This, of course, is incompatible with pursuing that goal, whatever it may be, as worth pursuing in itself.

It appears that virtue cannot be instilled by the method described by the *doux-commerce* thesis nor, more generally, by social systems that offer incentives for good behavior. Despite what I have said, however, someone might persist in believing that such approaches are nonetheless very closely and directly relevant to the promotion of virtue. More exactly, one might hold to the hope that something like this might be true: if people act as if they were

---

often results in bad behavior, while his peculiar system of socialist incentives can be manipulated in such a way that it only produces good behavior, so that his system would produce more virtuous behavior than the commercial one does. (See pp. 92-101.) Whether or not it is true that his system of incentives would produce good behavior, I would argue that the internal aspect of the behavior produced is no closer to virtue than the motive of material gain is. Greed can produce despicable behavior, but at least it does not involve slavishly subordinating one's own judgment of one's worth to the judgment of everyone else. Such subordination, when it becomes a major source of one's actions, clearly suggests a lack of self-respect.

(for instance) courageous, simply because they are offered an incentive to do so, they will naturally grow into acting that way out of genuine courage (or whatever the virtue involved might be). This would mean that the incentive caused them to have the virtue, though it was not the immediate cause. It leads to virtue by a process that, while perhaps not inevitable, is entirely natural.

It is true that I have said nothing to show that this is not possible, but I think that the burden of proof rests on the person who maintains that it is. The burden is a heavy one. One sort of trait that *can* arise as a natural consequence of socially presented incentives is habit: behavior that is consistently rewarded can form a habit that endures for a while after the incentive disappears. But I have already argued (I.3 & 11) that traits of character in general—and, consequently, the virtues in particular—are not habits. Actions that display such traits are distinguished by the reasons for which they are done, and I have argued in this section that the reasons that distinguish virtues are quite different from the motive of securing the benefits and avoiding the penalties that society offers. So the claim that such incentives would naturally tend to result in virtue amounts to saying that having one sort of reason for what one does would naturally tend to cause one to have a completely different sort of reason for it. More particularly, it amounts to saying that the motive of doing something because one is paid to do it (for that is what responding to an incentive really amounts to) can somehow cause us to act for the sorts of reasons that lie behind virtuous acts. I have argued that very different sorts of reasons lie behind different virtues, but they are all very different from the motive of doing something for pay.

4. Character in General

What I have just been saying about virtue can with more or less equal strength be said of character in general: that the offering of incentives is not closely and directly relevant to its formation. There is a fairly simple reason for this, and I think it is a compelling one no matter what theory of character one holds, so long as the theory is a more or less reasonable one. Whether traits of character are emotions, habits, skills, beliefs, or something more complex than any one of these things, any reasonable view of the matter must recognize, at least implicitly, that such traits have a certain important feature. If cowardice is an emotion, it cannot be fear of some particular person or thing. It must be about danger as such. If cowardice is simply fear, it must be the general level of fear with which one responds to various degrees of danger in general, or of some wide class of dangers. More generally, traits of character result in indefinitely many thoughts, feelings, and so forth, about particular objects and are not themselves about particulars. But the motives that Marx's argument reminded us are necessarily involved in responding to an incentive *are* about particular objects or states of affairs. They are, consequently, not traits of character and have no immediate or necessary effect on one's character.

This will become clearer if one considers the following story. Imagine a community in which people typically behave courageously when the occasion calls for it, and are almost never cowardly. For the most part, they readily face danger when the goal they are seeking is worth the risks it brings with it. Now imagine that some terrible calamity happens—perhaps a civil war breaks out, or a nuclear holocaust occurs—that drastically increases the amount of risk involved in almost any goal-seeking activity. The most ordinary actions, even leaving one's house, become dangerous. People will spend a good deal of their time hiding from danger, and a good deal less time than before pursuing many of the goals that matter to them. Their social situation is presenting them with incentives (in this case, penalties) that result in behavior that certainly resembles the behavior of cowards. Does this mean that these people really have become cowards?

Obviously not. They frequently feel fear and they frequently give up their purposes because of the risks they involve, but such behavior is compatible with courage and does not, so far at least, amount to cowardice. Of course, they experience more fear then they did before, and they are displaying a consistent and perhaps enduring pattern of fear-inspired behavior, but this is not a change in their character unless it is determined by a change in the way they respond to given degrees of danger. However, all that has happened, so far, is a change in the actual degree of danger with which their circumstances present them. A change in character, on any reasonable theory, would have to be a change in the deeper psychological sources of their fears regarding their particular actual circumstances. Clearly, it is possible for changes in particular circumstances to eventually result in such psychological changes, but such changes are not already wrought in the motives that are necessarily included in seeking or avoiding the rewards and penalties that the incentive structure of society offers us.

Again, these conclusions can be reinforced by taking up the theory I have defended in the earlier chapters of this book. Whether one is courageous or cowardly is a matter—among other things, but crucially—of the importance one places on safety. If one places any importance on safety, there will be circumstances in which one thinks that pursuing one's other goals does not allow one enough safety. As one's life becomes generally more dangerous, such circumstances will become more common. One will avoid hazards and fear them more often, and this would in part be *because* one's character has remained the same. Thus, the changes in the emotions and behavior of the people in my imaginary community are quite compatible with their being as courageous as they were before.

The theory I have defended here implies that to change from a courageous person to a coward, or the reverse, one must learn something (whether it is true or not) about the importance of safety in relation to the other goods that are ends of action. More generally, to acquire a trait of character one must learn something about what is right or good. If social institutions, or any other means of moral education, instill traits of character, they must enable us to acquire those beliefs that are the principles of traits of character. Simply inspiring motives by offering incentives is not enough.

VII

The Social Foundations of Character

1. Another Approach

In the last chapter, I treated the question of how institutions influence character by focusing mainly on two opposing arguments concerning a specific institutional arrangement: namely, commerce or trade. It turned out that, in the context of the larger question, what was most interesting about both of them was what they had in common. They both rested, one might say, on the same sort of model of the institutional arrangement involved: they both viewed it as influencing behavior by offering a system of incentives. It also turned out that modeling institutions as systems of incentives will not, by itself, enable us to see how institutions have the power to mold the character of the people who live within them. In the last section, though, I think we saw a clue to the effect that there is another general approach to modeling social institutions that might promise better results. One cannot acquire a trait of character without acquiring a belief about what is right or good. This suggests that we might do well to try to model institutions as sources of belief of this sort.

2. The Moral Foundations of Commerce

There is at least one way in which it is certain that one's institutional environment is relevant to the beliefs one holds about the right and the good. First, to take only the most inevitable and immediate point of relevance: the fact that a given institution exists simply *is*—at least in part and among other things—the fact that certain people share certain beliefs about what they should do. The fact that the institution of monogamy, or of polygamy, exists in a given culture includes, as a part of it, that some of the people in that culture share views about what sorts of conduct are permissible or obligatory. Further, in addition to beliefs that are absolutely essential if a particular institution is to exist at all, there are often other beliefs, some of which are about the right and the good, that must be shared by sufficient numbers of people if the institution is to persist securely as a going concern. I think we can take it for granted that there are social mechanisms that keep long-standing institutions in existence and these mechanisms, whatever they may be, must be able somehow to instill the necessary shared beliefs. If some of these beliefs are the sort that can serve as the basis of traits of character, then that might well explain how they could mold the character of the people who live within them.

Perhaps I can make these ideas more vivid and plausible by turning again to the case of commerce.

Consider, first, what a trade actually is. What sorts of things must be true if a commercial transaction, such as my buying your watch for five dollars, has taken place? Obviously, it is not sufficient, simply, that I come into possession of your watch and you come into possession of my five dollars. If you lose your watch while visiting my house and I lose five dollars while visiting yours, we have not consummated a commercial transaction. A trade is necessarily an intentional act. But what is the nature of the intentions that lie behind it?

What if I steal your watch and thoughtfully leave a five dollar bill in its place? That is not a trade either. More is needed than one person's intention to make the traded goods change hands. Nor have we made a trade if you steal the money from me while I, coincidentally, am breaking into your house to steal your watch. A mutual desire to take possession of the other person's goods will not do it either.

Trade does involve mutual intentions, but on both sides the intention is to do something more than simply take possession of something. To intend to acquire something by trade is to intend to possess it legitimately: it is to intend to get possession *and* to get the right to possess. If I want to buy your watch, I want to get the right to possess your watch. Where do I think this right would come from, if I were to acquire it? Obviously, from you. I think you now have the right to possess the watch. The idea that you have the right to possess it is a crucial part of the reason why I offer you something for it in trade. I am trying to get you to transfer your right to me. To accomplish this, I am trying to get you to consent to my having this right. I offer you the right to something I possess as a good reason why you should consent to my having the right to something you possess.

Thus, I can only enter a trade with you if I accept certain ideas. First, I must believe that people, at least sometimes, have rights to possess things. Otherwise I cannot have a certain intention that is absolutely essential to a commercial transaction: namely, the intention to acquire a right of this sort. Second, I must believe that such rights can be transferred by the consent of the holder. Otherwise, I would have no reason to use the means to acquiring rights that is also absolutely essential to commerce: offering something in trade.

The first of these two beliefs provides another sort of crucial support for commercial systems or, more accurately, for social systems in which trade is a prominent and enduring feature. Such a system can only exist if people make use of trade readily, as a matter of course. They will only do that on a permanent basis if they believe that the option of simply *taking* what belongs to another, without that other's consent, is somehow closed to them. Provided that it is deeply ingrained, the belief that people generally have a right to what they possess does have this implication: to believe in such rights is to believe (among other things) that such conduct is wrong.[1]

All of this is relevant to discovering the real implications of the Marxian argument I reconstructed in the last chapter. What this argument established, at least as I reconstructed it, was that, if we model commerce as a system of incentives, and if we study the effects it has on the internal aspect of human conduct simply in terms of the motives that are necessarily involved in responding to these incentives, then we can find (at best) nothing particularly admirable about the effects it has on us. What this means, more exactly, is that, if we wish to find something admirable in the effects of trade, this approach picks out the wrong aspect of commercial relations.

On the other hand, if we view commerce, as I just did, as based on a system of beliefs of a certain sort, the results are a good deal more promising. Commercial systems are founded on shared beliefs that people have certain rights, that they are capable of altering these rights in certain ways by giving their consent, and that individuals must not do certain things to them without their consent. These are obviously act-necessitating rules, and of course I have argued that such rules are the elements out of which certain virtues are formed. More specifically, one who acts on these beliefs will, at least if certain other conditions are fulfilled, display one of the traits that are traditionally viewed as part of justice, a trait that I believe people in the business world often call "integrity."

Contrary to what Marx suggests, commerce does not cause people to see each other as mere means to some end or other, as if they were inanimate tools, devoid of any moral status. Quite the contrary. The various social mechanisms that perpetuate the activity of trade by drawing people into the world of

---

[1] Most people who live in commercial societies believe that such behavior is not necessarily wrong when it is done by governments (through taxation or eminent domain, for instance), but that is another matter. They do not view such conduct as morally open to *them*.

commerce must somehow teach them the ideas that are essential to its continued existence. This means that they must teach them to regard people as beings with at least a certain sort of rights. Admittedly, these beliefs may not be the highest ideals to which human beings can aspire, but they are also far from the perspective of one who sees people as mere things to be manipulated just as one pleases.

Both the incentive-based model of commerce and the one based on act-necessitating rules are true: they simply pick out different aspects of the way in which trade brings people into relation with one another. One may wonder whether, for all I have said here, the incentive model picks out something that is somehow more important than the one that is based on beliefs. In some contexts, this is undoubtedly true. But as far as the effects that trade has on character is concerned, it is not. The immediate effect of the incentive structure of trade is simply irrelevant to character: it is quite compatible with both virtue and vice. The beliefs that underlie trade, on the other hand, are not irrelevant at all. Further, simply for the purposes of understanding trade itself, the belief-based model is in a way more fundamental than the other one. The motive that is necessarily involved in responding to the incentives built into trade is the desire to gain something from another person. This is the same motive that underlies fraud and theft.[2] Unless it is amended somehow, the incentive-based model I have been discussing contains nothing that can explain why people

---

[2] In a way, this was pointed out by Marx in the *Excerpt-Notes* from which I quoted in the last chapter, though the conclusions he draws from this fact are startlingly different from mine. Among his general comments about commercial relations are the following: "The intention to *plunder*, to *deceive*, inevitably lurks in the background, for since our exchange is self-interest on your side as well as mine, and since every self-interested person seeks to outdo the other, we must necessarily strive to deceive each other. . . . If the realm of physical force has been neutralized then we each attempt to delude the other and the shrewdest will get the better of the bargain." Karl Marx, "Excerpts from James Mill's *Elements of Political Economy*," *Early Writings*, trans. R. Livingstone and G. Benton (Baltimore: Penguin Books, 1975), pp. 275-76. Apparently, his idea is that trade is plunder that turns into fraud when the force that lies behind the law frightens us away from the cruder forms of predation. This commits him to the absurd empirical claim that trade always includes a desire to delude one's trading partner: something we all disprove several times a day, every time we make a purchase without even thinking of lying to the person at the cash register. He has built a model of trade that makes it impossible to distinguish it from fraud and theft, and takes this impossibility to mean that there is no essential difference between them. I take it to mean, rather, that his model is a superficial and impoverished one.

pursue the goal of gain *by means of trade* instead of by means of the obvious alternatives. The belief-based model I have sketched out here provides at least part of the needed amendment. Underlying trade-driven behavior, and essential to its very existence, are moral ideas that rule out these obvious alternatives as wrong.

3. Learning the Rules

Once again, as was the case in the last chapter, some of the ideas I have been applying to commerce can also be applied to other institutional arrangements. There is a broad range of institutions that propagate act-necessitating rules among the people who are influenced by them and that, consequently, have the power to influence character that flows directly from such rules.

An obvious example of such an institution is the law. Many laws, especially those that prohibit various forms of criminal behavior, are formulations of act-necessitating rules. When lawgivers issue a new law requiring or prohibiting some act that was not required or prohibited before, they give at least many people a reason, sometimes a sufficient reason, for doing or avoiding the act involved. Such laws are widely seen as commands issued by a body of persons with the authority to do so, and thus those who see it this way will see the fact that the law requires or prohibits something as by itself a reason for doing or avoiding the action involved. This is a reason for acting that is quite distinct from the intimidating negative incentives that the state attaches to breaking the law: some people simply think the law is right, and incorporate its rules into the ideas by which they govern their lives, even apart from the motive of avoiding punishment.

Another very important but less easily understood source of principles, including act-necessitating rules and other sorts of principles as well, is what I shall call social conventions. Consider an example of obviously conventional behavior. The first thing I do when I am introduced to someone I do not know is to grasp, squeeze, and pump the person's right hand. What makes it true that this act is convention governed? In part, it is the fact that I do not do it because the light of reason tells me that this squeezing and pumping is the right thing to do under the circumstances, as it might tell me, after an investigation, that to turn a screw counterclockwise is the thing to do when I want to loosen it. There is no investigation or reasoning involved. Rather, I do this just because this is what people (the people I know) do. Further, these other people act this way for the same reason. In these cases we are acting on shared notions about how one ought to behave. I call such notions "conventions" when they are believed in large part because others believe them, and these others believe them for the same reason.

The activities governed by conventions in this sense go far beyond apparently vacuous ceremonies like the handshake. They solve for us such substantive problems as when it is one's turn to be waited on in a store, how close one may stand to a person one is talking to, whether it would be rude or invasive to touch them, and so forth. Beyond that, convention obviously has a profound influence, for most of us, on our deepest convictions about what is right and good. Surely, most people do not live by a code they have constructed themselves, nor even by one they have thought about to any large extent. For the most part, they accept the principles they live by as conventions: they accept them because they are accepted by others, who accept them for the same reason.[3]

Although the beliefs that are essential for the existence of trade are codified in a vast array of complicated laws, the way in which we first acquire them is through social convention and not law at all. We first learn the relevant conventions—including those that establish the difference between mine and thine, the possibility of getting what belongs to another by means of trade, and the wrongness of taking it without the other's consent—when we are very young. We pick such things up from other people (especially our parents), who picked them up the same way. The same things are true of loftier ideals, which are usually not codified in the form of law, such as the idea that the good of others is worth pursuing in itself, or the idea that we should help others when they are in need. Except for those few people who believe such things on the basis of reasoning that they have done for themselves, these ideas seem to be placed in us by virtue of the immense power that convention has over the human mind. The conventions that govern a given society include a crucial core of act-necessitating rules that stipulate obligations and rights that people supposedly have, but in general it is possible, and probably very common, to acquire every sort of principle from this potent source.

We have reason to hope that laws and conventions can instill traits of character and even virtues in the people who are subject to them. I will now try to determine how solid our grounds for hope are. In the next section I will set out a difficulty that stands in the way of the idea that good laws and good conventions can instill genuine virtue in people. The eventual results of my

---

[3] For a more elaborate discussion of conventions, see my "Some Advantages of Social Control: An Individualist Defense," *Public Choice* 36 (1981): pp. 3-16.

efforts will show that institutions can help substantially in our quest to become better people. However, as we shall see, they will give grounds for worry as well as hope, since the power to instill admirable traits of character is also the power to instill despicable ones.

4. Difficulties

For the moment, we are considering sources of moral learning that simply cause someone to accept some principle of action. That is all they do. More exactly, I am discussing one model of the learning situation, one that represents one function of the situation and does not represent anything else that it does. The problem I want to present in this section has to do with those virtues in which one observes or looks out for the rights or interests of others. The problem is that there is reason to think that such models cannot explain how anyone can ever come to have such virtues. These sources of moral instruction do not seem to be able, by themselves, to provide any substantial support for virtues of this sort. What is particularly vexing is the fact that this is just the sort of virtue they would be most likely to support if they had any positive effect on character at all.

I will begin by describing an extreme case that has the characteristics that this sort of model picks out. We will then be able to see how this case reveals a serious shortcoming in the models themselves.

Peter's son, Paul, is six years old and no more concerned about the welfare of others than most boys his age. Peter decides that the boy will not grow up to be a truly charitable person unless he guides him in that direction. He lays down a rule to the effect that Paul must give his best toy to any needy child he meets. He gives his son hints that he will be punished if he disobeys, but he thinks this is probably not necessary: the boy almost always does what he tells him to do. Eventually Paul forms a painful habit of doing what the rule says. Before long, though, something unforeseen happens: he conceives a powerful disliking for children who have something "wrong" with them. Children who are lame or blind or sick become more odious to him than broccoli or spinach. This odium is in a way quite rational in the present circumstances and is based on something he has learned: namely, that people with disabilities are bad. He has learned this because his father *had made it true*. Peter has altered Paul's situation in such a way that people with disabilities have become bad in the sense that they are now *bad for him*, like poison. Even if, due to a certain level of natural sympathy with the sufferings of others, he minds sacrificing his interests to theirs less than he would have without it, it remains true that they are destructive of his interests. Since all the most powerfully visible evidence he has on the matter leads to this conclusion, it would actually be irrational of him not to draw it.

In a way, Paul has learned the principle his father meant him to learn. Peter meant to teach him that he should act in a certain way and he has learned it. He has assimilated a certain act-necessitating rule. But it is obvious that, in this story as I have told it, something has gone seriously wrong. Actually, at least two things have gone wrong. First, Peter has tried to instill a certain virtue that is based on an act-necessitating rule and, as we have seen (IV.2 and 4), no such trait is a genuine virtue unless one sees others as worthy of respect and concern. This requirement is plainly not satisfied in Paul's case. Further, as we saw in chapter V, genuine virtue in general requires a certain integration between the intellectual and the emotional parts of the self; one's desires and emotions must go in the same direction as one's beliefs about what is right and good. Paul's teeth-gritting giving, poisoned by regret and resentment, is only strength of character and not virtue at all. These two facts are clearly related. Because he does not see other people as worthy of respect and concern, or as valuable at all, he is unable to understand the *point* of the behavior that he believes, on the authority of his father, to be right. This makes it unlikely that he will *want* to do such things fully and without inner conflicts.

This remains true even if we alter my admittedly extreme example in a way that makes it more realistic. We might suppose, for instance, that Peter attempts to impart a rule about giving that is more moderate than the one I have him trying to instill. But any rule that requires giving to others would ensure that to some extent there is a conflict in Peter's mind between his own most deeply felt concerns and what he thinks he owes to others, thus opening the possibility of his drawing the conclusions I have him drawing. Again, we might expand his methods and have him *tell* his son that the point of all this is that others have dignity and importance as well as oneself, and that their welfare thus merits our concern. But there seems to be nothing in the story, thus amplified, that would enable Paul to even understand what this pronouncement means. He would think that it must be true just because his father says it is, but it is hardly self-explanatory. It stands in baffling conflict, whatever it might mean, with the facts as he finds them. For the facts, together with his beliefs about how he should act, imply that others are dangerous to him and therefore to be avoided insofar as they need his concern.

Notice, finally, that the story I have told does not assume that Paul has an ineradicable, natural instinct to be particularly "selfish." I have made three psychological assumptions about him, none of which commits me to a controversial theory of human nature. First, I have assumed that he has certain desires that run counter the rule he has learned, in that the rule requires him to lose things that are of value to him. He is emotionally attached to the toys he has to give away. Second, he does not *naturally* have an equally strong attachment to the idea that other people in general, including strangers, should have these things instead of him. Third, he really believes the rule he has learned. In a way, his thinking is not selfish at all. Indeed, I could go so far as to assume that he is completely incapable, due to the regard he has for his father's authority, of doubting the correctness of the rule without making the story end more happily. Such an assumption would only make the situation worse. Needy children have become so odious to him precisely because he *does* believe the rule. Whenever one of them appears on the scene, he thinks that something that is of value to him becomes rightfully theirs. He must lose it. This is painful to him, and all the more painful because he sees no point in the pain.

Of course, this is not what the moral development of most people, and of most children, is like. The question, though, is, Why not? Peter is using a certain method of influencing Paul's behavior: it consists entirely in causing him to believe a certain principle of action. In particular, the rule requires Paul to do things that naturally run counter to his own desires and serve to satisfy the desires of others. He also has a certain objective: to instill in Paul one of the virtues in which one observes or looks out for the rights or interests of others. Given only the method he is using, the nature of the rule involved, and the nature of his objective, and within the plausible assumptions I have made about Paul's psychology, there is no reason at all to think that Peter's method would turn out any better for him than it does in the story I have told. In the world we live in, moral education does not usually turn out this badly. What, then, is present in the world but missing from my story?

The same question applies, and with equal force, to the models of character formation I have been discussing in this chapter. In those models, laws and social conventions influence the character of the people who are subject to them simply by causing them to believe certain act-necessitating rules: namely, whatever rules are embodied in the laws or conventions involved.

There are many laws and social conventions that could conceivably impart other-regarding virtues such as the one Peter is trying to instill in Paul, but all these rules face problems, as far as this type of trait is concerned, that are the same in kind as the problem faced by Peter's rule. Some of these laws and conventions are like Peter's rule in that they require us to promote the interests of others, while others only require us to refrain from harming them. One might think that the difficulties that Peter encountered were due to the fact that he was teaching the first sort of rule, but in fact problems of the same kind are raised by the second sort as well. Rules that prevent us from harming others always either require us to forgo goods we could otherwise secure (by picking pockets, and so forth), or else they require us to give up some good we might otherwise keep (for instance, by refusing to pay our creditors for the things we have gotten from them). It costs us something to follow such rules just as, more obviously, it costs us something to follow rules of the sort that Paul was following.

It is obvious enough that it costs me five dollars to give five dollars to the poor. It is less obvious, but equally true, that it costs me five dollars to refrain from stealing the five dollars in your pocket. In both cases I do without something of value that I could otherwise have. Both sorts of rules —those that require us to benefit others and those that require us to refrain from harming them—present other human beings, if one accepts the rule, as a threat or obstacle to the satisfaction of one's own desires.

As I have suggested, though, what is most interesting is the fact that people who have mastered such rules do not see others in this way, at least not typically, and if they are virtuous they do not see them this way at all. Trade is made possible by the sort of rule that requires us to refrain from harming others. If I approach you to buy your watch for five dollars, I do so because I wish to give up the five dollars in order to get the watch. Underlying this fact, as I have already said, is the fact that I think the watch is yours (that is, by right). This is why I want to get the watch by means of giving up the money. But I know that it is possible to have both of them: I could steal your watch, or fail to deliver the money I have promised in return for it after you have foolishly supplied me with the watch in advance of payment. In a way, I am well aware that by engaging in trade I am forgoing the advantage I could gain through theft or fraud. I accept a rule according to which this would violate your rights and so would be wrong. But if I am a virtuous person, I do not feel you and your rights to be an *obstacle* to my self-enrichment.

Such feelings are not part of a virtuous person's emotional makeup. However, such feelings are perfectly compatible with believing in the rule and the rights involved. I can believe that it is utterly necessary to stop for all stop signs and yet be very irritated when one delays me in meeting an important appointment. I can feel a frustrated urge to run that sign. Why do virtuous people not see their fellow human beings in this light? The answer cannot lie in the rules that tell us what we must do or forbear doing; it lies, as I have suggested, in the fact that virtuous people respect persons in a way in which we do not normally respect stop signs. But this means that the existence of the virtues in which one looks out for or observes the rights or interests of others cannot be explained by a method of controlling behavior that does nothing more than cause people to accept such rules.

5. Learning from the Rules

If laws and social conventions cannot substantially support the formation of virtues that bear on the rights and interests of others, it is not easy to say what sorts of virtues they *could* support: other-regarding conduct is, after all, what the great bulk of them are about. It is tempting to draw the conclusion that the existence of virtue on earth depends entirely on individual insight and effort. If I am any good at all it is entirely because of what I have understood and done, aided perhaps by the understanding and the actions of individual human beings I have been lucky enough to know and wise enough to learn from. People can learn from other people, to be sure, but only as individuals. Virtue gains nothing from the institutional structures that human action builds and sustains.

This of course conflicts with the intuition with which I began the last chapter: that virtue, or at least character, is formed in part by the institutions in which people live. The basis of this conflicting impression is that two particular ways in which institutions might be thought to influence character in a positive way are not capable of having this effect. The one way to escape this conflict, other than admitting that I have simply gone wrong somewhere, would be to find some other way in which the structure of society might be able to encourage the formation of virtue.

As a matter of fact, we have already seen evidence that there is another way. Paul learned from Peter a certain principle about how he should act, simply by being told that the rule is right. This is one of the two possible means of influencing character I have already discussed at length. But as a *result* of learning this rule, he also learned something else; and although he learned it as a result of the rule, he did learn it, in a manner of speaking, on his own. He learned that people with obvious disadvantages and disabilities are bad, in that they are bad for him. This is a conclusion that he drew himself, and not something he accepted on someone's authority. He drew it because the rule he did accept on his father's authority made the further conclusion, once he had accepted the rule, obviously true. Believing the rule, he now felt that he automatically lost the right to something he valued as soon as a disadvantaged or disabled child appeared on the scene.

This process is not, strictly speaking, a part of either of the models I have discussed in this chapter and the last. It requires that we recognize a fact that is not part of either of these essentially simple models: that principles of action create new facts—or, more exactly, supposed or apparent facts—about which one can make observations, construct generalizations, or produce explanations. Further, in my imaginary story, the conclusions involved apparently had a real effect on the agent's character. It was a bad effect, but it is at least conceivable that the same mechanism could have positive effects as well.

An interesting example of such a positive effect can be found among the many ingenious speculations in Alexis de Tocqueville's *Democracy in America*. Tocqueville claims at one point that people who live in conditions of equality tend to acquire a trait he calls "individualism," which he defines as a "calm feeling, which disposes each member of the community to sever himself from the mass of his fellows and draw apart with his family and his friends."[4] If there is much of this sort of individualism going around, few people will take an interest in the public good, and the results of widespread indifference of this kind would be disastrous.

Of course, not all social arrangements have this result. In particular, aristocratic institutions do not. This is because they enable people to see aspects of life that, once seen, make it difficult to see life in an "individualist" way:

> As in aristocratic communities all the citizens occupy fixed positions, one above another, the result is that each of them always sees a man above himself whose patronage is necessary to him, and below himself another man whose co-operation he may claim. Men living in aristocratic ages are therefore almost always closely attached to something placed out of their own sphere, and they are often disposed to forget themselves.

This beneficial effect is produced by the hierarchical structure of aristocracies. Of course, equality destroys the hierarchy and thus demolishes the aspect of aristocracy that can teach people that they are connected with others who are outside the circle of their family and friends.

However, Tocqueville thinks that the democratic political institutions that often accompany conditions of equality can teach the same lesson. For instance, if an individual who lives in a society that is governed in this way finds that

---

[4] Alexis de Tocqueville, *Democracy in America* vol. 2, trans. Henry Reeve and Francis Bowen (New York: Vintage, 1945), p. 104.

it is proposed to make a road cross the end of his estate, he will see at a glance that there is a connection between this small public affair and his greatest private affairs; and he will discover, without its being shown to him, the close tie that unites private to general interest.

Tocqueville claims that such experiences, which are common in a democratic political system, are capable of producing in people a virtuous concern for the public good. His account of the way in which it is supposed to do this is interesting and deserves to be quoted at length:

> The free institutions which the inhabitants of the United States possess . . . remind every citizen, and in a thousand ways, that he lives in society. They every instant impress upon his mind the notion that it is the duty as well as the interest of men to make themselves useful to their fellow creatures; and as he sees no particular ground of animosity to them, since he is never either their master or slave, his heart readily leans to the side of kindness. Men attend to the interests of the public, first by necessity, afterwards by choice; what was intentional becomes an instinct, and by dint of working for the good of one's fellow citizens, the habit and the taste for serving them are at length acquired.[5]

It sounds almost as if Tocqueville is merely advancing a new version of the *doux-commerce* thesis, turning the old idea toward the defense of democratic institutions instead of aiming it at the defense of commerce. However, I think it should be obvious that this is not really what he is doing. It is true that he is saying that incentives that appeal to self-interested motives can result in an apparently virtuous concern for the good of others, but he does not suppose that these incentives and their related motives produce virtue directly and by themselves. The reason equality tends to generate what he calls individualism is that it lacks a certain aspect of hierarchial systems that makes the fact that people are related to one another saliently visible to the people themselves. If their public-spiritedness lacks this institutional support they can, so to speak, forget that they are members of a community. Free institutions, he thinks, tend to compensate for this lack, enabling us in their own way to "see at a glance" that we are related to the community in general.

Thus, the social system provokes and helps to preserve a certain understanding or insight in which one sees oneself as a member of a community. If the system does not also give its members reason for mutual animosity, as free societies in fact do not, the human heart will naturally tend toward benevolence. Apparently, there is a natural tendency toward taking an

---

[5] Ibid., pp. 105, 111, and 112.

interest in the good of others which develops into a virtuous disposition to act *if* the required understanding takes place, and this understanding is what the institutional framework helps to inspire. Both these elements—use of a notion of genuine benevolence and the causal role played by understanding —distinguish Tocqueville's idea from the purely motive-based and crudely egoistic scheme of the *doux-commerce* thesis.

However, although Tocqueville's idea is probably immune to the problems that beset the *doux-commerce* thesis, I do think it runs up against the difficulty I set out in the last section of this chapter. As you recall, I said there that simply absorbing the act-necessitating rules that are formulated by laws and social conventions cannot impart virtues of a certain sort: namely ones in which the agent observes or looks out for the rights or interests of others. The reason is that the process cannot produce the respect for other human beings that is essential to such traits if they are to be regarded as virtues, and can even stand in the way of producing it. Tocqueville is attempting to explain traits of this kind, and his idea is only directly relevant to my purposes if we use it to explain such traits *as virtues*. But if we do, we run up against what seems to be, in part, the same difficulty as before. Tocqueville describes a process in which the framework of society creates a certain environment—easily perceived relationships with one's fellows and an absence of reasons for hostility with them—in which benevolence then grows naturally. The problem lies in this assumed natural tendency to lean towards benevolence.

There are many things that at least could, conceivably, be produced by an entirely natural tendency, but it is not obvious that the way in which virtuous people value their fellow human beings is one of them. It is not difficult, for instance, to conceive that there could be a natural tendency to *like* our fellow human beings, but it does not seem possible that virtue, which leads one to treat everyone decently, could rest on one's liking everyone. Nor is it difficult to suppose that we have an inborn tendency to need the company of others—certainly, we all do need their assistance—but it does not seem that such needs are what renders the apparent burdens of decent behavior as little irritating as they are, or should be. The contrary supposition seems to blur distinctions that are crucial for understanding a number of virtues, including the distinction that separates the benevolence of a generous person from the unconscious manipulations of an inveterate flatterer.

It is at best uncertain that a natural bent or leaning could have the function that Tocqueville's idea would assign to it. The resolution of this uncertainty presupposes that we understand something of the foundation on which virtue actually does rest, of the view of one's fellows that it requires. I think I might be able to provide some of the needed understanding by making yet another beginning and offering another account of how institutions might instill other-regarding virtues in people, an account that is similar to the one I have drawn from Tocqueville, though differing from it in a crucial respect.

6. Ceremonial Rules

In sections 3 and 4 of this chapter, I focused my attention on laws and social conventions of a particular kind. Both are, as I have said, formulations of act-necessitating rules: they tell us what we must do or not do. In all the cases that I have cited, the rules involved also determine, in one way or another, the distribution of goods that, of course, exist independently of the rules that distribute them. In those sections I discussed models of the acquisition of traits of character in which one acquires the trait simply by learning a rule of this kind and learning it from the law or convention that formulates it. From some remarks by Tocqueville I extracted a different sort of account. Here there is a set of laws and conventions at work—namely, those that establish and maintain a system of democratic government—but the insight that imparts the trait of character that the account is to explain does not consist simply in learning the rules that they embody. Rather, these rules create a social world in which certain facts about life are very saliently visible, and the insight is a conclusion that we very naturally tend to draw if we find ourselves in such a world.

I propose, next, to construct a third sort of account, which differs from both of these in important respects. In this account, the rules play a role that is somewhat more central than the one they play in the Tocquevillean story, a role that makes it unnecessary to rely on natural tendencies. On the other hand, the rules involved lack both the characteristics that distinguished those found in the first sort of account: they do not distribute goods that exist independently of the rules themselves, and they do not tell us what we must do or not do.

Rules of the type that figured in my discussion in sections 3 and 4 can be contrasted with certain others, which I will call "ceremonial rules."[6]

---

[6] This distinction, as I will present it, is a reformulation of one made by Emile Durkheim. See chapter 2 of Erving Goffman's *Interaction Ritual* (Garden City, N.J.: Doubleday, 1967). The account of ceremonial rules given in this paragraph is largely drawn from Goffman. See also his *Relations in Public* (New York: Harper, 1971).

Ceremonial rules do not distribute goods or tell us what to do. Rather, they indicate to us ways in which certain activities can be carried out if we want or need to. Many of the activities I have in mind are familiar parts of everyday life. We begin an encounter with others by saying "hello" and asking how they are; we end it by saying "goodbye." We make requests and ask permissions; if granted them, we give thanks. If we do not do such things at the time or place that some act-necessitating rule requires, we make apologies and give excuses.

The activities that ceremonial rules might be said to regulate would not exist if rules of this kind did not exist. When we say "hello" we are engaging in an activity called a salutation and, if it were not for the rule that says that we can accomplish it by saying "hello," and other rules like it, there would be no such thing as a salutation. The same is true of making requests, giving thanks, and so forth. Further, in all these cases, the activity is important to us largely because of its expressive function. Ceremonial rules always regulate (or create) activities that, in one way or another, are supposed to express the agent's appreciation of the person toward whom they are done. One might say that the lesson of ceremonial observances is that other people must be approached gingerly and left with a benediction: we must not assume too much or handle them too roughly.

To see how a child might be brought to learn this lesson, consider the following story. Mary's daughter, Rebecca, wants to play with a pair of binoculars belonging to her uncle, John. He has let her use them in the past and, thinking that he wouldn't object to her having them now, she takes them. But Mary makes it clear to Rebecca that this is not the way one goes about getting what someone else has already got: you must ask him for it first, and say "please." Rebecca asks her uncle if she can please use the binoculars and is immediately told she has done it wrong: one says "may," not "can." If your request is granted, you say "thank you."

Rebecca soon masters these rules well enough. She does not doubt their correctness, since she has them on the authority of her mother. She even possesses evidence of their correctness: somehow, people become angry and unpleasant if you take something they have, even if they have no objection to giving it to you, without first saying words like "may," "please," and "thank you." If you say the words, however, they are soothed and happy. There are many ways in which one must avoid jarring people's feelings, and this is one of them. Rebecca has learned her lesson.

In an obvious way, however, Rebecca is really in the same position that Paul was in when, in section 4, Peter indoctrinated him with another sort of rule: she has faith in certain principles but does not understand them. Why do people have such volatile feelings about such things in the first place, and why do these words have the apparently magic power to soothe these feelings? If Rebecca had the sophisticated intellectual resources of a social scientist or a philosopher there would be many answers she could give to these questions. For instance, she might suppose that people are proud of the things they possess because such things show that they have the power it takes to accumulate them. Thus, they hate to have things taken from them because it is a challenge to their power: they would rather give or lend things than have them taken, since giving or lending shows that they have the power to dispose of what they have according to their whims and without any hindrance. Alternatively, Rebecca might think that people simply want to keep in their possession as many things as possible, and that they insist on the practice of asking permission because it enables them to say no, so that they can maintain the size of their hoard. Because she is only a child, however, Rebecca cannot indulge in such imaginative speculations.

Fortunately, she does not need to launch any such flights of fancy. The principles she has learned are embedded in various conventional ideas and practices that provide a context that clearly reflects on the meaning of these principles. A crucially important part of this context is provided by the notions of "yours" and "mine." The practices of asking, granting, and refusing permission are among those that mark the boundaries between what is yours and what is mine. Rebecca is aware that she need not seek permission to use something that already belongs to her; she also knows that she need not seek permission to come into possession of something that she is being given as a gift, or that she is taking in trade.

Sometimes, though, Rebecca wants to get to use, on her own initiative, something that is not hers and for which she offers nothing in trade. The practices concerning permissions make it possible to accomplish this without simply taking what she wants. The use of this complicated apparatus makes sense to her because she knows that it is one indication of the fact that, in the adult world, people are ordinarily seen as having a *right* to determine what happens to the things they possess: this is part of what it means to say that these things are *their* things. Asking permission is a practice that makes it possible for Rebecca to acquire something possessed by someone else without violating that right, which she would be violating if she were to simply take it. If she understands this, she can understand the moves in the game she has been taught in the way that adults understand them. By saying "may" rather than "can" she signifies that she is asking that a right be transferred from someone else to her rather than asking for information. By saying "please" and "thank you" she expresses an appreciation for the fact that the thing she is asking for is not already hers by right; that it comes to her, if it does, as a gift. The entire activity, then, expresses a respect for the boundaries between "mine" and "yours": more generally, it expresses a respect for the rights of others.

Clearly, if she comes to understand and pursue this activity in this way, a very important event has taken place in the development of the way she sees and values her fellow human beings. In seeing them as able to transfer or withhold their rights, she is seeing them as having a unique sort of power: the power to create moral facts. This is a profoundly important aspect of the way in which adults of all cultures view the world around them. As we see it, a friend who invites me to take a ten dollar bill from his or her wallet as it lies before me on a table thereby transforms what would be an act of theft into another one in which I accept a loan or a gift. A woman, by giving a man certain indications of consent, transforms what would be rape into something entirely different. If I enter your house at your invitation I am not committing trespass, and this fact is entirely due to the fact that you have invited me. One way to describe the exchange that has occurred in Rebecca's view of the world is this: She has come to see human beings as having a sort of status that no inanimate object has, a sort of moral sovereignty. Once an individual has absorbed this idea, it is possible to take it as a matter of course that it costs something to deal with our fellow human beings. Beings with this sort of moral authority are not so easily seen as *mere* obstacles to the satisfaction of one's urges, like a stop sign that threatens to make me late for an appointment. This means that, if Rebecca has learned the lesson I have described her as learning, she has acquired the basis of the respect for others that I have suggested must underlie the virtues in which one observes or looks out for the rights and interests of others.

As I have described it, the moral education Rebecca has undergone is more successful than the one Paul underwent earlier on, in section 4. This description is plausible, I think, because the educational processes themselves differ in important ways. Most important, they differ in the rules that the individual is learning and in the activities that these rules govern. The activity that Rebecca is learning obviously expresses something and so is quite mysterious to someone who, like Rebecca, does not understand what it expresses. As such, it *invites* her to understand it. But she cannot do so unless she grasps the idea that underlies the activity. The activity and its underlying idea are related to other ideas and practices in such a way that she can achieve the necessary insight. In Paul's case, the rule he was learning threw an obstacle in the way of gaining this insight, but Rebecca does not face this obstacle because she is learning her lesson from a ceremonial rule. It is true that her situation, like Paul's, does include an act-necessitating rule that requires one to relinquish or forgo something antecedently regarded as good. This is the rule prohibiting one from simply taking things that do not belong to oneself. Such rules, by themselves, would give her reason to see other human beings as mere threats or obstacles. But in her case, they are supplemented by ceremonial rules, which have a very different character. Ceremonial rules are generally relatively costless to follow.[7] It is not in itself against one's interest to ask permission (rather the contrary, in fact). This is true even if one knows in advance that the request will be refused.

Thus, if we take a situation in which the only moral ideas being learned are act-necessitating rules and add ceremonial rules to it, we change it into a system with a fundamentally different potential as a source of moral education. Before, it only contained rules that give us reason to see others as threats and obstacles, and no reason to place any other sort of value on them. Afterward, it contains rules that do not give any reason to see others in this way and which, once understood, also enable us to appreciate the point of rules of the other sort. Once we come to see people as beings that are able to possess, transfer, and withhold rights, we can understand the function of the act-necessitating rules that specify which rights people have.

I should add that among the important examples of this sort of system are the systems of commerce that exist in our world. The act-necessitating rules such systems contain—with their clear distinctions between mine and thine—also require the presence of ceremonial rules concerning the asking, granting, and refusal of permissions. If what I have said in this section is true, then, the conclusion of the Marxian argument is the reverse of the truth: commerce is

---

[7] Of course, this generalization has exceptions, but since the activities these rules make possible are important only because of their expressive function, the exceptions would probably be cases in which the meaning of the act is one that one finds unpleasant to express. An obvious case of this is the activity of apologizing, in which we express a conviction that we have wronged the person to whom the activity is directed. Also, in some cultures, there are conventions for greeting religious and political leaders by performing intrinsically self-abasing gestures, such as banging one's forehead on the ground. In addition, there may be some conventions that some people find abasing while others do not. It is conceivable, for instance, that some people find it unpleasant to say thank you because it includes an acknowledgment that people other than themselves have rights. However, I doubt that, in our culture at least, this experience is very common.

actually a potential source of virtue, at least of certain kinds of virtue. We will explore this idea further in chapters VIII and XI.

7. Institutions and the Formation of Principles

We have some reason, now, to think that institutions can instill or at least encourage the formation of a wide variety of traits of character, including virtues. Institutions can be sources of beliefs about what is right or good, either by teaching such beliefs in some more or less direct manner, or by creating situations in which it is especially natural to arrive at such beliefs. According to the theory of character I have defended in earlier chapters, if one has the right sort of belief about what is right or good and acts on that belief with some consistency, one already has some trait of character or other. Further, we have seen some evidence that institutions can instill or encourage not merely character in general but virtue in particular. If Rebecca learns the lesson I have described her as learning and acts on it consistently, then she has the most important elements of a certain sort of justice.

In this chapter, I have tried to dispose of a problem that presents us with reason to doubt that this way of forming character can support in some significant way the formation of virtue. I think I should pause, before going on, to say something about the problems I raised in the preceding chapter.

It is probably more or less obvious that the various objections to the *doux-commerce* thesis and purely incentive-based views in general do not apply to the view I am defending now. Stated in their simplest and most general terms, those objections amount to this (VI.3 and 4): such views cannot account for the formation of virtue because the mechanisms to which they appeal have no direct effect other than to inspire certain motives, and these motives are quite different from those internal states of the agent that distinctively drive virtuous action. They cannot account for the formation of traits of character at all, because the objects of these motives are simply particular things and states of affairs, while the internal states that distinguish traits of character are about broad classes of things and states of affairs. The mechanism to which the present view appeals has neither of these fatal characteristics. I have described institutions as imparting those principles that, according to my argument in the early chapters of this book, are distinctive of character, and they are about broad classes of things, and not mere particulars.

Another problem raised in chapter VI requires a more complicated response. This was the idea that it does not seem to be possible to have a philosophical theory about how institutions can influence human character because such an issue does not seem to be one that can be settled by philosophical means (VI.2).

If the analysis of character I presented in the early chapters of this book is correct, there are probably several ways in which reasoning that is philosophical in nature can result in theories about ways in which institutions can influence character. This analysis implies, to say it once more, that to acquire a trait of character one must acquire a belief about what is in some relevant sense right or good. As I have already suggested in various ways, this implication carries an important clue concerning the identity of the situations that are able to instill or effectively encourage the formation of traits of character. We can say that any situation from which we learn one of the relevant beliefs thereby makes a crucially important contribution to the formation of a trait of character.

Further, as I have also already said (section 2), the fact that a given social institution exists is, in part, the fact that certain people—those who live under the institution—share certain beliefs. Giving an account of which shared beliefs must be present if a given institution may rightly be said to exist seems clearly to be something that philosophical theories are competent to do. In some cases, such an account already tells us something important about how institutions can influence character. These are cases in which some belief that must be present if an institution is to exist at all is also the principle of a trait of character.

This is one way in which philosophical reasoning can produce a theory about how institutions can influence character. It was the method I was using in my discussion of trade in the second section of this chapter. Others are available as well. The beliefs that constitute an institution are sometimes not the only ones that it brings into the minds of the people whose lives are affected by it. In many cases, institutions bring with them certain supporting beliefs (how they do this need not concern us here) that encourage the sort of behavior that the institution requires: that the king enjoys his power by the grace of a god, that a gift of food that is not reciprocated turns to poison in the mouth of the ungrateful recipient, that people who do not pay their taxes are taking an unfair free ride at the expense of those who do, and so on. Most likely, the reader can supply more examples. Many of these supporting beliefs are of a sort that seems to be closely relevant to the principles one is able to hold or act on. As we will see in chapters VIII through XI, where I will rely heavily on considerations of this kind, a philosophical analysis of character can enable us to understand the nature of this relevance and its effect on the sort of character one has.

There is another way in which philosophical reasoning can be used to shed light on this subject, one that is more speculative than the others I have just mentioned but can nonetheless produce interesting results. This is the one I used in the cases of Paul and Rebecca, and in my reconstruction of Tocqueville's discussion of "individualism." In various ways, institutions create situations from which we can draw conclusions: they might create particular facts from which we can form generalizations, make some facts more salient than others, produce phenomena that call for an explanation, and so forth. Among the tasks that the concepts and techniques of philosophers can be used to carry out are those of representing and explaining the inferences that people are able to make. Brought to bear on the situations that institutions create, philosophical reasoning can delineate inferences that, for people who live in these situations, have enough circumstantial plausibility to be natural ones. We can then show what sort of effect these inferences would have on their character.

This method is obviously more speculative than the others I have just discussed, since it is often possible that different people will draw different conclusions from the same situation. Having learned the rules, they can learn different things *from* the rules. Yet this approach is not as speculative as it might seem. A theory of the origin of a trait of character does not state that from a specific concrete situation, in all its complexity and with all the features of it that individuals might perceive and to which they might respond, one specific result must emerge. Rather, it picks out certain features of many actual situations—as, for instance, that the people in them are taught a certain type of rule—and shows that these features support the formation of certain traits of character. This means that they can be expected, if certain specifiable conditions are present, to produce certain results: they can make people, in some respect, better or worse.

Such expectations can of course be frustrated by the fact that the needed conditions are not present. In particular, the effects of one aspect of an institution can be defeated by the contrary workings of other features of the institutional environment. The social world in which people actually live is in this respect extremely complex.

We will see, in the next chapter, that this complexity is sometimes actually a good thing. Some virtues are in tension with others, so that the fact that an individual possesses one of them to some extent makes it more difficult to possess the other. The tension between such pairs of traits can be assuaged if the aspect of the environment that supports one of them is balanced by a contrasting one, one that supports the formation of the contrasting trait.

VIII

Gifts

1. Questions

Whenever someone gives a party, they offer people various different things that are of value to them: food, drinks, music, an opportunity to meet people or be with interesting ones they already know, and so forth. Furthermore, they offer these things free of charge. You are entitled to them because you have been invited. Probably, every culture on earth has a practice that is at least very much like this one.

Imagine, though, that by some miracle this widespread practice were wiped out overnight and replaced, through a change in our social institutions, by another one. In the new setting, people either do not give parties or they do things that are *like* giving parties, but with one difference: these benefits are no longer offered for free. We sell admission to our parties.

More generally, imagine that all practices that have the same status as this one were wiped out by the same miracle. The status that invitations to parties have is that of a gift. A gift, in this sense, is something that one gives to another person, ostensibly because one thinks or hopes it would be of value to them, and not as a trade. Suppose that there were no more gifts and that, by virtue of some change in social conventions, people took it as a matter of course that anything we might give as a gift is rather to be sold, or kept, or simply abandoned.[1] Is there something we would lose by such a change, something that would indicate that it would really be a change from a better

---

[1] Ayn Rand describes a utopian community in which there is a custom to the effect that everything that in our culture is done as a personal favor is treated as a service to be paid for. *Atlas Shrugged* (New York: Random House, 1957), part 3, chaps. 1 and 2. One of the characters comments that "there is one word which is forbidden in this valley: the word '*give*'" (p. 714).

situation to a worse one? The answer to this question is, at least to me, not utterly obvious.

In case my hesitation on this point seems somewhat outlandish, consider the fact that it is not quite as easy to give a purely utilitarian answer to it, at least if we distinguish, as I hereby do, between gifts and charitable donations, or alms. Both gift giving and alms giving are practices in which some object changes hands from one person to another, and probably the most natural way to seek a utilitarian justification of such practices is to look at the efficiency of the resulting reallocation. It is easy to justify the practice of charitable giving in this way. Suppose that I have five coats, to none of which I am emotionally attached, and you have none and are cold. Moved by your need, I give one to you. I thereby increase the amount of utility or personal satisfaction in the world. Intuitively (and undeniably), you derive more value from the coat than I do, so that, while I lose something, you gain more. As far as individual satisfaction is concerned, a miracle that made such transactions impossible would produce a world that would be like ours except that many opportunities for social gains would be lost.

It is not possible to explain the value of gift giving in this way. Alms are, as such, a response to an objective fact about their recipients, by virtue of which one can be relatively sure that those who get them will value what they are given: they are cold; they are hungry; they are in pain. Gifts are not like this. A !Kung Bushman, asked by an anthropologist why he gave a gift of meat to someone who is not his kin, said, "He is an old man whom I like in my heart."[2] Although gifts are typically intended to benefit someone—as contrasted with rescuing them from some evil—they are not, as such, a response to any objective characteristics of the recipient and instead are apt, as in the case of the anthropologist's Bushman informant, to follow the promptings of the heart. Partly for this reason, and partly because it is not as easy to discover how to positively benefit someone as it is to find a way to save them from evils such as cold and hunger, there is no reason to suspect that any one object that is given as a gift is going to be more highly valued by the receiver than by the giver. Everyone knows this who has had to write a thank-you note for a well-meant but blunderingly chosen birthday present. The fact that a particular object changes hands as a gift does not always, and perhaps not usually, increase the amount of utility in the world. Indeed, the often capricious character of gift giving would seem to make the resulting

---

[2] Lorna Marshall, "Sharing, Talking, and Giving: Relief of Social Tensions among !Kung Bushmen," *Africa* 31 (July 1961): p. 240.

distribution of goods irrational no matter what standard one uses to evaluate it. Whether one thinks goods should go to each according to his needs, or intelligence, or virtue, or any other fact about the recipient, gifts will deviate with apparent arbitrariness from one's preferred pattern of distribution.

Of course, from a utilitarian point of view, there might be more of interest involved in the giving of a gift than in the fact that some object is thereby reallocated and the further fact that the people directly involved have certain feelings about the object. There is also the way they feel about the act of giving itself. One might expect this further fact to be relevant to the problem of the value of gift giving. It is true that, although the receiver sometimes wishes the act of bestowing had never taken place, the giver probably usually derives satisfaction from it.

But this satisfaction will not serve to answer the question I am entertaining here. The fact that people derive such intrinsic satisfaction from giving is simply the fact that they prefer giving, as such, over not giving. What our imagined miracle, in which the giving of gifts is obliterated, would accomplish is precisely to wipe out such preferences altogether. It would produce a world like ours except that the contrary preferences would exist. This means that some satisfactions in our world would be absent in the alternative one, but it presumably also means that the reverse would also be true. If our preference for giving implies that the alternative world is deficient, the preference that its inhabitants would have for not giving would have the same implications regarding ours. If these preferences are the only standards we have to judge them by, the two worlds are incommensurable.

To show that the actual world is better than the alternative one, we need something more than the actual preference for giving and the satisfaction it brings by itself. We also need more than the utility effects of the reallocation it brings about. Of course, this does not mean that we need to abandon the attempt to answer my question in the utilitarian manner. We could look for another preference, one that would be present in both worlds and less frustrated in the actual world than in the alternative one.

As a matter of fact, there is already an interesting literature on the value of gift giving, and one could read parts of it as asserting that such an additional preference does exist, and that the question I am asking here does have an answer. I will spend the next two sections of this chapter commenting on some of this literature and presenting my own answer. I will do so, however, in essentially nonutilitarian language. I think it would be possible to state my case in terms of preferences and their satisfaction or frustration, but to put the matter in that way would be somewhat misleading. I will try to explain the value of the practice of gift giving—and the limits of its value—in terms of its effects on the way we see ourselves and our relations with others. Ultimately, the point will be that, through these effects, it helps us to live lives that are better, in the sense that it helps us to acquire virtue. Of course, most of us have a preference for living lives that are in this sense better rather than worse, and a world without gifts would in some measure frustrate us in its fulfillment. But if I were to claim that this is why the alternative world is a bad one, I would thereby suggest, strongly and without any justification, that the badness of such a system is simply the badness that characterizes all frustrated desire. Such an approach to my question would only be particularly appropriate if this suggestion were true, and, of course, it may not be true: it could just be better to have the ways of thinking and acting that come with gift giving, quite apart from our preferring to have them.

Eventually, in sections 4 through 6 of this chapter, I will set out what I see as the limits of the gift as a foundation for virtue. For the present, however, I am concerned with its strengths rather than its weaknesses.

2. The Value of Activity

The general question of why the giving of gifts is a good thing has been asked by philosophers and social scientists from widely differing points of view. In one tradition, the answer given is fundamentally individualistic and egoistic. In another, it is, roughly speaking, collectivist, and probably is most interesting to people who hold strongly anti-egoistic principles. Despite their obvious differences, I think that these two positions are not only compatible but complementary, in part because one of them will not work unless it is combined with the other. In what follows, I will adopt or build on ideas from both these traditions. I set out a version of the more individualistic answer in this section and do the same for the contrasting, more collectivist answer in the next section.

One interesting statement of the former point of view can be found in book 9 chapter 7 of *Nicomachean Ethics*. There Aristotle is mainly concerned with solving a certain psychological problem. Though this problem is not identical to the one I am discussing here, the solution he offers for it includes something that could be seen as a partial solution to the one that presently concerns me. His problem is how to explain the fact—which some authors find "unreasonable"—that the givers of benefits are typically fonder of those they benefit than the recipients of those benefits are of those who have conferred them. Apparently, though Aristotle does not say this, the source of the appearance of paradox is our expectation that the recipient should appreciate the benefactor as a source of gain, while the benefactor should regret the recipient as the occasion of a loss. Aristotle's explanation is that there are reasons why the benefactor finds a certain value in the act of giving itself, so that the thing given is not a mere loss. That is, as one might wish to say, there are deeper preferences that are satisfied when we act on our preference for giving.

He spells out this explanation, in part, by offering a somewhat baffling analogy, or what at any rate appears to be an analogical argument:

> The same thing happens with the artist: every artist loves his own handiwork more than that handiwork if it were to come to life would love him. This is perhaps especially true of poets, who have an exaggerated affection for their own poems and love them as parents love their children. The position of the benefactor then resembles that of the artist; the recipient of his bounty is his handiwork, and he therefore loves him more than his handiwork loves his maker. [3]

On the face of it, this is a curious argument. Aristotle's claim that the recipient is the benefactor's handiwork or product (*ergon*) is obviously false if taken literally. However, Aristotle continues the above remarks with some others that indicate that this is not, or at least need not be, what he means:

> The reason of this is that all things desire and love existence; but we exist in activity, since we exist by living and doing; and in a sense the work [*ergon*] is its maker actualized, and so he loves his handiwork because he loves existence. This is in fact a fundamental principle of nature: what a thing is potentially, that its work [*ergon*] reveals in actuality. [4]

Obviously, these comments also contain mysteries, but it is possible to get something plausible out of them with a reasonable degree of certainty. Aristotle is saying that the reason for these partialities and fondnesses—of benefactor for beneficiary, and of the artist for the artist's product—is that we value activity, and we value activity because we value our own existence. The reason why valuing existence requires us to value activity is, apparently, that action is the only sort of existence of which we are capable. To be a

---

[3] Aristotle, *The Nicomachean Ethics*, trans. H. Rackham (Cambridge: Harvard University Press, 1926), 1167b34-1168a5.

[4] Ibid., 1168a5-10.

bundle of indefinite and unrealized possibilities does not count as existing, at least for us.

It seems that Aristotle introduces the case of the "artist," and especially the poet, because they illustrate most vividly the connection between existence and activity. Productive work, work that leaves a product behind, affords us a particularly vivid experience of our own existence. Not only do we actualize what we are potentially, but, in the product itself, our capacities become highly visible and endure after the act of producing them has been completed. Although beneficiaries are not literally the products of their benefactors, they can have the same sort of psychological significance: the benefactor has an effect on someone else's life that is visible (perhaps highly visible) and, in some measure, outlasts the act of conferring this effect. Our beneficiaries make us more aware of our own existence and, since this is something we value, they are valuable to us.

Actually, the last sentence in the above-quoted passage indicates that Aristotle is saying that the significance of the product (and, so, of the benefits we confer on others) goes rather deeper than I have so far made clear. That sentence says, to put it in stiltedly literal language, that what one's product does is to reveal, through activity, what one already is potentially. That is, one's product discloses, not merely that one exists, but that one exists as a being of a certain kind: namely, one that has the power to make a difference in the world and, in particular, the power to produce this particular result.[5] This implies that productive activity makes a deep and important contribution to one's self-knowledge.

The reasoning behind this notion could go more or less like this: An important part of the function of gift giving, from the giver's point of view, is to represent the giver's capacity to produce value. It accomplishes this most fully when the gift itself is the product of the giver's own efforts.[6]

---

[5] Not surprisingly, this idea that a gift represents the power of the giver was taken up and set forth with considerable emphasis by Nietzsche. In *Thus Spoke Zarathustra* he describes what he calls "gift-giving virtue" as the result of a spontaneously overflowing power in the giver and diagnoses stinginess and greed as symptoms of spiritual and, ultimately, physical impotence. See *The Portable Nietzsche*, trans. and ed. Walter Kauffmann (New York: Viking, 1954), pp. 186-88. For an extended discussion of his views on these and related themes, see my *Nietzsche and the Origin of Virtue* (New York: Routledge, 1990), chap. 6.

[6] These ideas probably constitute part of the basis for the notion, which one sometimes hears, that the best sort of gift is something one has produced oneself. As Emerson says: "Therefore the poet brings his poem; the shepherd, his lamb; the farmer, corn; the miner, a gem. . . . But it is a cold, lifeless business when you go to the shops to buy me something which does not represent your life and talent, but a goldsmith's." "Gifts," in *The Basic Writings of Ralph*

As I have reconstructed it thus far, Aristotle's explanation is independent of the metaphysical language in which he frames it. It also seems to be a plausible one: that is, giving does seem to offer the kind of opportunity for enhanced self-awareness that he alleges for it. But, as I have said, the problem he aims to solve is not quite the same as the one that concerns me. You might say that he is explaining why giving is better than receiving, while I am trying to explain why it is better than not giving. I have to show some way in which a life that involves giving is superior to a life from which it is absent.

However serviceable it might be for his purposes, it is clear that Aristotle's idea cannot achieve my aim unless something is added to it. What it says is that giving, as contrasted with receiving, enables one to be more vividly aware that one exists as a being that has the power to make a difference in the world. But this benefit is provided by any activity that differs from receiving in the same way, including action that is destructive of the interest of others. We can also become more aware of our own reality and power by causing pain to other people. In what way is giving superior to this sort of behavior?

We can amend Aristotle's explanation to answer this question in the following way. Human beings wish to see themselves as possessing powers of a certain sort. Most of our actions are directed toward some goal or other, and these goals are things that we regard as good. We wish to see ourselves as beings that can perform such actions, and this means seeing oneself as someone who can produce what is good. Indeed, we must see ourselves this way if we are to believe that we are able to live and act. Giving affords us an opportunity to confirm and vivify this vision of ourselves. When one confers a benefit on others, one knows through one's own direct experience that one has the power to produce pleasure, happiness, freedom, or whatever sort of benefit one has conferred. The same thing cannot be said of action in which one injures others.

Though this is admittedly a psychological speculation, it seems plausible enough. Still, it does not yet solve the problem I have set for myself. It indicates an end that is served by gift giving and is not realized by one alternative sort of behavior, but there are at least two other sorts of action that can carry out the same valuable function.

Waldo Emerson, ed. Brooks Atkinson (New York: Modern Library, 1950), p. 403.

First, if we wish to experience, vividly and with certainty, our ability to produce what human beings find valuable, there may well be no better way to do this than successfully to offer what we produce for sale. If others are willing to trade for my product, parting with things that are obviously valuable to them to get it, I cannot doubt that they find value in what I have produced.

Second, and perhaps more important, it is not clear that the account I have given so far explains the value of what seems to be the most crucial feature of gifts. The feature I have in mind is their benevolence: the fact that, at least typically, they are aimed at the good of someone other than the agent. This account claims that giving serves the end of enabling us to see ourselves as sources of what is good for human beings. Why can one not achieve the same result by doing things that are good, merely, *for oneself?*

I think these two serious deficiencies can be remedied, but to do so I will have to radically shift the sort of explanation I am offering, supplementing the account I have erected on the basis of Aristotle's and Emerson's remarks with another one taken from a different tradition.

3. The Value of Solidarity

The classic statement of this tradition is *The Gift*, by the French sociologist Marcel Mauss.[7] Though the focus of Mauss's book is on the many "primitive" or "archaic" social systems in which gift exchange is a much more conspicuous and important feature than it is in our system, he clearly—and I think correctly—believes that it has much to say about our system as well. His conception of the good that is achieved by gifts is vividly expressed by a native of New Caledonia who told an investigator that the feasts that it is their practice to give are "the movement of the needle which sews together the parts of our reed roofs, making of them a single roof, one single world." Speaking of a practice among the Kakadu of northern Australia of exchanging gifts after someone has apparently died as a result of sorcery (a circumstance that would normally cause a feud) Mauss says: "The exchange of objects is simultaneously an exchange of peace pledges and of sentiments of solidarity in mourning." If such gifts are exchanged, "no feud follows." More generally, he says of the objects that are given and

---

[7] Marcel Mauss, *The Gift: Forms and Functions of Exchange in Archaic Societies*, trans I. Cunnison (1925; reprint New York: Norton, 1967).

received in "archaic" gift-exchange systems that "the communion and alliance they establish are well-nigh indissoluble." More generally still, he says that the exchange of gifts teaches the human race deep and valuable lessons:

> Societies have progressed in the measure in which they, their sub-groups and their members, have been able to stabilize their contracts and to give, receive and repay. . . . It is in just this way that the clan, the tribe and the nation have learnt—just as in the future the classes and nations and individuals will learn—how to oppose one another without slaughter and to give without sacrificing themselves to others. That is one of the secrets of their wisdom and solidarity. [8]

According to Mauss, gift exchange serves, among other things, to bind society together or, to use a word he is fond of, to achieve "solidarity." Though he never articulates this idea very clearly, I think one may, by taking a few liberties, turn it into a position that is both plausible and reasonably clear. The most important liberty that should be taken here is to define the important term, "solidarity." I will say that the solidarity of a given group is the fact that the individuals in it are willing to incur costs for the benefit of other members, and expect the others to do the same for them.[9] Given this definition of solidarity, it is almost obvious how the practice of exchanging gifts, if widely followed, would support it. In this sense of the word, solidarity consists of two parts: a certain readiness to act on the part of the individual and an expectation that others will act the same way. The fact that I, for example, follow the practice of gift giving is itself typically an instance of this very readiness on my part. The fact that others follow it as well is, by the same token and to the same extent, evidence that I may reasonably expect others to act for my benefit, and it will naturally tend to inspire such an expectation in me. The gift supports solidarity because it is an instance, of a vivid and memorable sort, of precisely that benevolent behavior that is the subject matter of solidarity. "If friends make gifts, gifts make friends."[10]

---

[8] Ibid., pp. 19, 83 and 84, 31, and 80.

[9] My usage here is drawn from Mary Douglas, *How Institutions Think* (Syracuse, N.Y.: Syracuse University Press, 1986), p. 1.

[10] Marshall Sahlins, *Stone Age Economics* (New York: Aldine de Gruyter, 1972), p. 186.

It is a way in which people signal to their fellows that they are willing, even glad, to make donations to the good of others.

What I have just said is perhaps most obviously true of what Malinowski called a "pure" gift, "in which an individual gives an object or renders a service without expecting or getting any return."[11] But it is also true of any substantial gift for which, if there is a return expected, it is not expected to be equal in value, as far as the giver is concerned, to the thing or service that was given. In addition, it is true of the gift for which the giver expects some equivalent return, but does not expect it very soon, so that the gift is given in the face of the possibility of doing without its value until its eventual replacement. In all these cases, the gift is an instance of bearing a cost in order to benefit someone else.

There are some gifts, though, that are so small that they represent a trivial cost to the donor. There are also contexts in which the recipient is expected, by convention, to at least try to make a return that makes it worth the donor's while to have made the gift. There are even cases of gifts that, by convention, are reciprocated so swiftly and so exactly that they are sure to represent no loss to the donor at all. We read of cultures in which a gift of food is requited with a gift of the same dish, cooked according to the same recipe, or ones in which someone who receives a reindeer gives a reindeer in return.[12]

How do such gifts fit into the line of reasoning I have so far presented? I think that they, too, can effectively support solidarity, but in a somewhat different way than the one I have just described. Consider a case that is more familiar than the exotic ones we read of in the works of anthropologists. A group of men sitting in an American bar are liable to take turns paying for rounds of drinks until, at the end of the evening, each is in the same position, financially, that he would be in had he paid for all and only his own drinks. Such gifts, which cost the giver nothing (except in the *very* short run), obviously carry a weaker message from the more typical sort that do cost something, but both differ even more markedly from other ways of sending

---

[11] Bronislaw Malinowski, *Argonauts of the Western Pacific* (London: Routledge and Kegan Paul, 1922), p. 177.

[12] Claude Lévi-Strauss, *The Elementary Structures of Kinship* (London: Eyre and Spottiswoode, 1969), pp. 53-54. The author gives an interesting discussion of a French custom of reciprocating a gift of a bottle of wine, immediately, with a gift of a virtually identical bottle of wine on pp. 58-59.

the same message. Both are quite different, for instance, from verbal avowals of benevolence. They are not mere words, but actions: in both cases, one is contributing, in a positive way and through one's own agency, to the life of another. This fact has an inevitable emotional significance for the giver, even in the absence of a material cost. Many of the motives and feelings that can make one person hostile or indifferent to the good of another will also make it at least somewhat repugnant to *personally* contribute to their good. To take the extreme case, the very thought of feeding my mortal enemy with my own hands is repulsive, and the thought that he might feed me in return is also disgusting. Despite the fact that the costs of their gifts cancel each other out, the drinkers in the bar are saying, more eloquently than words could, "See, I am glad to fill your stomach." Here the wise cliche, "It's not the gift but the thought that counts," is literally true. If the gift is carried out with the right sort of style, it convincingly reveals a certain attitude of friendliness that can reasonably lead you to expect that, if relevant context should arise, the giver would be willing to incur costs for your benefit.

The gift as an entrenched and widely observed institution provides a social good that is quite distinct from the value of the things that are given. It indicates to all the members of the group that they live in a certain sort of society: one that is, to some extent, a society of people from whom they can expect benevolent behavior. Knowing that this is so is something that is profoundly important to human beings, both intrinsically and for its apparent implications for one's future well-being. It is an instance of the *philia* (roughly, "friendship") that Aristotle said seems to "hold cities together."[13]

The fact that gifts serve this important function solves the problem with which I ended the preceding section of this chapter: it explains why it is a good thing that people carry out some of their self-actualizing and power-revealing efforts in the form of gifts that are aimed at the good of someone other than themselves. It is plain that this social function is not served by actions that are good merely for oneself, nor by commercial transactions.

It is also true, though less obviously so, that it is not served by an entrenched and widely observed practice of charitable giving, either. Alms, unlike gifts, are discriminating as regards their recipients: they go to those who are perceived as being needy. They are also, so to speak, discriminating as to their source: they come from those who have something to offer to the needy, a group that is not likely to include everybody to the same extent. The

---

[13] *Nicomachean Ethics*, 1155a23. I am quoting here from the translation of Terence Irwin (Indianapolis: Hackett, 1985).

practice of charitable giving tends to shift goods from one segment of the population to another.

This is not likely to send the same signal to the same people that is broadcast by the practice of gift giving. Rather, it tends to send different messages to different people. To the extent that I am the sort of person who is perceived as needy, it indicates that I may expect benevolent behavior from others, and it fails to have this sort of meaning precisely to the extent that I am liable to have something to offer. To extent that people are members of the latter group, it would seem to broadcast the message that they are to be conduits through which benefits flow to others. If it is not offset by some other institution or some additional source of insight that conveys a contrary impression; we can expect it to indicate to them that they are to show benevolence and get none in return.

It is an important benefit of the practice of gift giving that it can offset this tendency and correct this impression. This practice has no restrictions as to recipients built into it and, consequently, everyone may be included among them. For this reason, it is able to indicate to everyone that they may expect benevolent behavior from others. This means that a characteristic of the gift that seemed to make it more difficult to defend—its capriciousness—is actually a part of its strength and a source of its social value. It helps to constitute a social world in which all may expect to be treated well.

Moreover, it is extremely unlikely that any other means of accomplishing this end can do it so well: no other way of sending this message would be at once so simple and natural to use, so easy to understand, so convincing, and so available to everyone.

In the first section of this chapter I argued that the value of the practice of gift giving is not easy to explain if one relies only on the sorts of considerations that spring most immediately to mind when one gives a utilitarian justification. In sections 2 and 3 we saw a reason why this is so. The value of the gift, so far as my discussion has been able to capture it, is not at all to shift resources to more highly valued uses. Its value is that of a symbol. In my amended version of Aristotle's account it represents the efficacy of the giver as a source of value. In Mauss's account, as I have reconstructed it, it symbolizes the giver's concern for the good of the recipient. In both cases, it is an opportunity, not so much to reallocate something valuable, as to reveal and confirm its presence. In both these ways, it symbolizes something we need to see revealed and confirmed. If gift giving were eliminated from our lives, we would loose an important means to understanding ourselves and our world.[14]

4. Limits of the Gift

Given this account of the value of the gift, one might wonder why all exchanges between people shouldn't take the form of gifts, so that life is carried on without any commercial transactions at all. If it is true, as Emerson says, that "it is always so pleasant to be generous, though very vexatious to pay debts,"[15] it also seems to be true that to be generous is also more noble than to give someone what is already theirs by virtue of some deal one has made. There are rather obvious economic reasons why it would not be a good idea to replace commerce with a pure gift-exchange system (as

---

[14] Perhaps this is the place to mention a problem that may be related to the symbolic character of gifts and their essential capriciousness. One sometimes encounters in the literature on the subject a certain preference for gifts which are not especially useful. Emerson, who recommends giving flowers because "they are a proud assertion that a ray of beauty outvalues all the utilities of the world" takes this view ("Gifts," p. 402), and Nietzsche seems to as well (*Zarathustra*, p. 186). This seems to be a widespread attitude in our culture. (Picture to yourself a friend who arrives at your door for a dinner party bringing, not a bottle of wine or a bouquet of flowers, but a gardening tool, such as a Toro Weedwhacker. What is wrong with this picture?) It seems to be common in other cultures as well. Among the Trobriand Islanders, the favored gifts are red necklaces and white bracelets. Among the Tarahumara, a corn beer known in local Spanish as *tesguino* has this status. The gifts at the *potlatches* of the Northwest Coast "consist almost entirely of treasure items," the "consumption utility" of which has, "especially in recent times, been negligible." H. G. Barnett, "The Nature of the Potlatch," *American Anthropologist* 40 (July-September 1938): p. 351. Concerning the American practice of exchanging Christmas presents, Lévi-Strauss has this to say: "Through the uselessness of the gifts, and their frequent duplication because of the limited range of objects suitable as presents, these exchanges . . . take the form of a vast and collective destruction of wealth." *The Elementary Structures of Kinship*, p. 56. It could be that the most common gifts around the world are not objects at all, but festivals, whether they are riotous *potlatches* and *tesguinadas* or gourmet dinner parties at which everyone eats food that is much fancier and less healthy than their usual fare. What might be the reason for this apparent bias in favor of nonuseful gifts? (After all, your friend's imagined gift of a gardening tool would be far more valuable than the bunch of flowers.) It could be that such gifts represent more effectively what the gift is meant to symbolize. For instance, it could be that when we give a gift, what we really want to give is happiness, and things that are immediately enjoyable represent happiness to us more vividly than things that are productive of some future good.

[15] Emerson, "Gifts," p. 402.

replace commerce with a pure gift-exchange system (as it might be called),[16] but they leave open the question of whether there are some reasons that carry some ethical weight. It might be, as far as the economic reasons are concerned, that any departure from a pure gift-exchange system represents a compromise between ethical ideals on the one hand and efficiency on the other, so that in a world of perfect virtue goods would only be exchanged out of motives of pure benevolence, as gifts. Is that indeed how things are?

I think the answer to this question is no: such a system would be objectionable on ethical grounds, in addition to the obvious practical ones. To see why, one must understand how a pure gift-exchange system differs from a commercial system of exchange.

We can see from my earlier discussion of the subject (mainly, VII.2) that there are certain things that are always true whenever there is a commercial transaction, or trade. In every case there are two agents, each of whom is undertaking to acquire the right to possess something over which the other agent presently has that right. Each tries to do this by offering to the other the right to something they themselves already possess, on the condition that the other transfer to them the right they are trying to acquire. If each accepts the other's conditional offer, the undertaking is successful and the rights involved change hands. These things are true whether the trade is a case of barter or of sale for money.

From these facts, one clearly important difference between trade and gift exchange is apparent. In a trade, two agents successfully determine, to some extent, what their own rights shall be. When gifts are given, rights change hands, and to this extent, gifts resemble trades: someone, at the end of the transaction, has a right to something that was not previously theirs. But they get this right on the initiative of the giver, and not on their own. Barter is not, as Mauss seems to suggest at one point, a case of two gifts that occur at the same time.[17] If I barter my basket of corn for your basket of fish, I get your fish because that is the condition on which I choose to give you my corn. On the other hand, if both objects are gifts, I transfer to you the right to my corn because I choose to do so, and I get the right to your fish simply because that

---

[16] In case readers do not find any of these reasons obvious, I can say that I have already hinted at one of them in the first section of this chapter. Such a system would drastically misallocate goods because givers, in contrast to people who trade, often have to guess what their recipients want. Also, unlike people who trade in market economies, they would have no way to respond to the interests of people whom they do not know personally.

[17] Mauss, *The Gift*, p. 35. For a similar but more sophisticated view, see Ludwig von Mises, *Human Action* (New Haven: Yale University Press, 1963), pp. 194-95.

to my corn because I choose to do so, and I get the right to your fish simply because that is what you choose. In that case, each of us is a passive recipient of the rights we derive from the transaction.

This passivity is compounded by the fact that there always seems to be a certain sort of pressure against refusing a gift. An anthropologist gives the following vivid description of this constraint, supplied by a !Kung Bushman informant:

> Demi said that, . . . [i]f a gift were to be refused, . . . the giver would be terribly angry. He would say, "Something is very wrong here." This could involve whole groups in tensions, bad words, taking sides—even "a talk" [something like a quarrel] might occur—just what the !Kung do not want. Demi said it does not happen: a !Kung never refuses a gift.[18]

Though the onus of accepting a gift is not as strong in our culture as it is in the nearly pure gift-exchange system of the !Kung, it is expressed in the same ways: as the imminent possibility of bad words, bad feelings, and perilous controversy. Mauss speaks of it as an "obligation to receive."[19] Whether it is always a genuine obligation or can take more subtle forms, it is obvious that people do not feel nearly as free to reject a gift as they do to reject an offer in a bargaining situation.[20] If I am unable to resist this pressure, then my rights do not merely come to me on the initiative of my benefactors, they are in a real sense imposed on me by them.

The pure gift-exchange systems that actually have existed in the world possess a feature that mitigates or balances this effect to some extent. In such systems, there is always an obligation to repay a gift received by giving another, often with interest.[21] Indeed, this obligation seems to be recognized in some form in all cultures. This, at any rate, was the opinion of Edward Westermarck, an author who is well known as a cultural relativist: "To

---

[18] Marshall, "Sharing, Talking, and Giving," p. 244.

[19] Mauss, *The Gift*, pp. 39-40.

[20] There is a rather obvious explanation for this fact. A gift carries with it a strong suggestion of benevolence on the part of the giver toward the recipient. Consequently, it is very difficult to refuse to receive a gift without suggesting that one is rejecting the giver's benevolence. None of this is true of bargaining offers. The very coolness and impersonality of trade brings a compensating freedom of choice.

[21] Mauss, *The Gift*, pp. 40-41.

requite a benefit, or to be grateful to him who bestows it, is probably everywhere, at least under certain circumstances, regarded as a duty."[22] We are familiar with a vague and weak survival of this obligation in our own culture, as when we feel that we should invite the Joneses to dinner because they had us over last week. In pure gift-exchange systems the obligation to repay is much more clear and strong, and is universally regarded in the anthropological literature as an essential part of such systems: Mauss defines "the archaic form of exchange" as "the gift and the return gift."[23] The exchange consists of the first gift and the obligatory second one that requites it. The whole exchange is initiated by the first giver. There is one obvious reason why pure gift-exchange systems *ought* to have a strong obligation to repay. Without it, one would have no way to try to acquire the rights to things that others possess, except to beg for them and place oneself at the mercy of the other person's own free choice. With it, one can place another under an obligation to give to oneself by giving them something first.

This fact implies that our role in acquiring new rights is not utterly passive. Nonetheless, it does not grant us the sort of power we have in a trade situation, because it does not enable us to determine, by our own actions, which new rights we will acquire. It must still be up to the other person's discretion what the return gift will be.

One might say, then, that the connection between the first giver's actions and the rights that eventually result from those actions is weaker in such gift exchanges than it is in trade. For rather different reasons, one could also say that the rights themselves are weaker. An anecdote should help to explain what I mean by this and why. It was told to an anthropologist who was investigating the gift-exchange system of the Tarahumara Indians of Northwestern Mexico. The anthropologist was asking an informant, a Mexican rancher who had spent many years trading with the Indians, to explain certain Tarahumara concepts, namely, *kórima* (in some contexts, gift), *yama* (giving), and *kuyama* (return giving). The anthropologist was puzzled by the fact that the Indians would explain *kórima* by saying it is simply a gift, though it often seemed to function merely as a payment for something one had received. Is this return "gift" really a gift or only a payment? The informant answered by telling a story:

---

[22] *The Origin and Development of Moral Ideas* (1908), quoted in "The Norm of Reciprocity: A Preliminary Statement," Alvin W. Gouldner, *American Sociological Review* 25 (April 1960): p. 171.

[23] Mauss, *The Gift*, p. 45.

Last year, Lazaro [a Tarahumara trading partner] said to me: "I have a lot of
corn down here along the path. Please take my corn up to my house for me."
I said, "Sure, I'll take it up there by burro, as *kórima*." That is, I'm not going
to charge anything for doing it. So I took the corn up to his house. Then he
said: "I'm giving you this *kórima*," and he gave me two sacks of corn. This
kórima was a payment. [24]

The two sacks were Lazaro's attempt to pay him for hauling the corn, and
he accepted it as such. On the other hand, by calling his making the trip (a
journey of about two days) *kórima*, he was saying he wouldn't charge for it.
In English, calling something a gift carries the same implication. "It's a gift"
means "no charge." Lazaro's request was an overture to a relationship that, at
that point, could have been a purely commercial one: the informant could have
agreed to move the grain *on condition that* a certain payment was made. By
presenting his service as a gift, the informant was refusing to make such
conditions. This is what enables us to see what he has done as a gift, despite
the fact that both he and his recipient share a principle according to which a
return gift nonetheless ought to be made. But it means that he was committing
himself to a special relationship to the obligatory return gift. He placed himself
in a position from which there is liable to be little he can do to secure the return
gift. To *claim* it as his due would be a very delicate operation, because it would
suggest that he *is* charging something for the first gift, that it was given subject
to certain conditions. It could even raise the possibility that he thinks he has a
right to take his "gift" back. This would mean that he is violating the earlier
commitment made by presenting it as a gift. That is why we are generally
willing to make such claims only when we are growing desperate, or when our
relationship with the recipient is already foundering.

We can see both these transfers as gifts because the first one was not made
subject to any conditions, and the second was not made in fulfillment of such
conditions. This is consistent with the fact that the one was made with the hope
and expectation of a return, and with the fact that the second was
obligatory—that is, with the fact that it was a payment.

The first gift was made with the knowledge that it is rather unlikely that the
donor would be able to secure a return by his own personal efforts. This is a
consequence of the very fact that it *was* a gift. For the same reason, the return

---

[24] I have translated and transcribed this from my own recording of the interview, at which
I was present. The anthropologist, to whom thanks are due for tolerating my presence, was
Jerome Levi of Carleton College.

was made by the second giver in spite of the fact that it was unlikely that it could be exacted from him, even by the gentle methods of moral suasion.

The interest that the first giver has in securing a return gift ordinarily cannot be entered as a claim against the person who owes the return, and the reasons for this are apparently moral ones. One can easily doubt whether such an interest can properly be called a right at all. At any rate, it seems weak in comparison with the rights we secure by our own efforts through trade. Compare the behavior of someone who is seeking a return gift with the alacrity and firmness with which a shopkeeper informs you that you have forgotten to pay for your purchase. That is the sort of behavior that asserts a clear and indisputable right, and its unhesitating and unashamed forthrightness is never available to the givers of gifts. If the first giver has a right to a return gift, it is often a right that is as if it were not.

Further, the power that the obligation to repay a gift brings to those who give first is further diminished by the fact that the same obligation applies to them in the event that they are given something by someone else. In that case, one suddenly becomes subject to an obligation, and this obligation is heteronomous in the most literal sense of the word. It is imposed by another person without one's own active participation, except for the consent one gives, and is difficult and awkward to avoid giving, by accepting what one is given in the first place.

Finally, while the duty to give is a duty of imperfect obligation, the duty to repay is, by comparison, a duty of perfect obligation. The duty that the first giver fulfills allows considerable latitude for one's own inclinations in deciding what to give, to whom, and when. If one is under an obligation to repay, all these things are already determined or constrained. One must give to one's benefactor; one cannot give something insultingly paltry in comparison to what one has received. One cannot take too long in doing it nor, in many cases, can one do it too soon, since that can carry the insulting suggestion that one hates to be beholden to one's benefactor. Though the first gift is by nature capricious, the return gift is not. "For, to return the benefit we are obliged ethically; we operate under a coercion which, though neither social nor legal but moral, is still a coercion."[25]

---

[25] Georg Simmel, *The Sociology of Georg Simmel*, trans. and ed. Kurt H. Wolff (New York: MacMillan, 1950), p. 392. Because of this element of "coercion," as Simmel calls it, receiving can be an unenviable position to be in; giving can even be used as a weapon against the recipient. An anthropologist describes a group of Indians who use it in just this way, to get back at some rude guests at a feast they are giving: "This was no way for guests

We would lose a great deal if gift exchanges were entirely to displace the role that commercial transactions play in our lives, and this loss would not simply be a matter of economic inefficiency. In a commercial system of exchange, people have a certain power to determine what their rights and obligations are regarding the material resources they use to survive and to enjoy their lives. In a pure gift-exchange system, they would lack this power. To a substantial extent, they would be the passive recipients of the sorts of rights that, in a commercial system, they would have been able to create for themselves. Perhaps more important, unless the gift-exchange system lacks an obligation to repay, it would also be one in which people passively receive obligations from the will of others. These obligations are the sort that, in a commercial system, are self-prescribed. When I barter my corn for your fish, I create for myself an obligation to hand over my corn. I do so by accepting the conditions on which you gave up your fish, and accepting them was something I had nothing like a moral obligation to do. If your fish were a gift, on the other hand, I would have an obligation to make some return just because you chose to give up what you had, and I would not have had the same moral freedom to refuse that I have in a trade situation.[26]

5. A Mixed System

A gift system that is not balanced and moderated by the presence of a system of commercial exchange would be very different from the system we

---

to behave, and it soon became apparent that they were intimidating Kaobawä's group. Still, he and his followers continued to supply them with all the food they needed, keeping their complaints to themselves. They did not want it to be known that they were worried about running short of food. Instead, they planned to conduct the feast on a scale that would be difficult to reciprocate." Napoleon A. Chagnon, *Yanomamö: The Fierce People* (New York: Holt, Rinehart and Winston, 1968), p. 107.

[26] In political philosophy, social contract theories explain our proper relations with the state on the basis of an idea that has its home in commerce: namely, the idea of contract. What would a *social gift* theory of the state be like? If the theory posits the state as the giver and the subject as recipient, the results would have to be very different from those that are typically generated by social contract theories. Actually, folk versions of such theories were often invoked in support of the despotisms that preceded the democratic revolutions of the modern era. They maintained that the sovereign (the little father, the sun king, and so forth) showered benefits on his subjects (like one's literal father, or the real sun)—including even the gift of life, since most of us would have little chance of surviving without the sort of public order that is provided by the state. Though you did not ask for these benefits and cannot refuse them, you owe him something in return for them. And what could repay gifts that are so great? Your life. This is essentially the argument Plato attributes to Socrates in the *Crito*.

know. Our system of exchange is a mixed one, including as part of itself a limited but important element of gift giving and an extensive system of commercial exchange. The composite character of our system makes it different from a pure gift-exchange system, and I have argued that some of these differences give us reasons to prefer it to such unmixed systems. I also claim that these reasons have considerable ethical weight. As the reader can probably guess from the general drift of the preceding chapters, grounds for this claim have to do with the relations between these systems and the character of the people who participate in them. More precisely, they lie in the fact that the two aspects of our system support the formation of quite different sorts of virtues, ones that cannot easily be combined to an exemplary degree in the same individual soul.

It cannot have escaped notice by now that the giving of gifts, as I have characterized it, bears a certain resemblance to the subject I have already discussed at length in chapter III: namely, generosity. This resemblance, however, is a very limited one: the differences between them are profound. If I give you a bottle of wine solely in order to curry your favor—only, for instance, to get you to do something for me in the future—what I do is not generous, though it still can be called a gift. In general, the giver of a gift is not necessarily pursuing the good of another as an end in itself. In this respect, gift giving is different from generosity. Further, though return gifts in a pure gift-exchange system can be called gifts, they cannot be called generous because they are given in order to fulfill an obligation: they are simply attempts to fulfill the requirement placed on one by accepting the gift for which the return is being made. Any act that is done solely for this reason is not a generous one (III.1).

Yet, as deep as these differences are, the resemblance between generous acts and gift giving is real and, for our purposes, important. Some of the things that disqualify a bestowal from being generous also indicate that it is not a gift. The wine is not a gift, no more than my giving it is generous, if I borrowed a similar one from you last week and am only giving this one to you to set matters straight.

A certain analogy can even be drawn between generous acts and return gifts, despite the fact that all cultures recognize some sort of obligation to make such returns, and despite the fact that the intention to fulfill an obligation is in itself incompatible with the generous intention. This is true in any system, such as ours, in which the obligation to requite a first gift is vague and weak. One reason for this is the fact that, to adapt a comment I have already made in a similar context (III.2), people in such systems sometimes do not find the relevant act to be *clearly* binding, and, when that happens, they often act on intentions that are vague as to whether they are fulfilling an obligation. An act based on such an intention can be said to be both generous and done to fulfill an obligation, just as a vague statement can be said to be both true and false. Further, in such a system, it often happens that people who make return gifts do not think that they are obligated to do so, so that they are not acting under the compulsion of a moral obligation. In addition, it is particularly difficult for the first giver in such a system to *confront* the recipient with such an obligation by making a claim for a return, as one can with an obligation to return borrowed goods or with a contractual obligation. Even when recipients do believe they are obligated to make a return, they know that, in a sense, they do not have to make it. In the intention that lies behind the return gift there is a sort of freedom that, in a weak but salient way, mirrors the gratuitousness of the generous intention.

In a system like ours, what is true only to a limited extent of return gifts can be applied much more obviously and directly to first gifts. Though such gifts can be given as a devious way to serve the agent's own ends, they are typically given (to some extent and among various other motives) out of a friendly regard for the good of the recipient as something worth pursuing in itself.

Despite the fact that they are limited in extent, the similarities between gift giving and the virtue of generosity are deep enough to enable the institution of the gift to teach us some of the things we need to learn to be generous people. If the resemblance were merely a matter of external behavior—if it began and ended with the fact that both sorts of behavior involve handing over our own property to other people—the institution might only succeed in teaching us to go through certain motions that resemble generosity but have none of the spirit that lies behind the generous act. But there is more to the resemblance than that.

Though it is true that gifts can be given without any regard for the good of their recipients, it is also a fact that they typically are not, and this fact is not a matter of chance. People use the practice of gift giving to disclose their friendly intentions to other people, and if it were not typically true that the disclosure is genuine and the intentions are real, they would not be able to use this practice in this way. The practice of gift giving as we know it broadcasts, by means that speak louder than mere words, that people typically believe that the good of others is worth pursuing in itself, and thus will have that strong influence over the human mind that beliefs that are obviously widely held always have. This effect is reinforced by the adages—such as "It's the thought that counts," "It is better to give than to receive"—by which, in our system, people express their common understanding of the spirit of the practice of gift giving. Further, it is in the nature of the practice of gift giving to broadcast, by means of people's actions, their common conviction that it is worthwhile to benefit others despite the fact that there may be no means, either gentle or harsh, by which they can extract the benefit from you. One is thus told that, at least to this extent, giving *freely* is a good thing to do.

The gift aspect of our composite system of exchange inculcates ideas that are important elements of the virtue of generosity. This, by itself, is an interesting and important fact. It becomes much more interesting, though, when we notice that this aspect of our system coexists with another one, one that supports the formation and use of virtues of radically different kinds. As I argued earlier (VII.2), commerce instills ideas that are important aspects of a certain sort of justice: the ideas that people have certain rights, that they are able to determine which rights they have by giving their consent or withholding it, and that there are many things individuals must not do to others without their consent.

We have also seen evidence that suggests another connection between the commercial system and virtue. The power possessed by all the individuals taking part in trade to determine their own rights and obligations is an instance of what I earlier on called moral sovereignty (VII.6), the power to create moral facts. It would be difficult to exaggerate the importance this power has in cultures such as ours. Our ability to determine our own rights to material resources, subject to the constraints that are built into the nature of trade, is a crucial part of the conception we have of ourselves, and it is important, in part, for ethical reasons. It means that a profoundly important part of our rights and obligations are our own doing. It gives us continuous and salient evidence that we are to be treated as human beings and not as inanimate things, and that we have the dignity characteristic of persons. As such, it supports the thoughts and feelings that lie behind a certain sort of self-respect: the sort, namely, that is expressed in our willingness to stand up for our rights when they are challenged and that requires us to see ourselves, to some extent, as individuals who are not to be trifled with.

We have here the elements of a solution to the problem with which I ended chapter III. Some virtues stand in relations of mutual tension. Because they presuppose ways of looking at the world that are radically different and not easily compatible, each has a certain tendency to retard the development of at least one of the others. If this tendency were realized to its ultimate potential consequences, the result would be tragic. What factors might serve to prevent or discourage this from happening?

If the point of view I have defended in chapters VI and VII is correct, we cannot fully understand individual moral development simply by examining the psychology of the individual. Such factors as the unique internal structures of individual traits and the personality types they presuppose are not the whole story. Individual character, as I have contended at length, is helped in developing along certain lines and hindered from pursuing others by the social setting in which the drama of development is acted out. Virtues that require radically different psychological profiles can rest on foundations embedded in radically different institutions, sectors of the social structure that foster different ways of looking at the world.

Life as we know it would be very different if our civilization had a well-developed commercial system and no institution of gift giving at all. In that case, correspondingly well-developed virtues such as respect for one's own autonomy, the form of justice that is involved in keeping one's word, and a bookkeeping sort of prudence might well have driven generosity and related traits off the field. Fortunately, though, history has not placed us in such a system. Commerce is not the only sector of society that has a measure of power over the development of character. Its power is checked by that of other sectors, including especially the radically contrasting institution of the gift. Its calculating, success-driven impersonality is balanced by an alternative realm in which all relationships are personal, one's intentions are what matters, it is better to give than to receive, and waste or capriciousness often barely count as objections to a given course of action. Everyone, however deeply submerged they might be in the commercial way of seeing things, is subject to the influence of this other sector of life. The two realms are equally part of the culture we live in, and we all inhabit both of them.

The stability they lend to disparate virtues is all the greater for the fact that both these sectors are themselves solidly grounded in enduring natural interests of the individual participants. The commercial sector is a field of action in which individuals enter into relationships for mutual benefit, and the fact that each of the participants benefits immediately from his or her own actions within it gives them a reason to continue to observe and support its various rules and practices. The gift is a readily available and effective means by which individuals can do certain things that, to some extent or other, they seem to want to do: to experience their capacity to make a positive difference in the world, and to disclose to one another their willingness to incur costs for the benefit of others. Anchored in these enduring institutions, radically different virtues can acquire a stability they would lack if left to their own psychological devices.

Partly because generosity is a very different sort of trait from justice and self-respect, these traits can only be effectively supported by institutions that are segregated in different sectors of society. If we imagine our mixed system of exchange replaced by a simpler but still workable system that does not include the radical distinction I have observed between commerce and gifts, we are imagining a system that cannot provide as solid a foundation for all three of these virtues as the mixed system can.

It is important to realize exactly why this is so. Consider, first, that such an alternative system must be a system of *exchange*. Unless people are to dwell at or below the level of prosperity afforded by the most technologically debased sort of subsistence agriculture, they must work within a division of labor of some sort. This means that they will necessarily consume goods they do not themselves produce and produce goods that they cannot consume. In that case goods must somehow be passed from one individual to another. Since it would be both unworkable and undesirable to set up a central authority to dictate to whom all these surplus goods should go, people must voluntarily give at least some of them to each other. These donations must, at least sometimes, be part of an exchange of some sort: otherwise, one would have no way to acquire the rights to the surplus of another person, except to beg for them.

These voluntary donations must be either conditional, in the sense I have specified in section 4 of this chapter, or in the corresponding sense unconditional. In the latter case, the donations will be gifts, while, in the former, they will be commercial in nature. Further, if a pair of reciprocal donations constituting a given exchange begins with a gift, the other donation must be a gift as well, while, if the first donation is a commercial one, the other must likewise be commercial.[27] Thus, any given exchange must consist exclusively either of commercial acts or of gifts: there is no third alternative

---

[27] If I offer to give you three fish on condition that you give me a basket of corn, and you respond by simply giving me the corn as a gift, you have rejected my offer and there is, so far, no exchange of goods, but merely a unilateral transfer. On the other hand, if I make you a gift of three fish and you offer to give me a basket of corn for it—that is, if you offer to buy them from me—then you are proposing to transform my act into a commercial one and, if I accept your offer, that is what it will become.

type of exchange that somehow combines aspects of both trade and gift exchange.

The only workable alternatives to our mixed system of exchange, then, that are simpler in the sense that they do not include a distinction between commerce and gifts are, on the one hand, a pure gift-exchange system and, on the other, a commercial system unaccompanied by gifts. As a foundation for the three virtues I have claimed are anchored in the mixed one, each of these simpler systems is demonstrably poorer than the more complicated alternative.

In the first place, as I have recently suggested, it does not seem possible that a commercial system unchecked by an institution of gift giving would do anything to encourage generosity. Though it is true that, as proponents of the *doux-commerce* thesis might tell us, such a system would encourage people to act *as if* they were generous, and despite the obvious fact that this is a considerable benefit for a social system to provide, it is nonetheless also true that the trait thus encouraged is not what ethical theory calls generosity.

On the other hand, if the rules and practices of commercial transactions were plucked out of the world and gift-exchange were carried on without them, the resulting system, regarded as a foundation for the sort of self-respect that consists in showing an adequate appreciation for one's rights, would thereby be severely damaged. In such a system, human beings would entirely lack certain powers that, as I have said, are a powerfully salient feature of individuals in a commercial system of exchange. The inhabitants of a pure gift system would see themselves as essentially passive in relation to a fundamental class of rights and obligations. They must take it as a matter of course, much more than we do, that their rights and obligations fall on them without their own consent, in ways that often allow them no way to escape them if they should want to. In such a world, self-respect would lack some of the support it is granted in ours.

The same thing is true of the relevant sort of justice, and for the very same reason. The conditions in which the inhabitants of such a world find one another are precisely the same as those in which they find themselves, as far as the relevant classes of rights and obligations are concerned. This is also true of the commercial sector of a mixed system of exchange, except that in the one case everyone is fundamentally passive, while, in the other, everyone is a creator of many of their own rights and obligations. This feature of commerce—the fact that everyone in it sees everyone else, as well as themselves, as a creator of moral facts—enables it to instill respect for other people (see VII.6).[28] As I argued in chapter IV, section 2, respect for others is necessary if justice is to be a virtue. The capacity to instill respect for others that is possessed by a commercial system is essential to the power it has to support the particular sort of justice that is distinctive of such a system. A pure gift-exchange system would lack this capacity. It is true that it might effectively teach people to treat one another benevolently, but that is an entirely different matter: as I have argued earlier, benevolence is not the same trait as justice and the respect on which it depends, and it does not even form part of the foundation of justice (IV.4).

So far, the prospect of eliminating the complexity of our system of exchange appears to present us with a dilemma: if we embrace commerce unchecked and unadorned we can expect, other things being equal, to give up generosity to some extent; if we adopt a pure gift-exchange system we can expect, other things being equal, to sacrifice some measure of justice and self-respect.

Actually, the dilemma is worse than that. A pure gift-exchange system would not even be as well suited to provide a basis for generosity as would a practice of gift giving that has to coexist with a well-developed commercial system. Though this statement admittedly might seem paradoxical at first glance, the reason behind it is simple. It lies in the fact that a pure system, precisely because it must do all the work of a system of exchange by itself, must include a strong obligation to repay a first gift with a return gift. To the extent that it does include such an obligation, and to the extent that the system is in good working order, everyone in it who makes a first gift does so with the expectation that it will be repaid. This would certainly blunt the power such acts have to broadcast the message that people typically believe that the good of others is worth pursuing in itself.

It is true that in such a system first gifts, and return gifts, too, are well enough suited to the task of supporting solidarity, because they broadcast the message that people are willing to incur costs for the benefit of others, at least in the short run. Solidarity, as I have defined it, can exist provided only that people realize that their interests are so intertwined with those of others that they must incur costs for the benefit of others if they expect others to do the

---

[28] It is perhaps worth pointing out that this point is immediately relevant to the problem of tensions between the virtues, insofar as there might be any tensions between self-respect and virtuously just treatment of others. We have here a social basis for self-respect that can only be provided to one member of the system if it is provided to all and, for the same reason, also encourages one to view others as the virtue of justice requires. That is, these two virtues are institutionally connected.

same for them. Generosity, however, requires more than this. It involves, not merely pursuing the benefit of others, but doing it in a certain way: as an end in itself. Accordingly, it needs rather a stronger message than the one that suits solidarity well enough.

6. The Blessings of Compartmentalization

Despite what I have said in its defense, I am sure that the idea of segregating different virtues in different sectors of society will be more or less disturbing to some people. Indeed, there seems to be something about the notion of compartmentalizing the ethical life that is distasteful to all of us. Mauss was apparently moved to write *The Gift* by a longing for a world in which there was no hard distinction between business relations and relations between friends, in which the same act could be—and often was—an exchange, a personal avowal of benevolence, and even a ritual with religious meaning. Probably, most thoughtful people are susceptible to this same sentiment to some degree or other. When we reflect on the fact, for instance, that the Tarahumara word for "trading-partner"—*norawa*—is also the word for "friend," we are apt to feel at least a twinge of nostalgia for a world in which potentially clashing functions are integrated and life is whole and harmonious. It is difficult to deny the power of this nostalgia.

But what do we think is the harm in compartmentalizing life, so that generosity has its home in one sector of the social world, while self-respect and the sort of justice that is displayed in keeping one's word have their home in another, entirely different one?

The only plausible answer I can find runs more or less as follows. In a culture like ours, both gifts and trades are pervasively widespread phenomena. Not only are exchanges between people divided into two very different types but, as a consequence, there are two radically contrasting types of relations between people. On the one hand there are relations among trading partners and economic competitors, wherein exchanges are commercial. On the other hand, there are a range of relationships that are based on exchanges that are really gifts—free donations to the well-being of another person. These include friendships, love relationships, marriages and other relations within the family, and, to some extent, relations between neighbors: what we might call, for lack of any better term, "affiliations."[29] What is frightening about compartment-alization is that it suggests we can expect that the virtues that have their homes in these radically contrasting sectors of life will, so to speak, *stay* at home. In that case, commercial relations will be brutally tough-minded and, while technically staying within the letter of the principles of justice, will otherwise be coldly predatory, while affiliations will be sentimental and imprudent —even, on occasion, self-destructive. As a matter of fact, I must admit that this is more than a mere possibility: to some extent, the society we live in really is like this.[30]

If this is the reason for the longing for primordial simplicity, however, it embodies only some of the truths that are important in the present context. Though the greater complexity of society as we know it clearly brings hazards with it, it also affords moral resources that would not be available in the simpler alternative systems. These virtues can stay at home, but they can also be exported, and in the latter possibility lies one of the peculiar blessings of the division of moral tasks among institutions.

---

[29] For an interesting discussion of ethical issues raised by such relations, see Hugh LaFollette's *Personal Relationships: Love, Identity, and Morality* (Cambridge, Mass.: Blackwell, 1996).

[30] In effect, I am suggesting an account of the moral hazards of trade that contrasts sharply with the one given by Marx. He says that, because we live in a society with a strong commercial sector, "the only intelligible language that we speak to one another consists in our objects in relationships with one another. We would not understand a human speech and it would remain ineffective. . . ." That is, we are unable to either make or receive a request in which help is asked for simply as a free donation to someone's well-being: "on the one hand it would be seen and felt as an entreaty or a prayer and thus as a humiliation and therefore used with shame and a feeling of abasement, while on the other side it would be judged brazen and insane and as such rejected." "On James Mill," in *Karl Marx: Selected Writings*, ed. David McClellan (Oxford: Oxford University Press, 1977), p. 121. He is saying, I take it, that the traits of the commercial sector *displace* those of the gift-exchange sector altogether. The facts, I think, are not nearly that simple. It is true that, if I find I must ask a perfect stranger for a small favor (for instance, I have no change and need to ask for a quarter to make a telephone call), I will find my own request embarrassing and the stranger might find it annoying. However, it is also true that if I ask a small favor of a friend (for instance, "As long as you're up, could you get me another beer out of the fridge?"), I feel no embarrassment at all. Of course, if I ask for a very large favor, I might be embarrassed in both cases, but the difference in the degree of felt awkwardness is so great that it signals a difference in kind. We are related to intimates very differently from the way in which we are related to strangers and other nonintimates, and commercial relations have not destroyed this difference by making friendly relations impossible.

The reasons for this are implicit in a number of things I have said about various virtues. First, consider the fact that, as I have recently pointed out, the gift sector of a mixed system is better suited to provide a basis for generosity than a pure gift-exchange system would be. Second, to the extent that the institution of the gift does effectively support generosity, it encourages a trait that is an enduring impetus to action with a scope that is potentially very broad. The principle of generosity is utterly general and can be applied to any context in which the agent finds an opportunity to benefit someone. It does not apply merely to some narrowly specified range of contexts (Christmas and birthdays, for instance) in which convention urges the giving of gifts. This means that the gift sector opens the way to an indefinite variety of forms of conduct that would not be so readily available to people who, other things being equal, were not subject to the influence of such an institution.

Moreover, there is reason to expect that these forms of conduct *will* invade the commercial sector of society. Admittedly, it is true that the basic rights that constitute the fundamental institutions of commercial exchange are compatible with heartless behavior. It is quite possible to refrain from the force and fraud that these rights proscribe while, at the same time, squeezing every bit of benefit we can get from our trading partners. As far as the moral foundations of trade are concerned, such harsh conduct is always one's right. However, it is also true that to refrain from doing something harmful or annoying to another person, when one has a right to do it, is to confer a benefit on them (III.5). In other words, the possibilities of gentler conduct in commercial relations are also opportunities for generosity. Further, the gift element of the exchange system will enable people to see them as such. They see the end toward which the opportunities aim as something that is good and worth pursuing in itself.

If they conduct business under the influence of the gift element of the system, people will be more likely than they would otherwise have been to supplement the fundamental commercial institutions with traditions of fair play and restraint that counteract its potential for excessive toughness. The extent to which they will actually do so is, of course, a matter of individual insight and choice. The point, however, is this: a practice of gift giving that does not do all the work of a system of exchange by itself can function as a resource on which individual conduct can rely in other sectors in the system.

We find analogous effects if we look at influences that run in the other direction, from the sector of commercial relations to that of affiliations. Relationships that are based on unconditional donations to the well-being of another person are not measurably less hazardous than commercial relations.

They are merely dangerous in an entirely different way. However, as we will see, their hazards are diminished if their influence is checked by relationships that are based on trade.

To found a relationship on unconditional giving is a risky thing to do, especially in a culture that has few clear and strong obligations to reciprocate them. In commercial relationships, anything we give to our partners is given on the condition, more or less explicit, that we get something in return. Since each such exchange is voluntary, we always specify conditions that are such that what we expect them to accomplish for us will be more valuable to us than whatever we give. Because this is true of everybody involved, every step in the formation of the relationship serves—provided only that our expectations are borne out—our mutual advantage.

Nothing like this is true of affiliations, and this fact alone is enough to make these two sorts of relations profoundly different. First, in affiliations there is no explicit understanding concerning what the participants are to get out of it, and consequently there are no very definite rules about what any one of them may do or not do. If friendships and families are like little states, they tend to be like states with no laws and no constitution. Second, not only is there no explicit understanding as to what the participants have coming to them, there is not even very definite tacit understanding of such things.

The reason for these features of affiliations is very simple: it is that, as I have said, such relations consist of unconditional donations to the well-being of one's partner. Obviously, this fact is inseparable from features of affiliations that make them profoundly important to us: they have, at least, incomparably more emotional importance than commercial relations have. We do not attach conditions when we give things to our friends and lovers, or when we make a gift of our time and effort simply by doing things for them, precisely because we value their well-being as something good in itself and trust them to do the same by us. To do otherwise would be to suggest either that we value our partners for what we can persuade them to give us, or that our trust that they will reciprocate is not real.

However, trusting someone is always somewhat hazardous. Some of the hazards involved have little to do with the character of the individual one is trusting and, in fact, have deep implications for the nature of affiliations as such. Like relations based on trade, affiliations—at least between adults—are voluntary. Even when these relations are based on unchosen connections such as relations of blood, we remain personally connected with the people involved, if we do, by choice. This means that, in general, we expect that participating in these relationships will be more valuable to us, in that they will produce more of whatever it is that we regard as good, than not participating in them. This, after all, is part of what the trust that such relationships rest on is all about: we trust our partners to care about our aims and about our notions about what is good. However, the fact that this trust is and must be expressed by unconditional donations creates an environment in which it is easy to violate it.

Given the absence of a clear obligation to reciprocate unconditional donations to the good of another, such relationships can drift into a state of affairs that, for one of the parties involved, produces less good than would be produced by withdrawing from the relationship. As the relationship develops, donations can tend to flow from the more gullible and generous partners to the ones who are more aggressive or more skillful at expressing their "needs" and imposing them on others.[31] The result is often a relation between parties of dangerously unequal power, which, nonetheless, everyone involved takes for granted. Relations that are based on mutual acts of unconditional benevolence are an ideal field for exploitation: to become an exploiter, one need only accept the benevolence of another and fail to *really* respond in kind. Because no one is aware of any explicit conditions attached to the benevolence of the victim, such behavior can be very difficult to notice and even more difficult to remedy. And yet it seems imperative that the victims do both of these things. Their degraded position, after all, represents a serious threat to their self-respect.[32]

---

[31] Talk of one's "needs" is a familiar technique used by exploitative friends and lovers: in this context, such talk is no more than a coercive way of presenting one's wants as a law that binds others to one's service.

[32] These reflections suggest a sociological hypothesis that, if it were fully developed, might be described as a non-Marxist theory of exploitation and class conflict. It states that classes of exploiters tend to emerge when one group of people is supported by obligatory unconditional donations from another group of people, provided that the participants in the system do not believe that any particular donation entitles the donor to a particular requital from the recipient class. The fact that these transfers are both obligatory and unconditional would mean that the donors would not withhold the benefits of their largesse in the event that the recipients do little or nothing in return. The exploitation would consist in the fact that, not surprisingly, the recipients as a group do little or nothing in return. Two examples of groups that, according to this theory, would tend to become exploiting classes would be governments (together with their dependents) and priestly castes. The theory would predict that governments would tend to be exploiting classes because taxes are a clear example of donations of the relevant kind. More precisely, they are examples of a certain subclass, since they are not only unconditional and obligatory, but compulsory (that is, enforced by physical coercion). Priests are sometimes supported by unconditional acts of beneficence that, though not compulsory, are regarded as obligatory. The anthropologist Jonathan Parry writes that

The fact that love and friendship lack the rigid framework of rights and obligations that we find in commercial relations means that they present us with an opportunity for perfect liberty of action, but they also bring the threat of undetectable and irremediable oppression. Individuals who are faced with the difficult task of noticing and remedying the fact that they are being victimized can find a powerful resource in the principles and practices that form the basis of commercial relations. Whatever remedy the victim might try to use, the point of the remedy *must* be, assuming the relationship is not abandoned altogether, to transform it into one that really is mutually beneficial. Further, there is liable to be no effective way to achieve this other than, either implicitly or by means of explicit threats, attaching conditions to the exploiter's continuing to receive something of value that the victim provides. Victims can do this by indicating somehow that the relationship is a voluntary one and that they are capable of ending it if it is not good for them. Alternatively, the victim may simply cut the supply of some benefit the victimizer used to enjoy, whether that benefit is money, sex, kind and civil treatment from the victim, or something else of value.

If they are successful, these methods will have the effect of making the victim's contributions to the relationship (at least some of them) conditional on the erstwhile victimizer's good behavior. This would mean that the relationship is being repaired by making it more closely resemble a trade. The most powerful protection against the pitfalls of an affiliation is momentarily to commercialize it.

Of course, such protection brings with it hazards of its own. Victims who defend themselves in these ways are posing a threat to the continued existence of the relationship. They are admitting that they do not entirely trust their partners and this, together with the fact that they are countering covert

---

the pilgrims to the holy city of Benares consider it their duty to ply the priests there with a sort of gift known among them as *dana*, "a voluntary and disinterested donation made without . . . expectation of *any* kind of *this*-worldly return": "Though there are no comparable figures for the present day, Bayly reports that at the beginning of the nineteenth century there were more than 40,000 Brahmans living off religious gifts, that is between 17 and 20 per cent of the total population." "On the Moral Perils of Exchange," in *Money and the Morality of Exchange*, ed. J. Parry and M. Bloch (Cambridge, Mass.: Cambridge University Press, 1989), p. 66. The feature of this story that suggests, at least to me, the possibility that these people constituted to some extent a class of exploiting drones is not the fact that the services they performed were priestly in nature; it is the fact that, as Parry points out, "*dana* is a *gift* and *not* a reimbursement for priestly services, which are rewarded . . . by a separate emolument" (p. 71).

manipulation with open and frank manipulation, involves a more or less open admission that the relationship may lose its character as an affiliation altogether. Such methods are not friendly ones. Nonetheless, the protection of their own good might require such a desperate response.

These methods of safeguarding affiliations against their own hazards can have a very important meaning for the people who use them. In protecting their own good in this way, they are creating new rights for themselves, and they are creating and protecting these rights by means of their own ability—perceived and confirmed by others as well as themselves—to produce something of value to other human beings. In this way, what they are doing lends powerful support to their sense of their own dignity and their continuing ability to preserve and enhance it. The means by which they are protecting their own interests function as moral resources that support crucial elements of their self-respect.

More obviously, these protective measures also work to make the relationships that threaten these interests less unjust—that is, they serve to make the positions occupied by the threatened individuals less unfair than they were before. As a matter of fact, they do more than that. Until and unless individuals who are connected by affiliation manage to reach agreements that create rights between them, the way they treat one another probably cannot be characterized by the virtue of justice at all. We can only treat a person justly, in this sense, if we do whatever it is we are doing because we think it is that person's due. To the extent that the ties that bind us to someone are the sort that are created by gift exchange, we do whatever we do because we think it is good for them. There are two very different sets of concerns at work here: justice and well-being. Aristotle tells us that "if people are friends, there is no need of justice between them."[33] I have argued, in effect, that this is actually not true: there sometimes is a need to impose justice on affiliations. But it is an imposition. It is in the nature of such relations to run on a very different set of principles, within which we seek the well-being of others and trust them to seek ours.

To the extent that people participate in a commercial society, they have learned certain principles to the effect that rights can be created by agreement, and by certain skills that enable them to protect their interests by granting or withholding their consent to supply benefits that others wish to acquire from them. Indeed, the fact that people participate in a commercial society simply

---

[33] Aristotle, *Nicomachean Ethics*, Rackham trans. slightly altered, 1155a27.

is the fact that they act on such principles and exercise such skills as these. But these principles and skills are like the principle of generosity in that they can be applied to a broad class of situations that reach far beyond the narrow context in which they have their home. People can rely on them in any context in which they seek better treatment from those who have some benefit to gain from them, provided only that they are able to decide whether to grant this benefit or not. These contexts include all affiliations of any kind. By definition, such relations are ones in which the individuals involved make reciprocal free donations to one another's well-being, and such donations are actions that they are quite capable of either doing or not doing, at their own discretion.

These safeguards against the manipulation and exploitation that threaten affiliations are available to people because the live in a system in which some relations are not affiliations but are instead commercial relations. Further, since commercial relations consist precisely in the fact that people do use the principles and skills on which these safeguards rely, they would *only* be available to people who live in a society that to some extent or other includes a commercial sector. In a pure gift-exchange system, they would simply not exist.

IX

Punishment and Revenge

Hatred and anger are the greatest poison to the happiness of a good mind.
—Adam Smith, *The Theory of Moral Sentiments*

1. Character and the Minimal Functions of the State

In the course of defending the American Revolution, Thomas Paine made a statement that neatly distinguishes between the functions performed by various institutional arrangements:

> Some writers have so confounded society with government, as to leave little or no distinction between them; whereas, they are not only different, but have different origins. Society is produced by our wants, and government by our wickedness; the former promotes our happiness *positively* by uniting our affections, the latter *negatively* by restraining our vices. . . . The first is a patron, the last is a punisher.[1]

Part of what Paine meant to express here was a conception of government that for a long time had considerable influence in this country. This was the idea that, as Paine says elsewhere in the same pamphlet, "security" is "the true design and end of government."[2] That is, government should only carry out what might be called the minimal functions of the state: those in which it either discourages the use of force and fraud by exacting retribution from those who use them or compels such offenders to make amends for what they have done by compensating their victims. What government does is negative: it corrects human misbehavior. For the rest, Paine meant to say that the positive benefits we can expect from our institutions must come from "society," which is simply

---

[1] Thomas Paine, *Common Sense*, in *Tracts of the American Revolution*, ed. Merrill Jensen (Indianapolis: Bobbs-Merrill, 1977), pp. 402-3.

[2] Ibid., p. 403.

the nongovernmental part the social world. These benefits include positive effects on our character, or what he called "the affections." One clear implication of this is that the state can have no positive effect on character. Indeed, this idea seems to be logically connected, for Paine, with his minimalist conception of government: the proper business of government is to carry out its minimal functions and we *therefore* cannot expect it have a positive effect on what sorts of people we are.

At times one of these ideas, or one of their presuppositions, has been used to defend a conception of government that in one respect is the opposite of the one Paine held. George Will has argued that the minimalist conception of the state is wrong on the ground that government ought to engage in "soulcraft," in the activity of making better people of us. Though his conclusion is the opposite of Paine's, there is an assumption lurking behind it that is identical to one that Paine relies on: if the state does not deliberately perform any functions but the minimal ones, it will have no reliable positive effect on the character of its subjects.[3]

In this chapter I will argue that this assumption, shared by the radical individualist Paine and the conservative communitarian Will, is not true. I maintain that, as states perform their minimal functions—in particular, as they enforce the criminal law—they do tend to have a certain beneficial effect on the character of the people to whom their laws apply. This effect is a result of certain morally important differences between the way in which states exact retribution and the way in which it would be exacted by the victims and private individuals acting in their behalf: by displacing private retribution, the state helps to drain revenge from the community it governs. It does so by means that also serve to ease the tension that we earlier saw exists between forgiveness and self-respect (IV.5). It has these effects, not as the result of artful intentions on the part of legislators, but inevitably and spontaneously.

In this chapter I will give reasons for thinking that my thesis is true, and will try to make them more vivid by asking the reader to imagine what would happen if the minimal functions of the state were performed by private protection agencies, business firms that, for a fee, would exact retribution from individuals who victimize their clients.

---

[3] Will does not actually say this, but his book on this subject, which is otherwise very intelligently written, would be a massive non sequitur without it. See George F. Will, *Statecraft as Soulcraft: What Government Does* (New York: Simon and Schuster, 1983).

2. Punishment

I will begin by pointing out some linguistic facts, certain differences between the ways we speak in different circumstances. In a later section of this chapter I will provide evidence that these differences in speech reflect real and important differences between the facts we are speaking about in those circumstances, but I will not be concerned with that just yet.

Suppose that a friend of mine does something to offend me. Overcome by anger, I slap him for it. There are a number of things that might be said about such behavior, but no one, I think, would say that I have punished him. No one would say, "You punished him too severely" or "It's barbaric to punish your friends with violence—use more civilized methods." This is what we call "getting back at" someone, or "getting even." Whatever I might do to my friends and however harshly or gently I might do it, I cannot be said to punish them. On the other hand, when parents slap their children, that is the sort of thing that *can* be called punishment. We observe this distinction even if we think in both cases the slapped person had it coming.

Why is it that one of these acts is not a punishment while the other is? One might think that the reason why the first case is not called punishment is that it is a "selfish" act: I hit him just because I don't like what he did *to me*. That is what "getting back at" someone is. But it would still not be called punishment if I had slapped my friend for offending my brother. I can get back at someone in someone else's behalf—altruistically, one might say.

It will be easy to give a more adequate account of the differences between these cases, though still only a partial one, if we consider a few more examples. The charges that my bank levies against me when I carelessly over-draw my account resemble the fines a government might exact from me, except that while what the government thereby does to me can be called a punishment, what the bank does cannot. If the Israeli government assassinates a Palestinian terrorist in Lebanon, that is not called punishment, even if the killing is ordered because the terrorist killed fifty Israelis the week before, and even if it is carried out because the terrorist is thought to deserve it. On the other hand, if the same government executes an Israeli subject for killing someone, we do call that punishment (even if we think that the subject is innocent or the penalty is excessive).

From these examples we can extract certain general principles that, I think, are all true. People are not said to punish their friends; businesses are not said to punish their clients; governments are not said to punish their external enemies. Governments are said to punish their subjects, parents are said to punish their children. There is a pattern here that is perhaps obvious by now: in the case where one is said to punish, one is thought to have authority over the person one punishes; in the other cases this is not so.

"Punishment," as we ordinarily use the word, is not identical to what Nietzsche called "the drama" of punishment: "a certain strict set of procedures" such as, to use Nietzsche's grim examples, drawing and quartering, boiling in oil, or dropping a millstone on the malefactor's head.[4] We have also seen that punishment is not identical to retribution, either; we still do not have the concept of punishment if we add to the idea of "the drama" the notion that such things are done to give the victim what he or she deserves. One must add—at least—that the one who does it is in a position of authority over the one to whom it is done. This does not mean that only those in such a position have a right to punish; only they may do something that *counts as* punishing.

Punishment is generally spoken of as a perfectly proper human activity. The alternative sorts of retribution, most often called "revenge" and "vengeance," are treated quite differently, as something ignoble. Their names seem to function in our language as the names both of passions and of vices, and even when treated as passions they are generally referred to with disapproval.

Here, as elsewhere, though, one needn't follow the way people generally speak. One can take at least two different points of view on the conventional relations between punishment, authority, and revenge. On the one hand, we might think that punishment is the same human activity as revenge; we simply *call* it punishment when it is done to us by our superiors. The enormous emotive difference between "punishment" and "revenge" merely signifies that we accept from our superiors a sort of treatment that we would not stand for from our equals. What seems to be a great moral difference is simply a symptom of human servility. On the other hand, we might take the view that these are two genuinely different forms of conduct and that there is something in the nature of authority, or of some kinds of authority, that makes this difference possible. People in authority, or some of them, are in a position to do things that are proper and not ignoble.

While the first of these two points of view is surely not entirely false, I think the second is entirely true. Before I try to show this, I should say something about what authority is.

---

[4] Friedrich Nietzsche, *On the Genealogy of Morals*, in *Basic Writings of Nietzsche*, trans. and ed. Walter Kaufmann (New York: The Modern Library, 1968), pp. 498 and 515.

3. Authority

We can divide authorities into two kinds. On the one hand, some people are said to be authorities on certain subjects, such as numismatics or economics. On the other hand, some people have authority over other people, such as their children or their employees. One may be an authority *on* a subject or *over* people. I will call the former sort "theoretical" authorities and the latter "practical" authorities.

One exercises theoretical authority by making statements. If someone with this sort of authority makes a statement within the sphere of his or her competence, that is a good reason for believing what that statement says. If Joe DiMaggio says, "This is the way to hold a baseball bat," his saying so is evidence that this is the way to hold a baseball bat. Note that this means that one may be a theoretical authority on practical matters—on what is to be done. Theoretical authority is not distinguished from the practical kind by its subject matter. Practical authority is exercised by issuing orders. If a mother tells her five-year-old son to go to bed, that is a good reason for the son to go to bed. When a practical authority issues an order, it is a good reason to do what the order tells one to do.

It is not difficult to see why both sorts of authority are called by the same name: in both cases, an authority is a creator of reasons. But there is an important difference between them that is relevant here. Theoretical authorities are not said to punish people. Accordingly, when I say "authority" in what follows, I will mean practical authority.

What I have said about authority is admittedly brief and sketchy, but it enables us to ask with some clarity whether and in what way it is necessary for states to possess either the reality or the appearance of authority. It seems easy to imagine a state that carries out its minimal functions without claiming to have any authority over its subjects. Such an organization, it seems, could pursue and catch people who violate the rights of others and then do such things as taking their property, confining them in prisons, or killing them. Its representatives could execute murderers without claiming that the reason they should have refrained from murder was that the state had laid down laws *telling* them to refrain. They may simply hold that murderers should not act as they do because it violates the rights of others. They need not tell murderers that they are putting them to death because they disobeyed the state; they may just claim that they are killing them because they are murderers. They might even claim that, on grounds having to do with risk and procedural justice, they are the only ones who have the right to exact retribution for such behavior.

None of this would amount to claiming authority, because in none of it do they claim that their say-so by itself constitutes a reason why their subjects should do what they say.[5] But what I have said earlier clearly suggests that a state that claims no authority cannot make one particular claim that all states do in fact make, one that seems essential to the nature of the state: it suggests that they cannot claim that, in doing such things as putting people to death, they are punishing them. In this way, at least, the concept of authority does seem to be essential to understanding the state.

The short account of the nature of authority that I have given suggests one possible way to explain why only practical authorities can punish. Only practical authorities can issue orders that are reasons for doing what the order enjoins. Thus, only they can enforce such orders; only they can harm people for disobeying authoritative orders *that they have issued.*

Unless this account is amended somehow, it will surely do my case no good, because it does not show how punishment could be superior to nonauthoritative retribution. In fact, unless it is augmented, it rather tends to show the reverse. If this is all there is to it, authorities, when punishing people, would seem simply to be trying to get back at them for ignoring their orders and thus insulting them by implicitly denying their authority. This would mean that punishment is simply a sort of revenge that is peculiar to people who claim to possess authority.

Actually, there is another reason for thinking that this account is in fact not complete. If this were a full explanation of the conceptual connections between authority and punishment, all practical authorities would be treated as competent to punish, but in fact they are not. This can be seen by considering a few examples. Employers are treated as having authority over their employees: they give orders and, normally, they are obeyed. Yet, although they can enforce their orders by threatening their subordinates with unpleasant things, such penalties are not generally referred to as punishments. Doctors are typically viewed as practical as well as theoretical authorities—we take "doctor's orders" to be reasons for doing whatever it is the doctor orders. Teachers are thought to exercise a sort of authority over their students, but the

---

[5] Nonminimal states must claim authority because, unlike minimal states, they require us to do things that we had no reason to do before the state began to require them. Everyone has reasons for being generally helpful to people in need, but a government that requires us to help the needy through our taxes requires us to give a certain amount of money to a certain organization to help the needy, and *that* is something we had no reason to do before the relevant laws were passed.

low grades they give students who do not do their work are not called punishments.

What reason might there be for regarding these authorities as not competent to punish? They have a number of relevant characteristics in common. In each case, the authority of the person is the result of a contract into which that person and his or her subordinates have entered freely. They have come together, not to pursue a whole way of life together, but only to satisfy certain specific desires with relatively limited objectives. In the examples I have cited, these desires include the desire for remunerated work, the desire for medical treatment, and the desire for knowledge. Punishment requires an area of concern that is in some sense broader than the sort involved here. For instance, authorities, in punishing, may thereby express a concern for their subordinates' true welfare (as when parents punish their children for playing with fire and paternalistic governments punish their subjects for using heroin), or they may express a concern for whether their subordinates' behavior is morally right or wrong (for instance, whether it constitutes a wrongful use of force). Both of these concerns are typical of the two practical authorities I have mentioned that are regarded as competent to punish: parents and states.

4. The Problem of Revenge

This is no doubt an incomplete explanation of why some authorities can punish, but it already has implications regarding the question that most immediately concerns me here: how can the punishments that at least some authorities perform plausibly be held to be morally superior to revenge? I have said that the fact that some authorities are not regarded as competent to punish has something to do with the way in which the actions of those authorities are prompted by the desires of certain people. It can be argued, on the other hand, that certain authorities that *are* said to punish people are in a position to plausibly claim that, when they punish, their own desires are not involved in the same way and to the same extent they would be if their punishments were acts of vengeance. It can also be argued that when this claim is true, what they do is morally superior to revenge.

To show this, some definitions are needed. "Resentment" is an emotion that is inspired by the thought that one has been wronged. If I experience resentment, it is because I interpret the thing that was done as wrong *and* because I realize that this thing was done *to me*. It is a quite different sort of passion from what I will call "indignation," which is provoked simply by thinking that a wrong has been done. When I am indignant either I am upset about a wrong done to someone else, or I am upset about a wrong done to me *just as I would be* if it were done to someone else. The fact that it was done to me is not part of what makes me feel this way. It does seem possible to be merely indignant about a wrong done to oneself. I say "merely" because resentment has a peculiar, poisonous intensity that indignation generally lacks.

In the sense in which it is the name of an emotion, "revenge" (or "vengeance") is the sort of resentment in which the crucial interpretation—that someone has wronged oneself—gives rise to a felt desire to harm the one who has done the wrong. It is a desire for retribution.

What is wrong with revenge, regarded as a passion? First, it is easy to find objections to the sort of behavior that typically flows out of revenge. Such conduct has a number of undesirable consequences. Partly because it is such an intense passion, it tends to make us overestimate the wrong we have suffered and thereby tends to make us exact more retribution than strict justice would allow. In the same way, it goads us into harming the innocent. Both these excesses provoke vengeful reactions in others, which begins the vicious spiral of feuding.[6]

What is much more important for my present purpose is the fact that, even apart from these consequences, the passion of revenge tends to have bad effects on people who experience it. Because of these effects they are liable to become worse human beings and live worse lives than before. The effects involved follow not so much from vengeful behavior itself as from the passions and standards of value that lie behind it. When wrongs that have been done inspire resentment, the individuals who experience it think about those wrongs more than they would have otherwise. They brood over them. The more they think about their grievances, the more resentful they feel. If left to itself, this cycle can spiral into a monomania that pushes more rational interests aside and clouds the principled concern for right and wrong that inspires resentment in the first place. Even if they do not do anything, they become *willing* to do things that they would have considered beneath themselves before. Through resentment, their principled rejection of wrongdoing undermines itself.

Revenge unsettles one's reason. The cycle it begins is difficult to break because, although, as Adam Smith said, there is "something harsh, jarring, and

---

[6] These are among the "inconveniences" of the "state of nature"—that is, of a world without government—named by John Locke and Robert Nozick. See Nozick's *Anarchy, State, and Utopia* (New York: Basic Books, 1974), pp. 10-11.

convulsive"[7] about resentment, there is also something curiously *pleasant* in the cruel fantasies it brings with it. It leads to ways of thinking, irrational and out of control, that seem bad in themselves, but at least as important is the content of this thinking and of the resulting behavior. It tends to distance us from other people, resulting in a certain all-too-familiar objectification of the other and a resulting indifference and hostility to their well-being. In other words, it undermines the values that forgiveness promotes: our concern for the good of others and our connection with them.

All these objections to revenge, regarded as an emotion, are compounded by the fact that it is closely related to a vice that sometimes goes by the same name, though it is more often called "vengefulness" or perhaps "vindictiveness." The most troublesome aspect of this relationship is, simply, that experiencing the passion can easily cause one to also have the vice.

The emotion of revenge, being a species of resentment, is based on a standard of value. In this way it is like any other emotion (see V.8). In the case of resentment the standard is one that implies that something that has been done to oneself is wrong. This standard might be shared by many other people, including ones who are incapable of revenge. Revenge includes something in addition to this: it also contains a felt desire to get back at the one who did the harm, a desire that arises from the belief that the wrong was done to oneself. As a passion, however, revenge does not include a belief that doing such harm is *justified*. When one is in the grips of vengeful feelings, harming the enemy *seems* like the thing to do, but this is a matter of emotional interpretation. It is partly for this reason that the passion of revenge can be a mere episode, unrelated to one's enduring character.

As a passion, revenge can be experienced and acted on akratically: one can act on it despite the fact that one does not believe that vindictive behavior is really justified. The akrasia begins to disappear when one begins to accept a certain principle that, unlike the one that lies behind resentment, is not shared by all sorts of people. This is the notion that wrongs to oneself do justify getting even with the perpetrator. The justification need not be the sort of thing that a contemporary moral philosopher would think of as a moral justification. It might be based on a medieval conception of honor or a mere belief in the absolute necessity of maintaining an appearance of invulnerable power. The transformation of revenge into a trait of character is complete if this principle, whatever it might be based on, becomes a settled part of one's own behavior.

---

[7] Adam Smith, *The Theory of Moral Sentiments* (Indianapolis: Liberty Classics, 1976), p. 92.

As I have said, one of the hazards of the passion of revenge is the fact that it can lead to the formation of the vice of revenge. The brief description I have just given of the vice indicates part of the reason why the passion is liable to lead to it. Ordinary life, unfortunately, brings us many occasions, both petty and grand, for the passion of revenge. People who experience an emotion persistently are under some pressure to see it as justified. This is particularly true if they act on it. One feels called on to rationalize the emotion by developing views that would justify it, and this lends some appearance of rightness to the actions that flow from it. But this change in how our actions appear is the sort of change that I have just said is essential to hardening the passion of revenge into an entrenched trait of character. Once we have undergone this transformation, we accept a principle to the effect that wrongs to oneself justify getting even with the perpetrator.

Further, if what I have said about vengeful behavior and the passion of revenge is true, this trait of character is a vice. All the objections raised against them applies to it as well, but with greater force. To have this trait of character means to increase the frequency of these intense feelings and confused thoughts, with a corresponding increase in the undesirable practical consequences. But the difference the trait of character makes is not just a matter of quantity, of more of the same bad things happening. As long as my vengefulness is a matter of having the episodic thoughts and feelings that come to most of us from time to time, they come to me unbidden and perhaps unwelcome. However much I am to blame for my reactions to them or what they lead me to do, I can still say that they do not represent who I am or what I stand for. If my vengefulness becomes a trait of character, however, this saving truth is no longer available to me. I am no longer the weak victim of my thoughts and feelings: I have gone over to the enemy's side. Not only am I somehow deluded into thinking that these things that I am doing are right, but this error of mine is the *reason* I am doing them.

Clearly, it would be desirable to do something about the passions of revenge and resentment, if that is possible. But what should we do about them? There is certainly no question of eliminating both of them from our lives altogether. Even if that were possible I submit that, paradoxical as this might sound, it would not be desirable.   Part of the reason for this lies in some psychological facts that I will assume are familiar ones. It seems to be inevitable that most of us are upset when people victimize others. It seems almost as inevitable that most of us believe in the moral appropriateness of retribution of some sort. Of course, not all of us live by the principle that "everything is dischargeable, everything must be discharged" (see IV.2), but most of us do think that retribution of some sort is at least a fitting response to wrongdoing and is often the right thing to do. There are probably good reasons why we *should* think this, but for the present the point is that most of us do think that way and will probably continue to do so.

Given this, eliminating resentment would amount to replacing it with indignation: if we somehow eliminated the highly personal negative emotional responses to wrongs done to us, we would experience the impersonal one instead. That is, we would be upset about wrongs done to ourselves just as we would be if they were done to someone else. This would mean being utterly indifferent to one's own dignity in the sense in which I have been using it, in which dignity is the fact that one appears, in one's own eyes, to be a worthy human being. Wrongs committed against oneself are always assaults against one's dignity in this sense (see II.5).

This is part of the reason we are so upset when we think someone has wronged us. This psychological fact seems, once again, to be more or less inevitable. The only way to avoid being upset for this sort of reason, other than having a sense of one's own worth that is so invulnerable that it cannot be touched by the world, would be to be unconcerned about one's worth at all. The former way seems quite impossible for most of us and the latter is highly undesirable. But this means that one component of one's upset about wrongs done to oneself will be that one realizes that it was done *to oneself*, and this means that it constitutes resentment and not mere indignation.

This concern with our own dignity, necessary and desirable though it is, stands at the beginning of a process that, if it is not hindered, causes serious harm to the community and to the character and well-being of the individual. The common belief that some sort of retributive response is appropriate to wrongdoing provides those who are its victims with a ready antidote to the hurts their dignity has suffered. If someone has mistreated me, that is palpable evidence that I am unable to prevent such things from being done to me. As such, it is evidence (maybe smartingly good evidence) that I am impotent. If I manage to exact some sort of retribution, even if it is retribution of a mild sort, that would tend to show that I lack this negative characteristic and have instead a certain positive one, namely, efficacy. Depending on the context, my efficacy will indicate to me various other positive traits, including perhaps courage, resourcefulness, and various sorts of skill. But if one wants to take this solution one is not merely resentful; one is experiencing the passion of revenge.

The line between self-respect and revenge is very thin. Concern with one's dignity, together with ideas and traits that are perfectly reasonable and normal, seems to lead very naturally to an emotion that has an explosive power to do harm. The problem is how interrupt the process by which this happens.

Most likely, this interruption must occur after the beginning of the process: suppressing all concern for one's dignity is not an option, and as long as there is any such concern the potential for revenge is there. In the scenario I have presented, revenge does not come from excessive concern for dignity, but from reaching for the wrong antidotes to a sense of degradation that may, for all that, be perfectly legitimate.

A more modest sort of solution to our problem would be to introduce the interruption fairly late in the process: instead of trying to obliterate all concern for one's own dignity, or all forms of resentment, or indeed even revenge itself, we might try to contain the influence that the passion of revenge has over the workings of our minds. Revenge, after all, seems to be the proximate cause of the trouble I have described. As we have already seen, we can to some extent contain the passion of revenge if we can prevent it from growing into a settled trait of character. Both the power of revenge and its badness increase greatly if one accepts a principle that justifies it. Essentially, it is this acceptance that transforms it into a trait of character. Without this transformation, one's resentment either remains an isolated episode or, at worst, a temperamental disposition against which one can struggle akratically. To the extent that this transformation can be prevented, a particularly virulent form of resentment will have been contained, and without simply repressing it from consciousness.

5. A Solution

Even this relatively modest approach to the problem might seem dauntingly difficult. It does require of me that I exert control over the influence my emotions have on the rest of my life, and it is not obvious how this can be done.

Actually, it is not as difficult as I have perhaps made it seem. As we have seen in the last three chapters, my efforts to alter or preserve my character do not take place entirely in the solitude of my own mind. Around me are institutions that act as a sort of moral furniture, supporting me in this enterprise. In particular, the state performs this sort of service as it carries out its minimal functions. To the extent that its authority and the conventions that surround it are accepted by its subjects, it helps to drain malicious resentment from the community it governs. It does so by discouraging thoughts that justify revenge and extend its power over us.

Parents sometimes claim that in punishing their children they are doing it for the children's own good. We often find this claim a plausible one because we believe—with some reason—that concern for the child's welfare is natural in parents and can be stronger than anger at the child's misbehavior. Thus, at least on occasion, we can reasonably believe that parental punishment is not a vengeful act.

Governments, by means of various symbols and ceremonies, and also through direct statement, make the same sort of claim. The beliefs thus fostered, and the trust that arises from them, are probably indispensable conditions for the stable existence of states. In the case of governments, such professions of disinterestedness are much more plausible than they are in the case of parents. The misdeeds for which parents punish their children are often things that harm or irritate the parents themselves: the child has ruined an expensive machine or been distractingly noisy, and so forth. This means that occasions for parental punishment often present temptations for parental vengeance. Except in a small number of cases (such as treason) this sort of thing is not true of the misdeeds for which states punish their subjects. One can imagine the officials of a state being irritated with a burglar for showing so little respect for their laws against theft, but they are not *victims* of the theft, and the provocation they have suffered is a far less serious insult than what the victim has suffered. The state generally does not have that personal stake in the matter that is required by revenge: it is what Locke appropriately calls "an indifferent judge."[8] For the most part, when it punishes someone, it is not getting revenge for harm done to it.

Nonetheless, what the state does would still be vengeful if it were seeking retribution for the victim's sake—this is the sort of thing I would be doing if I slapped my friend for offending my brother. But in various ways governments claim, more or less convincingly, that insofar as they enforce the criminal law for the sake of someone's interests, they do it for the sake of the community in general: more precisely, they do it to deter the sort of injustice the criminal has perpetrated and, thus, to protect the community from danger. This, officially, is part of what distinguishes the laws thereby enforced as criminal, in contrast to the civil law which affords remedies to private individuals.

Moreover, most states disseminate the belief that what motivates their officials is to a large extent not a goal at all, not even the goal one seeks out of honest indignation: rather, they are moved to act by the law and by their understanding that the law requires that this be done. Indeed, if this were not true of a given state, it is doubtful that it could be said to have a legal system

---

[8] John Locke, *The Second Treatise of Government*, in *Two Treatises of Government*, ed. Peter Laslett (Cambridge, England: Cambridge University Press), section 125.

at all, since guiding the conduct of those who administer it is one of the indispensable functions of the law.[9]

What is more important, for our purposes at least, is the fact that the subjects of the state tend to share these beliefs: they generally think that the state exacts retribution coldly, impersonally, as a matter of policy. If I, a subject, believe a certain further presumption that all political authorities make—namely, that the seeking of retribution is solely the prerogative of the state—I will think that this cold way of proceeding is the proper way, and I will also think that seeking retribution in my own behalf is literally none of my business: it is a matter for the police and the courts. Thus, the state and the beliefs that conventionally come with it discourage me from having vengeful thoughts. That is, they discourage me from thinking that wrongs against me justify *my* exacting retribution for them. In addition, by accomplishing what would have been accomplished by personal revenge (namely, by hurting the person who has hurt me) they remove a large part of the *point* of having such thoughts. Thus, they tend to prevent episodes of temperamental revenge from growing and hardening into a trait of character and a vice.

If the state, by accomplishing the palpable results of vengeful action, were also to afford its subjects the emotional gratification that is characteristic of such action, it would probably inflame vengeful passions rather than discourage them. However, it offers very little in the way of such gratification. To a vengeful person, it is most gratifying to achieve such results oneself. It is less gratifying, but typically still acceptable, to hire someone to do it (e.g., to hire a thug to break the malefactor's legs); in that case, retribution is exacted through something one does and for one's own sake, although it is not done directly by oneself. It would also be satisfying, though still less so, if an ally were to step in and express sympathy with the vengeful person by "evening the score" without being asked to do so; at least the one for whom the score is evened can feel that he or she personally had *something* to do with it.

Adam Smith identified two things we want when we act vengefully: we want those who have mistreated us to "be made to repent and be sorry for" what they have done, and we want this to come about "by our means."[10] If my enemy is accidentally crushed to death by a falling rock, that may be an occasion for some gloating, but it will not gratify my revenge because it fails to achieve either of these purposes. Both of them, and especially the latter

---

[9] Lon Fuller, *The Morality of Law* (New Haven: Yale University Press, 1969), pp. 81 ff.

[10] Smith, *The Theory of Moral Sentiments*, pp. 138 and 181.

one—that the lesson comes about "by our means"—are necessary if our feeling of lost dignity is to be displaced by a clear demonstration of our efficacy. It is precisely the latter purpose, however, that is *not* served by state punishment. I am aware that the government's legal apparatus can teach my enemy a lesson—insofar as that is possible—but I know that this will not be done by me, through me, or even for me. Without this, the retribution gained does not promise to be the intense source of pleasure it would otherwise be.

So far, then, such punishment counteracts revenge by counteracting the belief that hardens it into a trait of character and, in addition, by depriving it of emotional gratification. But it acts against revenge in ways that go further and deeper than this. One of the beliefs that tend to be widely shared within a political system, held by both the sovereign and its subjects, can prevent resentful feelings from arising in the first place, at least to the extent that victims of aggression accept it. This is the familiar idea that the wrongdoer is to be seen simply as one who breaks the law: lawlessness is what is wrong with what the criminal does. This has a very important result, one that was identified long ago by Nietzsche: "from now on the eye is trained to an ever more *impersonal* evaluation of the deed, and this applies even to the injured party himself."[11] To the extent that injured parties accept this idea, their attitudes toward retribution tend to some extent to lose the reference to oneself without which resentment is impossible.

The benefits of a state that performs its minimal functions are difficult to perceive because we live with them, but they should show up more clearly if we consider what sort of community we would have if private firms did the same work. Suppose that I live in such a community. I come home one day to realize, with horror, that my apartment has been robbed and maliciously vandalized. The protection agency to which I subscribe discovers who the culprit is, catches him or her, and exacts retribution.

Does their retribution constitute punishment? If we follow ordinary usage the answer is clearly no. As private businesses, they cannot be said to punish their clients or their employees, much less could they be said to punish someone who is a stranger to them, as the culprit in this case may well be. They cannot be said to punish at all. According to some remarks I have made earlier, this is because they derive what authority they have from a contract that all parties enter into to satisfy certain desires with relatively limited objectives. For the same reason, what they deal in is in fact revenge. More specifically, this is due to the nature of the desires that the contract satisfies. If I subscribe to their

---

[11] Nietzsche, *On the Genealogy of Morals*, p. 512.

retribution-exacting service, it will be, as far as this issue is concerned, just as though I had paid a thug to beat up people who have harmed me: they would be peddlers of broken bones. If they are successful, they afford me the satisfaction of revenge: not the intense satisfaction I would have had by doing it myself, but at least the sort that I can secure by having hired agents of mine—competent professionals, presumably—to do it for me.[12]

In such a system, no cultural barrier interposes itself between the goals of self-respect and the means employed by revenge. The benefits of a system in which there is such a barrier cannot be perceived directly, but we can identify them conceptually by contrasting such a system with one in which retribution is private. In the private system, offenses against oneself are directly relevant to one's self-respect, and the vengeful solution is made all the more attractive by the fact that it is visibly and effectively carried out. On the other hand, to the extent that a state performs its minimal functions, and to the extent that one accepts the ideology that comes with the relevant governmental institutions, neither of these facts is the case. One's revenge is not being gratified and, more important, the offenses are not relevant to self-respect at all. Insofar as I adopt the impersonal evaluation of the offense, it loses its character as an affront to my dignity. What the offender offends against is not my dignity but an impersonal system.

In such an environment, the conduct in which we act on and seek to protect our sense of our own worth is somewhat less likely to take the form that is familiar to us from tales of Renaissance Italy or the Wild West, in which individuals fight with each other over offences against themselves. It is at least a little more likely to take the form of conduct that is more productive of good and less adverse to forgiveness and related traits.

---

[12] These remarks may be read as a criticism of the individualist sort of anarchism defended, among others, by David Friedman in part 3 of *The Machinery of Freedom* (New York, Harper Row, 1973). Some individualist anarchists sidestep the sort of problem I am pointing out here by saying that in their system punishment would not exist. Its place would be taken by compensation of the sort found in our current system of tort law. Once that move is made, I suppose the issue becomes why they are so sure that retribution will not exist in their system, but that lies outside the constellation of topics I have limited myself to here.

X

The Politics of Envy

... fear, that reigns with the tyrant, and envy, the vice of republics ...
—Henry Wadsworth Longfellow, *Evangeline*

1. Introductory

I have just argued, in chapter IX, that certain functions that all states perform tend to decrease the amount of revenge in the world. In this chapter I will discuss the differential effects that various political arrangements have on another trait that, like revenge, is frequently spoken of as an emotion but is also generally regarded as a vice: namely, envy. In sections 2 and 3 I will try to show that we have good reasons for avoiding whatever envy is produced by the institutions within which we live. In sections 4 and 5 I will argue, roughly, that certain political institutions can actually decrease the envy in the world. More precisely, I will argue that a shift from one sort of political arrangement to another can have this desirable effect, although I will leave it to the reader to decide whether this transition would be worth whatever costs it might involve. I will not try to argue that the latter sort or arrangement is on the whole better than the first. As in the preceding several chapters, I am only interested in the effects that institutions have on character, and, for the present, I am only interested in one trait. I am not discussing any of the other factors that are relevant to the value of our institutional arrangements.

2. The Badness of Envy

Some of the reasons for avoiding envy are obvious. The sorts of human action in which envy most commonly expresses itself are hostile and aggressive, and virtually all of us already believe behavior of that sort is bad in itself—especially when it is motivated by envy. Further, such behavior tends to lead to fighting. Fighting tends to have destructive effects that fall on all participants, and on third parties as well. At the very least, it tends to wastefully burn up resources of various kinds.

Such considerations give all of us some crudely self-interested reasons to reduce the amount of envy in the world if we can. Of course, they may not weigh heavily with people who are in the grips of envious malice, but that does not mean that such reasoning only applies to a certain group of people: namely, those who are not envious. Envy can strike anyone, whether rich or poor, incompetent or talented, and we should not assume that we know who will be next.[1] If we happen to live in a society that fans the flames of envy, the effects that we *can* assume will fall on us are uniformly undesirable.

Some of the obvious reasons for avoiding the envy-producing effects of institutions derive from commonly held principles concerning our obligation to treat one another decently. Others are based on a purely utilitarian concern for the effects of envious behavior. In addition, if we take a closer look at the sort of trait envy is, we can see, after some reflection, that there is another, less obvious reason why we must avoid systemic envy if we can: even apart from its consequences, envy conflicts with our commitment to live rationally.[2]

There are indefinitely many things for which I can envy someone: good looks, wealth, power, having a clever and handsome spouse, reputation, knowledge, and so on. Still, the possible objects of my envy are limited in two ways: I can envy people only if I see them as possessing something good and only if I see them as possessing more of that good thing than I. I must see them as occupying a higher position in the world than I do. Further, the objects of envy are facts about the present, and not their antecedents in the past. If I am

---

[1] Benjamin J. Stein once remarked that one reason contract disputes in the movie industry are so prolonged and vicious is that the two sides of the disputes envy each other. Producers are wealthier than writers and directors, but they envy them nonetheless. They envy them mainly because writers and directors have immensely greater prestige than they do and because they are not required to bear, as producers are, the business risks involved in cinematic ventures. It is interesting that, though their envy is not directed at anyone's wealth, the behavior it causes is just what one would expect if it were so directed: they try to get the best of the writers and directors in money matters. ("Rich Man, Poor Man," *New West* July 1981, pp. 101-2.) Envy is not something that characterizes one economic class (the "have nots") and is directed toward another class (the "haves").

[2] Contrast with this the view of Charles Frankel: "Why is envy 'Irrational'? . . . It is a genuine human emotion, and its satisfaction, if a man feels it, is as much a part of his self-interest as the satisfaction of any other interest." "Justice and Rationality," in *Philosophy, Science and Method: Essays in Honor of Ernest Nagel*, ed. S. Morgenbesser, P. Suppes, and M. White (New York: St. Martins, 1969), pp. 409-10.

hostile to you because I think that you acquired your superior position at my expense (because, for instance, I think that the reason you have a car and I don't is that you *stole* my car from me) then I am being vengeful, perhaps, but certainly not envious. Envy is about states of affairs and not at all about their origins. It is, one might say, "ahistorical."[3]

More generally, the objects of envy are, one might say, extremely "abstract": I can only be envious about the difference between someone else's position and my own. If I really dislike the fact that you have more of something than I do because I think that you are no more deserving than I am then, perhaps, I am being resentful. I am not, however, being envious. As I have already indicated, envy also includes a certain behavioral response to these facts about people's positions. If I respond enviously to an unfavorable difference between my position and that of my neighbor, I regard that difference as *in itself* a reason to take steps to reduce that difference, either by raising my position or by lowering that of my neighbor. Partly because it is usually easier to damage someone else than to help oneself, envy is typically hostile and aggressive. It typically includes a desire to pull others down.

In light of these facts, consider a certain oddity in the way envy is traditionally viewed. It is often depicted in fiction as a trait that is peculiarly evil. Nathaniel Hawthorne attempted to portray the evil of revenge by depicting the gradual moral degeneration of the character of Roger Chillingworth in *The Scarlet Letter*, showing "the effects of revenge, in diabolizing him who indulges in it."[4] In sharp contrast to this, Herman Melville made John Claggart in *Billy Budd* diabolical from the outset. Claggart is an envious person and not a vengeful one, and it seems to be his envy that enables the reader to accept him as something of a devil in human form on the basis of the minimal characterization provided by the author. To descend from the world of high art, something of the same satanic quality is embodied in the character of "Baby Jane" Hudson in a ghastly movie by Robert Aldrich. Indeed, Milton represents Satan himself as a prototype of envy.

Artists tend to depict envy in more lurid colors than they lavish on other vices, such as revenge or greed. Obviously they are not projecting an attitude that only they hold; they are relying on the fact that their audience also tends

---

[3] See Robert Nozick's remarks about the "historical" nature of love and of certain principles of justice in his *Anarchy, State, and Utopia* (New York: Basic Books, 1974), pp. 152-60, 167-68, and 199-204.

[4] Nathaniel Hawthorne, *The American Notebooks* (Columbus: Ohio State University Press, 1972), p. 278.

to see envy as somehow more contemptible than revenge or greed. This is odd, because it does not seem to have worse social consequences, on the whole, than the other vices do. Why, then, do we tend to find envy so repellent?

The very brief account of the nature of envy I have given so far suggests that a good part of the answer may be that envy is gratuitous in a way in which other vices are not. In revenge, one is moved to hostility by something bad someone has done. In greed, one is moved to seek something good (namely, wealth) because one sees it as good. As bad as these traits may be, there is at least some tincture of sense in them: it makes sense to seek what is good and be moved to hostility by what is bad. In envy, however, we are often moved to hostility by what is good. We only envy people for things we believe are worth having. The abstractness of envy seems, at first sight, to rule out any intelligible explanation of this fact. The hostility involved would seem to be provoked by the mere fact that the good things are possessed by someone other than oneself. As far as the envier knows, this other person's having these goods may be perfectly innocent. What, beyond a mysteriously pointless malice, could account for such antipathy?

Although the apparent gratuitousness of envy might explain why we find it peculiarly repellent, it leaves us with another problem: how is it possible that the well-being of others inspires the envious person with hostility? We must answer this question if envy is to make any sense to us.[5]

3. The Self-Esteem Explanation

The following is a simple but, I think, quite plausible answer to this question.[6] When one reacts enviously to the difference between one's position in the world and that of someone else, it is because that difference undermines one's self-esteem. We often see certain goods (and which goods these are varies from one person to another) as indicating value in the person who possesses them, in such a way that the amount of that good the person

---

[5] Of course, we could decide that the question is unanswerable. This is the alternative taken by Melville, who uses his sinister master-at-arms to symbolize his own Platonic conviction that evil is unintelligible. But this alternative is only reasonable if we first try to answer this question and find that we cannot do it.

[6] Perhaps I should warn you that my answer is not original. More or less the same answer is taken for granted both by John Rawls in *A Theory of Justice* (Cambridge: Harvard University Press, 1971), p. 535, and by Robert Nozick in *Anarchy, State, and Utopia*, pp. 239-46.

possesses is taken as evidence of the degree of value of the possessor. My having less of it than others have tends to show that my worth is inferior to theirs. If my envy flares up, it is because this tendency is felt to be strong enough to threaten my self-esteem.

Seen in this way, there is a certain amount (perhaps very small) of logic in envy; it is based on a perception that something constitutes evidence for something else. Of course, some people would be inclined to think that, beyond this modicum of reason, envy is in fact utterly illogical for the simple reason that the evidence it is based on is necessarily worthless: facts about others can never be evidence of my own worth or lack of it and should have no effect on my self-esteem. They are simply irrelevant.

That, at least, is what one might think. But such a thought, plausible though it is at first, is too facile.[7] The things that support our self-esteem are always things we have and a certain number of other people do not have. Mere literacy can be a basis for self-esteem in a largely illiterate culture, but not in ours. Things that everybody has cannot provide such a basis. Because of the nature of self-esteem, judgments to the effect that there are certain differences between ourselves and others do seem to provide evidence that affects the relevant judgments about our own attainments. To that extent, judgments about others do seem to be relevant.

There *is* an element of rather gross illogic in envy, but it lies not necessarily in these judgments themselves, but in the relationship between the judgments and the desires that, in envy, arise from them. These are desires that are satisfied by simply reducing the difference between one's own position and that of someone else: that is, they are desires that can be satisfied by pulling the other person's position down. The relationship involved is the fact that these judgments are the source of these desires. If I have an envious desire to pull someone down, it is because I see their higher position as evidence of a certain lack of worth on my part. To the extent that this is the nature and source of my desire, what I want is simply to destroy evidence that I would still know was there after I had destroyed it. Since it is the mere existence of the evidence that annoys me, and not the fact that someone else knows about it, I could only be trying to conceal it from myself. This would mean that the point of envious malice is self-deception.

The self-esteem explanation of envy, as I will call it, can explain a certain strange furtiveness in the nature of this trait. People who suffer from it are

---

[7] The argument that follows here is drawn from Nozick's *Anarchy, State, and Utopia*, pp. 243-45.

seldom aware that they do, often taking their feelings of ill will as representing some other emotion, such as moral indignation. According to the self-esteem explanation, the cause of the felt desire to pull the other person down that is typical of envy is the fact that the envier interprets the other's higher position as evidence of the envier's own inferiority. This cause is something of which I, if I am envious, would naturally try to avoid being lucidly aware. Such awareness would be painful. If I have no other explanation for these desires, my felt ill will inevitably seems to me to be mere pointless malice.

I can avoid this if I can find the cause of my feelings in some fault or flaw in the person who is the object of those feelings. Because of the abstractness of envy, this would mean that these feelings were not really feelings of envy at all, but something else. For instance, if I explain my envious ill will toward you by finding ways (real or imagined) in which you have wronged me, then, in effect, I have disguised my envy as resentment or revenge. After all, if these feelings really had arisen from my interpreting you as having wronged me, then they really would have been feelings of resentment or revenge and not of envy.[8] A particularly easy way to disguise one's envy is simply to see the person who is its target as arrogant and insulting. This is easy because the envied qualities, since they wound the envier's self-esteem, have the very same effect that an arrogant insult has. It literally *feels like* one has been insulted, and this can be expected to give verisimilitude to the thought that one has.[9]

Ironically, this strategy can even take the form of maliciously denying that the people we envy possess the very things for which we envy them. Melville's Claggart envies Billy Budd, in part, because Billy is obviously a much better person than he is, but he covers up this fact by thinking that Billy is only more contemptibly devious and hypocritical than others are. Professor X envies Professor Y for Y's brilliant scholarly achievements, but he protects himself

---

[8] The process here is fundamentally the same as the one that I presented as concealing jealousy from the person who suffers it in V.7, above.

[9] This response is wonderfully illustrated throughout part 1 of Yuri Olesha's novella *Envy*. Kavalerov, Olesha's narrator, envies an important official for his bustling efficiency, his involvement in the world, and his intense purposiveness, and he perceives the official's quiet absorption in his work as if it were a deliberate insult to him: "A man, staring at a sheet of paper, is digging in his ear with a pencil. Nothing special. But everything about him says: You, Kavalerov, are a bystander." *Envy and Other Works by Yuri Olesha*, trans. Andrew R. MacAndrew (Garden City, N.J.: Anchor Books, 1967), p. 8. Olesha makes it eloquently obvious that Kavalerov suspects that he really is "a bystander." The official is only innocently and inadvertently reminding him of it.

by believing that Y's work, despite its superficial cleverness, is entirely derivative of the work of Professor Z.

If such self-deceptive responses to one's own envy are very common, it may be impossible, in practice, to distinguish envy from various other traits. In principle, though, I think it is plain enough how they differ. The other traits all include negative value judgments one makes about the object of one's malevolence. Envy, on the other hand, is a hostile trait that includes as parts of itself only positive judgments concerning the value of the person toward whom one is hostile. In itself, it is a more inevitably sincere form of flattery than imitation is. Nonetheless, envy can cause the envier to make negative judgments about the envied person; to understand what it is, we must be careful to distinguish these judgments from those that are part of envy itself.

Envy is a constitutionally confused and self-deceiving trait. Individuals who want to see themselves and those around them in a lucid and noncontradictory way—and this includes everyone who wants to live rationally—have good reason to avoid coming under its influence. This gives us another reason, in addition to the ones I set out in section 2, to avoid envy if we can. But the question remains of whether and how this might be done.

4. Institutions and Self-Esteem

I can distinguish only two widely influential views concerning the power of institutions to abate envy. For reasons that will be obvious, I call them "the left-wing view" and "the right-wing view." Those who hold the left-wing view claim that institutions, especially political ones, can reduce envy, and that the way they can do this is by eliminating to some extent the objective occasions of envy: since envy is a response to the perceived differences between the amounts of good things that people possess, we need only reduce these perceived differences. According to the right-wing view, social institutions, especially political ones, cannot significantly reduce the envy in the world. Envy is a problem for the psychotherapist, not the legislator or the voter.[10]

In what follows, I will try to show that neither of these views, as I have stated them, is true. I will argue against the right-wing view simply by indicating how institutions (specifically, political ones) can work to reduce envy (and increase it as well). The left-wing view requires a more direct sort of attack.

---

[10] Helmut Schoeck defends the right-wing view in *Envy* (New York: Harcourt, Brace and World, 1966), pp. 254-55 and 299-301. Schoeck attributes the left-wing view to a number of socialist and equalitarian writers, for instance on pp. 250-51 and 252.

In light of what I have said so far, we certainly should not regard it as obvious at the outset that the way (that is, the only way) to reduce envy is to equalize the good things people have. To so regard it would only make sense if envy consisted merely in one's awareness of inequalities that are unfavorable to oneself. It *is* obvious that the only way to get people to see fewer ugly things is to reduce the number of ugly things in the world (e.g., perhaps by banning tasteless billboards), since the alternatives are plainly either impractical (for instance, teaching people to repress their awareness of many things) or undesirable for some other reason (like blinding everyone). But we have already seen that envy is not like seeing something: it does not consist simply in some effect that follows whenever one's attention is turned toward a certain object. If envy were that simple, it might well be true that the only feasible way to get rid of the effect would be to get rid of the object. There is, however, more to it than that.

According to the self-esteem explanation, there is also the weak self-esteem that produces the envious response to inequality. This explanation implies that if one is not vulnerable to doubts about one's worth one will have no envy, and thereby implies that if such vulnerability is somehow reduced one will be less envious. This would mean that if institutions could increase the self-esteem of those who live within them, they could thereby decrease their envy. This view has been defended by John Rawls. He claims that, despite the fact that the just and well-ordered society he describes in his *A Theory of Justice* would allow inequality to exist, its institutions would discourage envy. They would do so, he argues, by ensuring that "the less fortunate have no cause to consider themselves inferior."[11] This is an alternative to both the left-wing and right-wing views, and, though it is much less influential than they are, it certainly deserves careful consideration.

Can institutions ensure that those who have smaller shares of good things will not be moved by that fact to doubt their own worth? Or, if we consider a weaker version of the thesis than the one Rawls defends, we might ask: Can some institutions at least guarantee that there will be fewer such doubts on the whole than there would be without that institution? While any decent person would no doubt hope that at least one of these questions can truthfully be answered with a yes, there are quite general reasons for suspecting that the answer to both is no, at least if we require (as it seems we should) that the self-esteem our institutions are to foster is rational self-esteem.

---

[11] Rawls, *A Theory of Justice*, p. 536.

Consider Rawls's account of self-esteem: To have self-esteem, he says, is to believe that (1) what Rawls calls one's "life-plan" is worth carrying out and (2) one is able to carry it out unless circumstances external to oneself prevent it.[12] If we take this account as adequate for our present purposes, it seems to follow that to have rational self-esteem would be to believe these two things on the basis of good evidence. Further, people do not have good evidence for such beliefs unless they have actually tried to carry out their life-plans. They must do something that indicates that their plans of life suit their own psychological makeup and that they are able to carry these plans out if not hindered. Such doings are virtually the only things that could count as evidence at all. While it is true that, as Rawls points out, the approval of others has something to do with self-esteem,[13] it is only rational to be influenced by their approval if one has reason to believe that it is based on evidence, and one can only have such reasons if one has *done* something that could provide the necessary evidence.

This would seem to mean that there are only two things institutions can do to provide strong support for rational self-esteem. First, they can make it possible for people to choose and carry out plans of their own. Second, they can include clear and settled standards of thought and discussion that enable people to evaluate choice and performance in a rational way. Unfortunately, the chance to choose and act does not only indicate the presence of worthiness and ability when they are present: it also indicates their absence when they are not. The opportunities provided are opportunities to fail as well as to succeed. Worse, the standards of thought and discussion, for the same reason, would expose failure for what it is and in that event would generate self-doubt and self-contempt rather than self-esteem. This would mean that if institutions do something that strongly supports the rational self-esteem of some people, they do something that, with equal power, prevents it for others.[14] Thus, we must

---

[12] Ibid., p. 440. Rawls uses "self-respect" instead of "self-esteem" in this passage, but the two words, as he employs them, are interchangeable.

[13] Ibid., p. 441.

[14] This is true even if we suppose that, as in Rawls's just and well-ordered society, self-esteem is to some extent protected by the fact that people are "democratic" in their judgments of one another: that is, they recognize the good of all activities provided they are consistent with the requirements of justice and insofar as they are complex and realize the capacities of the agent (*A Theory of Justice*, pp. 442 and 426). It is all too easy, even with the best of intentions, to choose a way of life that does not fit this description and, if people do fail in this way, this democracy of judgments will not help them out. It may well make

face the depressing possibility that a society that supports rational self-esteem might also generate more self-doubt and self-contempt than one in which people are less able to form rational convictions about what they are worth. From this follows another depressing possibility: such a society might produce more envy.

This conclusion is reinforced if we consider another likely consequence of the freedom and opportunity to chose one's own way of life. As Rawls suggests, a society that to some considerable extent provides its inhabitants with such benefits will tend to dissolve into "a plurality of associations. . . with their own secure internal life."[15] Freedom and opportunity tend to prevent the pyramid structure that distinguished what Tocqueville called aristocracy. Rawls claims that this pluralistic arrangement "tends to reduce the visibility, or at least the painful visibility, of variations in men's prospects."[16] No individual will be very sharply aware of members of other groups and, since the society as a whole has no acknowledged hierarchical structure, people will compare themselves only to individuals who resemble them.

Such an arrangement, Rawls thinks, would promote self-esteem. We can see, however, that it will also promote the opposite of self-esteem if we recall the

---

their failure more bitterly painful if they believe that their fellows are not being the least unfair in seeing more good in the actions of others than in what they do. In addition, Rawls claims that people in his ideal society would derive self-esteem from the fact that they are given basic rights and liberties (p. 544), but he also points out (on the same page) that these things would be distributed equally. This runs up against the difficulty, which I discussed earlier, that people do not seem to derive self-esteem from goods they possess equally. Beyond that, I doubt that it is rational to derive self-esteem simply from being allowed to do things that no one has a right to stop one from doing, and I would imagine that the citizens of a just society would believe that no one has a right to stop them from exercising their rights and liberties. Rawls also holds that the less favored in his society have no reason to feel inferior on account of the larger shares received by others, since the larger shares are only allowed on condition that the less favored received compensating benefits (p. 536). But since these compensations do not express anyone's opinions about the life-plans of the less favored or their ability to carry them out, it would be quite irrational of them to derive any self-esteem from being granted them. On the other hand, being granted a benefit one has no hope of reciprocating can be a perfectly good reason to feel inferior. (Kavalerov, the character in the novella by Olesha I mentioned above in footnote 9, loathes the official for having fished him out of the gutter and given him a warm place to sleep. It is not difficult to see a sort of logic in this.)

[15] Rawls, *A Theory of Justice*, p. 536.

[16] Ibid.

fact, which I discussed above, that people seem to base their self-estimates on comparisons between themselves and others who seem to be either better or worse than themselves in some respect. A caste system presents, as its denizens look out into the world around them, a hierarchy in which, for better or worse, they can locate themselves in a clearly visible scale of excellence. A society that lacks such hierarchy also lacks the support such a structure gives to the self-esteem of the people who are able to locate themselves above the bottom of the social pyramid. It might well be that such people, if they lived in a freer and more equal system, would be much more confused and uncertain about their worth and much more vulnerable to serious doubts about it. According to the self-esteem explanation, this means that freedom and opportunity might well produce envy.

I think it is safe to assume that we have a powerful preference for a society in which freedom and opportunity are widespread and plentiful, and that most of us would prefer such an arrangement even knowing that it may produce envy. Sometimes we must put up with the bad effects that good things have. On the other hand, we should also want to find some means to interrupt the process by which a society of freedom and opportunity could produce envy. If it can be done at a reasonable cost, we should try to compensate for the unwelcome effects of welcome things.

5. Politics and Envy

The search for such means might seem to bring us back immediately to eliminating the objective occasions of envy, the relevant perceived disparities between oneself and others. This, however, would be a rather hasty conclusion to draw just yet. It sometimes happens that the objective occasions confront people who are afflicted with weak self-esteem and yet they do not develop envy as a result of this experience. Sometimes, a perception of one's inferiority to others results in some quite different passion or trait of character, such as a yearning to improve oneself, defeatism, or a craving for self-punishment. It is quite obvious that at least some of these traits can be helped or hindered by their social surroundings, and without altering either the disparities involved or the wounded self-esteem resulting from them.

Consider, for example, the craving for self-punishment. People whose self-esteem is weak are likely to believe that they are flawed in some way. Consider what can happen to such people if they live in a certain strongly moralistic culture, one in which convention holds that any sort of flaw whatsoever is deserving of punishment. The conventions specify, for instance, that physical underendowments, such as poverty, are never caused by a lack of talent, much less by bad luck, but by moral turpitude, and that any person who suffers them is a deserving object of the wrath of God. If such people subscribe to these conventions, they will be likely to regard their supposed flaws as reasons why they ought to suffer pain and misfortune, and in that case they will have good reason to inflict such things on themselves. We should not be at all surprised, then, if that is what they do. Obviously, these conventions would not have these effects if their self-esteem were not weak in the first place; just as obviously, though, this weakness would be likely to develop into other forms of thought and action in the absence of social surroundings of this kind.

One can give an account of how an institution can transform weak self-esteem into envy that is similar to this account of self-punishment except that it does not assume the existence, at the outset, of an ideology that would justify the thoughts and actions involved. Imagine a group of people who belong, together, to an organization from which none of them can resign. Each member has particular amounts of various goods that are capable of being transferred among the members as they, collectively, decide. These goods are distributed unequally among them. Their decision-making authority, however, is distributed equally: collective decisions are made by voting and each person has one vote. Finally, suppose that the number of votes needed to constitute a collective decision on any issue is less than 100 percent.

I have just described an institution that is wonderfully suited to achieving the aims of envy. If N is the number of votes needed for a collective decision, and N voters agree in envying the same group of members, they can easily assuage the pain of their envy simply by voting to transfer some goods from that group to themselves.[17] In fact, this system offers its members an incentive to act as if they were envious even if they are not. Someone who, merely out of greed, is organizing a coalition to loot a section of the population would do well to choose as his or her victims those who are richest in transferable goods. This would increase the organizer's chances of both offering rich gains to possible coalition members and at the same time attacking a group that is small enough to be relatively helpless.

This system would tend either to produce envy or to exacerbate whatever envy it happens to contain already. To see why, consider, first, the obvious fact that the organization I have described is simply a schematic version of a

---

[17] It may be worth noting that envy can motivate someone to join the coalition of N or more voters even if possession of those particular goods is not the reason one envies the people in the victimized group. See footnote 1, above.

democratic state. It is an organization with virtually no constitution other than the practices that are necessary to make it a state and a democratic one. Further, as I have described it so far, this state has an inveterate tendency to lure its citizens into achieving the goal of maliciously envious behavior, namely, worsening the positions of the people they believe are better off than they are. They would be doing this in ways that would reduce the differences between their own positions and the positions of these other more favored individuals. Indeed, as I have so far described this system, such behavior would in the long run be quite visible and obvious to everyone.

For the most part, people resist seeing themselves, when they participate in the political process, as mere looters. They want to believe that whatever they strongly and visibly tend to do in their role as citizens must be more noble than that. In addition, the persons who run the states they live under do not want people to see their governments as mere instruments of plunder. Through education and propaganda, states and political parties try to help their subjects see things in the desired way. To accomplish this, they must convince people that the differences between the positions of different people are, in themselves, reasons for taking steps to reduce such differences. In this way, the results of the political process would imprint themselves on the conscience.[18]

The belief thus imprinted on the minds of the citizenry, or at least those of its members who are sufficiently impressionable, makes it possible for envy to exist in places where it did not exist before. If the self-esteem of some of the members of this system has been damaged by their thinking that others are in some way better off than they are, they suffer from a personal problem and need a solution to it. This belief, if they happen to hold it, offers them a solution to this problem, and it assures them that this solution is entirely legitimate. It assures them that the difference between their positions and the positions of those who are better off is a good enough reason for narrowing

---

[18] One could complicate my rather simpleminded little model and make it more realistic (and more similar to the system we inhabit) by supposing that those who are richer in transferable goods try to capture the machinery of government by some stealthy means or other to prevent equalization from taking place and perhaps quietly transfer goods in their own direction. We would then have a system with two opposed tendencies: one toward the erosion of disparities and the other away from it. But the latter tendency (supposing it is not entirely invisible) would be one in which most people would not see themselves as complicit, so that they would thus not feel any need to justify it. Consequently, this more complicated system would have the same effects on the consciences of most people as the one I have described.

that gap. If, not surprisingly, they accept the offered remedy and want to do what it proposes, they are envious.

Further, the belief this system encourages people to hold is precisely what is needed to transform the passion of envy into a trait of character in my sense of that term. Envy, for all I have said about it so far in this chapter, can be a mere emotional episode. The felt desire to pull another person down, if it is present, may be an experience that hits me in spite of myself. If I am experiencing envy, then I interpret the disparity between my position and that of the other person as calling for some such course of action, or at least some remedy that would reduce the painful disparity, but this interpretation need not be something I believe. I may in fact be horrified to find myself looking at other people in such a way.

As long as this is the nature of my envy it is, in a way, something that I suffer from. Perhaps my neighbors ought to feel some compassion for me, even if—to my own disgust and regret—my envy prompts me to do something malicious. Such behavior would after all be akratic and not vicious. But the day I begin to see such disparities as justifying such conduct is the day that my character begins to take on a quite different ethical status. Before, my envy victimized me almost as if it were an alien force that I opposed; now I have gone over to its side and joined forces with it. My envy begins to cross the boundary that separates an emotion from a trait of character and (if my argument in sections 2 and 3 is sound) a vice.

This brings us back to the issue of the viability of the left-wing view. I argued earlier that the policy it recommends is not necessarily *the* way to reduce envy by institutional means. We can now see that at least at times it may not even be *a* way: the political procedures I have just described as contributing to envy are precisely those the left-wing view recommends to reduce it. The people who hold that view only see one of the effects of the policy they recommend: that it would eliminate some of the objective occasions for envy. This is true but, as I have just tried to show, it would also increase the inclination to respond to the occasions that remain in an envious way.

Given these two opposite effects, it is an interesting question whether the net result of such a policy would be to elevate the general level of envy in the system or to diminish it. The two effects are produced by two quite different sorts of state activity. In one case the state functions as an agency that makes events happen. It causes moveable goods to change hands. In the other, it functions as a teacher, a generator of ideology. In particular, it generates justifications for the events that it makes happen. It may be impossible to know much about the differential effects of two so widely disparate sorts of state activity on the lives of the citizenry. If the policy recommended by the left-wing view were to be carried out with more ideological noise than practical results—a state of affairs that is not untypical of a democracy—it will be sensible to suspect that it will increase the level of envy in the system rather than decrease it. In that case, the state will have done relatively little to remove the disparities that occasion envy while doing relatively much to rationalize the activity of dragging down those who are more fortunate than oneself.

This suspicion gets some additional support from the self-esteem explanation of envy, which raises the possibility that the state's efforts to remove disparities, considered in their own right even assuming that they are effectively carried out, might do little or nothing to reduce envy. It is often true of people with weak self-esteem that they, so to speak, *look for* reasons to think ill of themselves. If I suffer from this malady and feel inferior because my neighbor has a better car than I do, I probably will not suddenly feel good about myself when the troublesome vehicle is destroyed in an accident. I am likely to feel inferior about something else my neighbor has, or someone else has. If this is what envious people are like, then the self-esteem explanation indicates that, as painful discrepancies between envious people and their supposed superiors are eliminated, they will be apt to be pained by some other differences that they hadn't noticed before.[19] This would mean that the envy-abating effects of destroying such differences could be very small indeed.

As sensible as these suspicions might be under certain circumstances, however, they are obviously based on more or less plausible speculation. Are there any political arrangements about which we can confidently predict that their net result would be to diminish envy?

Consider, as a way of answering this question, how we might try to achieve this confidence by modifying the policy I have just been criticizing. The political process I have described exacerbates the tendency toward envious responses to disparities because it transfers goods from some citizens to others and because these goods are transferred for certain reasons. There are only two ways in which we can modify this process with any hope of avoiding the promotion of envy.

The first way is to specify, as part of the state's constitution, that the political process not transfer goods at all, or at least not make transfers that equalize the positions of citizens. This modification of the original process, however, would

---

[19] See L. P. Hartley, *Facial Justice* (London: Hamilton, 1960).

not have net results that we can predict with any confidence. The reason is that, as I have pointed out, the equalizing efforts we would be eliminating may have an envy-abating effect as well as an envy-producing one. We would be eliminating the former, benign effect from the system along with the latter one.

The second way to modify the process is to specify, again by some sort of constitutional provision, that transfers not be made for the reasons they are made in the system I have described. This provision would be satisfied by a policy in which people receive transfers only because of some fact about their own positions and never because of the disparities between their positions and those of others. They only receive such payments because, for instance, they are sick, or disabled, or for some other reason cannot provide themselves with the necessities of life.

The second of these two ways does not have the defect from which the first one suffers. If we do not wish to risk losing whatever envy-abating effects the state's efforts at equalization might have, this policy would not force us to do so. If we want to, we can place limits on the reasons for which particular transfers may be made without reducing the tendencies such transfers have to make the positions of citizens more equal. This simple fact seems to have a very important implication. Supposing the analysis I have presented here is true, it seems to mean that a state that pursues the left-wing policy could be *certain* to reduce the envy-producing effects of that policy if it were modify it into a suitable version of the second alternative policy, one that has the same equalizing tendency that the left-wing method has. However, the new system would only have this effect because the transfers that occur within it are not made *in order to* equalize what people have.

One should notice that, to have this effect, the system would probably have to place more stringent limits on transfers than I have so far suggested. The intent behind this policy is to achieve this effect by creating a safety net for people who fall into certain categories without setting off a general scramble after the goods held by others. This is perhaps more easily said than done. Imagine a system in which transfers can only constitutionally be made to people who belong to various categories, such as the sick, the disabled, and so forth. Suppose, however, that the constitution leaves the question of which categories are to count open to democratic collective choice. In that case, individuals who wish to extract transfers from others can form coalitions and press to have themselves declared one of the categories entitled to such benefits. I suspect that this is a fair description of the system in force in the United States today. It is merely a slightly more complex version of the schematic democracy I have described earlier, with the same struggle carried on in a slightly different manner. Coalition leaders would be obligated to invent suitably defined categories to which their constituencies belong, but this merely makes their task a bit more complicated than the one that faced them in the simpler system. The more complex system offers them the same incentives to form coalitions that achieve the very same effects as those in the simpler one. It consequently would have the very same results: a visible and persistent tendency to lure people into achieving the aims of malicious envy.

It seems likely that the constitutional arrangement I have described could only have the effect I have claimed for it—in fact, it could only really *be* a system in which the reasons for transfers are limited in the relevant way—if it were to specify fairly clearly which categories count. This would represent no small change from the system under which we presently live, in which the question of which categories count is left wide open and the problem of who counts and who does not is often a central issue in public choice controversies. If what I have said here is true, however, we could expect that a shift from our present system to one in which choice is constitutionally constrained in this way would reduce the amount of envy in our world. To that extent, we could all expect to gain from such a change.

XI

Character and the Survival of Liberalism

Liberalism—it is well to recall this today—is the supreme form of generosity; it is the right which the majority concedes to minorities and hence is the noblest cry that has ever resounded on this planet. It announces the determination to share existence with the enemy; more than that, with an enemy that is weak. It was incredible that the human species should have arrived at so noble an attitude, so paradoxical, so refined, so acrobatic, so anti-natural. Hence, it is not to be wondered at that this same humanity should soon appear anxious to get rid of it.
—José Ortega y Gasset, *The Revolt of the Masses*

1. Introductory

As a political reality, liberal democracy began in America and Europe with the revolutions of 1776 and 1789 and has since then settled securely in every inhabited continent. By both violent and peaceful means, it has dealt death-blows to its major ideological enemies, including slavery, authoritarian monarchy, fascism, and communism. Today, it looks as if the final and complete victory of liberal democracy is within sight at last.[1]

Despite this fact—the fact, that is, that things *look* this way—I propose in this chapter to examine reasons for thinking that liberal democracy is in the long run not really a viable system. If a single political system is about to spread over the entire world, that system might not be liberal.

More precisely, I will entertain and take seriously the possibility that liberalism as a political system is inherently unstable, that it tends to

---

[1] In case this claim seems too apocalyptic to be very plausible, the following more reserved one will do as well, for the present purposes: "Now, outside the Islamic world, there appears to be a general consensus that accepts liberal democracy's claims to be the most rational form of government." Francis Fukuyama, *The End of History and the Last Man* (New York: Avon, 1992), p. 211. Fukuyama's book, however, is in part an argument that the more apocalyptic claim is actually true.

undermine itself. In sections 3 through 6 I will argue that we have good reason to expect it to encourage the formation of a trait of character that drives individuals to do things that undermine liberal institutions and that prevents them from caring about certain values on which such institutions are based. It leads people to do illiberal things, moreover, precisely in the name of liberalism. However, I will also argue in sections 7 and 8 that there is at least one sort of liberalism that does not have this sort of instability. This is because it fosters traits of character that work in ways contrary to the vicious one encouraged by the other sort of political culture.

It will be evident that our own culture has, so to speak, not decided which sort of culture it will be. As Ortega y Gasset said in a related context:

> It is not that the present situation may appear to us good from one viewpoint, and evil from another, but that in itself it contains the twin potencies of triumph or of death.[2]

Before I try to show any of this, though, I must say something about what, as I take it, liberalism is.

2. Minimal Liberalism

Liberalism has taken many different forms, but it always rests on attachments to two goods that are taken to be of fundamental importance. These two basic values are liberty and equality. The relative strength of these attachments, and the political principles that articulate them, are among the things that distinguish one form of liberalism from another.

Both these basic values have been interpreted very differently by different liberal thinkers. The liberties affirmed may include extensive rights to do things that have profound effects on others, or they may be limited to the rights to regulate one's own purely "private" affairs and to express one's opinions. The equality involved might include rights of equal access to the education and medical care systems, or it might be far more restricted.

There is at least one limit, though, to the ways that the varieties of liberalism can differ one from another: though the extent to which each of

---

[2] José Ortega y Gasset, *The Revolt of the Masses* (London: George Allen and Unwin, 1961), p. 59. The quotation at the head of this chapter is from p. 58 of the same edition. For anybody interested in the subject I am treating here, most of Ortega's book—chapters 1 through 13—will repay a close and thoughtful reading.

these fundamental goods are affirmed may vary widely, in neither case may the affirmation be reduced to utter triviality. Some liberals seem inordinately attached to liberty, while others appear to be very partial to equality, but no ideology could be called liberal unless it affirms the value of both goods. At a minimum, liberalism must include something equivalent to two familiar principles: (1) people have a right to freely express their views, and (2) they have a right to the equal protection of the laws.

Further, liberalism does not treat the two fundamental goods in precisely the same way. In a certain sense, liberals, properly so called, value liberty (at least *some* liberties) above equality: whatever the liberties are that the liberal holds sacred, he or she will not sacrifice them for the sake of equality.[3] At a minimum, this means that the liberal (in contrast to most nondemocratic socialists) will not try to bring about a more egalitarian society by suspending freedom of speech, not even as a passing stage on the way to a better world. These two principles, together with this constraint, comprise what might be called "minimal liberalism."[4]

---

[3] John Rawls can be interpreted as adhering to this requirement when he gives his first principle of justice (which specifies the nature of his commitment to liberty) "lexical" priority over the second one (which gives the content of his egalitarianism). See his *A Theory of Justice* (Cambridge, Mass.: Harvard University Press, 1971), p. 61.

[4] I emphasize that the characterization of liberalism that I have given covers very widely disparate views, probably including both the extremely egalitarian liberalism defended by Ronald Dworkin in his "Liberalism," in *Public and Private Morality*, ed. Stuart Hampshire (Cambridge, England: Cambridge University Press, 1978), and the laissez faire, market-oriented liberalism defended by Ludwig von Mises in his *Liberalism* (San Francisco and Irvington, N.Y.: Foundation for Economic Education and Cobden Press, 1985). Some people (though not the same ones) would argue that one or the other of these authors is not a genuine liberal, but both are probably covered by the description I have given. Equality is a much less important idea for von Mises than it is for most liberals, but he does insist on a right to equal protection and consequently does not fall outside the boundaries of liberalism as I have described it. See *Liberalism*, pp. 27-30. Dworkin is more problematic, since he explicitly argues that equality is a more fundamental value than liberty, and that we actually have no right to liberty at all. See, with regard to this last assertion, "What Rights Do We Have?" in *Taking Rights Seriously* (Cambridge, Mass.: Harvard University Press, 1977), pp. 266-78. However, Dworkin does think we have important rights to various liberties (in the plural, not the singular: a distinction that he makes much of), which include extensive rights to free expression, and he apparently would not sacrifice such expression rights for the sake of equality. Thus, he seems to be, at any rate, what I would call a minimal liberal.

The instability that tends to afflict certain sorts of liberalism has to do with the two principles of minimal liberalism. It arises from the fact that, in the sort of society liberalism brings with it, they can easily become incompatible, so that one of them operates to interfere with the secure operation of the other. One way to express the nature of this interference would be this: The first principle indicates that a liberal order rests on tolerance; if not on the virtue of tolerance, then at least on tolerant behavior in which one forbears to interfere with the expressive conduct of others.[5] The second principle, however, can place such behavior in conflict with the natural and legitimate concerns of self-respect. When this happens, we can no longer expect people to adhere to the first principle.

I will only be able to make my thesis plausible if I first try to describe, briefly and impressionistically, what liberal society is like. The relevant features will perhaps stand out in clearest relief if I contrast it, also broadly and impressionistically, with the sort of institutional arrangements that liberal institutions have tended to displace wherever they have appeared.

3. The Preliberal World

For two hundred years liberalism has been making a revolution in the circumstances of everyday life so great that it is very difficult to understand it adequately. This is partly because the revolution is still well under way, and, in consequence, we are all participants and carry all the biases that participation brings. It is also due in part to the fact that the break with the past was deep and surprisingly complete. As Ortega says, "never in the course of history had man been placed in vital surroundings even remotely similar" to those that liberalism brought with it.[6]

Throughout history, most human beings have found themselves confronted by an array of practical requirements, of things that must be done. If they cared to consider how well their lives were going, they did so by considering how well these requirements were being met. Will I have enough food for the winter? Can I avoid angering the gods? Can I pay my taxes? These requirements they saw as placed on them by beings external and superior to

---

[5] For an interesting discussion of related issues, see Stephen Macedo, *Liberal Virtues: Citizenship, Virtue, and Community in Liberal Constitutionalism* (New York: Oxford University Press, 1990).

[6] Ortega, *The Revolt of the Masses*, p. 42.

themselves. Their superiority was established by, if nothing else, the fact that it was from them that these standards came.

Ortega describes the general character of the preliberal parts of human history like this:

> For the "common man" of all periods, "life" had principally meant limitation, obligation, dependence; in a word, pressure. Say oppression, if you like, provided it be understood not only in the juridical and social sense, but in the cosmic.[7]

What Ortega calls the "cosmic" sort of pressure is undoubtedly very important for understanding the difference between liberal and preliberal societies. Liberalism brought with it a striking degree of relative prosperity, which liberated huge masses of people from the need to devote most of their time to the simple end of producing what they needed to stay alive. However, the sort of pressure that I wish to single out and discuss is the other one mentioned by Ortega, the sort he calls juridical or social.

Most people in the societies that immediately preceded liberalism were confronted with a considerable and burdensome array of obligations that were placed on them by tradition. In one way or another, this is true of people who live in any sort of society, but certain of the traditional obligations in preliberal societies have two characteristics that, jointly, separate their world from our own. Together, they distinguish these social systems as instances of what, following a famous discussion by Sir Henry Maine, I will call "societies of status."[8]

First, in such societies, the traditional mores defined groups of people, and, in addition, they defined various obligations in such a way that, once an individual is a member of one of these groups, that individual cannot avoid a very significant burden of obligations of that sort. Second, membership in these groups was itself not a result of any voluntary action on the individual's part. Tradition placed obligations on individuals in a way that excluded individual choice. These obligations are the unchosen consequences of involuntary group membership. A few examples might help to reveal exactly what this means.

---

[7] Ibid., p. 43.

[8] Henry Sumner Maine, *Ancient Law* (New York: Henry Holt and Company, 1888), p. 165.

The example of a society of this sort that comes most readily to mind is a caste system. In a pure caste system, there are customs or laws that assign important obligations to people simply by virtue of their membership in their political or economic class. The obligations involved both require and enable these people to carry out the political or economic functions that, again simply by virtue of class membership, are properly theirs. Because they are attached to class functions in this way, these obligations are identical throughout a given caste and are not shared with the rest of the human race.[9] To the extent that people inherit their caste membership from their parents, and cannot abandon it by individual choice (the peasants, for instance, are tied to the land), it is obvious that such systems fit the description I have just given of the assignment of obligations in societies of status.

Another example, somewhat less obvious, of a system that answers to this description is one in which the family structure is characterized by a certain sort of patriarchy. A rather extreme instance is to be found in the early Roman Republic as described by Maine. According to him, this was a system in which the law and its obligations only served to regulate the foreign relations between families. Within the family the only law, if we may call it that, was the will of the "despot enthroned by each hearthstone," the head of the family.[10] In the earliest and purest form of this system, this meant that sons and daughters were subject for life to the arbitrary decrees of their father, which he could enforce with any sort of punishment, including death.[11] Thus, the individuals who occupied the status of son or daughter were vulnerable, just because they belonged to those categories, to a stream of unavoidable obligations. Of course, the status of son or daughter is, except in some cases of adoption, one that is occupied involuntarily.

As this example indicates, the sort of society I have described does not necessarily involve fixed duties that are unalterably built into the position occupied by the person to whom they apply. In principle, the obligations

---

[9] Here I am using caste in the sense employed by Ludwig von Mises. See his "The Clash of Group Interests," in *Money, Method, and the Market Process: Essays by Ludwig von Mises*, ed. Richard M. Ebeling (Norwell, Mass.: Kluwer Academic Publishers, 1990), p. 204.

[10] Maine, *Ancient Law*, p. 162.

[11] "The parent . . . has over his children the *jus vitae necisque*, the power of life and death . . .; he can modify their personal condition at pleasure; he can give a wife to his son; he can give his daughter in marriage; he can divorce his children of either sex; he can transfer them to another family by adoption; he can sell them." *Ancient Law*, p. 133.

involved may be flexible, or even unpredictable. What makes a system a society of status in my sense is not the content of the relevant obligations but their source. The arrangements that Maine attributes to the early Roman Republic qualify by virtue of the fact that important obligations are based on group membership, and because membership in these groups is, at least typically, not the result of the voluntary conduct of the individual member. That is sufficient.[12]

4. The Liberal World

Liberal democracy has shown a powerful tendency to build a world that is very different from the ones I have just been describing. My brief discussion of liberalism in section 2 suggests one very likely reason for this: it is very difficult to reconcile these earlier arrangements with either of the two basic values of liberalism: liberty and equality.

Anyone who places a high value on liberty would, to the extent that they do so, be uncomfortable with the idea that there can be significant obligations unilaterally imposed on one, either by tradition or by a human overlord set up by tradition. Such authorities—for that is what they are—seem to function at the expense of individual freedom. People who are strongly attached to the value of liberty will sacrifice it only if it is necessary to do so. As liberal society has evolved, these particular sacrifices of liberty

---

[12] It is also possible, though I have no reason to stress this point, to interpret the gift-exchange systems I discussed in chapter VIII as societies of status. As I pointed out there (VIII.4), such systems inevitably generate significant obligations (obligations to make return gifts) by a process that is substantially outside the individual's control. As anthropologists have noted, in such systems gifts are reserved for exchanges between members of one's own group. To the extent that people are perceived as falling outside one's group, commercial exchange is used, and, in some cases, people who are completely alien are treated without moral constraints at all. See Marshall Sahlins, *Stone Age Economics*, (New York: Aldine de Gruyter, 1972), p. 162. To be a member of the group is, in part, to participate in a tradition-defined process that, by its nature, brings a flood of obligations with it. Since membership in such groups is typically by birth or adoption—the former always and the latter usually an involuntary one on the recipient's part—such societies are clearly ones in which an important body of obligations are the unchosen consequences of involuntary group membership. Gift-exchange systems differ from many societies of status in one important respect: in many societies of status, the obligations are owed to someone who is either above or below oneself in some hierarchical order. As I use the term, however, societies of status does not refer to systems that are necessarily hierarchical. The same is true of Maine's usage.

have lost their original appearance of necessity: other principles of social order seem to have served at least as well.

In much the same way, the old ideas have proved to be unattractive to people who value equality. When liberalism first became a formidable political fact in Europe, the serious competitors it encountered were examples of a particular sort of society of status: they were remnants of caste systems, in which many people were trapped in groups that played subservient roles in relation to other groups. This imputation of subordination seems to be an inevitable feature of such systems. The functions served by the various groups—such as ruling, fighting, tilling the land, and so forth—always seem to be such that people have more or less definite notions to the effect that some are superior to others. In practice, this has always given the impression that the members of at least one group are inferior to the individuals outside their group to whom they owe their obligations. This is true even when the social system is divided into groups each of which have duties to all the others, so that it realizes in some way the moral ideal of reciprocity.[13] The subservience meted out by these systems was particularly severe when there was no way the individual could escape it.

Of course, the liberal conception of equality is not incompatible with hierarchy of every sort, but it does mean that, if we are to burden people differently, there must be some good reason for doing so. Over the years, people who live in the liberal nations have found it increasingly difficult to give good enough reasons for the traces of preliberal hierarchy that remained in their world.

The tendency of liberalism has been to develop moral traditions that are altogether inimical to traditions in which individuals are assigned to groups and obligations are assigned to them as group members. Naturally, there must be obligations that are not the result of voluntary actions of the

---

[13] A certain hierarchical attitude is often openly displayed in the writings of the classic apologists for such systems. One clear example is Plato's *Republic*. Another is John of Salisbury's defense of the medieval caste system in the *Policraticus*. The latter author compares the commonwealth to a human individual, with some parts performing the functions of the feet and others doing the work of the soul. The commonwealth is healthy when "the higher members shield the lower, and the lower respond faithfully and fully in like measure to the just demands of their superiors, so that each and all are as it were members one of another by a sort of reciprocity. . ." *The Portable Medieval Reader*, ed. J. B. Ross and M. M. McLaughlin (New York: Viking Press, 1949), pp. 47-48. Such reciprocity is, as John says, between superiors and inferiors, not between equals.

individual who has them, but with the destruction of the old way the only such obligations that can remain are ones that apply to everybody.

Clearly, however, no moral tradition could consist solely of such universal obligations. A society thus limited would be one in which what each individual owes to all the others is absolutely identical; it would in this sense be devoid of what one philosopher has called "moral particularity."[14] For many reasons, including a sufficient number of obvious ones, the moral entanglements of unique individuals must be to some extent unique. Liberal societies have avoided unarticulated sameness by relying on certain moral practices that, while some of them can probably be found other sorts of social systems, have nonetheless assumed unprecedented importance in the liberal democracies. This transformation has resulted in the formation of systems that, again following suggestions from Maine, I will call "societies of contract."[15]

To the extent that individuals live in such a society, they see their differential obligations, the obligations they do not share with all of humanity, as foreseeable consequences of their own voluntary conduct.[16] Sometimes, the conduct involved literally is the signing of a contract of some sort or other, but perhaps more often it is one of the many other sorts of intentional actions by which we become entangled in the lives of others, including joining a club, enrolling in a school, entering a profession, or

---

[14] Alasdair MacIntyre, *After Virtue: A Study in Moral Theory* (Notre Dame: University of Notre Dame Press, 1984), p. 220.

[15] See footnote 8, above. Friedrich Hayek gently criticizes Maine's formula as follows: "The true contrast to a reign of status is the reign of general and equal laws, of the rules which are the same for all, or, we might say, of the rule of *leges* in the original meaning of the Latin word for laws—*leges* that is, as opposed to the *privileges*." *The Constitution of Liberty* (Chicago: The University of Chicago Press, 1960), p. 154. While Hayek's comment is quite true, I think it misses the point of Maine's distinction, which is to explain how people in a given society come to have *differential* obligations. General rules equally applied (as long as they are described no further) cannot explain that.

[16] I should emphasize that a given society is a society of status or of contract *to the extent that* it answers to one definition or the other. It is no part of my thesis that all systems answer to one or the other, or that a pure instance of either sort of society has ever existed.

taking part in the give and take of an intimate relationship over a long stretch of time.[17]

Such actions, unlike the preliberal sources of differential obligation, are not violations of our freedom: they are actually expressions of it. Further, the obligations involved arise from conduct that, in principle, any adult can do, and not from membership in a group that sets one above or below other people. Thus, moral particularity, on the face of it at least, is created in ways that are compatible with the liberal ideals of freedom and equality.[18]

---

[17] Admittedly, my (and Maine's) use of the word "contract" here is somewhat inexact. Yet, though many of the moral and legal practices toward which I am gesturing here are not contracts, still they resemble contracts in three important respects. Consider the following example. In our culture, the obligations one has toward one's children are not based on one's status as their biological ascendant. This is shown by the fact that we see exactly the same obligations as attaching us to our adopted children, while on the other hand we see none of these obligations as attaching us to children we might have given out for adoption. Yet such obligations could not be based on contract either. The only contract that could provide such a basis would have to involve the children as parties, and many of them are not competent to enter into contractual relations. Apparently, the obligations are based on an act on the part of parents or guardians (perhaps having the children in their homes and *not* taking steps to find other homes for them) that differs from entering a contract in that it can be unilateral. But it otherwise resembles a contract in that (1) it is voluntary, (2) it has an obligation as its foreseeable result, and (3) any adult in principle can do it.

[18] I should point out that, though I use a phrase from MacIntyre here I am radically disagreeing with what he uses it to say. Consider this important passage: "We all approach our circumstances as bearers of a particular social identity. I am someone's son or daughter, someone else's cousin or uncle; I am a citizen of this or that city, a member of this or that guild or profession; I belong to this clan, that tribe, this nation. . . . As such, I inherit from the past of my family, my city, my tribe, my nation, a variety of debts, inheritances, rightful expectations and obligations. These constitute the given of my life, my moral starting point. This is in part what gives my life its own moral particularity." *After Virtue*, p. 220. What he is expressing here is clearly a preliberal way of creating moral particularity. Both in this passage and throughout this enormously influential book, MacIntyre ignores the liberal way of achieving the same result. This omission is essential to the argument of *After Virtue*. If I understand it rightly, the relevant part of that argument goes as follows: MacIntyre eloquently presents, in broad outline, various features of preliberal moral systems that established differential obligations among the people who lived within them. He then notes that this description does not apply very well to liberal democracies. He concludes that the moralities on which such societies are based must be ones in which the only obligations that exist are those few that can be attributed to everyone. Within the wide limits established by these bloodlessly universal obligations, little of moral importance happens: mainly, life is a series of brutal conflicts between nakedly self-interested individuals or factions. See *After*

5. Finding Out Who One Is

Insofar as earlier societies were based on status rather than contract, they presented people with a prefabricated array of moral obligations. They did so, moreover, in a particular way: by presenting them, in a certain sense, with a prefabricated identity. If I were born into the hereditary caste of priests—or musicians, or tillers of the soil—this classification would indicate to me a significant part of what I would be doing with my life, and of what would be important to me as I lived it. This classification would tell me something important about my obligations and—at least as important—these obligations would indicate how important this classification was. They would indicate to me that my caste membership is not just another fact about me, like my being tall, deep voiced, or blonde: it indicates to me *what I am.*

Admittedly, there is a sense in which, even after status has been replaced entirely by contract, one could say that society still presents the individual with a prefabricated identity. Convention gives a certain meaning to words and phrases such as "intelligent," "slovenly," "of Italian ancestry" and it may be that, independent of my own voluntary actions, these conventions indicate that I am all of these things. Someone who is willing to make a certain philosophical assumption might conclude that it is in that case true by convention that these things are true of me and that, consequently, it is society—the social group that is governed by these conventions—that makes it so.

Even if this is so, however, there is still a large difference between this social group and a status system. If these words and phrases apply to me by linguistic convention, they do so merely as an unassorted collection of epithets. These conventions do not indicate to me which of them are important and which are trivial. This is of course what people are wondering about when they seek to find out who or what they are, when they seek to discover their own individual identity: they wish to know, not merely which attributes do they have, but which are the important ones. This latter question is what, in large part at least, a status system settles for us. In such a system, there may be little need to seek to find one's own identity; it is, to some extent, settled.

Virtue, chap. 3 and pp. 250-51. This argument, if it really is his argument, simply assumes, without any proof, that preliberal ways of achieving differential obligations are the only ones there are.

What Maine called "the movement from status to contract"[19] makes it possible for a social system to contain differential obligations without assigning individual identities. To the extent that this transformation has occurred, it is possible to sever being from doing, to separate the question of who or what I am from that of what I morally ought to do. This would mean that I am able to find out what special obligations I have toward others without knowing who I am—without considering my race, class, or gender, for instance—but simply by considering what I have done.

To the extent that a social system develops under the influence of liberal ideas, it seems inevitable that this separation should occur. As I have already suggested, it seems unlikely that any society can function unless its method of assigning moral obligations allows different people to have different obligations. We cannot bear our obligations simply as members of an undifferentiated mass. Yet liberal societies are constrained as to how they bring about the needed differentiation. They must avoid presenting their inhabitants with prefabricated identities. Dictating to people who they are to be represents a highly undesirable sacrifice of liberty. Moreover, since one's identity always seems to be in some way good or bad, it constitutes a very serious sacrifice of equality as well. Of course, liberal institutions must be based on assumptions about what people are like. It would be desirable, however, to make no assumptions about any one person, independent of their overt behavior, other than basic principles that apply to everyone: for instance, that people are able to think, to make choices, to act on their choices, and to accept responsibility for foreseeable consequences.[20] But a contractual system can be based on precisely such universal principles as these. Thus, it seems inevitable that, unless there is some powerful counteracting force at work, liberal societies will, so far as it is feasible to do so, complete the transition from status to contract, and thus free themselves from the necessity of socially assigning identities.

This suggests rather strongly that in such a society the solution to the issue of individual identity is entirely up to the individual. Finding the answer to it is a solitary enterprise, something the individual does alone. This suggestion, if anyone should take it and believe it, would be an error. The reason it would be an error is, simply, that it is doubtful that there is such an

---

[19] Maine, *Ancient Law*, p. 165.

[20] See John Rawls, *Political Liberalism* (New York: Columbia University Press, 1993), pp. 29-35.

entirely solitary enterprise as (successfully) finding out who one is. At least, it is not an enterprise on which, in any society, the general run of humanity might be embarked.

This is a far from trivial fact, and it helps to explain deeply important features of liberal regimes. I will discuss these implications in the next section but, before I do that, I should briefly recount some of the reasons (in case they are not sufficiently obvious) why the search for identity is something individuals cannot not be expected to do entirely on their own.

First, there are probably many individuals who, to some substantial extent, inevitably absorb their ideas about themselves from other people. The opinions of others exercise an influence over them that they cannot come close to entirely resisting. They accept some of the opinions of others, not as conclusions that they are able to confirm somehow, but simply because they are opinions and are held by someone. Discovering their own identity, insofar as such individuals are able to accomplish it, is to a significant extent not their own doing.

Of course, it is likely that not everyone is like this. There probably are people who avoid, with at most trivial exceptions, this sort of uncritical absorption of the ideas that others have about them. Rather than substituting the judgment of others for their own, they think for themselves. Yet to the extent that it produces any real understanding, this thinking for oneself is seldom, if ever, something that is done entirely *by* oneself, at least when the thinking that is done is about oneself.

One reason why this is so can be found in the fact that the self, as a subject matter of inquiry, presents the inquirer with some serious difficulties. My own identity is something about which I have very strong motives for deceiving myself. As I have already suggested, it always seems to be either good or bad. The traits I am most likely to find important—traits of character, skills or incapacities, and emotional dispositions are obvious instances—are seldom if ever entirely neutral. They are usually something to be either proud or ashamed of. If I am left entirely to my own devices, the promptings not only of vanity but of the perfectly normal need for self-esteem will certainly lead me to suppress, augment, or slant the evidence.

Further, whether we distort it or not, this evidence is peculiarly difficult to collect. Simple introspection, direct inspection of the contents of one's own mind, is of far less value in these matters than one tends to think it is. The most important statements about ourselves do not take the form of descriptions of simple mental events.[21] Consequently, to know whether some such statement is true requires that I do something more than to turn my mind's eye inward and see whether some event has occurred within me. To some extent they seem to function more like explanations of events rather than descriptions of them, and usually serve to explain an array, often a large one, of occurrences both mental and physical.

Knowing whether one of them is true has all the prerequisites that the art of explanation has. Among other things, I must be aware of other plausible explanations for the same facts, and I must have good enough reason to believe that the one I am giving is the best of them. Does my inability to accomplish much lately indicate that I have become self-indulgent, or does it mean that I have become understandably depressed because life has disappointed me so many times? Perhaps it is merely some undiagnosed physical illness that has lowered my spirits. The picture presented by the available evidence is often radically incomplete. It is understandable if my desire to think well of myself steps in and paints over the white spots on the canvas.[22]

Clearly, substantial difficulties stand in our way as we try to acquire solidly based conceptions of who we are. The ones I have just described, however, are not hopelessly insurmountable. There are routes by which they can sometimes be circumvented, and the most readily available ones by far involve relying on the participation of other people.

This is probably most obvious with regard to the problem of resisting one's urge toward self-deception. With few exceptions, I can rely on others to be far less biased in my favor than I am. It is not, of course, that I am biased and they are not: their biases are rather in other directions than mine. We can rely on each other, as individuals with clashing and thus complementary prejudices, to test and check our ideas of ourselves.

---

[21] Gilbert Ryle, *The Concept of Mind* (New York: Barnes and Noble, 1949), p. 15 and *passim*.

[22] Traits of character present an additional difficulty. When we want to know whether we have a given trait of character, we are mainly interested in whether the trait we have is an instance of virtue or of vice. This requires us to find out whether the principle it is based on is true or false. To have any well-grounded ideas about this at all, we must to some extent be able to solve problems about the nature and value of the proper ends of human action and about the legitimate constraints on the means we should avail ourselves of as we pursue our ends. I can only have good reason to deny that my actions are cowardly if I have good reason to deny that they reveal that I value safety too highly. Such reasons, in turn, can only be mine if I have some notion, more or less well founded, of what *would* constitute overvaluing safety. Such issues of course are complex and endlessly contestable.

Similar things can be said of our efforts to overcome the problems that are inherent in the explanatory nature of many of the relevant ideas. Finding all of the most plausible explanations for something and finding the best reasons for preferring one explanation to another are undertakings that rely on one's powers of imagination. In difficult cases, even when the thing to be explained is my own behavior, my best chance of success requires me to avail myself of imaginations that are not my own. Possibilities that are invisible to me might be visible, even obvious, to other people.[23]

We learn from points of view that differ from our own, and this especially includes ones that are adverse to ours. This adversity is an indispensable source of insight. A look of surprise on someone's face as I say something that seems obvious to me can, and often should, lead me to reconsider my ideas and either abandon them or be sure I have good reasons for keeping them. It is at least arguable that no one ever arrives at a substantial sort of self-understanding without at some point gaining insight from collision with the viewpoints of others. What is more than arguable is the fact that, for most people, finding out who they are is not something they do on their own.

6. Identity as a Datum and as a Task

To the extent that it withdraws from people their socially prefabricated identities, liberal society has not compelled them to find out who they are on their own. The search for one's identity cannot be a solitary enterprise, not at any rate if it has a reasonable chance of being successful. Yet it seems it must be carried on somehow or other. People seem to have an ineradicable need to have some definite and well-grounded notion of who or what they

---

[23] Again, essentially the same things can be said of the problems arising from the notions about good and bad, right and wrong, that undergird ascriptions of character. The fact that, here too, our self-understanding depends on others is strongly suggested by the history of ethics. All these notions are the work of a long line of people working with and against each other. One reason why this is so is that it is only in the context of discussion and debate that human beings can gain an insight into the troubling question of how adequate are their notions about what is good or right. It is possible to have a rational basis for such ideas, but this is secured mainly by taking positions on relevant issues in the context of reactions of other people who have positions of their own. Under the pressure of comments both friendly and hostile (especially the latter), our ideas have been constantly checked, altered, and—we hope—improved.

are.[24] How then can the search be carried on in a liberal society? An answer to this question is already implied by what I have said in the preceding section of this chapter. I will now make it explicit.

The attempt to understand who we are, like any investigation, must be carried on by means of symbolic behavior, behavior (such as using words, making pictures, or putting together mathematical formulae) that communicates messages by representing things. This means that one of the ways in which investigations can be classified is in terms of this symbolic behavior: who is doing the representing, and to whom are these things being represented? Based on how these two questions are answered, we can classify these processes as "monological" and "dialogical."[25]

To say that an investigation is dialogical is to say that at least some of the symbolic behavior by which it is carried out consists of an exchange between two different representers, in which each one serves both as author of a message (or messages) and as audience for the message(s) of the other. At least some of the messages sent by each side are received by the other and influence in some significant way subsequent messages sent by the other. (For these purposes, messages can be questions.) Examples of such symbolic behavior include courtroom cross-examinations, Socratic dialogues, most ordinary conversations, and many wordless encounters between individuals that transpire by means of looks and gestures only.

---

[24] No doubt there are many reasons for this, some of them profound and poorly understood, but one grossly obvious one is simple self-interest. Whatever is good for me is good for just the sort of person I am, and will often not be good for other sorts of people. This means that I am not likely to find out what it is that is good for me without finding out what sort of person it is that I am; and if I do not find out what is good for me, I am not likely to get it.

[25] Here I am borrowing my terminology from Charles Taylor, who in turn borrows it from M. M. Bakhtin. See Taylor's "Multiculturalism and 'The Politics of Recognition,'" *Multiculturalism and the Politics of Recognition: An Essay by Charles Taylor with Commentary by Amy Gutmann, Steven C. Rockefeller, Michael Walzer, and Susan Wolf,* ed. Amy Gutmann (Princeton: Princeton University Press, 1991), pp. 25-73. Taylor uses "monological" and "dialogical" to say things that are very different from and to some extent opposed to the things I am using them to say, and it is quite possible that he does not mean the same things by these words as I do. For that reason, I hesitate to use the same terminology he uses, since I might thereby lead readers who are familiar with Taylor's essay to misunderstand what I am saying, or to think that I have misunderstood what he is saying. However, these words so perfectly express what I have in mind—better, indeed than they fit what he is saying—that I can see no better alternative. I will comment on the differences between Taylor's message and mine later on. That, I hope, will prevent some confusions.

On the other hand, an investigation is monological to the extent that the relevant symbolic behavior is not dialogical: if either (1) the representer and the audience are identical or (2) one functions only as representer and the other only as audience. An example of this sort of symbolic behavior can be found in Descartes's *Meditations*, in the thoughts the author attributes to him as he sits quietly by his stove, finding out what he knows and what he does not know.

Among the processes in which people putatively find out who they are, an obvious example of a monological one would be the sort that is carried out (assuming this ever happens) when individuals figure out who they are entirely on their own. This of course is the asocial process that I have said is not on its own a feasible way to find out who one is. Another instance of a monological process, however, *is* social in nature and has proven over the centuries to be entirely feasible. This is the one that is distinctive of preliberal societies.

In these cases, the party that sends the messages, and in so doing attributes an identity to someone, is not an individual human being but some superindividual entity, such as law, custom, or tradition. The audience is the individual to whom the identity is attributed. If the relevant entity informs me that, in one important respect, what I really am is a farmer or the son of a living father, there is no possibility that I will be able to send messages—such as questions, objections, or denials—back to it.

Things are very different when the process by which identity is found is, as I am putting it, dialogical. In that case, no one involved in the procedure is elevated to the position of an unanswerable speaker and no one is trapped in the role of a passive audience. On the contrary, any message can be answered, and the answer can influence subsequent messages from the other side. The outcome of the process—the message that the participants come away from the process believing or acting on—is determined by the give and take among all who have participated in it. It is a cooperative enterprise in which no one participant has the power to determine the final outcome. Indeed, there is no outcome that is final, in the sense of being unrevisable; there is only the outcome of the moment. Further, that outcome, for each participant, consists only in what he or she is actually convinced is so. Thus, the result of any one process is not only revisable but also (at least potentially) plural.[26]

It seems obvious that liberalism requires the dialogical approach. As I have said, identity must be sought either monologically or dialogically. For all the reasons I gave in section 5, the sort of monological process in which the definer and the defined are the same person is not feasible, at least most of the time and for most people.

The other sort of monological procedure cannot coexist with liberalism for very long. This is the one in which the definer and the defined are different persons, the latter occupying the position of mere audience in relation to the former.

One reason for this incompatibility has to do with the first of the two principles that I attributed to minimal liberalism in section 2, the one that maintains that people have a right to freely express their views. This right opens all important subjects to dialogue with other individuals, including the subject matter of the monological process. An American teenager's immigrant parents tell him that ancient tradition dictates that his place in society requires that he obey his mother's older brother or prepare for the priesthood; he may find this fact impressive. In a liberal society, however, he will hear a clamor of many voices speaking on this issue, and the other

---

[26] One difference between Charles Taylor's use of "monological" and "dialogical" on the one hand and my own on the other (see footnote 25, above) lies in the fact that he restricts the use of monological to investigations of identity that are asocial, in which it is "something each person accomplishes on his or her own." (*Multiculturalism and The Politics of Recognition*, p. 32.) Other differences are to be found in his suggestions that throughout history the search for identity has always been almost completely dialogical (see p. 34) and his tendency to speak of the monological as an "ideal" that is inadequate because it "seriously underestimates" the inevitable "place of the dialogical in human life" (p. 33). All of this suggests that for him "monological" and "dialogical" mean simply "asocial" and "social," respectively. That, of course, is not what they mean when I use them. But these terminological differences, if that is what they are, seem to be connected to deeper ones. A central claim of his essay is that liberalism, when it arrived, stepped into a world that was thoroughly dialogical (in his sense) and then proceeded to interfere with the smooth working of this process (pp. 34-35). Another is that the only solution to the problems caused by this interference is to change liberal society so that it is more like preliberal society (as I have characterized it) (see pp. 51-61). I think that the first of these two claims has more than a little truth in it. However, given that the word "dialogue" and its cognates inevitably suggest a dynamic process involving an open exchange of conflicting views, it is also profoundly misleading to state this idea as he does, by describing preliberal society as dialogical. I shall presently argue that the second claim—that only the preliberal approach offers a hope of a solution—is not true.

voices will, unlike the voice of ancient tradition, answer questions and give reasons if challenged. As many immigrants to liberal countries have testified, the eventual effect of these voices is to take away the tendency to believe what the monological messages say, and, with it, the will and faith needed to help transmit them eventually goes as well. The liberal dialogue washes away the preliberal monologue.

This means that, in a liberal society, people must for the most part seek their identity dialogically.[27] This in turn indicates that life in a liberal society will not be experienced by all as an absolutely unmixed blessing. Previously, one's own identity was to some extent a given; now it is simply a task, and one that to a significant extent is carried out in concert with others. Why this should diminish the blessings of liberalism can be seen by analogy with another important feature of liberal society as we have known it: the creation of differential obligations by means of contract.

The last time I lived in an apartment, the rent I owed for my home was not set by obligations I had to a lord to whom I was bound by the unavoidable accident of birth, nor was it imposed by tradition. Nonetheless, my obligation to pay the rent was obviously not entirely my own doing. The matter of whether I owe rent, and how much, and to whom, was settled by me *and* by my landlord. I could not have had any particular obligation in the matter unless we both agreed that I had it.

---

[27] I should emphasize something that I have already suggested but perhaps have not yet made explicit enough. The enterprise of seeking self-understanding through dialogue is not unique to liberal society. It must have existed throughout human history and at times was widespread even before the birth of liberalism. Henri Pirenne argued eloquently that, by the late twelfth century, relations among the merchants and artisans of the time took place in conditions that were remarkably free of the restrictions that characterize societies of status. This, however, was apparently only true of relations *among* these individuals. Relations with individuals *outside* the group were a different matter. Pirenne argued that these people regarded their freedom as a caste privilege and jealously guarded it as such against the rural peasants whom they held in subjection and regarded as their inferiors. See his *Medieval Cities: Their Origins and the Revival of Trade* (Princeton: Princeton University Press, 1952), chaps. 7 and 8. See also his *Economic and Social History of Medieval Europe* (New York: Harcourt Brace, 1937), chap. 2. The point, however, is that most people, including most of these lucky individuals, were given some portion of their identity by the moral and legal structure of their societies, and they have generally felt that this was an important portion of it. In addition, those who were not so fortunate had little opportunity or inclination to inquire what, in addition to this portion, constituted who they were. They knew who they were and that, at least, was the end of that. In liberal societies, this source of putative insight into one's own identity is for the most part not present at all, for anyone.

This means that we both acted under constraints that were sometimes strongly felt. The rent always seemed high to me and went painfully higher every year. I regretted that I could never find a landlord who would rent a similar apartment to me for less money. My landlord, on the other hand, often complained that the rent was so low that he could barely make money on our building after his expenses were paid. He probably was sorry that he apparently could not find an equally reliable tenant who would pay more than I would. My obligation to pay the rent, and my landlord's right to that rent, was the outcome of a process that we both found painfully frustrating at times. The reason was that we both participated in the process fully: unlike the lords of old, neither one of us could have things his own way.

What I have just said about the task of determining one's obligations by means of contract can also be said, at least if we speak on a sufficiently high level of abstraction, of the task of discovering one's identity dialogically. That is, in each case the task is carried out by means of an activity in which we cooperate with others, and, in roughly similar ways, the necessity of the other's participation can be painfully constraining.

I want to have a low price for my home and for everything else I must pay for, and in a contractual system I am free to influence my trading partners in that direction, but they will not prove to be completely malleable. I make certain conjectures about who I am, mainly very flattering to me, and I try to convince my fellow participants in the dialogue to confirm these conjectures. They, however, have perspectives of their own, and are not biased in my favor in just the way I am. They are not likely to confirm my preferred self-conception in every detail. Their behavior may even attribute to me a failed or deficient identity. They might, for instance, attribute vices to me or imply that I lack admirable skills. I may not be able to think that I am who I would like to be. Just as the contractual system does not allow me to pay just what I want, so the liberal dialogue may make it difficult to think just what I want about myself. I may even find it very difficult to achieve self-esteem.

In a liberal society this a constant danger. This fact poses a problem for the stability of liberal societies. If what I have been saying here is substantially true, liberal society thrusts us into a situation in which the words of other individuals, and all their conduct capable of communicating thoughts about us, have great power both to help and to harm us. How will the inhabitants of such a world be apt to use this power?

In such a society most people, or most influential ones, accept the first principle of minimal liberalism, the one that grants them freedom of expression.

To the extent that they do accept this principle, they will apparently feel free to use their considerable power as they see fit. This would mean that they will feel free to withhold from us the support without which self-esteem may be difficult or impossible to achieve.

However, the constant threat of damage to which the first principle thus exposes us runs counter to the values represented by the second. The second principle, which promises the equal protection of the laws, identifies as a basic function of the liberal system the provision of security from harm by others.

The problem for the stability of liberal society lies in the fact that, to the extent that people are influenced by this idea, they will tend to react in a particular way to the insecurity created by the first principle. Looking at the world from the vantage of the second principle, we tend to view acts that harm others with suspicion, and we tend to view acts that do serious harm with strong suspicion. What we would suspect is that these acts are injustices, for what the principle promises is a certain security from harm as a matter of right. Of course, against harms to oneself one will be ready to respond with particular intensity.

The effect is reinforced by the liberal value that the second principle serves to formulate: the value of equality. The liberal dialogue exposes the individual to the possibility of a daily bruising. The acts by which the bruises are inflicted are challenges to one's self-respect: they are degrading or demeaning. On the other hand, those who do such acts often appear high-handed, as if they are somehow lording it over us. Thus, the insults, derogatory comments, and the mere cold refusal to support one's preferred self-conception are typically felt by those who suffer them to establish a certain relation between higher and lower, in which the sufferer is subordinated to the one who is inflicting the suffering. Often, the bruised individual feels an emotion that is the inner correlative of a shouted accusation: "Who do you think you are!?"[28]

7. A Vice without a Name

Part of the problem is this. These suspicions, the suspicions that other people are committing acts of injustice simply by expressing their views, together with the fact that the apparent injustices are degrading to oneself, place terrific pressure on the principle of forbearance that underlies the virtue of tolerance.

---

[28] Later, I will briefly discuss some authors who claim that such acts really do in some way subordinate people. Here I am only saying that this is how such actions are often perceived. See footnote 43, below.

Together, they can make it seem necessary to react to such acts in ways that include censuring them and, often, go a good deal further than that.

What this means is that a liberal society will tend to produce a trait of character that acts in ways that are directly contrary to tolerance. This trait will be a particular sort of resentment. It will differ from other sorts of resentment in that it will be directed against the communicative behavior of others, and in particular against failures to support one's preferred conception of oneself and against expressions of opinions that conflict with this conception. It will differ from the *emotion* of resentment in that it includes notions that appear to ensure the legitimacy of the anger that accompanies it. The liberal notions of equality and immunity from harm are notions about what is just and what is unjust; when we are angry against those who violate them we are angry on principle and not merely out of personal vanity.

Though this trait seems clearly to be one that some people do possess, it does not seem to have a name in our culture. For lack of a more appropriate term, I will call it "hypersensitivity." We should not be surprised if people who are hypersensitive in this sense sometimes fail to support liberal institutions that guarantee freedom of expression. Such institutions serve, as part of their normal functioning, to permit others to cause them pain, to protect the acts that do so as a right. Their fondness for these institutions is apt at least to be dampened by the realization that this is so. The problem, however, is deeper than that: hypersensitive people are not merely hurt, they are offended. Their resentment is based on certain notions about justice. These notions include, in some form or other, the principle that symbolic behavior that damages the self-esteem of others is wrong. This would mean that, to the extent that institutions protect people who do such painful things, they serve merely to protect wrongdoing.

People who hold this view might well decide that these institutions are simply unjust, reasoning that institutions that protect injustice are themselves unjust. Those who arrive at this conclusion can be expected to denounce such institutions and actively undermine them when they have a chance to do so.

The object of such active attempts at undermining would be to control the dialogue through which, in liberal society, people discover who they are, to determine what participants are to say or refrain from saying. To the extent that they succeed, the search for identity will take place monologically and not dialogically. The monologue will be delivered by whoever does the controlling. What hypersensitive activists seek, in part, is a self-monologue conducted through the controlled behavior of others.

Exercising this sort of control is just what people who are afflicted with hypersensitivity will be inclined to do, unless some other factor intervenes and prevents them. Those who are in the grips of this trait see what some people say as an injustice, as violating the liberal proscription against harm and the ideal of equality. Anyone who is faced with such injustice would obviously be justified in using more or less coercive means to put an end to it.[29]

Of course, this would not necessarily mean making threats of physical sanctions such as beatings, incarceration, or the expropriation of the offender's wealth. At a minimum, however, it would mean the use of psychological manipulation or threats (perhaps veiled) of informal sanctions such as shunning and other nonviolent expressions of hostility and moral blame. Such methods can be very effective. If they work their effects often enough, dialogue on relevant subjects will come to an end, replaced by monologues or by silence. Perhaps a more likely result, if there are many hypersensitive people trying to control each other, is a social world that simmers with snarled threats and hints of reprisals, a world in which dialogue is intermittent and dangerous.

Hypersensitivity need not, however, lead one to become an open foe of the legal and political institutions of liberalism. Some people who feel its promptings can also be strongly attached to the first of the two principles of minimal liberalism. They can, in other words, both believe in free expression and in their right to curb expression. Such a position is not a comfortable one, since it seems clearly contradictory, and people who find themselves in it will (assuming they are averse to self-contradiction) believe or hope that there is some way to interpret the two principles of liberalism that will strike some reasonable compromise, a balanced view of their relative importance.

Despite its appearance of moderation, this position is in its own way just as opposed to liberalism as the openly hostile one. As I have already said, an essential element of liberalism is the idea that the freedom of expression protected by the first principle is *not* to be sacrificed for the sake of the values protected by the second. Such a sacrifice is, of course, what the balanced view sought by those who hold this position amounts to.[30]

---

[29] "'What is a sensitive person?' said the Cracker to the Roman Candle. 'A person who, because he has corns himself, always treads on other people's toes.'" Oscar Wilde, "The Remarkable Rocket," in *The Fairy Stories of Oscar Wilde* (New York: Peter Bedrick Books, 1986), p. 68.

[30] Traditionally, countries that consider themselves liberal democracies have curbed speech of various different kinds, but their legal theories have taken sometimes heroic measures to make the limits imposed entirely compatible with freedom of discussion. Sometimes the speech that is curbed is interpreted as part of an action in which something illegal is not merely said but *done*, as in the cases of conspiring, inciting, or making fraudulent promises.

If a society constituted by liberal ideas tends to produce people who suffer from the principled resentment I have been describing here, it plainly is planting the seeds of its own destruction, whether the stance that this resentment takes in relation to liberal institutions is straightforwardly hostile or whether it is ambivalent and reformist. The system would, in either case, be an unstable one.[31]

Other communicative acts are made actionable because they have demonstrably bad effects on the victim's reputation or on some other thing that can be thought of as the victim's property, as in the law of libel and slander. Still others are interpreted as the appropriation of facts that do not rightfully belong to the speaker, invasions of privacy being one of several possible examples. Finally, as in the case of obscenity, they are sometimes prohibited on the basis of principles (involving, for instance, community standards or appeals to prurient interest) that are meant to single out for legal prohibition the communicative act itself or the way it is expressed, as contrasted with any thoughts or feelings that might have been expressed in them. Of course, it is debatable whether these theories are all fully plausible or genuinely consistent with liberalism. All I wish to insist on here is that they represent a great effort to avoid curbing communicative action simply because it expresses an opinion or feeling that is deemed to be bad. If we attempt to amend liberalism to find a more reasonable balance between freedom of expression on the one hand and equality and harm avoidance on the other, we do precisely that. What we are striking at is not the communicative act itself, nor its physical consequences, nor the misappropriation of information. The enemy we are trying to neutralize, the source of the painful and degrading threats to one's identity, is the human mind that lies behind the utterance, with its uncontrollable power to form opinions, have emotions, and weigh the values of things. This is an undertaking that liberal societies have tried very hard to avoid.

[31] It would also seem to be flawed in another way, since hypersensitivity appears to be a vice. It is related to but distinct from what I called "quarrelsomeness" and "petty vanity" in II.7. Those traits involved taking the concerns of self-respect too far. Hypersensitivity need not involve an overvaluation of such things. It is defined rather in terms of what the individual is willing to do to other people about such things. While the other traits are faults in the agent's view of the good, hypersensitivity raises grave doubts about the agent's justice. Providing an argument that it does involve such a breach would require a lengthy argument and one that I am not prepared at this time to give. There is another reason for thinking this trait is a vice, one that is probably more obvious and can no doubt be stated more briefly: it is the same reason that, as I have claimed earlier, envy is a vice (X. 2 and 3). The hypersensitive person does not merely believe that it is permissible to prevent, by means more or less coercive, the damaging communicative act. Such a person positively *wants* to do so. Where does this desire to indulge in coercion come from? It springs from a wish to maintain one's preferred conception of one's own identity. The point of the coercion would be to protect one's self-esteem from erosion caused by the expressive acts of others. But why would the expressive acts of others constitute a threat to one's self-esteem? The most obvious reason is that the opinions that others have about us as are in such cases experienced as evidence about who we are. But the coercive acts involved here only aim at stopping people from communicating their opinions, and obviously do not destroy the opinions

8. A Viable Liberalism

We have reason to think that the sort of resentment that I described in the preceding section is a good deal more than a theoretical possibility. There are a number of recent developments in current liberal culture that seem to indicate a heightened sensitivity to degrading expressive conduct by others and a spreading belief that forcibly silencing the expressions is a just cause.

Perhaps the most important single development of this sort is one of which many Americans seem to be unaware. Many liberal democracies currently have laws on the books that prohibit the expression of views or feelings that are offensive to members of various races or ethnicities, or to people with certain sexual preferences. In Austria one can be sent to prison for denying or "minimizing" the Nazi genocide. In Denmark one runs a serious risk of criminal prosecution by saying in strong language that homosexuality is morally wrong. Laws punishing racist speech are very widespread. The United States seems to be the only industrialized nation in which it is still entirely legal to express racist opinions.[32]

The United States does not yet have such laws, largely because it has a written Bill of Rights guaranteeing freedom of speech and of the press, and because of the way its legal system presently interprets these guarantees. However, it has been the setting for a number of pervasive cultural developments that seem to arise from relevantly similar principles and motives. Probably the most obvious and widely discussed instances are the campus speech codes in force at many colleges and universities. These codes often give administrators wide discretion to use sketchily defined powers in disciplining students and professors for saying things about various protected groups (including women, racial minorities, and

---

themselves. What could explain why people would want to protect their self-esteem by such means? It is only because of the opinions, which are untouched by the act of suppressing their expression, that these expressions are at all relevant to one's own conception of oneself. Since the goal that is sought in it is the preservation of *one's own* conception of one's identity, the point of the coercion would seem to be to hide the evidence from oneself.

[32] For more examples of national speech codes, see Jonathan Rauch, *Kindly Inquisitors: The New Attacks on Free Thought* (Chicago: University of Chicago Press, 1993), chap. 1.

homosexuals) that are deemed to be derogatory. That is, they punish expressive conduct, and do so on account of the views that the conduct expresses.[33]

Other developments that are fundamentally of the same sort can be found in recent changes in rules governing the workplace, in both the public and private sectors. The rules regarding sexual harassment, which in a great many places of employment have been changed in recent years, are very much to the point. Traditionally, harassment, as a prohibited act, did one of two things: either it involved offers of work-related benefits in exchange for sexual favors, or it involved unwanted bodily contact. The former sort of act obviously violated the contractual rights of the employer and the latter in many cases just as obviously constituted a hurtful incursion against another's body. Both are the sort of act that may be prevented by more or less coercive means within a liberal order.

Recently, however, such means have been used to contend with "harassment" that consists simply in expressive conduct that creates a "hostile" work environment for some individual. In a great many cases this conduct need not express any hostility on the part of the individual who is doing it: it is enough if they express attitudes or feelings that are demeaning to certain people. In such cases the rules will be seen from a liberal point of view as doing precisely what a campus speech code does, as abridging the freedom of people to express their views.[34]

A distinct but related development in the American workplace is the widespread introduction of compulsory "diversity training." This involves requiring workers to attend sessions that are explicitly meant to look into and improve their attitudes and feelings about their minority and female coworkers. In the course of doing so, the people who run these sessions have been reported

---

[33] For examples of such rules, see Dinesh D'Souza, *Illiberal Education: The Politics of Race and Sex on Campus* (New York: The Free Press, 1991). A more recent treatment of the subject, with much material on other, closely related cultural developments, is Richard Bernstein, *Dictatorship of Virtue: Multiculturalism and the Battle for America's Future* (New York: Alfred A. Knopf, 1994). Both authors are critical of these phenomena, but there seem to be no book-length journalistic descriptions of the subject of which this is not true.

[34] The speech code now in effect at my own university *is* a harassment rule. It defines harassment in such a way as to include the making of comments that are demeaning to members of one of a list of protected groups.

as using methods that are psychologically intrusive and painful to the workers who are subjected to their training.[35]

My point here is not that all or any of these policies are bad.[36] It is that each of them represents in some way an abridgment of the freedom of expression in order to protect the values embodied in the second principle of minimal liberalism, especially immunity from harm. Moreover, it is just the sort of harm that prompts hypersensitive people to attempt to silence the expressions of others. That is, each of these policies is a step away from liberalism, and it is just the sort of step that a hypersensitive person would take. I cannot argue here to what extent they actually are due to hypersensitivity—it would take me too far into the fields of journalism and sociology—but one thing that can be learned from what I have said already is that liberal institutions definitely are vulnerable to the sort of damage that hypersensitivity will cause if it is not somehow prevented from doing it.

This raises the question of how a liberal culture can protect itself against such damage. As long as it consists simply of what I have called minimal liberalism, there is no such protection at all. The question, then, is: What can be added to minimal liberalism to provide such protection?

One plausible solution to this problem would be to rely—perhaps more strongly than we have—on a certain institutional arrangement that is already part of our culture, and is probably part of all cultures. The most important part of the dialogue in which we find our identity is the stream of day-to-day, face-to-face encounters we have with other individuals. In it, we are able continuously to develop and learn about our individual natures. One thing that helps to prevent hypersensitivity from putting a halt to this process is the fact that it takes place within an ancient institutional framework that serves to protect individual identities from the sort of bruising to which hypersensitivity is a destructive reaction: namely, what is sometimes called etiquette.

This framework includes the ceremonial rules I discussed in an earlier chapter (VII.6) together with many other rules that seem to proscribe all the ways in which we might give offense to others, including being too blunt, taking more

---

[35] See Heather MacDonald, "The Diversity Industry," *The New Republic*, July 5, 1993, pp. 22-25. According to MacDonald, p. 23, one of the goals of the "diversity consultants," as they are called, is to detect and remove undesirable ethical beliefs, such as the idea that "fairness equals treating people the same."

[36] I do think that the argument of this chapter could be used as part of a larger argument against all policies of this sort, but that would require lengthy discussions that would take us far away from the subject of this book.

than one's share of something, getting out of turn, and so forth. These rules enable us to show (or give the impression) that we value the people we encounter, and care enough about their dignity to take their feelings into consideration. Emily Post said:

> Rule of etiquette the first—which hundreds of others merely paraphrase or explain or elaborate—is: Never do anything that is unpleasant to others.[37]

Regarded as a solution to the problem of hypersensitivity, etiquette protects the dialogue by preventing us from provoking the hypersensitive into damaging it. As such, however, it has at least one serious drawback, which is suggested by Post's broad statement of the function of etiquette. As it stands, this statement is an obvious exaggeration, since it is clearly unrealistic to enjoin people to avoid ever displeasing anyone. But it does come close to stating what codes of etiquette are for, and this very fact indicates a hazard that they all bring with them. The fact that some action that causes pain to someone—especially if the pain consists in some sort of trauma to that individual's self-esteem—very often makes it possible for the pained individual to object to the action as rude or, in more recent parlance, "insensitive." The danger is that, if such objections were raised frequently enough, our day-to-day encounters with others would be seriously damaged.

In particular, they would be damaged as means to revealing the truth. The truth is often unpleasant in one way or another, and the truth about who or what we are is especially likely to hurt. If every plausible charge of rudeness (or insensitivity) were raised and pressed vigorously, we would have very strong reasons to express ourselves—at least when our message has any bearing whatever on the conception our auditors have of themselves—with politely tortuous indirectness or not at all. In such an environment, the truth is not likely to flourish.[38]

---

[37] Emily Post, *Etiquette* (New York: Funk and Wagnalls, 1937), p. 43.

[38] Partly on the basis of his own observations, Jonathan Rauch argues at some length that, at least as regards its achievements in science and scholarship, Japan is a case in point here. In Japanese culture, criticizing other people's ideas is considered rude. As a result, ideas are seldom debated openly. Instead, they are traded on "a kind of gray market" in which "people criticize privately." The result, Rauch says, is a culture that is very good at following the lead of others but surprisingly poor (considering its large, well-educated, and extremely hard-working population) at producing new ideas. *Kindly Inquisitors*, pp. 126-27. See also his *The Outnation: A Search for the Soul of Japan* (Cambridge: Harvard Business School Press, 1992).

Though etiquette is no doubt part of the solution to the problem of hypersensitivity, it can also become part of the problem itself. Undeniably, this is something that does sometimes happen. Most of us have had the experience of knowing someone who is so quick to object to slights that talking to them feels like a hazardous undertaking. Usually, we simply avoid such people or restrict our talk with them to impersonal or superficial matters. Someone might wish to remind us at this point that such problems are the exception rather than the rule, that the dialogue, at least so far, is for the most part not sabotaged by accusations of rudeness and insensitivity. This is true, and it gives us some ground for hope. But then the question is: Given the pains that can be caused by self-discovery through dialogue, and given that hypersensitivity seems to be on the rise, what reason can we have to expect that this will continue to be true?[39]

There is a brief answer to this question that is, it seems to me, somewhat too brief. It is that, in a certain way, etiquette is a self-correcting system. Accusing people of breaches of etiquette is unpleasant to others and, for that reason, the rules prohibit doing so too readily and too directly. To do so is itself a breach of etiquette. The system prevents those who adhere to it from using it as a club with which they can beat dialogue to death.

The reason this answer is too brief is that it assumes that people who act according to the strictures of etiquette will do so consistently. If they do, this itself requires an explanation. How might we explain the fact that people generally adhere, as consistently as they do, to a system that assures them that various acts that cause them pain are wrong and *also* heavily constrains their efforts to defend themselves against such acts?[40]

---

[39] A closely related problem would be to explain why a polite aversion to offending others does not, by itself and aside from charges hurled by putative victims, stifle vigorous debate. Whatever it is that prevents this from happening, Jonathan Rauch's view seems to be that it is absent from Japanese culture: the Japanese are too polite to accuse one another of being offensive, but their horror of giving offense often has the same suffocating effect on discussion. See footnote 38, above.

[40] The thought of people rebelling against such constraints is far more than a theoretical possibility. This, in fact, is one of the differences between traditional etiquette and the new standards of "political correctness," or what might be called the new ethic of sensitivity. Racist, sexist, or homophobic insults are obvious breaches of etiquette, and people who advocate new standards of linguistic sensitivity to combat such insults are sometimes called the "new Victorians," suggesting that what they are trying to do is simply to bring back etiquette as we once knew it. Yet there is at least one very large difference between etiquette on the one hand and these new standards on the other. Intemperate accusations of rudeness are always violations of etiquette, but accusations of racism, sexism, or homophobia, no

Good manners as we know them do not seem to be self-supporting. They seem to rest on something outside themselves. One support that seems very important is a certain cultural value, one that is not itself a matter of etiquette. What I have in mind is the value that is embodied in a saying that parents sometimes tell children to say to themselves when they feel an urge to hit someone for something they have said: "Sticks and stones may break my bones but names will never hurt me."

This idea has been ridiculed by advocates of restrictions on free speech.[41] It is not difficult to see why: it seems on its face to be false. If, as I have argued here, liberal society consigns us to developing and discovering our identity in dialogue with others, then clearly we will be profoundly affected by the contributions others make to the dialogue, and this will certainly include the names they apply to us. I have already given reasons for thinking that these effects can be both good and bad. To deny this seems to be foolish, and worse: it seems to discourage people from protecting themselves against the bad effects.

But there are other aspects of the sticks and stones proverb that are not so easy to dismiss. First, it clearly implies that the effects of being hit with stones is radically different from the effects of being pelted with words. Second, because it is something that people are supposed to remember and repeat to themselves, it suggests that the things the would-be victim thinks are relevant to the effects of the latter sort of pelting. Words do not have effects by themselves, but depend on a contribution from their audience.

---

matter how reckless they might be, are never "politically incorrect." None of the recent campus speech codes contained any explicit instructions to the effect that such epithets should not be flung about carelessly. What we are witnessing is the formation of codes of conduct that resemble etiquette except that their enforcement is unconstrained in precisely the way I am considering here. For a discussion of other ways in which these new codes differ from traditional etiquette and morality, see Gertrude Himmelfarb, *The De-Moralization of Society: From Victorian Virtues to Modern Values* (New York: Knopf, 1995), "Postscript: The 'New Victorians' and the Old."

[41] "A child may chant 'sticks and stones may break my bones, but names will never hurt.' Names do hurt, though. That is why she chants. . . . Words can break bones. 'Shoot her' might break a few. . . ." Rae Langdon, "Speech Acts and Unspeakable Acts," *Philosophy and Public Affairs* 22, (Fall 1993): p. 302. Interpreted in this way, the idea becomes a mere piece of wishful thinking, so deeply confused that it is contradicted by the very reason for wishing for it: it is precisely because words do hurt that the child tells herself that they can't. For similarly dismissive comments, see Stanley Fish, *There's No Such Thing as Free Speech and It's a Good Thing Too* (New York: Oxford University Press, 1994), p. 110.

This suggests an alternative way of reading this quaint aphorism, not as an incredibly naive and inaccurate statement of fact, but as an attempt to change the facts, a thought that makes itself true. As such, though it is clearly optimistic, it can be regarded as resting on a principle that is no more obviously false than its most popular alternative. Even its optimism may be methodologically sound.

What might the relevant difference between a word and a stick be? A word, as applied to me, can only hurt me (in the relevant sense) insofar as it purports to represent what I am, and only insofar as its being applied to me leads to my accepting this representation as just. Nothing like this is true of the way that sticks hurt us.

One respect in which words seem to be different is that between the hurling of the word and the harm that it does me are a number of things that I can be said to *do*: I listen to it, understand it, see myself in light of it, and so forth. Of course, we can also say that being hit, being cut, and bleeding are also things that we do. They are also alike in that both sort of events are normally more or less involuntary. But one important difference, and one reason why the former sort of events are more action-like, is that they and only they can *become* voluntary. One cannot bring oneself to bleed by an act of will, but one can bring oneself to understand or to fail to understand.

If that is true, then the sticks-and-stones principle, as I have read it, is a plausible one. It rests on the idea that we are able to withhold some step that is essential to our being seriously harmed by what others say about us, and that such harm only comes when we believe what is said simply because it is said. What the principle says, in effect, is that we ought to exercise this sort of control, that we should not absorb the thoughts that others have about us but rather should form and act on our own individual judgment about such things. What the naive-sounding proverb serves to do is to inculcate a certain trait of character, in which giving in to the inaccurate and adverse opinions that others have of oneself is regarded as wrong. Obviously, this trait is closely related to self-respect, and is probably a more important basis for it than conduct in which we stand up to tyrants and quarrel with our enemies. I will call it "independence."[42]

---

[42] After I had chosen this word for this trait I noticed that Ayn Rand used the same word for what is almost the same trait, the only difference being that the trait she is naming seems to govern one's thinking about everything, and not just oneself. "The virtue of Independence," she says, is "one's acceptance of the responsibility of forming one's own judgments and of living by the work of one's own mind." *The Virtue of Selfishness: A New Concept of Egoism* (New York: New American Library, 1964), p. 26.

Independence, in this sense, is one thing that can help etiquette to continue to exist. It can do so by, in a way, actually reducing the importance of etiquette. Those who possess this trait are to that extent less likely than others to see the value of and—this of course is the point—insist on the protections for delicate feelings that etiquette affords. Thus, they will not mind as much as they otherwise would constraints on their power to seek that protection.

In a way, however, independence merely pushes our problem back another step. The problem is, how can a liberal culture avoid spawning a hypersensitivity that undermines its own institutions and ends the dialogue that they normally foster? If independence is part of the answer, then it, too, requires some explanation. Its exercise is difficult and painful, and silencing others is a genuine alternative to it, one that offers obvious advantages. What can be added to our picture of liberal culture that might help independence to grow and do its work?

A partial answer to this question is already before us. Independence is based on the sticks and stones principle, which is itself a part of our moral and political culture. It is an idea that people accept, in part, because it is part of this culture and continues to be passed on from parent to child. If it exists together with the liberal notions of liberty, equality, and protection from harm, the result is a particular form of liberalism. In it, independence serves to protect liberty from being engulfed by equality.

I will call this sort of liberalism, including any culture that shares the same principles, "individualist liberalism." It is distinguished from the other sorts of liberalism by the fact that it possesses a certain source of immunity to the sort of instability I have been describing in this chapter. It is possible to select from among the other varieties of liberalism one that probably cannot have any such immunity at all. This is the variety that results if one takes the distinguishing ideas of individualist liberalism and replaces them with ones that are directly opposed to them.

The distinguishing ideas of individualist liberalism are the sticks-and- stones principle and the assumption on which it rests, that people can distance themselves in some way from what others say about them. Suppose that these ideas are replaced by a way of thinking that begins with the ideas that the identities of individuals are a product of the groups to which they belong, that this in turn is decisively influenced by the way other people classify them, and that the influence of the classification depends on the way those others characterize the groups involved. For want of a less awkward term, we can call this way of thinking "identity collectivism."

People who have absorbed a liberal political culture that includes this notion would face an excruciating dilemma to the extent that they find, as we all do sooner or later, that others characterize them in some unflattering ways. They would view the liberty of others as a source of serious damage to themselves, and respect for that liberty as acceptance of the inevitability of such damage. No one should be surprised if such people try to seize some sort of coercive control over what other people say and, perhaps, think. The society that such a culture would produce would of course not be a liberal one.

9. Prospects

It is not obvious whether our own political culture more closely resembles the individualist sort of liberalism or the nonindividualist sort I have just described. It is certain that it has contained strongly individualist elements, at least until recently, but it is also well known that identity collectivism has been gaining influence, especially among intellectuals.[43]

---

[43] Charles Taylor seems to adopt some form of this idea in his *Multiculturalism and The Politics of Recognition,* cited in footnote 25, above. It is also, in one way or another, fundamental to much of the recent literature that calls for new restrictions on "hate speech." Much of it insists that, in the words of Stanley Fish, epithets directed at a group to which one belongs cause "lacerating harms" that are "grievous and *deeply* wounding," and are not a matter of hurt feelings. This idea, as used by Fish and other authors, seems to involve some very direct connection between speech and the harms it does, as if people are affected simply by being expressly classified in unfavorably characterized groups. Stanley Fish, *There's No Such Thing as Free Speech and It's a Good Thing Too,* p. 109. See also the first three contributions to *Words that Wound,* ed. Mari Matsuda, Charles Lawrence, Richard Delgado, and Kimberlè Crenshaw (Boulder, Colo.: Westview Press, 1993). In recent years some philosophers have advanced a claim that can be interpreted as an interesting variation on this idea. The claim is that, in characterizing a group adversely, one is not merely saying something about them, one is performing an act, what J. L. Austin called an "illocutionary act," and that there is reason for legally forbidding such acts. See Andrew Altman, "Liberalism and Campus Hate Speech: A Philosophical Examination," *Ethics* 103, January 1993, pp. 302-17, and Rae Langdon, "Speech Acts and Unspeakable Acts," cited in footnote 41. One of the illocutionary acts one is performing, according to these authors, is the act of "subordinating" someone. The argument for forbidding them seems to involve the notion that this act is done *to* someone—the group's members—and is thus not a victimless offense. Since it would make little sense to legally forbid an act on such grounds if it has no effect on the person to whom it is done, this notion seems to involve the additional idea that the act itself must somehow alter the people toward whom it is done: if I subordinate you then you have (in some nontrivial sense) been subordinated. The idea that one can be changed by such purely symbolic means is what identity collectivism amounts to. I personally doubt that this version of the idea of group responsibility is philosophically defensible, but that is

The coexistence, within the borders of the same national culture, of the individualist variety of liberalism together with a variety that I have argued is unstable raises a certain problem about the viability of the individualist variety itself. The advantage, as to stability, that individualist liberalism enjoys rests on independence and the sticks-and-stones principle. The problem is that, in the event that a culture with individualist elements also has aspects that are hostile to this principle, the principle and the trait of character that is based on it might not survive. If they die, the system seems doomed to develop into some newer, less stable sort of system.

So far, the institutional support for the survival of liberalism consists in the fact that this principle has the status of a social convention. Such conventions, as I have pointed out (VII.3), do seem to provide some degree of support for the widespread acceptance of principles of action, but it is doubtful that the sort of support they can provide is sufficient to solve the problem we are now confronting. They support principles by presenting us with a certain reason for accepting and following them, the reason being that others accept and follow them. The problem at present is that here we are dealing with principles that some people have keenly felt reasons *not* to accept or follow. Such reasons might well be stronger than the one the convention presents on the other side. Is there any way a culture could provide some additional reason for accepting the principle, in such a way that the convention itself has some further institutional support?

Actually, what the sticks-and-stones principle counsels us to do is something we already have additional reason to do. It tells us to protect ourselves from a certain sort of harm that others can cause us. We already have reason to avoid harm. But it also counsels us to use certain methods for avoiding this harm. It advises us to avoid the harm the opinions of others might do by refusing to accept those opinions. Someone has no reason at all to accept this advice if they think that this method cannot actually be used. If they think that they *cannot* avoid absorbing the adverse opinions others hold about them, then the sticks-and-stones tradition and the rugged independence that is based on it will make little sense to them. There seem to be a significant number of people who

---

beside my point here. The point is that the idea itself seems to be gaining adherents, and that we should expect it to have certain institutional and characterological effects unless other factors intervene.

do think this way.[44] To the extent that this way of thinking spreads, the sticks-and-stones tradition will necessarily lose ground.

People whose minds function in this way believe they lack a certain skill: namely, the ability to understand the opinions of others without at once succumbing to them. The problem we are now considering would be alleviated if there were institutional arrangements that somehow teach people this skill or encourage them to acquire and use it. To the extent that people do learn this lesson, an otherwise insuperable obstacle to accepting the sticks-and-stones principle has been removed.

One institutional arrangement that does perform this task can be found among the systems that I have called societies of contract. These are societies in which the differential obligations of individuals are foreseeable consequences of their own voluntary acts. The institutional arrangement I have in mind is a certain variety of society of contract, one that has historically been closely related to liberal democracy: namely, the competitive market. This is a contractual system in which people who might become obligated to us have

---

[44] A number of authors have suggested that—contrary to what I am assuming here—that this way of thinking, or something relevantly like it, is actually true, and that it is true of everyone. Mari Matsuda offers the following anecdotal argument regarding racist opinions: "At some level, no matter how much both victims and well-meaning dominant group members resist it, racial inferiority is planted in our minds as an idea that may hold some truth. . . . In conducting research for this chapter, I read an unhealthy number of racist statements. A few weeks after reading about a 'dot busters' campaign against immigrants from India, I passed by an Indian woman on my campus. Instead of thinking, 'What a beautiful sari,' the first thought that came into my mind was 'dot busters.' Only after setting aside the hate message could I move on to my own thoughts. The propaganda I read had taken me one step back from casually treating a fellow brown-skinned human being as that, rather than as someone distanced from myself." *Words that Wound*, p. 26. Matsuda's anecdote suggests an interesting idea, one that may well be true, but it does not support the conclusion she draws from it. The possible truth is the idea that, in understanding the statements of others, we often see the world momentarily as they do—this in fact may be an essential part of understanding what another person is saying. It may also be the case that—as this story suggests—such statements sometimes irresistibly compel one to see things from the other's point of view. But this is an as-if sort of seeing, similar to the "interpretations" that I argued in chapter V are an essential part of the emotions, and not the sort of vision of the world that is involved when one actually believes something. It may be that, when I try to understand a racist idea, I experience (in an as-if sort of way) a psychological distance from members of the race that the idea is about, something that mimics the distance experienced by the racist. But this is not the vicious sort of alienation that I would presumably undergo if I really thought that these people are, or really might be, my inferiors. That is, what might be true of everyone is *not* the idea that the statements of others have an irresistible control over our beliefs, but something quite different.

alternatives to doing so. Those who are indebted to me were not stuck with me, but could have dealt with someone else instead.

In a way, it might seem paradoxical to claim that such systems can help people to gain independence from the opinions of others. In any sort of contractual system, the opinions of others, at least some others, are very important. To the extent that we live in such a system, we can only deliberately acquire claims against other people by offering them something they want. To do this, we must be able to understand—and be interested in understanding—the wants of others, and to do this we must to some extent be able to understand and be interested in their thoughts as well.

This is true especially of the competitive market. Under competition, the other person, as I say, has alternatives to dealing with us. Such a system penalizes us, not merely for failing to divine the wants and thoughts of others, but for failing to do it *fast enough*, for delaying until someone else discovers the unsatisfied desire and satisfies it. Such a system exerts a continual pressure on us to attend to the possible desires and thoughts of potential trading partners. For that reason it might discourage the emergence of character types that essentially involve contemplating one's own thoughts and completely withdrawing from the points of view taken by other human beings: including proud Byronic heroes, Walden Pond hermits, and vision-questing shamans. It is more likely to produce test-marketing consultants, pollsters, and organizational yes-men.[45]

This is the truth—or one of them—behind the *doux-commerce* thesis I discussed earlier (VI.2). Important as this truth undoubtedly is, however, it should not blind us to another one, one that is even more important in the present context. This is the fact that, while competitive markets penalize us for being oblivious of the facts about other people's thoughts and wants, they also penalize us, and with the same sort of rigor, for taking them to be *more* than facts. An entrepreneur who always accepts, as if they were the word of God, the beliefs and desires of the consumers regarding his or her product would be at a severe disadvantage in facing a more independent competitor. For

---

[45] As Georg Simmel put it, competition tends to bring people to an awareness of "the innermost wishes of the other, even before he himself becomes aware of them." This fact is somewhat obscured, he points out, by the tendency to think of competition as a sort of fight. If it is a fight, it is a "simultaneous fight *against* a fellowman *for* a third one." *Conflict: The Web of Group Affiliation*, trans. and ed. Kurt Wolff and Reinhard Bendix (Glencoe, Ill.: The Free Press, 1955), p. 61-64. Competitors do tend to trample one another, but the ultimate reason for this is that they are all rushing to offer their customers whatever they want.

instance, if the product I offer is a very popular one and I simply adopt the consumers' attitude toward it—which in this case is strong approval—as my own, I would be unable to detect the shortcomings in that product and would be at the mercy of a competitor who *could* detect them and offer a product the consumer would prefer. Investors during wartime who are swept up by a general mood of optimism into thinking that their country will win are apt to lose money if this thought proves to be a self-gratifying illusion, while those who are immune to such collective fervor stand to profit.

These observations can easily be generalized. Competitive markets, and contractual systems in general, reward us for satisfying the desires of others, but only for satisfying desires they in fact do have at the time we attempt to satisfy them, and only for doing things that in fact do satisfy those desires. Any susceptibility to factors that cloud one's awareness of these facts is a liability, even if these factors are the thoughts and wants of the people we seek to please. If a nation's wartime optimism proves to be tragically misguided, and its rulers must find ways to pay reparations extorted by a ruthless victor, they will be eager to borrow money from whomever can help them pay. People who foresaw this need are, other things being equal, more likely to be in this position than those who succumbed to the popular belief that this day would never come.

Things look quite different if we imagine moving from such a society to one that lacks the one feature that is essential to contractual systems. Such systems are constituted by the fact that, to some extent or other, obligations in such a system are voluntary. If I have an obligation to you that, in contrast to this, is completely independent of my ability to choose, then you are not and never were under any pressure to entice me into accepting or keeping this obligation. This removes from your shoulders the peculiarly strong reason you would ordinarily have, in a contractual relationship, to take my desires and beliefs seriously.

I, on the other hand, may have such a reason, a stronger one than exists in a contractual relationship, and fundamentally different in kind. Suppose that the obligation is to perform some set task in a manner to be specified by you. Then I have a good reason to be alert to information about how you want this job done. Depending on the exact nature of our relationship, I can probably avoid problems if I can somehow collect information about your preferences. But I so far have no reason at all to discover a method of performance that, in your terms, is better than the one you want, one that would make you even happier. That is, I have a reason to take your wants and beliefs seriously without the reason that is present in contractual relationships, and heightened in ones that are disciplined by competition, to approach those wants and beliefs at some critical distance from them.

Both these features intensify as the relationship becomes less and less voluntary. At the limit, in a completely involuntary relationship—slavery —there is probably little incentive to operate as an independent mind at all. If you are literally my master, your whims are the most important single factor in my life (or nearly so). Perhaps the most obvious reason for this is the fact that I can avoid savage punishments by divining your whims in advance. But I gain little or no benefit from thinking about whether they are right or whether your beliefs are true.[46]

An uncritical sensitivity to the inner experiences of others, at least of one other, is a valuable trait for a slave to have. This is not true of the inhabitants of a contractual system. It encourages sensitivity of a sort, but it rewards those who combine it with a certain critical distance. I should probably emphasize, since there is sure to be misunderstanding otherwise, that I am not saying that this feature of contractual systems is uniformly beneficial as far as its effects on human character are concerned. An organizational yes-man who is taken by his boss's delusions is at a disadvantage when competing with one who is merely (but convincingly) pretending to be, but he may be a less despicable person. As far as anything I have said in this section is concerned, competitive markets might have bad effects on character, and might even, on balance, do more harm than good. The trait I am talking about here is a neither a virtue nor a vice but a skill, and can be put to either virtuous or vicious uses.

In the present context, what matters is that this skill removes an otherwise insuperable obstruction in the way of acquiring the cognitive independence that I have argued is crucial to the survival of liberalism. To someone who can understand the opinions of others without succumbing to them by mere contagion, the sticks-and-stones principle will seem as sensible as it did to many of us when we were children, but to someone without it, it will seem as cruelly nonsensical as its critics are now saying it is. To the extent that someone does follow its advice, however, they will have no reason to defend their self-esteem by silencing others.

---

[46] In such a situation, there would probably be considerable advantage to me in absorbing your beliefs and desires as my own as much as I can. I might be better at anticipating the behavior of an agent who has the same beliefs and desires that I have myself than I would be at guessing the behavior of an agent with a mind really different from my own. I would have no need to imaginatively put myself in your shoes, I would already be wearing your shoes.

Postscript: Toward a Society of Status?

I would like to close by saying a few more words about the nonindividualist liberalism I described in section 8, in which the sticks-and-stones principle is replaced by the collectivism of identity. I will call the resulting sort of culture "collectivist liberalism." It deserves our attention if only because it may represent an important part of the future of our own political culture. If what I have said in this chapter is close to the truth, we have reason to be very worried about this.

As I have described it, it represents a return to the society of status. It seems to represent status renascent and reformed along egalitarian lines. Traditional societies of status were hierarchies, in which a small and fixed collection of groups were clearly ranked, with some groups higher and others lower. Because of liberalism's commitment to equality, collectivist liberalism is permanently wedded to the idea that all groups are on the same level. In addition, in contemporary liberal society there are an indefinite number of relevant groups. Where the traditional systems were hierarchical and closed, the newer one is egalitarian and open-ended. Yet it shares with them one of their essential characteristics: in each case, the individuals who inhabit them acquire their identity monologically from some human agency or other.

Collectivist liberalism, as we see it in our culture, also possesses the other essential feature of societies of status: membership in the relevant sort of group brings unchosen obligations. Being liberals of a sort, adherents to this way of thinking are apt to think of the regime in favor as granting rights rather than imposing obligations. Various groups are to have an enforceable right to be spoken of in ways that are not demeaning to them. But of course in each case this means that the members of another group—that is, all nonmembers of the group that possesses the right—have the obligation to speak as the right prescribes.

This combination of egalitarianism, open-endedness, and status could represent a particularly explosive combination. It is very doubtful that it could possibly achieve the static sort of order that preliberal societies sometimes came close to attaining. Unless it abandons its commitment to equality, it cannot allow one group to impose its view of the social world on all the others, as societies of status have done in the past. Given that, there seems to be no way that it could arrive at some official truth about who everyone is and what is their worth.

The result would seem to be an analogue, within the realm of symbolic behavior, of the politico-economic system I described at the end of the chapter (X.5): an endless squabble between increasingly numerous groups, each of whom presses for their right to speak while seeking to control what others are saying about them. Advocates of collectivist liberalism need to explain what would prevent such a regime from disintegrating into what one critic has called "a simmering sort of mutual dislike on the level of everyday discourse,"[47] and perhaps into something much worse on the level of political activity.

When people think about these issues they often arbitrarily limit the groups who will press claims to some finite list. They often ignore, for instance, creationists who try to compel schools to eliminate textbooks that describe evolution as scientific fact, on the grounds that such ways of speaking demean them by branding their views as unscientific, or Moslem fundamentalists who seek to suppress books that wound them by satirizing the Prophet Mohammed.[48]

Ignoring them, and the indefinite number of others who have equally sincere and well-founded complaints, amounts to assuming that there could be some equivalent of the constitutional provision I discussed earlier (X.5), in which the groups that are going to count is strictly limited. But this seems clearly inconsistent with identity collectivism itself, which indicates that we are *all* radically vulnerable to the symbolic behavior of others and have a profound and ineradicable interest in controlling that behavior.

---

[47] Richard Bernstein, *Dictatorship of Virtue*, p. 9.

[48] See Jonathan Rauch, *Kindly Inquisitors*, Ch. I.

Index

About the Author

LESTER H. HUNT (b. 1946) is professor of philosophy at the University of Wisconsin - Madison, where he has taught since 1984. He received his Ph.D. from the University of California in 1976 and before settling in Madison taught at a number of colleges and universities, including Johns Hopkins University, the University of Pittsburgh, and Carnegie-Mellon University. He is the author of *Nietzsche and the Origin of Virtue* (Routledge, 1991) and of articles on ethics, philosophical psychology, political philosophy, philosophy of law, and philosophical ideas in literature. He lives in Oregon, Wisconsin, with his wife, Deborah Katz Hunt, and their son, Nathaniel. Among his many hobbies are cooking, off-road travel, and playing the violin.

DATE DUE
